Orello Cone

The Gospel and its Earliest Interpretations

A Study of the Teaching of Jesus and its Doctrinal Transformations in the New

Testament

Orello Cone

The Gospel and its Earliest Interpretations
A Study of the Teaching of Jesus and its Doctrinal Transformations in the New Testament

ISBN/EAN: 9783337188177

Printed in Europe, USA, Canada, Australia, Japan

Cover: Foto ©Lupo / pixelio.de

More available books at **www.hansebooks.com**

THE GOSPEL

AND ITS

EARLIEST INTERPRETATIONS

A STUDY OF THE TEACHING OF JESUS AND
ITS DOCTRINAL TRANSFORMATIONS
IN THE NEW TESTAMENT

BY

ORELLO CONE, D.D.

SECOND EDITION, REVISED

G. P. PUTNAM'S SONS

NEW YORK   LONDON
27 WEST TWENTY-THIRD STREET   24 BEDFORD STREET, STRAND

The Knickerbocker Press

1894

Electrotyped, Printed and Bound by
The Knickerbocker Press, New York
G. P. Putnam's Sons

PREFACE.

THANASE COQUEREL'S little book on The
First Historical Transformations of Christianity
furnished the suggestion of this work. More than a
suggestion, however, it cannot be said to have supplied.
For while it is conceived in accordance with a generally
correct insight into the relations of the different writings
composing the New-Testament literature, its critical
point of view may be regarded as now in many respects
antiquated.

The object of this work is to elucidate the teaching of
Jesus and to present both in their relation to it and to
one another the principal types of religious doctrine contained in the New Testament. The pursuit of this object
has led to a consideration of the resemblances and differences which exist between the word of the Master and the
interpretations of it by his followers who composed the
several writings of that book. While the classification of
the New-Testament literature results from critical processes, it was not consistent with the limits proposed to
enter upon a detailed discussion of them, and no more
has been attempted in this direction than to present those
grounds of the classification adopted which are apparent
from an analysis of the writings.

Instead of undertaking to make a complete exposition

of the theology of the New Testament I have endeavored to discuss only its more important features in such a manner as to present in outline the principal teachings of Jesus and the interpretations and transformations which they underwent in the books composing the Christian canon. If the result has been to show in these a greater or less departure from the simplicity and the practical, humanitarian, and religious interest of the original gospel of the great Teacher in the direction of a theological speculation conducted through a combination with it of the ideas of the age with which the several writers were in touch, there have also been made apparent, it is hoped, the worth and preëminence of that gospel in contrast with the philosophical interpretations of it by his earliest followers, and its importance as the basis of character, an inspiration to right living, and the only ground of permanent Christian union.

The work has necessarily been grounded upon a critical and exegetical study of the New Testament, and in its prosecution assistance has been derived from the commentators. I am also under obligations to the scholars to whose works reference has been made in detail in the notes, particularly to Pfleiderer, whose classification of the New-Testament literature has been in the main adopted, Wendt, Weizsäcker, Immer, and Baur.

I desire to express my obligations to Dr. C. H. Toy of Harvard University, who kindly read the work in manuscript, for important suggestions which have aided me in its revision.

Dr. C. C. Everett's work on The Gospel of Paul did not, I regret, come to hand in time for reference.

As I do not pretend that my interpretation of the course of the development of religious thought in the New Testa-

ment or of individual passages is faultless, I shall be
thankful for any criticisms which are calculated to lead to
a more complete understanding of the subject than I may
have been able to attain.

ORELLO CONE.

BUCHTEL COLLEGE,
   March, 1893.

CONTENTS.

THE GOSPEL

EARLIEST INTERPRETATIONS.

INTRODUCTION.

THE HISTORICAL AND CRITICAL TREATMENT OF THE NEW TESTAMENT.

RELIGION is a product in the origin and development of which human nature is so largely participant that, like all other human products, it has a history. Its history is the record of its formation and its transformations. To designate religion as a product is, indeed, to speak quite indefinitely of it and, perhaps, to provoke inquiry as to its factors. But to enter upon this inquiry would divert us from our present purpose, which is historical. We may, then, well leave the investigation of the nature of religion to anthropology and theology, while we proceed to study in its phenomena that particular form of it which appears in the New Testament, and is known as Christianity. The historical view of the formation of religion and of the modifications which it undergoes in the course of time concerns only its manifestations in life and in literature. The antecedent influences which affect the form or the development of any particular religion this view may, indeed, take into account if they lie in the domain of history, regarding the message which a religious teacher delivers in its relation to his environment and to his predecessors. But these human aspects of religion mark the limitations of history. Foreign to its occupation are all speculations and presumptions regarding the superhuman influences which may be supposed to have determined or affected the message of a teacher or the lives of believers. Inspiration may be a fact, but it is not a fact for the historian, and is not, indeed, historically demonstrable.

The historical study of religion has been greatly impeded by the dogmatic interest in which it has been maintained that this or that form of religion, the form of it which each advocate regards as the true religion, is final and unchangeable or absolute. Yet this position finds no support either in history or in philosophy. For nothing is historically more evident than that religion, like science, art, institutions of society, government, and all other things finite and human, is constantly undergoing modifications in accordance with the changing knowledge, needs, and civilization which the development of human nature and the general progress of man bring about. Again, it is clear that religion cannot in its nature be fixed, and that absoluteness cannot be predicated of it. Setting aside as confusing and inadequate all definitions of religion which deprive it of its "theologic crown," * it is manifest that whether we regard it with Schleiermacher, as consisting in " a feeling of absolute dependence" upon God or in sentiments of love and worship toward Him, it has the qualities of relativeness and limitation which belong to all conditions and expressions of human nature. The

* See Martineau, A Study of Religion, etc., 1688, vol. i., p. 4.

case is not changed if we view it upon its reverse side as "a mode of thought," and take account of the knowledge real or supposed which is implied in it as the matter of feeling. For whether we assume man to acquire his knowledge of God by the use of his natural faculties, or to become possessed of it as a revelation through inspired teachers, this knowledge is conditioned by the limitations of his nature. If, then, religion as a mode of thought consists of a knowledge which is relative, and as a mode of feeling is the feeling of a relation, it is evident that nothing can be more irrational than to affirm absoluteness of it. One might, perhaps, assert without fear of contradiction that no greater truth has been attained by man or revealed to him than, for example, that fundamental doctrine of Christianity, the Fatherhood of God ; but to affirm this truth to be final would be to set limits either to human attainment or to the revealing divine grace. Such an affirmation would be purely speculative and without any ground either in experience or reason. Moreover, the relativity of our apprehension of this truth is manifest from the fact that we know it only according to the analogy of a finite human relation, that of parentage. Its indefinite transformability appears when in its communication it is found to be variously apprehended according to the point of view and the degree of the affectional and intellectual development of the recipient. Accordingly, every thought concerning the Deity which man thinks, in whatever way he may come to think it, assumes in the first place the complexion of his own nature and limitations, and is in the second place subject to unlimited modifications as it is apprehended by different individuals. This is not a presumption, but an induction from the nature of man, from human experience, and from a scientific study of the records and history of religions.   It is also the point of view from which the purely historical treatment of the Christian religion and its documents must proceed.

A prepossession which has seriously hindered the progress of an historical and critical study of the New Testament, is that of the unity of doctrine in all its books. The writers of the various Gospels, Epistles, the Acts, and the Apocalypse have been assumed to have been inspired in the sense that they were capable of producing works which are free from error.   This inerrancy has been supposed by some to extend to all the minutiæ of words and minor details, and by others to include only a sort of general accuracy in matters of fact, a correct reproduction of the words of Jesus, and infallibility in all statements and expositions of Christian doctrine. From this point of view the writers of the Gospels, who are supposed to have been precisely the persons whose names are attached to them, are believed to have composed biographies of Jesus which can not only be brought into a substantial harmony in all matters of chronology and arrangement of material, but also shown to present no important divergences in their apprehension of his teachings. Individual peculiarities in the use of words and in style are, indeed, conceded ; but here the line is rigidly drawn, and it is regarded as but little short of blasphemy to teach that the evangelists have contradicted one another in matters of fact on the one hand, or on the other have presented widely divergent apprehensions of the nature, mission, and doctrine of Jesus. The teaching that the Gospels contain legendary or mythical accounts is denounced as destructive of the historical credibility of every other part of them, and the student is asked to reconcile with his reason and historical sense the propositions that two such representations of the character and teaching of Jesus as those of the first and fourth Gospels can have proceeded from two men who were his original disciples, and that they are in substantial accord with each other. According to this theory there are no strongly marked divergences of opinion, no oppositions, irreconcilable tendencies, and conflicting interpretations of Christianity in the several writers of the Epistles, the Acts, and the Apocalypse, but all their teachings are cast in the same mould, and constitute in perfect harmony one substance of doctrine. Substantially the same view of the teaching of Jesus and of the mission of Christianity is held to be represented in Romans and the Epistle to the Hebrews, and Galatians and the Epistle of James are accordant in the sense of presenting " different sides " of one and the same doctrine. These conclusions follow legitimately from the premises which assume the infallibility of the New-Testament writers in matters of fact and doctrine, and they have been defended with a degree of assumption and dogmatism than which the history of theology presents no more deplorable example.

That the theology of the New Testament constitutes a distinct department of theological science in general, and that its object is to ascertain and set forth the doctrines of the several writers and the teachings of Jesus, is a proposition which better describes the point of view from which most of the treatises on the subject have proceeded than the character and results which they have generally exhibited. In accordance with the fundamental principle of Protestantism that the doctrines of the Protestant Church should be nothing else than the exposition of the teachings of Scripture, the early reformers consistently founded their dogmatics upon a rigid exegesis of biblical texts. This is especially true of Melanchthon and Calvin, the former founding on the Epistle to the Romans in his *Loci Theologici*, and the latter proceeding in his *Institutio Christianæ Religionis* upon the assumption of the immediate relation of Scripture and dogmatics. But it was not long until the dogmatic system gained the supremacy, and Scripture was subordinated to it, until texts from the Bible were chiefly sought and prized for the use to which they could be put in fortifying the traditional theology and refuting its opponents, until exegesis was pressed altogether into the service of dogma, and only that interpretation of biblical passages was recognized as valid which squared with the accepted theological tenets. The attempts which were made toward the end of the seventeenth century to effect a real separation of Scripture from dogmatics and to consider the proof-texts or *dicta probantia* by themselves, particularly in the works of Sebastian Schmidt, Hülsemann, Baier, and Weissmann, appear to have been undertaken in accordance with a right apprehension of the true nature of biblical theology and of its scientific requirements, but the dogmatic view so far prevailed as to effect an unhistorical arrangement of the proof-texts and to vitiate the treatment of the subject.

The opposition to the theological system of the Church in which the spirit of the age found expression toward the end of the eighteenth century contributed in a one-sided and superficial way to the placing of biblical theology upon a basis independent of dogma, when Bahrdt, Teller, and others opposed the popular orthodoxy by weapons drawn from the Scriptures themselves. The criticism of Semler and the biblical theology of Zachariä also contributed to the establishment of the scientific study of the Bible in independence of the dogmatics of the Church. The point of view of Zachariä's very important work may well be commended to many modern theologians. He would have the student forget temporarily the system of the Church and seek to determine by an independent, careful investigation of the entire Scriptures the theological doctrines which they contain. The theology thus derived, he remarks, one may rightly call the real biblical theology, and one may compare it with the doctrines of the Church which are declared to be grounded in Scripture, in order to convince oneself of their correctness, and, if they are not so grounded, to have an insight into the actual biblical teaching. One must, as it were, forget all the truth that one has learned, in order to be unpartisan enough to recognize and express what the holy Scriptures teach without regard to whatever this or that party, this or that divine, holds to be true and right. But with all the fair promise of these words the author was not able to cut loose from dogmatics, and his work loses greatly in scientific value from the attempt to institute a criticism of the doctrines of the Church which, he assures his readers, far from suffering by his fresh investigation, will rather appear to be set forth in a new light. There are found intimations only of the true historical method of treating biblical theology in the other writers at the close of the eighteenth century, among whom Ammon and Storr are deserving of particular mention. The former, for instance, rejects the ordinary method of throwing the several writers of the Bible together, and recommends a regard for the peculiarities of each and for the people for whom and the age for which they wrote. But this idea appears to have exerted little influence upon the execution of his work, and the limitations of a dogmatic bias are evident in the application of his method for the purpose of illustrating the progressiveness of divine revelation. The distinction between dogmatic and biblical theology was clearly expressed by Gabler to the effect that the former, so far as it rests upon the Bible, has as its task to gather from the biblical teachings what is universally true, with the help of philosophy to discover this out of what is merely local, temporal, and individual, and scientifically to establish and combine it. Biblical theology, on the other hand, deals solely with the actual ascertaining of the ideas of religion which are contained in the biblical writings, and must therefore take up the merely local, temporal, and individual, because these are most characteristic of the mode of thought of a time and of particular persons.

In reviewing the historical course of the early treatment of the New Testament, it is difficult to classify every writer whose works are of sufficient importance to come under consideration as representing one distinctive tendency only. We have already seen how a writer sets out with a promise which he does not keep ; and since a prominent theologian of the first years of the nineteenth century, G. Lorenz Bauer, begins as a genuine historical critic and ends as a rationalist, occasion may be taken at this point to define and illustrate the latter of these tendencies in contrast with the former. Bauer in his work in four volumes on the biblical theology of the New Testament defines this science as a development of the theory of religion held by the Jews before Christ and by Jesus and his apostles, kept free from all foreign ideas, and derived from their writings according to the different ages and the varying views and knowledge of the sacred writers. This is a tolerably clear and accurate definition of biblical theology regarded from the point of view of historical criticism. For the historical and critical treatment of the biblical writings proceeds upon the presumption that they are literature, and applies to them the canons of literary and historical criticism. It is so far regardless of results that it does not permit them to influence its procedure or determine its conclusions. It is indifferent to the relation which its results may hold to any doctrines or traditions however cherished and venerable. Its sole aim is to ascertain the facts. These it leaves to the dogmatic theologian who may make of them whatever he can.

Now, in attempting to carry out these principles, Bauer furnishes an illustration of a tendency which is as much opposed to them, in fact, as is the dogmatism in opposition to which they have been laid down and maintained. Indeed, it is only to another sort of dogmatism that he commits himself in adopting the method of rationalism, when he turns aside from the pursuit of a purely historical purpose to investigate and determine what is a universally valid truth and a universally valid Christianity, and when he lays down the principle that whatever in the teaching of Jesus and his apostles contradicts the results of experience and the conclusions of sound reason is to be regarded as an accommodation to erroneous popular ideas. Of a like dogmatic character was his procedure when he sought by means of biblical theology to decide the great question whether Christianity is a rational and divine religion. For this is not an historical question, and in attempting to answer it one brings into the domain of history one's own subjective opinion of what is rational and divine, and sets up the purely dogmatic presumption that wherever the biblical writers do not agree with that opinion they accommodate themselves to the ideas of their time. This principle is of essentially the same dogmatic character as that in opposition to which it was laid down, for there is no essential difference in the two affirmations, that the biblical writers were infallibly and verbally inspired, and that whatever they thought and intended to express was in conformity with truth and reason. Both are *a priori*, both imply a presumption which has a tendency to determine the results of the historical and critical process, and both are accordingly incompatible with this process. When theologians, then, flee from the old orthodoxy or the new, indeed, to rationalism, they only escape from the servitude of one sort of dogmatism to put themselves under that of another.

As to its basis of rationalism, it may be characterized as philosophical in contradistinction to the principle and method of history and criticism applied to the New-Testament writings. Kant's doctrine of moral interpretation expresses its essential idea in the argument that, because the moral betterment of man is the object of religion, it must contain the supreme principle of biblical interpretation. Obviously no more thoroughly dogmatic presumption than this can be conceived, and Kant had the frankness to admit that the sense arrived at by this method is not, indeed, to be given out as that had in mind by the author interpreted! This remarkable candor of the great philosopher is, in fact, an admission that the so-called moral interpretation is decidedly no interpretation at all, but consists simply in reading a writer in the light of what one thinks he ought to say for the moral improvement of mankind, that is, in reading into his writing one's own preconceived ideas of what the moral betterment of mankind is, and what teaching will contribute to it. Now, the rationalistic method of treating the New Testament, which has played a very important part in the history of theology, and still thrives vigorously in some quarters, has always proceeded upon essentially this Kantian principle, that the biblical writers actually do teach or must at all events be made to appear to teach what is preconceived to be true and rational. Since, then, according to the presumption of rationalism, the supernatural is not acceptable to reason, it cannot from this point of view be supposed that the New-Testament writers intended to record accounts of miracles, and hence in recording what appear to be such they must really have meant to record something else. Likewise, since such beings as Satan and demons cannot rationally be supposed to exist, and to influence or to possess men, the evangelists did not actually intend to represent them as existing and taking a part in affairs, but quite another meaning may and must be put upon the words in the Gospels which appear literally to convey such a teaching.

Much of the older and the more recent theology abounds in examples of the application of this rationalistic principle. Since the serpent cannot be supposed to have talked with Eve or Balaam's ass with his master, the narratives of such conversations are assumed to convey what passed in the minds of the persons concerned. In like manner the appearance of Satan and the words which he is said, in the first and third Gospels, to have spoken to Jesus in the temptation are intended to express in a figure the struggle which the latter underwent with certain tendencies in himself before entering upon his ministry and the considerations which prevailed in the issue. From this point of view the author of the Acts in recording the Pentecostal phenomena really intended to relate nothing which may not be explained by the supposition of unusual religious excitement and the appearance of electric sparks. It is our error if we take literally what was meant to be understood as figurative. Assuming the unbroken and universal prevalence of natural law, rationalism declared that the biblical writers did not intend that their accounts of phenomena which appear to imply the suspension of the usual order of things should be understood as teaching a direct divine intervention, but that these narratives took the form which they have from the oriental religious view of the world that traced all natural events to the immediate agency of Deity. Accordingly, the story of the descent of Jahveh in flames upon Mount Sinai is really only an account of a thunder-storm; it was a stroke of lightning under which Saul fell on the road to Damascus; and the wonderful deliverance of Paul and Silas from the prison at Philippi was in fact nothing but the result of an opportune earthquake. It is even supposed that in those accounts which contain no intimation of a natural cause this has been overlooked by the narrators, or they have through ignorance taken for an immediate intervention of God what has in fact a sufficient explanation in accordance with the regular order of events. Thus the accounts of resurrections of the dead in the New Testament, including that of the resurrection of Jesus, are to be interpreted as actually relating awakenings from a state of suspended animation, and the miracle of Cana becomes a mere wedding-jest, since Jesus really caused the jars to be secretly filled with wine. Refinements of explanation are resorted to in dealing with words by this method, so that, for example, Jesus' walking on the sea is made to be a walking on the shore of the lake, and the piece of money

which was to be found in the mouth of a fish becomes
the money which was to be received from the sale of the
fish. Thus was the real meaning of words distorted, and
whole passages and sections were made to convey the
opposite of the sense intended by the writers to such a
degree that Zeller's judgment is not too severe when he
says that no account of miracles was so evidently such
that the rationalistic interpreters would not transform it
into a natural occurrence, and no difficulty so great that
their acuteness could not overcome it. * For violent
exegesis, sophisms, and unlimited torture of texts, the
rationalistic dogmatism may well dispute the palm with
its opponent, the orthodox supernaturalism. Rationalism
has, indeed, rendered an important service to theology as
a method of transition. More than a method of transition, however, it cannot be regarded ; and as a theological
point of view it may be characterized as a halting-place
in the progress from the old orthodoxy to the historical
and critical treatment of the Bible.

Rationalism appears to have laid a spell upon the
human mind, and its influence has been overcome with
difficulty. The historical method has, however, made
slow but sure progress. The important works on biblical
theology, by Kaiser and De Wette, both published in the
same year, 1813, contributed not a little to this progress,
although neither of them furnishes an example of the
purely historical and critical treatment of the Bible. The
former, in attempting to consider the extra-biblical
religions in connection with the biblical and to discover
the principle of the ideally true religion, vitiated the
historical procedure by introducing a subjective standard

* Die Tübinger historische Schule, Vortäge und Abhandlungen
geschichtlichen Inhalts, 1865, p. 272.

of the universally true and valid.   To the latter belongs the merit of treating biblical theology not according to the different writers, but according to the characteristically different periods.   But in attempting philosophically to distinguish the essential from the unessential in religion, he subordinated the purely historical to the religious and dogmatic interest, and placed himself upon rationalistic ground.   The works on biblical theology by Baumgarten-Crusius and Von Cölln, issued in 1828 and 1836 respectively, mark no important departure from the methods and points of view already considered.   The former occupies essentially the ground of traditional orthodoxy in the attempt to set forth the religion of the Bible as a connected whole without distinction of the two Testaments, and in ignoring all differences of doctrine among the apostles and between them and the original teaching of Jesus.   The latter undertook to furnish a treatment of biblical theology from the purely historical point of view, and to carry it out in all its strictness and purity in distinction from the false endeavor after a practical and popular method of treatment and the incorrect idea of the relation of biblical theology to the theological system, to the universal history of religion, and to the philosophy of religion.   But in the execution of the work the attempt to distinguish between the symbolical and the unsymbolical in the teaching of Jesus and the apostles introduced an arbitrary and indeterminable principle whose application could not but be unfavorable to the purely historical method.

At this point the criticism and the theology of the New Testament received from Strauss' Life of Jesus and the discussions which it called forth an impulse which exerted a most important influence upon their development. Two vital questions received such a treatment in the criticism of Strauss that they became and have remained for half a century central points of theological controversy. These are the question of the miraculous in the Gospel-history and that of the credibility of this history in view of the relation of the various narratives to one another. Strauss took his position, in the first place, upon the ground that the criticism of the New Testament must proceed, like that of all other writings, in entire freedom from presumptions. Its task being to ascertain the historical facts from the reports before it, it must treat these reports according to the general canons of historical and critical investigation. It was his opinion that, since the indissoluble connection of natural causes and effects is found to exist in every other department of human history and affairs, it is an unallowable presumption that it did not hold in the domain of biblical history. He maintained that those traits which in all other ancient documents we recognize as certain signs of an unhistorical character cannot be assumed to give a superior historical quality to various narratives in the Gospels. The question, then, regarding the credibility of a narrative of a miracle resolves itself, from the historical as opposed to the dogmatic point of view, into the question: Which is the more probable, that something really happened here which contradicts the analogy of our whole experience, or that the tradition which has handed down the report of such an event is false? Now, in our experience there are numberless examples of inaccurate observation, untrustworthy tradition, intentional or unintentional fabrication, and in general of incorrect reporting, while there is not a single example of an authenticated miracle, that is, of a result which did not demonstrably follow from the natural connection of things. Accordingly, from Strauss' historical point of view, the foregoing question contains its own answer.

As to the question of the credibility of the Gospel-narratives in view of the relation which they hold to one another in the matters of agreement, chronological arrangement, apprehension of the person and work of Jesus, etc., it cannot be denied that results of the greatest importance for the theology of the New Testament have come from Strauss' work and the numerous writings which it called forth. It was believed by all who at first engaged in the contest that the criticism of Strauss could only be overcome by establishing the apostolical origin, and accordingly, as was supposed, the entire credibility of the four Gospels. This task proved to be much more difficult than was supposed. Neither the traces of a later origin which they show in themselves, nor the striking differences which appear in them when they are compared with one another, particularly in regard to the person of Jesus and the relation of Judaism and Christianity, could with all the exegetical art which was applied be removed from the Gospels ; and that school of criticism is now regarded as conservative which constructs the Gospel-history upon the priority of Mark, and derives Luke and our Greek first Gospel from this and a collection of sayings or logia supposed to have been written in Aramaic by Matthew, while the fourth Gospel has been so much disputed as an apostolical writing that its legitimate use as an original source for the teaching of Jesus is open to the gravest question.*

---

* A good illustration of the influence which the discussion of the origin of the fourth Gospel has had upon conservative scholars is shown in Wendt's ingenious but artificial eclectic treatment of the discourses contained in it for a construction of the teaching of Jesus. Die Lehre Jesu, ii., 1890.

Whoever, then, would at the present time write a life of Jesus or an account of his teachings must give heed to the fact that the existence of any immediately apostolical source is in a high degree questionable.

This condition to which criticism has brought the study of the Gospels has a most important bearing upon any treatment of the life and teachings of Jesus. Since we can know his doctrine only mediately, that is, through the statements of the writers of the New Testament, and particularly of the Gospels, it is evidently of no slight importance whether the authors of the writings which must be depended upon for information were eye-witnesses, that is, whether their relation to the events and the sayings of Jesus was such that they were able in writing of them to produce histories in the proper sense of the word, or whether they were so far separated from the time of which they wrote that a considerable modification of their material must be supposed on its way to them through the channels of tradition. This consideration is of great importance, not because if the latter alternative be taken there remains no trustworthy source of information as to the general character of the teachings of Jesus and even as to the principal and essential particulars of it. But it is evident that the acceptance of one or the other of these alternatives must greatly affect the method of treating the subject and the nature of many of the results arrived at. If, for example, one does not regard the evangelists as simple reporters of the words of Jesus one will avoid the violent exegesis of the old harmonists in treating passages which, while seeming to be parallel, differ widely in the relation of time and the connection of thought. From this point of view also the treatment of the Gospels cannot but become less dogmatic and mechanical, and give more room to what is called critical divination, or the insight of historical criticism, than is possible by the old method of studying them. This critical insight or divination, which in the first place is a faculty, and in the second place is cultivated by transporting oneself into the environment of an ancient writer and making it in a sense one's own, has produced the most satisfactory results in the study of the Greek and Latin classics, and in view of the conclusions of criticism is the means which must now be chiefly resorted to for the elucidation of those Christian classics which the Gospels are, since, indeed, they have now come to be regarded as literature.

If, then, with all the reactions since the time of Strauss the tendency of the critical study of the Gospels has steadily set against the method of treating even the synoptics as writings cast in the same mould and in most respects accordant, in a much greater degree has the difference between these and the fourth Gospel been accentuated. The latter has, in fact, come to be very widely regarded as containing a unique type of the conceptions of Jesus and his mission which were formed during the first century after his death. The necessity has been forced upon students of the Gospels of deciding between the first three and the last in seeking for the historical source of the life and teachings of Jesus. The decision which has so often been made to the prejudice of the synoptics seems now likely to turn against the fourth Gospel as a writing of a marked theological and ideal tendency. The more this is done, however, the more is stress laid upon the historical character of the synoptics as writings in whose common tradition has been preserved the kernel of the most that can be really known of the life and teachings of the Nazarene.

It was from this point of view that the relation of the

synoptics and the fourth Gospel was regraded by F. C. Baur, the founder of the Tübingen historical school, whose thorough and acute criticism of the latter Gospel marks an era in the study of the New Testament. While the publication of Baur's principal writings was subsequent to that of Strauss' Life of Jesus, the former was in no sense a follower of the latter. The underlying principles and aims of the two men were fundamentally different. The criticism of Strauss was both negative and inadequate. It was negative in tending to overthrow the historical credibility of the Gospels, and inadequate in that, while it sought to establish the mythical theory as an explanation of certain portions of the Gospels, it left other very important parts of them unexplained ; since the myth, as legend unintentionally formed, does not account for those features of these narratives which are marked by a decided intention and dogmatic interest, and, far from being, like the myth, common to all, are in various forms peculiar to one and another. The criticism of Strauss proceeded from a philosophical point of view, and was rather a criticism of the Gospels than of their history. In his zeal to remove from the Gospels all unhistorical constituents he failed to construct, or to indicate how there might be constructed, a positive historical portrait of Jesus. Baur's procedure was essentially different from this, and perhaps might be said to have been opposed to it. He did not begin his investigations with a criticism of the Gospels, but with a study of their history, that is, of the conditions out of which they sprang. His point of view was that, if our Gospels are not simple historical narratives, if rather religious interest and dogmatic reflexion had an important part in their origin, they are, nevertheless, documents which show the spirit of the ancient Church

and the views and interests which existed in it.   Important
information in regard to these various views and interests
may be obtained from other witnesses in part older and
more immediate than the Gospels themselves, that is,
in the other New-Testament writings, in the statements
of early writers of the Church, and in the extra-canonical
remains of the ancient Christian literature.   Now, if with
these aids we attempt to form the most accurate possible
view of the Christian Church of the first centuries, of the
oppositions and parties contained in it, and of the entire
internal development of original Christianity, we shall not
only have gone far beyond the Gospel-criticism of Strauss
with reference to its extent, but we shall have supple-
mented its negative results by results which are historical
and positive.   Besides, we may hope in this way to obtain
a clearer insight into the life and teachings of the Founder
of Christianity.

Baur, accordingly, in seeking for a tenable ground of
further historical combinations, began with a study of
those writings of the New Testament which appeared to
him as the oldest documents of original Christianity to be
best adapted to this purpose, the genuine Pauline Epistles,
that to the Romans, the two to the Corinthians, and that
to the Galatians.   He drew from these the conclusion that
the ordinary view of the apostolic age was incorrect, which
regarded it as a period of harmony and unbroken peace.
In expressions of Paul himself and by means of inferences
from historical notices of the later Ebionites and from the
pseudo-Clementine literature he found evidences of the
oppositions and strifes in which the apostle to the Gentiles
was engaged with the Jewish-Christian party and even
with the original apostles themselves.   It was from this
point of view that Baur's study of the Gospels proceeded.

These he regarded as historical products of their age,
based upon tradition and antecedent writings, and composed in the interest to a greater or less degree of one or
the other side of the contest over the Pauline apprehension of Christianity, or, in general, in the interest of a
theory of Jesus and his mission which chanced to be the
favorite one of the author or editor of each. This predilection of the writers he called a " tendency," and hence
" tendency-writings " became in the Tübingen school of
criticism a standard term descriptive of the Gospels. A
single exception was made in this respect of the Gospel of
Mark which was regarded as a neutral, colorless writing
composed from the first and third Gospels. The relation
of the synoptic Gospels, then, to the facts of the Gospel-
history being mediate, these cannot have, in Baur's opinion,
the full importance of an authentic source of the teaching of Jesus. Its actual contents can, in fact, be determined through them only approximately, since the subjectivity of the writers is a factor always to be taken into
the account. Yet, notwithstanding the fact that the writers
of the four Gospels are not to be regarded as mere reporters, their writings have no little importance as sources
of the teachings of Jesus. For in each of the Gospels the
consciousness of the time to which it belongs is represented
in a new and peculiar form, and the farther we must separate them according to the difference of the time of their
origin and the individuality of their authors, the more
important documents do they become for the history of
the development of New-Testament theology.*

The historical method of studying the New Testament
reaches its culmination in the principles and processes of
the Tübingen school. The requirement that the various

* Baur, Vorlesungen über neutestamentliche Theologie 1864, p. 24.

writings which compose it shall be investigated with reference to the conditions and influences in the midst of which they originated, and studied independently of all dogmatic prepossessions, is rigidly observed. The contention that in sacred history laws and principles should be accepted as valid which are not recognized in other history is not admitted. "Christianity," says Baur, "is an historical phenomenon, and as such it must submit to be historically considered and investigated." * When he is charged with the design of placing Christianity in an historical connection in which all that is supernatural and miraculous in it would become a vanishing moment, he answers: "This is certainly the tendency of the historical method of treatment, and in the nature of the case it can have no other. Its task is to investigate whatever happens under the relation of cause and effect; but the miracle in its absolute sense dissolves this natural connection; it sets a point at which it is impossible, not for want of satisfactory information, but altogether and absolutely impossible, to regard the one thing as the natural consequence of the other. But how were such a point demonstrable? Only by means of history. Yet from the historical point of view it were a mere begging of the question to assume events to have happened in a way contrary to all the analogy of history. We should no longer be dealing with an historical question, as that concerning the origin of Christianity incontestably is, but with a purely dogmatic one, that of the conception of a miracle, [that is] whether contrary to all historical analogy it is an absolute requirement of the religious consciousness to regard particular facts as miracles in the absolute sense." It were certainly an error to regard this attitude

* Die Tübinger Schule, 1859, p. 13.

of the founder of the Tübingen school as identical with that of the rationalists who rejected the miraculous "in the absolute sense" on purely *a-priori* grounds, and then proceeded to apply a violent and artificial exegesis to the Gospels. On the contrary, it is not from a philosophical but from an historical point of view that he approaches the subject. It is not, indeed, unusual from the apologetic side to urge that those who thus deal with the miraculous are equally with the dogmatist and the rationalist under the influence of a presumption, that is, of a presumption against the supernatural. This view is, however, in the highest degree illogical. For it is not at all a presumption from which the historical critic takes his departure, but precisely and only an induction. From historical phenomena in general, from human affairs and experience, the induction is derived that events happen under the relation of natural causes and effects. The historian proceeds, and must proceed, to judge them accordingly, so long as the phenomena before him admit of an explanation by this principle. That myths and legends grounded upon the supernatural which are found in the prehistorical records of ancient peoples are to be regarded as history, and that it is to be taken for a fact that Jove or Jahveh at any time interfered to turn the scale of battle, he would hold to be most illogical and unscientific presumptions. To enter upon a philosophical discussion of the supernatural would be foreign to his purpose, and there remains nothing for him to do but to proceed upon the accepted scientific inductions which lie at the basis of the science of history.

The keen and thorough discussion to which the theories and conclusions of the Tübingen critics have been subjected for more than half a century has no doubt shown that they were in many respects one-sided and over-wrought. The historical view of the schism in the early Church which they maintained has not been supported in its full extent, their doctrine of "tendency" in the Gospels has been considerably modified, and their opinions regarding the date of the Gospels and some matters touching the history of the canon have not, indeed, altogether been sustained. But it cannot be disputed that Baur's general historical view of primitive Christianity has exerted a far-reaching and permanent influence. The different and even conflicting points of view of the New-Testament writers can no longer be denied, and "tendency" is a term which is likely to be always recognized in Gospel-criticism. The opinions of scholars regarding the fourth Gospel have been so much modified that it can no longer be looked upon by the learned as the favorite and most trustworthy source for the life and teachings of Jesus. By those who feel the influence and appreciate the spirit of the higher criticism it is not now regarded with the enthusiastic, sentimental devotion which was rendered to it by Schleiermacher and Neander. As to the strictly historical method of treating the New Testament which Baur contributed more than any one else to establish and make prevail, there can be no doubt that it has taken a permanent place in biblical criticism, and has practically driven from the field both the traditional and the rationalistic dogmatism. The ghost of the old harmonizing method still, indeed, haunts the domain of theology, but wherever criticism prevails there prevails the principle that each biblical writer is to be studied with reference to his age, his environment, and the questions which can be historically shown to have been mooted in his time. That the New-Testament writings are to be

regarded as literature; that they have an historical setting; that they are amenable to the principles of literary
criticism; that whatever spiritual truths they may contain, they are human productions, and must be judged as
such; and that they are to be studied in accordance with
methods established by inductions from history and
experience—this is the incontestable point of view from
which scholarship now proceeds in the investigation of
all the literary remains of the primitive Christian Church,
whether they are canonical or uncanonical.

The opposition to the Tübingen school has been
directed more against some of the results of its criticism than against the method itself. The denial of the
genuineness of all but four of the Epistles ascribed to
Paul and the relegation to the post-apostolic age of
the greater part of the New-Testament writings could not
but be vehemently contested. But the method is of
greater importance than particular results of its application; and, as might have been expected, after the smoke
of the first contests cleared away it became apparent that
just this method and no other was prevalent and likely to
be permanent. Although opposing conclusions have been
reached by those who have employed it, and bias and
prejudice have not been absent in its application, it has
come to pass that no work on biblical theology of great
importance and influence has recently been written in
which it has not been followed with more or less rigidity
and consistency. It is only necessary for confirmation of
this statement to glance at the divisions of such works as
those of Reuss * and Weiss.† The former is composed of

* La Théologie chrétienne au Siècle apostolique, third edition, 1864.
† Lehrbuch der biblischen Theologie des Neuen Testaments, 3te Ausg.,
1879.

the following books: 1. Judaism; 2. The Gospel; 3. The Apostolic Church; 4. The Jewish-Christian Theology; 5. The Pauline Theology; 6. The Theology of Transition; 7. The Johannine Theology. The latter, following not less strictly the historical method, divides his material into: The teaching of Jesus; The Original Apostolic Type of Doctrine; Paulinism; The Apostolic Doctrine of the post-Pauline Age; and finally, The Johannine Theology. These books, while written by men who by no means accept the conclusions of the Tübingen school, mark a decided advance upon the old apologetic method of treating the theology of the New Testament. Though pursuing a different aim and governed by a different tendency from these, Hausrath * and Pfleiderer † furnish fine exemplifications of the same method, and the New-Testament Theology of Immer ‡ is deserving of especial mention in this connection.

Instead of entering upon a further consideration of the works on the New Testament which illustrate the historical method, it may, perhaps, be best to give a little space to the answering of objections to it which many readers may be supposed to entertain. If it be objected that this method has a tendency to subvert the traditional faith in the Scriptures as the inspired and infallible word of God, it should be borne in mind that if criticism is once admitted as a legitimate means of ascertaining the nature, date, authorship, and true interpretation of the books of the Bible, it must be allowed to take its natural course. If the conclusions which it reaches are unfavorable to the doctrine of the infallibility of Scripture, then

---

* Neutestamentliche Zeitgeschichte (in three volumes), 1868–1873.

† Das Urchristenthum, seine Schriften und Lehre, etc., 1887.

‡ Theologie des Neuen Testaments, 1877.

the objector may well ask himself on what grounds that doctrine rests, and whether it can be logically and securely established by any other process than this same critical and historical one to which he is opposed. It would result that his objection was not so much to the method as to its conclusions, and he would be in the position of an advocate of the Ptolemaic system who should have objected to astronomy because the study of it resulted in establishing the Copernican system.

No little prejudice exists against the historical and critical method as applied especially to the New Testament because it often results in the conclusion that some of the Gospels and Epistles were not written by the men to whom they have been traditionally ascribed. This result is, however, shocking rather to the sentiments of men than to their intelligence. For if one will fairly consider the facts in the case one cannot but see that there is very little evidence of any sort, and none that can be called immediate, for the authorship of many of these writings. Of traditional evidence there is, indeed, abundance, of contemporary evidence there is none for the authorship of the Gospels. But experience in historical investigation soon teaches us to receive the testimony of tradition with great caution. Precisely what, then, in brief, are the facts? The earliest traditional testimony to the authorship of our first Gospel, for example, dates from a period about seventy years after its supposed composition, does not relate to the existing Greek recension of it at all, and runs to the effect that Matthew wrote the sayings ($\lambda\acute{o}\gamma\iota\alpha$) of Jesus in Hebrew. Traditionally, then, Matthew is connected with the composition of a writing which probably furnished the basis of our first Gospel. When the Greek first Gospel was composed, by whom, how it stands related to this original Hebrew work ascribed to the apostle, how much of the latter was included in it, how much other material and from what sources derived was employed by the Greek writer of it—of these things our informant, Papias, tells us nothing, perhaps knew nothing. He does not even mention the Greek Matthew, and the first knowledge that we have of its existence dates from Justin Martyr, about the middle of the second century, and he gives no information as to its authorship. As to the other supposed apostolical Gospel, the fourth, there is a trace, much disputed, however, of its existence in Justin Martyr, but not until near the end of the second century do we find any one ascribing it to John. Papias, who is said to have been a disciple of John, does not appear to have known of its existence. It must be conceded by every unbiassed mind that such data are altogether inadequate to establish the genuineness of the writings in question, which are here taken as examples in this respect of a considerable number of the New-Testament books. There are certain things very necessary to be known about this testimony before we can put much reliance upon it, which we cannot find out, for example, what the nature of the information was which those early writers had who ascribe a book to a particular author, whether they had trustworthy evidence, or followed a current tradition without examination. In all that they say on this subject there is no indication that they made a critical examination of the genuineness of any of the books in question. They either accept tradition or give fantastic reasons for their belief. It is, accordingly, a significant fact that the most trustworthy information that we have regarding the origin of the greater part of the New-Testament books is not to be credited to the Christian writers who lived from sixty to one hundred years after they were written, but to the historical criticism, so much suspected in some quarters, which took its rise some seventeen hundred years later.

That no earnest attention was given in the early Church, that is, for about a century after the composition of the oldest of our synoptic Gospels, to what we now call the canonicity of a New-Testament writing, is a fact incontestably established by history. The writers of this period do not appear to have concerned themselves greatly about the authorship of a book, provided only that the book served their purpose. Along with our Gospels or instead of them were used others which often deviated from them. The Jewish Christians and the Gnostic Christians used different Gospels, and neither party recognized those of the other. Justin Martyr along with our first and third Gospels used another containing matter different from anything which is found in our canonical Gospels ; and as late as the end of the second and the beginning of the third century writings of trifling importance, more distinguished for their weakness and puerility·than for any qualities of worth, were treated with great consideration, and even thought to be inspired, by eminent leaders in the Church. These facts show very clearly how much importance is to be attached to the opinions of the so-called witnesses of the early Church as to the genuineness of New-Testament books, and furnish a complete justification, if, indeed, any justification were required, of the rigid application of historical criticism in order to ascertain whatever can be known regarding their origin.

Again, if it be objected to the historical and critical method of studying the New Testament and its times that its conclusions show some writings to have been falsely ascribed to men who had no part in their composition, it should be considered that this result of the inquiry is not to be charged to the method but to the character of the age in question. Nothing is easier than for pseudonymous writings to pass unquestioned in an uncritical age, particularly when they are favorable to a prevalent religious interest. That the critical spirit was not abroad during the first two centuries of the Christian Church scarcely needs proof to an intelligent reader. Men, certainly, were not critical who could with the utmost confidence and *naïveté* quote the Sibylline Books in which Messianic prophecies are put into the mouth of the ancient Sibyl, and that was not a critical age in which even an Origen could defend these writings, and Clement of Alexandria quote from Aristobulus shameless falsifications of the Greek poets, in which Orpheus is made to speak of Abraham and Moses and the ten commandments, and Homer to discourse of the sacredness of the Sabbath. No one will regard it as improbable that pseudonymous writings should circulate undisputed in such an age who reflects upon similar cases in more recent times, and recalls that Fichte's Criticism of Revelation was in its first anonymous edition almost universally ascribed to Kant; that in the collection of Hegel's works were included a treatise by Schelling and one by F. von Meyer ; that the authorship of many of Shakespeare's plays is doubtful ; that the Memoirs of the Duchess von Brieg were long regarded and quoted as genuine ; and that the Eikon Basilike was, in spite of the objections of Milton and fifty years later of Toland, devoutly believed to be a genuine writing of the " martyr," Charles I. of England. Besides, no one acquainted with the history of literary deceptions of the kind in question will be surprised to find them in the early Christian centuries. Frauds of this kind were committed in perfect *naïveté* and even good faith in ancient times. Of about sixty complete treatises and fragments from the Pythagorean school attributed to the master the greater part are demonstrably spurious, says Zeller, and were written by new-Pythagoreans about a century B.C., in order to give authority to certain innovations. If this could happen, as it did in great part in Alexandria, it is not to be wondered at that pseudonymous writings should easily gain currency and acceptance among the fathers of the Church, who were credulous enough to accept the most fabulous and absurd traditions, and even to believe and circulate the marvellous and extravagant promise of the Messianic vineyards as a genuine word of Jesus.

Should any devout person be shocked at this conclusion, and be inclined to repudiate the critical method by which it is reached, let him reflect that it is not so sweeping as it may at the first glance appear to be. There is, indeed, no good reason why criticism should offer an apology for itself; but in the interest of clear views of this matter it should be said that the conclusion in question affects only certain New-Testament books, and that most of these are of subordinate importance. A distinction should also be made between the conclusion that a writing is not genuine, and that which declares it to be an intentional counterfeit. A writing would come under the latter classification if its author expressly ascribed it to another person. But this is not the case with the writer of any one of our canonical Gospels, * which may have been designated as

---

* The last chapter of the fourth Gospel was probably not written by the author of the rest of the book, and even verse 24 does not ascribe the

"according to" Matthew, John, etc., without any intention of an ascription of authorship.   But, in fact, we do not know by whom these titles were prefixed.   Even the Tübingen criticism does not dispute the genuineness of the four great Pauline Epistles, and finds in the synoptic record an historical basis for the teachings of Jesus.   As to the charge that the conclusion in question makes Christianity and the Christian Church a product of fraud and deception, it is almost too superficial to merit consideration.   It originates in the erroneous identification of Christianity and its literature, and proceeds upon the assumption that there was not a Christianity long before there were any books written about it, and that the authorship of a book is, indeed, a matter of vital importance.   Besides, even if some of the books of the New Testament were by later writers intentionally ascribed to apostles, it by no means follows that this was done with conscious deception.   For how such an act is to be morally judged depends upon the way in which such a procedure was regarded at the time when the forgery was committed.   In a time when the personality of an author counted for little or nothing, when critical investigation of the authorship of writings was not undertaken in order to establish their credibility or importance, and when the principal consideration was whether or no a given book favored the good cause, it cannot be surprising that it was not thought to be morally reprehensible to credit a work written with good intentions in the interest of the common faith to some man of renown whose name would give it currency.   The wide prevalence of this practice in ancient times and even in the early years of

work to John, but to "the disciple whom Jesus loved," who is not in the Gospel said to have been John.

the Christian Church should make one cautious about denying the possibility of its existence in the time immediately succeeding that of the apostles. *

It remains to be said that the historical method can be logically applied only to materials of history, that is, to facts and phenomena which have had an historical course and development. Here lies the distinction between it and the dogmatic method of dealing with the New-Testament writings. The latter sets out from the presumptions that all these writings contain one and the same type of revealed truth, and that they present an unbroken unity of doctrine which excludes all conflicting tendencies and all important variations of thought and opinion. These tendencies and variations this method cannot allow, and accordingly from its point of view all oppositions of teaching are only apparent, and may be resolved by an accommodating exegesis into a unity acceptable to the believing mind. The former method, on the contrary, permits no presumption to govern its processes, but goes straight forward in the application of the principles of historical investigation intent only on reaching a scientific conclusion. From the latter point of view the last book in the New-Testament canon marks the limit beyond which extends the wide domain of the history of doctrines, the history of conflicts, errors, triumphs of faith, and tragedies of unbelief. The application of the former method shows that, far from being a unity, the New Testament presents varieties of teaching, conflicting tendencies, oppositions, a progress of thought, and an evolution of dogma—reveals in itself the fermentation of elements, processes of growth, and the real beginning of the history of Christian doctrines.

* See Zeller, Vorträge, etc., *ut supra.*

3

In treating of the gospel of Jesus and its earliest interpretations, the discussion in this work proceeds upon the judgment that the synoptic Gospels are the sole historical records of his teaching; that the fourth Gospel contains a transformation of it effected under the influence of Hellenistic thought; that the doctrine of Paul must be derived from Romans, 1 and 2 Corinthians, 1 Thessalonians, Galatians, and Philippians; that Hebrews, Colossians, Ephesians, and 1 Peter are to be classified as deutero-Pauline writings composed toward the end of the first century; and that 2 Peter, Jude, the Pastoral Epistles, and the so-called Epistles of John are to be regarded as anti-Gnostic writings of the early years of the second century.

CHAPTER I.

THE TEACHING OF JESUS.

I.—DOCTRINAL ANTECEDENTS AND ENVIRONMENT.

ALTHOUGH the religion of Jesus, regarded as his personal feeling and experience of relation to God, and regarded again as to certain fundamental moral and spiritual principles, was essentially new, yet the right study of it must proceed from a consideration of its historical connection with the religious doctrines of the Jewish people. A clear distinction must, indeed, be made between it and the so-called theological system, yet it would be manifestly as erroneous to say that it was not grounded upon certain theological conceptions, as to maintain that all of these or even the greater part of them were new and original. If Judaism could not have produced Christianity without Jesus, neither could Jesus, historically regarded, have become what he was without the great teachers of his people who preceded him. As something absolutely new, then, the teaching of Jesus is no more to be regarded than as a mere continuation of the law and the prophets. Genius, indeed, creates, but it does not create out of nothing. Accordingly, in the mind of the wonderful religious Genius who was the Founder of Christianity, the religion of his ancestors underwent one of those great transformations to which every product of human thought, or, if one like the phrase better, every divine truth that takes on a human expression, is subject, and to which, in fact, his own teaching did not long wait to be subjected.

Fundamental in the Jewish religion antecedent to and at the time of Jesus was the monotheistic conception which, though perhaps not held in absolute purity, that is, to the exclusion of the existence of other beings of a superhuman nature, practically included the unity and aloneness of the Supreme Being. Not only was He the omniscient, omnipresent, and omnipotent Ruler of the world, having, however, an especial care for Israel, but He possessed, as a most prominent attribute, holiness, and was in particular regarded as the Holy One of Israel, to whom all impurities whether physical or moral are an abomination, and in whose eyes even the heavens are not clean. This quality is not conceived as isolated and in-operative, but as having effective spiritual relations with the chosen people, upon whom holiness is enjoined be-cause God is holy. According to a very beautiful passage in the second Isaiah,* the divine holiness is also brought into immediate connection with grace and mercy: " For thus saith the high and lofty One who inhabiteth eternity, whose name is Holy, I dwell in the high and holy place, with him also who is of a contrite and humble spirit, to revive the spirit of the humble, and to revive the heart of the contrite ones." As just, truthful, and faithful is the divine Being also represented in the Old Testament. He holds with equal hand the scales of award, and not to the theocratic nation of His choice alone, but to all men dis-tributes impartial justice and wreaks vengeance on His enemies. According to the Deuteronomist, " He is the Rock, His work is perfect ; for all His ways are judgment ;

* Isa. lvii. 15.

a God of truth and without iniquity, just and right is He." * " All His works are done in truth," and " He is not a man that He should lie, nor the son of man that He should repent." †

The doctrine that Israel was the chosen people of God and the ideas which are connected with and follow from it held a prominent place in Jewish thought. The theocratic conception in general is not, indeed, peculiar to the Jews, but no other nation has held it with such intensity of conviction and tenacity of purpose and with so vast an influence upon the religious thought of mankind. In their thought the choice of the nation by Jahveh was purely arbitrary, grounded upon no merit of theirs, and an act of pure condescension on His part to the least among the peoples.‡ The continued protection of Jahveh was, however, dependent upon the fidelity of the nation to Him, on condition of which they should be a " peculiar treasure " to Him " above all people," or His private property more than all, § and attain extensive dominion in the earth. This indomitable passion for temporal power which finds expression in nearly all the literature of the Jews, far from being regarded as incompatible with their religious strivings and aspirations, appears to have been entertained in so close a connection with the latter that the cause of the nation as a political power was identified with that of Jahveh as the national Diety. A striking warmth and enthusiasm appear in the poetic fervor with which the relation of Jahveh and the people of His choice is expressed under the conception of a " covenant," which was symbolized by the marriage-tie, and the breaking of

* Deut. xxxii. 4.
† Ps. xxxiii. iv.   Numb. xxiii. 19.
‡ Deut. vii. 7.   § Ex. xix. 5.

which was represented as conjugal infidelity.* Along
with this particularism one could not expect to find, as,
indeed, one does not find, any well-developed conception
of a general divine providence. But entirely consistent
with it was the persistent Messianic expectation which
outlived through ages a multitude of misfortunes in
internal dissensions, defeats, captivities, and political an-
nihilation. This was in general a direction of the hope of
the people towards an ideal future in which the political
and religious aspirations entertained by the noblest
minds of the nation and nurtured by the prophets
and psalmists should be gloriously realized. The
Messianic time is sometimes represented as a restoration of the splendors of the Davidic age ; sometimes its
fulfilment is to be accomplished through a King or Messiah ; and again it is depicted without mention of this
personality as a time when misfortune and sorrow shall
have ceased, when the restoration of the people and the
state shall have been consummated along with the return of
the captives out of bondage and the reunion of the twelve
tribes. A prominent feature of this time, according to
some of the prophetic delineations, will be the forgiveness
of the sins of the people and their spiritual purification,
when the law of God shall be in their inward parts and
written in their hearts, and all shall know Him from the
least unto the greatest, for He shall forgive their iniquity
and remember their sin no more. Finally, the prophetic
optimism reaches its culmination in the extravagant vision
of recognition by foreign nations of Israel and Jahveh.
when " the mountain of the Lord's house shall be established in the top of the mountains * * * and all
nations shall flow to it ; * * * for out of Zion shall

* Hos. ii. 2, 19 f ; iv. 12, 15 ; Jer. iii. 9.

go forth the law, and the word of the Lord from Jerusalem." * It is by the intervention of Jahveh that this great spiritual transformation of His people is to be effected—of Him who " retained not His anger forever, because He delighteth in mercy." He will " subdue the iniquities" of the people and " cast all their sins into the depths of the sea." † Again, the thought is expressed, which has been called the profoundest in the Old Testament, that the suffering of the innocent servant of Jahveh, probably the pious remnant of the nation in the captivity in Babylon, will have as its result the repentance of the people and their return to God. ‡

The Jewish conception of the relation of the Deity to human affairs is that of an immediate divine direction. This is a corollary of the theocratic idea, and governs the pragmatism of the biblical writers who paid little regard to secondary causes. Historical events are not conceived as following a natural course, but as brought about by the power of God who is a worker of wonders, getting the victory by His " right hand " and His " holy arm." § The all-sufficient divine efficiency is made even more striking by belittling the human agencies through which it operates, which are sometimes chosen with great arbitrariness and, indeed, by means of very trivial tests.‖ All this appears to have the twofold object of glorifying Jahveh and taking from man all occasion for boasting.¶ The subject of the theocracy was, however, by no means held to be free from responsibility in the midst of this vigorous and obtrusive

* Isa. ii. 2, 3 ; see also Micah iv. 1–4, vii. 11–13 ; Zech. viii. 20–23.
† Micah vii. 18, 19 ; see also Ezek. xxxvi. 25-27.
‡ Isa. lii. 13–liii. 12.
§ Ps. lxxvii. 15, xcviii. 1 ; Ex. xiii. 3, xiv. 31.
‖ Judges vii. 2–7.
¶ Ezek. xx. 14, 22, 44, xxii. 22, xxxvi. 21–23.

divine regency. It is for him to obey, and strict account is taken of his transgressions. The divine righteousness demands the righteousness of man, and is offended at the sight of sin, which may indeed be forgiven to the penitent, but must be atoned for, that is, " covered " by sacrifice, an elaborate system of which appears in the Pentateuch, and is recognized in the post-exilian books. The sin may be atoned for by punishment, by sacrifices, or according to one great writer by the sufferings of an innocent person. The prophets and some of the psalmists attained a higher conception of God's dealing with sin, and declared that the sacrifice of a broken spirit was the one acceptable to Him, who would have no more the offerings of victims and took no pleasure in bloody altars.

Although the governmental conception of God was fundamental in the theocracy, and was so held in the earlier development of the Jewish religion as almost to exclude from thought all other divine attributes, the progress of the people could not but eventually bring about the recognition of the humane sentiments and the consequent ascription to God of qualities which were regarded as noble in man. The mercy of God as the Ruler of the chosen people is a theme on which the writers of the Pentateuch and the prophets and psalmists frequently dwell with great fulness and fervor of expression.* It is, however, generally under the particularistic, national limitation that the divine attributes of love and mercy are conceived, although special personal applications of them are not wanting, notably in the Psalms. The idea of God as a Father is not, indeed, foreign to the Old Testament, but it generally appears only in an especial application to Israel.

---

* Ex. xxxiv. 7 ; Num. xiv. 18 ; Deut. vii. 9 ; Neh. xiii. 22 ; Ps. xxv. 10, lxxxvi. 5, 15, etc.

Jahveh is represented now as the father, now as the husband of His people.* A more general conception of the divine fatherhood appears to be expressed in the beautiful words of a psalmist: "A father of the fatherless and a judge of the widows is God," and again: "Like as a father pitieth his children, so Jahveh pitieth them that fear Him."† In one of the later Psalms the limits of nationalism are broken over and the goodness of God is sung as including foreign peoples. The divine mercy is invoked that the way of God "may be known upon the earth," His "saving health among all nations."‡ In some of the Old-Testament apocryphal books are found conceptions of the universal divine providence and love which remind us of the teachings of Jesus. Here we read that the mercy of the Lord is upon all flesh, chastening, disciplining, teaching;§ that he pities all, loves all things that are, and abhors nothing that He has made, for if he had hated anything He would not have created it.‖ It is probable, however, that these doctrines must be regarded as greatly in advance of the prevailing opinions, since under the influence of the dominant nationalism they rarely come to expression in the literature of the people. They appear to be the views of a few advanced thinkers who in part anticipated by two or three hundred years the great Teacher of his nation and of the world.

From the time of Ezra to that of Jesus, the legalistic conception of the relation of the people to Jahveh held undisputed sway, and was especially upheld by the Pharisaic party. The misfortunes under which the nation had

* Jer. xxxi. 9, ii. 1 ; Hos. xi. 1 ; Mal. ii. 10.
† Ps. lxviii. 5, ciii. 13.   ‡ Ps. lxvii.
§ ἔλεος δὲ κυρίου ἐπὶ πᾶσαν σάρκα, κτλ. Sir. xviii. 13.
‖ Wisdom xi. 24 f, ἀγαπᾷς γὰρ τὰ ὄντα πάντα, κτλ.

suffered in the destruction of their city and in the Baby-
lonian exile being regarded as divine punishments for their
infidelity to Jahveh, they thought to secure His favor and
the fulfilment of His promises by a strict observance of all
the requirements of the law. Accordingly, while they
still suffered from wars and oppression, and bore the
burden of ritual and ceremonial, they were ever eagerly
inquiring when the kingdom of God was coming. Such
a period of unrest, suffering, revolt, and expectation was
well calculated to produce an abundant apocalyptic literature which undertook by means of a prophetic representation of divine interventions, cataclysms, and violent
subversions of the historical course of affairs, to solve such
problems as the reconciliation of the accumulating misfortunes of the people with God's choice of them as His own,
as the true interpretation of His ancient promises, as their
own national inferiority to the great and victorious world-
powers about them, and as the relation which the true
religion of Israel ought to assume towards the foreign
culture, beliefs, and worship. * With regard to this last
problem, three tendencies existed, that which favored a
toleration of foreign beliefs, that which vehemently
opposed such an attitude, and the syncretism of the Jews
of the Dispersion who had felt the influence of Hellenic
culture, and of whose views and aims the Alexandrian
philosophy as developed by Philo may be regarded as the
most finished expression.

In several matters of importance, however, a general
agreement existed among both Palestinian and Alexandrian Jews.   1. The writings which had been handed
down from ancient times, and regarded as clothed with
canonical authority, were looked upon as given by the

* See the Apocalypses of Daniel, Enoch, Baruch, Esra, etc.

inspiration of God, and held in superstitious reverence. Nothing could be farther from the thought of a Jew of the time of Jesus, or, indeed, of some centuries before and after, than to question the infallibility of the sacred books of the nation. These were the centre of all religious interest, the subject of learned inquiry, and the basis of instruction in the schools and of edifying discourse in the synagogue. It is almost needless to remark that it did not accord with this point of view to apply critical inquiry to these books in order to ascertain the facts regarding their authorship, date of composition, and authenticity. The traditional ascription of authorship was sufficient, and that Moses wrote the Pentateuch, and that the entire book ascribed in the canon to Isaiah was the work of that prophet, were propositions which no one thought of questioning. But with all this literalism and worship of the Book post-exilian Judaism was degenerate and spiritually dead. The priest had succeeded to the prophet; the teachers were occupied with artificial and refined interpretations of the sacred books; and in the endless course of an obtrusive ceremonial were unheeded the admonitions of the great prophets of Israel's golden age of religious life, enjoining righteousness, fidelity, truthfulness, mercy, and justice, with consideration for the poor, the feeble, the widows and orphans. If this literalism and spiritual degeneracy may be placed in the relation of cause and effect, no better illustration could be furnished of Paul's great saying that " the letter killeth." 2. The conception of the Deity tended to assume a more spiritual character towards the Christian era and to become more puristic and transcendent. The name of God was removed from common use, regarded as unspeakable, *

* ἄῤῥητον.

and avoided as much as possible in the oath and in ordinary speech by means of other terms. The Alexdrian translators rendered it throughout by the Greek word for Lord, *κύριος*, and Sirach forbids the naming of the Holy One.* Philo also expressly designates the divine name as an *ἄῤῥητον*. The attempt was made to trace back this concealment of the name of Jahveh to ancient times, and to support it by the authority of Moses.† In accordance with this puristic idea, and perhaps in consequence of more refined conceptions of the divine Being, appears to be the endeavor to alleviate or remove the anthropomorphism which in the Old Testament ascribed to Him a human form, members, senses, etc., and the anthropopathism according to which He was represented with human passions. The Septuagint, the Samaritan Pentateuch, and the writings of Philo and the other Alexandrian philosophers show this tendency in differing degrees. 3. In immediate connection with, and perhaps dependent on, these views of the nature of God was developed a more complete angelology than appears in the early literature of the Jews. Not unknown, indeed, to the earlier Hebraism was the conception of angelic beings who served as messengers of Jahveh, shared in His counsels, and formed His court. But towards the time of Jesus this originally *naïve* and poetic idea assumes a more dogmatic expression under the influence of Persian doctrines, and we find angels named and classified. The divine manifestations and interventions are supposed to be effected through the agency of these intermediate beings or by the hypostasized glory of God (Shechinah) or by the Word (Memra). Thus the Deity is thought of as withdrawn from direct participation in the affairs of men

* *ὀνομασία τοῦ ἁγίου*, xxiii. 9.   † Levit. xxiv. 11-16.

in accordance with the extreme conception of His holiness. 4. To Persian influence must without doubt be ascribed the doctrine of evil angels which does not appear in any of the pre-exilian books. The most striking appearances of Satan, *i. e.*, Adversary, are in the books of Zechariah and Job. In Job he appears among "the sons of God," and is not represented as an enemy of the Deity or an outcast from His presence, but as a member of His court. In the former book his opposition to God is more distinctly set forth, and in 1 Chronicles he appears as a tempter of the king to an act of disobedience which in 2 Samuel is represented as done at the instigation of Jahveh himself. In 2 Chronicles xviii. 20 f, a "lying spirit" is spoken of as coming forth apparently out of the group of angels surrounding the throne of God and offering to entice Ahab to destruction. Here the Satan of the book of. Job appears as a demon who enters into and speaks through false prophets, if any connection may be supposed to exist between the two conceptions. At any rate this appearance of the Jewish belief in demons is not without importance for the later doctrine of "possession." Starting from the legendary account in Genesis of the "sons of Elohim" who had intercourse with the daughters of men, there was developed a doctrine of fallen angels, which in the apocryphal book of Enoch is worked out in great detail. In the books of Tobit and Baruch evil spirits play an important part as crafty and powerful enemies of mankind, and in Josephus appears a well-developed demonology which deviates from that of the book of Enoch in representing the demons as the spirits of bad men. The exorcism of evil spirits by means of the fumes of the heart, liver, and gall of a fish is mentioned in Tobit vi. 6, 7, viii. 2, 3.

The intense Messianic expectations of the time shortly before and after Jesus appear in the Palestinian apocalypses and the frequent revolts. The pre-Messianic and the Messianic periods were designated respectively as " this age," or " the present age," and " the age to come." * The signs of the coming of the Messiah were thought to be tribulation, natural convulsions, and political upheavals,† and Elias was expected as a forerunner.‡ In connection with this Messianic expectation was held the doctrine of a bodily resurrection, which the Sadducees denied, while the Essenes and the Alexandrians contented themselves with a belief in a purely spiritual immortality. The allegorical method of interpreting Scripture should also be mentioned as a striking phenomenon of this age. It was practised by Philo and the Palestinian scribes, though strangely combined by the latter with a most rigid literalism. §

2.—THE KINGDOM OF GOD.

The consideration of the teaching of Jesus respecting the kingdom of God naturally comes first in order, because it is with the proclamation of this kingdom that the

* αἰὼν οὗτος, αἰὼν μέλλων.

† Dan. xii. 1 ; 4 Esr. xv. 5, xvi. 22, 23 ; Matt. xxiv. 7, 8.

‡ Mal. iii. 1 ; iv. 5.

§ On the subjects treated of in this section see especially Holtzmann, Judenthum u. Christenthum, 1867 ; Toy, Judaism and Christianity, 1890; Weber, System der altsynag.-paläst. Theol., etc., 1880 ; Langen, Das Judenthum in Paläst. zur Zeit Christi, 1866 ; Keim, Gesch. Jesu, i. 1867 ; Wendt, Die Lehre Jesu, ii. 1890 ; Nicholas, Des Doct. rel. des Juifs, 1860 ; Noack, Urspr. des Christenthums, i. 1857 ; Gfrörer, Das Jahrh. des Heils, i. 1838 ; Havet, Les Orig. du Christianism, iii. 1884 ; Hausrath, Neutest. Zeitgesch, i. 1868 ; Immer Neutest, Theol., 1887 ; Kuenen, The Religion of Israel, iii. 1875.

story of the Gospels opens. The oldest Gospel connects the New Testament with the Old by applying to John the Baptizer the theocratic words of the second Isaiah which announce the coming of Jahveh in His kingdom: " The voice of one crying in the wilderness, ' Prepare the way of the Lord, make straight His paths.' " * Our first canonical Gospel places before this announcement the statement that the preaching of John was summed up in the terse and comprehensive words: " Repent, for the kingdom of heaven is at hand." † In like manner the first Gospel represents Jesus as beginning his ministry after the baptism with precisely the same proclamation, and the second Gospel puts into his mouth the words: " The time is fulfilled, and the kingdom of God is at hand; repent, and believe the glad tidings." ‡ This term, kingdom of God, or of heaven, was not original either with John the Baptizer or with Jesus, and in opening his ministry with its announcement, as we must believe he did, since the oldest Gospels so represent, Jesus connected his mission with the history and the theocratic-political hopes of his nation. The kingdom of God was an expression well known to the Jews of his time, and was understood by them in the genuine national theocratic sense as the ideal realization of that kingship of God over His people which through the entire canonical and apocryphal literature is regarded as the normal relation which would subsist when the promises of the prophets and the theocratic-

* Mark i. 3 ; *cf.* Isa. xl., 3.

† Matt. iii. 2. In the first Gospel "kingdom of heaven," βασιλεία τῶν οὐρανῶν, is always used, with four exceptions. Mark and Luke employ "kingdom of God," βασιλεία τοῦ θεοῦ.

‡ Mark i. 15. The third Gospel omits this announcement, and describes the beginning of Jesus' ministry vaguely thus: " And he taught in their synagogues, honored by all," iv. 15.

religious hopes of the people should be fulfilled and realized.

That the traditional Jewish conception of the kingdom of God was in important respects modified in the teaching of Jesus there is no doubt, and these modifications will be considered further on ; but in respect to the temporal character and theatre of this kingdom his teaching was a continuation of that of the prophecies and apocalypses which preceded him. We have seen that at the beginning of his ministry he took up the announcement of the Baptizer that the kingdom of God was at hand. That it was not only near, but had already come, is implied in the saying that "from the time of John the Baptizer until now the kingdom of heaven suffereth violence and the violent seize upon it." * As a proof that it has " already come," he adduces his casting out of demons " by the finger of God." † When asked by the Pharisees as to the time of the coming of the kingdom, he answered that it was not to come in such a manner as to be watched for, but that it was there already in the midst of them. ‡ In the explanation of the parable of the tares, which is announced as a parable of the kingdom of heaven, the field is said to be the world, and the sower of the good seed the Son of Man, while the distinction is clearly drawn between the existing kingdom and the future " consummation of the age," § in which the perfection of the former is to be effected by a process of purification. In the series of parables to which this one belongs that of the leaven which should effect a universal transforma-

* Matt. xi. 12 ; Luke xvi. 16.
† Matt. xii. 28 ; Luke xi. 20.
‡ Luke xvii. 20, 21.
§ συντέλεια τοῦ αἰῶνος τούτου, Matt. xiii. 39.

tion, and that of the grain of mustard which grows to a great tree "so that the birds of the air come and lodge in its branches," both prophesy the development of a spiritual world-kingdom. The temporal point of view also obtains in the injunction not to be anxious about food and raiment, but to seek first the kingdom of God and His righteousness in the assurance that He whose providence clothes the lilies will care also for men. The blessing pronounced upon the poor in spirit and upon those persecuted for righteousness' sake implies the present existence and possession of the kingdom of heaven.* It already is, and its privileges are enjoyed by the poor in spirit and the persecuted. As an existing economy the publicans and harlots are said to be entering into it before the chief priests and the elders.† As introduced into the world, it is not necessarily limited by national boundaries, but may be taken from one people and given to another. ‡ It is evident, then, that the kingdom of God in the thought of Jesus was the realization in human society of the highest moral and spiritual ideals. Its perfection would be attained when the will of God should be done by men on the earth as it was conceived to be done in heaven by the angels. Jesus was no dreamer, brooding over nebulous philosophizings as to the solution in a celestial future of the problems of life and destiny, but a practical reformer, God-inspired and filled with a divine enthusiasm of righteousness, who would overcome wrong, selfishness, and sin upon the earth by the heavenly powers of truth, love, and holiness. He was a new preacher of the old, sound, strong religion of conduct by which

* Matt. v. 3, 10.
† Matt. xxi. 31.
‡ Matt. xxi., 41.

4

his nation had attained all its greatness, and in which alone it had then, broken and disheartened, any hold upon the future. He was a disciple and continuator of the great prophets of Israel who, in the midst of a flood of adverse fortunes and overwhelming defeats, never ceased to proclaim their faith that God could and would establish upon the earth a kingdom wherein should dwell righteousness. Not less than theirs was his confidence in God, and with all the ardor and earnestness of a great nature he devoted himself to the fulfilment upon the earth of the promises of the prophets and of his own prophetic hopes. The first historic departure from this great purpose occurred through the weakness and superstition of his followers when, after the tragedy which ended his earthly career, they began, " gazing up into heaven," to revel in visions and apocalypses of his second coming; and the latest infidelity to this heroic faith is presented in the absorbing occupation of modern Christendom with refinements of theological speculation and problems of future salvation.

If, however, Jesus regarded the kingdom of God as introduced among men by his teaching, it was not yet completed and consummated. He and a few followers who did not half comprehend him were alone its representatives against an unfriendly world. Out of these feeble beginnings his indomitable faith beheld a future growth of the kingdom to greatness and power. Through all his teaching there runs the apparent paradox that the kingdom is here, and that it is yet to come. He asserts that a greater than any of the old prophets had announced it, and that with himself it had come into the world, yet he teaches his disciples to pray that it may come, and that in its coming God's will may be done upon the earth.

He compares it to a grain of mustard which is yet to grow to a great tree, and to leaven whose vast process of transformation is yet to be accomplished. It is evident, then, that to his prophetic insight the kingdom of God, his kingdom, was destined to have an historical development and to be a victorious transforming force among the earthly powers of the future. But heavenly Patience and Faith must watch over its processes, and withhold the rash hand which would pluck up the tares to the destruction of the wheat.* In the consummation whatever the enemy has wrought will be condemned and rejected, and the good will be garnered and preserved. Not according to the idea of the Baptizer did Jesus bear in his hand the winnowing-shovel. He had the patience which was wanting to the fierce prophet of the desert, and with more comprehensive mind and farther sight saw in the processes of the ages the consummation of his kingdom.

Here we might leave Jesus' conception of the future of his kingdom in the world, with nothing to mar it as a product of a noble and sound intelligence, of moral earnestness and a great faith in the truth and in God, were it not that some words are ascribed to him in the Gospels which appear to represent an altogether different view of the matter. For nothing can be more opposed to this sane and rational conception of the development of his kingdom, which we have seen to be expressed in the parables of the grain of mustard and the leaven, than is the idea of a sudden crisis and a hasty consummation within the generation then living, which appears to be conveyed in the words: " Truly do I say to you, there are some of those standing here who will not taste of death till they

* Matt. xiii. 24–30.

have seen the Son of Man coming in his kingdom."* A violent interference with the order of natural development and a catastrophic descent and establishment of the kingdom with the aid of celestial powers are indicated in the explanation of the parable of the tares. At the "consummation of the age," † or, as the words are commonly rendered, at "the end of the world," "the Son of Man will send forth his angels, and they will gather out of his kingdom all the stumbling-blocks and those who do iniquity, and will cast them into the furnace of fire; there will be wailing and gnashing of teeth." The parable of the net is made to close with the introduction of similar mythological features: "So it will be at the consummation of the age. The angels will come forth, and separate the wicked from among the righteous, and will cast them into the furnace of fire; there will be wailing and gnashing of teeth." ‡ This also is said to be a parable of the kingdom of heaven. We meet here with an expression which appears strange in the mouth of Jesus, "the consummation of the age." A related expression is also found in other sayings ascribed to him in the Gospels, as in that with reference to the sin against the Holy Ghost, which he is made to say would "not be forgiven in this age or in the age to come." § These latter terms also appear in the very materialistic promise to the disciples put into the mouth of Jesus in answer to the implied question of Peter as to what they were to get who had left all to follow him: "There is no one who hath left

* Matt. xvi. 28.   Mark reports the saying differently: "Till they have seen that the kingdom of God hath come with power," ix. 1, and Luke softens it into: "Till they have seen the kingdom of God," ix. 27.

† συντέλεια τοῦ αἰῶνος.

‡ Matt. xiii. 41–43, 49, 50.

§ Matt. xii. 32.

house, or brothers, or sisters, or mother, or father, or children, or lands, for the sake of me and of the glad tidings,
who will not receive a hundred-fold in the time that now
is, houses, and brothers and sisters, and mothers, and
children, and lands, with persecutions, and in the age to
come [ἐν τῷ αἰῶνι τῷ ἐρχομένῳ] everlasting life." *
According to the first Gospel these material rewards are
to be enjoyed " in the renovation † when the Son of Man
sitteth on the throne of his glory," and to the apostles
the promise is added that they shall "sit on twelve thrones,
judging the twelve tribes of Israel." ‡

There can be no doubt that these passages present
grave difficulties to those who regard them from the
point of view of the unity of doctrine in the Gospels, and
also to those who suppose that the views of Jesus regarding the nature of his kingdom and the manner of its consummation underwent a gradual change from the beginning to the end of his career. The former theory puts
too great a strain upon exegesis, and requires in short
nothing less than the reconciliation of irreconcilable oppositions, of a process by evolution with a swift completion by convulsions effected through celestial agencies, of
sober practical judgment and faith in the divine order
with dreams and visions of Jewish Apocalypses. As to
the latter hypothesis, it does not, indeed, require us to

* Mark x. 29, 30.

† παλιγγενεσία, "that restoration of the primal and perfect condition of things which existed [as was supposed] before the fall of our first
parents which the Jews looked for in connection with the advent of the
Messiah, *and which the primitive Christians expected in connection with the
visible return of Jesus from heaven.*" Grimm-Wilke's Clavis N. T. *sub
voce;* Gfrörer, Das Jahrh. des Heils, ii. p. 101 ; Weber, System der Altsyn.-
paläst. Theol. p. 380 f ; Cremer, Bibl.-Theol. Lexicon of N. T. Greek,
p. 150.

‡ Matt. xix. 28–30.

attempt impossibilities, but so radical a change in Jesus' conception of the kingdom of God as it supposes should not be assumed unless an adequate cause for it can be found in his environment. It is not at all improbable that the attitude which the Jewish authorities assumed towards him near the end of his ministry may have cooled the ardor of his early hopes in the success of his cause, but the theory that this circumstance could entirely change his conception of the nature of his mission and of the agencies by which its good fortune was to be secured, and lead him to believe that he must invoke the aid of the celestial powers, and come on the clouds of heaven in order to establish it, is too bold and violent by far. It implies in the first place the assumption that he must have regarded the fortunes of his cause as dependent on a merely local and temporary condition, and, indeed, in general, upon the reception which it might have among the Jews of his time. This is to suppose an almost total collapse of that heroic faith which we have seen that he had in the historic fortune of the kingdom of God and a resort to superstition, the refuge of little minds and the last stage of the degeneracy of a feeble faith. Besides, great difficulties attend the attempt to show that Jesus held different views at different periods of his ministry, and especially that there was a marked development in his opinions as to the nature of his mission and the character of the kingdom of God, for the reason that the chronology of the Gospels is sometimes uncertain and again altogether indeterminable. But apart from these difficulties, it cannot but appear strange to the historical judgment that Jesus, who had repeatedly declared that the kingdom of God was already among men, and that his public ministry had introduced it, should speak of it, as in the passages previously quoted, as if it were yet to come, and should employ the expressions, "the age to come," and "the renovation," which could only be understood according to the usage of the time as referring to the Messianic age, or the age of the kingdom of God, still in the future. Did he at one time think that he had actually introduced the kingdom of God, and that it was to have an historical development, and did he afterwards waver and doubt? Did he teach both that its coming was not as of something to be "watched for," that it was already "in the midst" of men, and also that it was yet to come with *éclat*, with the Son of Man riding on the clouds attended by a troop of angels? Did he at one time plainly teach by implication that the judgment of his kingdom was moral, silently executing itself in the lives of men and discriminating between honesty and hypocrisy, between penitent harlots and self-righteous Pharisees, and at another time declare that this judgment was to be dramatic and apocalyptic, executed by "angels" who should "come forth" and cast the wicked into a furnace of fire? Did he at one time teach his disciples that it is the law of the kingdom of God that he who would be first among them should be their servant, and at another that in the "renovation," or the apocalyptic kingdom, they should sit on twelve thrones judging the twelve tribes of Israel? Did he give them at one time the sane and sober assurance that they should drink of his cup and be baptized with his baptism—a promise which was indeed not only fulfilled in their experience, but has been fulfilled in that of all his true followers since—and did he at another time expressly implant in their minds insane hopes of dominion and thrones to be enjoyed within that generation—hopes which were never realized, and never could be—dreams of Jewish apocalypses?

In attempting to answer these questions and to determine what was Jesus' real conception of the consummation of the kingdom of God, whether it was an historical or an apocalyptical conception, we must first of all renounce those exegetical subtilties by which it is sought to reconcile things that are irreconcilable, and for which all difficulties disappear by a reference to figures of speech. The question to be answered is, " Is it more probable that Jesus used this apocalyptic language than that it expresses the hopes and expectations of a later time? " It should be borne in mind that no grounds exist for a definite settlement of this question, and that the greater probability must be the end of the inquiry. If Jesus conceived of the Messianic mission in accordance with the ideas of his time, there is nothing improbable in the supposition that he may have used such language as that quoted from the Gospels in the preceding pages. But it is certainly difficult not to think that his ethical conception of the kingdom of God should exclude, should render impossible to him, such apocalyptical ideas and such unrealized and unrealizable hopes. We may say, indeed, that " his ethical purity and greatness are independent of all such local opinions," * but it is not easy to reconcile his holding of them with the intellectual greatness, sobriety, and strength, with which we see that he elsewhere conceives and unfolds the idea of the kingdom. The question has often been asked: How can we account for the expectations of such an apocalyptical consummation of the kingdom of God which are found in the Gospels and Epistles if Jesus did not speak substantially as he is reported? This diffi-

* Toy, Judaism and Christianity, p. 358.

culty may not be capable of an entirely satisfactory explanation, but it appears much less formidable than before, after one has read the passages relating to the second coming in connection with the apocalyptical writings which influenced Jewish thought in the first century after Christ, and when one also considers that the belief of the early Christians in the Messianic mission of Jesus could not be satisfied without a second manifestation which should efface the ignominy of Calvary, institute a judgment upon the enemies of the good cause, and reveal the defeated and humiliated Jesus of history as the real and victorious Messiah of the " age to come." The Jewish Messianism which finds expression in the half-despairing half-hopeful words ascribed by tradition to two disciples on the road to Emmaus, " But we are hoping that it is he who is to redeem Israel," * considered in connection with the demonstrable tendency to exalt and glorify the person of Jesus which set in soon after his death, furnishes fruitful suggestions as to the origin of apocalyptical passages in the Gospels and Epistles. † A careful and candid consideration of the facts in the case, then, appears to show a preponderating probability for the opinion that the apocalyptic passages in question are not accurately reported words of Jesus. Out of his strong faith in his cause he may very likely have prophesied the future glory and triumph of the kingdom of God upon the earth, and may

---

* Luke xxiv. 21.

† Georgii, Eschatolog. Vorstellungen der neutest. Schriftsteller, Theol. Jahrbücher, iv. 1–25 ; Baur, Vorles. über neutest. Theol. pp. 105–112 ; Keim, Gesch, Jesu, iii. pp. 219, 335; Weiffenbach, Wiederkunftsgedanke Jesu, 1873; Immer, Neutest. Theol. p. 142 f ; Weiss, Bibl. Theol. des N. T. 3te Ausg. 1879, §§ 32–34 ; Toy, Judaism, etc. p. 358 f ; Wittichen, Art. " Zukunft" in Schenkel's Bibel-Lexicon, v., p. 725; Von Cölln, Bibl. Theol., 1836, ii. p. 153.

have connected with his foresight of its fortunes some conception of the judgment which would attend its historical course. But that in the tradition of the early Christians, to whose feverish Messianic hopes the real advent of the Christ was a coming " in power " which was still in the future, his prophetic words should have assumed the highly-colored and extravagant expression of Jewish apocalypses is very probable, and to the historic sense, to say nothing of the sentiment of reverence for Jesus, is more probable than that he should himself have employed such terms. Since nearly half a century elapsed from the time when the words of Jesus were spoken before our synoptical Gospels were written, and since no one of these is the immediate record of a personal disciple, the conditions are not wanting for such a transformation of his sayings regarding the future as this theory requires.

The exclusion of these sensuous and apocalyptic features from the teaching of Jesus finds support in the manifest fact of his spiritual apprehension of the kingdom of God, not, indeed, at a particular period of his ministry, but throughout its whole extent.   It was not the Jewish kingdom of God with its theocratic-national and political features which he preached. He surpassed the greatest of the prophets and the noblest minds of his own time not only in having the courage and faith to declare that this kingdom had already come, but also in conceiving of it not as a condition in which external prosperity and freedom were inseparably connected with an ethical-religious transformation, but in which the former were to be absolutely subordinated to the latter. In fact, one may say that in his thought the kingdom was not a thing to be so much wished and sought for as moral and spiritual fitness for it. The stress is laid in all his teaching upon the ethical and religious renewal of the people, and while it cannot be denied that he occasionally referred to matters of temporal interest, and showed himself, as has been maintained, a patriot * ; that he called Jerusalem in the words of a patriotic Psalm " the city of the great king " ; that he wept over the obduracy of its inhabitants ; and that he warned his fellow-countrymen that unless they repented they would all perish after the manner of the victims of Pilate's wrath, † yet the opinion maintained by Hase and Keim that he conceived the kingdom of God as a theocratic-political institution, or at least that he did not exclude from it earthly and sensuous features ; that " he never transformed the sensuous Messiah-idea into a purely spiritual one " ‡ ; and that " on the way to his death he lifted the banner of the theocratic Messiah aloft even into the heavenly regions," § has against it almost the entire testimony of the synoptic Gospels on which these scholars rely, and finds, of course, not the least support in the fourth Gospel. It results from an examination of the evidence adduced in support of this opinion that it rests to a great extent on those passages which should rather be regarded as expressing the Messianic expectations of the early Christians than included in the genuine teaching of Jesus. The theory that he secretly cherished hopes of a worldly dominion, but refrained from declaring himself as a temporal Messiah from fear of the Roman power, rests on nothing but a conjecture, and is hardly reconcilable with his integrity in view of his open and repeated assertions of his spiritual purpose. The general tendency of his teaching

---

* Hausrath, Neutest. Zeitgesch., p. 367 ; Keim, Gesch. Jesu, ii. pp. 42 f.
† Luke xiii. 3.
‡ Keim, Gesch. Jesu, ii. p. 49.
§ Hase, Gesch. Jesu, 1876, p. 418.

and his whole demeanor are opposed to this theory.   The
subjects of his kingdom were to have the gentleness of
the little child rather than the spirit of the warrior, and the
disposition of the helper and minister rather than that of
the ruler. His ministry was to the humble and poor, and he
made no overtures to the rich and powerful, but rather
declared that those who had great possessions would with
difficulty enter the kingdom.   He forbade the use of the
sword, and though on one occasion he spoke of the conflicts which the entrance of his teaching into the world
would bring about, there is no reason for supposing that he
had in mind a contest for political supremacy.   His triumphant entrance into Jerusalem and his authoritative purification of the temple can hardly be interpreted as an attempt
to assume temporal dominion, in the absence of an appeal
to arms and of a single threat, even by a hint, against the
Roman power.   "To Cæsar the things that are Cæsar's,
and to God the things that are God's," is not the motto of
a revolutionist.

If the foregoing conclusions are valid, there can be
but little room for a difference of opinion on the question
whether Jesus' conception of the kingdom of God was particularistic or universal, that is, whether he conceived it as
a Jewish kingdom or a world-kingdom.   The chief difficulties which this question presents arise from the peculiar
character of the records, or from what may be called the
"tendency" of the writers, by reason of which they appear consciously or unconsciously to favor in their representations of the teachings of Jesus the Jewish-Christian
or the Pauline view of the Gospel.*   Our first and third
Gospels in which the tendencies are more marked than in

* See the author's Gospel-Criticism and Historical Christianity, 1891, pp.
291-305.

the second must, accordingly, be used with discrimination in the study of this question. Mark as well as Luke represents Jesus as not confining his ministry to the Jews, but as visiting the contiguous territory on occasion,* and the first Gospel mentions the journey into Tyre and Sidon.† On the contrary Mark and Luke omit the injunction to the disciples, which the first Gospel records, not to go to gentiles or Samaritans.‡ On the critical theory that Mark is the oldest Gospel, there would appear to be good reason for supposing that this prohibition did not belong to the original tradition of Jesus, but was added to the first Gospel by its author or editor in its present form, since this record contains other Judaizing traits, and appears on the whole to have been written in the interest of the Jewish-Christian party. There is an apparent conflict of tendencies in this Gospel, which complicates the question of the actual attitude of Jesus towards Jews and gentiles, but the difficulty is somewhat relieved when one discriminates between the actual words of Jesus and the general drift of the record. It is not improbable, too, that Jesus expressed himself differently at different times, and that a sentiment of fidelity to the tradition may have determined the editor of the first Gospel, as well as the author of the third, to retain sayings which appear to conflict with one another. Jesus appears suddenly to have changed his attitude towards the gentiles in the case of the Syrophœnician woman § to whom he at first refused aid with the harsh words, " It is not allowable to take the children's bread and throw it to the

---

* Mark vii. 24, 31 ; Luke ix. 52.
† Chap. xv. 21.
‡ Matt. x. 5, 6.
§ Matt. xv. 21 f.

little dogs," afterwards granting her request because of her " great faith."   In the case of the centurion's servant, however, no hesitation is recorded, and Jesus is said to have commended the heathen officer's faith in a manner far from favorable to the Jews.   If we exclude the commission to preach to and baptize all nations and the sensuously-colored saying that many should come from the east and the west and recline at table with Abraham [*] from the genuine teachings of Jesus, it does not seem to be an improbable conclusion even from the first Gospel that, while Jesus occupied originally the particularistic point of view of the Old Testament,[†] his experience of the susceptibility to his doctrine on the part of the heathen and of the obduracy and hostility of most of the Jews had a tendency not merely to produce in him a sudden impulse, as in the case of the Syrophœnician woman, but to confirm the conviction of the universal destination of the kingdom of God which he would naturally hold by reason of his doctrine of the fatherhood of God and the brotherhood of man.[‡]

3.—THE RIGHTEOUSNESS OF THE KINGDOM OF GOD.

In Jesus' doctrine of righteousness as compared with that of the Old Testament is presented an example of those great transformations of ethical-religious ideas which are inevitable in the course of the spiritual progress of mankind.   The impulse to which these transformations are due often proceeds, as in this case, from a great reli-

[*] Matt. xxviii. 18, viii. 11, 12.

[†] His respect for and observance of the law, Matt. viii. 4 ; Luke xvii. 14 ; Mark xiv. 12 ; Matt. xxvii. 17 ; Luke xxii. 7–9.

[‡] See Matt. v. 43–48, and compare Paul's teaching that the Israelites are first called, the gentiles afterwards, Rom. ix. 30–33.

gious genius. At bottom the idea of righteousness* is a moral one, but it followed the usual course of moral conceptions in assuming a religious application in reference to man's relation to God. Accordingly there appear in the Old Testament two sorts of righteousness, a righteousness of the law and a righteousness of the heart. According to the former conception he was righteous who observed all the statutes of Jahveh, the ceremonies, purifications, festivals, etc., and kept himself from the foreign cults. This legal righteousness is celebrated in many of the Psalms. He is pronounced blessed whose delight is in the law of Jahveh, and whose meditations are on it day and night. The author of the 51st Psalm is unable to free himself from it in the last verse notwithstanding the spirituality of the rest of the composition. The 119th Psalm is conceived throughout in the spirit of this formal righteousness, and some of the great prophets often reveal their limitation by this point of view. The later scripturalism of the scribes tended to develop still further the legalistic conception of human righteousness until it resulted in Phariseeism with its statutory rigor and casuistry. Many passages in the book of Sirach express the profound respect which was felt for this legal righteousness. But together with this artificial righteousness was taught and enforced another which was more profound, and struck its roots deeper into the past. This was a noble moral earnestness touched with the religious emotions of love and trust towards God. It was a righteousness which sprang out of a sense of immediate relation to God, and its law does not fail of expression even in the midst of the mass of legalism which composes the book

* δικαιοσύνη. On the relation of the biblical to the classical Greek sense see Cremer, Bib.-Theol. Lexicon, etc., *sub voce* δίκαιος.

of Deuteronomy: "Thou shalt love Jahveh thy God with all thy heart and with all thy soul and with all thy might." Accordingly it is said that Abraham's trust in God was accounted as righteousness, and there are sung in many of the Psalms the praises of inward righteousness, as purity of heart, innocence, humility, trust in God, benevolence to the poor and destitute. Side by side with the legal conception of righteousness are found in the canonical and apochryphal books of the Jews impassioned expressions of the higher righteousness which is born of the human sense of dependence in which the spirit "cries out for the living God," and the soul pants for Him in its hunger and thirst "as the hart panteth for the water-brooks."* Even when, shortly before the appearance of Jesus, the statutory righteousness predominated and the schools of the scribes were flourishing, the book of Wisdom represents the truly righteous man as one whose understanding is not perverted to evil, and describes him as a friend of mankind.† Righteousness consists, according to this writer, in a knowledge of God.‡ Hillel, an immediate predecessor of Jesus who "embodied in himself all the devotion and all the gentleness of Phariseeism," gave expression to some conceptions of ethical righteousness which for the times were broad and liberal, perhaps even lax, especially in respect to divorce. Words very similar to the Golden Rule of Jesus are attributed to him: "What thou wouldst not have another do to thee do not thou to another." But his teaching was moral rather than religious, and one is

* Ps. xlii. 1, 2.
† Wisdom iv. 11, xii. 19.
‡ τὸ γὰρ ἐπίστασθαί σε ὁλόκληρος δικαιοσύνη, xv. 3. Compare John xvii. 3, "This is the everlasting life, to know Thee," etc.

hardly justified in calling him with Renan "the true teacher of Jesus." *

The fundamental opposition of Jesus' ethical conception of righteousness to that of the teachers and the official orthodoxy of his time appears in his declaration to his disciples that unless their righteousness should exceed that of the scribes and Pharisees they should not enter the kingdom of heaven.† This saying appears to be directed against the hollow externality and legalism which then prevailed, and probably implies that the true righteousness of the kingdom consists in an inward, upright relation to the law spiritually apprehended. That its possession by men is conditioned on moral earnestness and effort is plainly expressed in the injunction: "Seek first His kingdom and His righteousness."‡ Here righteousness is placed foremost among the objects to which the will should be directed, just as in the beatitude, "Blessed are they who hunger and thirst after righteousness," it is made the supreme object of desire. Wherein the righteousness of Jesus differed from that of the Pharisees, and was in some respects opposed to the Old-Testament legislation is shown in detail in the Sermon on the Mount in the passages which emphasize the contrast between the external works and the internal disposition.§ The false prophets are such because "inwardly they are ravening wolves." Not alone the outward act of homicide is murder, but the inward fractricidal

---

* On Hillel see Geiger, Das Judenthum, etc., 1 Abth., 1865, pp. 104 f ; Jost, Gesch., iii. pp. 111 f ; Keim, Gesch. Jesu, i. pp. 268 f ; Toy, Judaism, etc., pp. 264 f.

† Matt. v. 20.

‡ $\delta\iota\varkappa\alpha\iota o\delta\acute{v}\nu\eta$ $\alpha\dot{v}\tau o\tilde{v}$ [$\theta\varepsilon o\tilde{v}$], *i.e.* the righteousness required by God and acceptable to Him, not that given by Him.

§ Matt. v. 21-48, vii. 15.

5

hatred.   The lustful desire is adulterous.*   Profanity is rather the levity with which the name of God is employed than the solemn oath.   The marriage-tie is sacred, and should not be violated by taking advantage of the legal permission of divorce.   Not an eye for an eye and a tooth for a tooth, but rather the endurance of wrong than the returning of evil for evil.   What was " said to those of old time," is surpassed by the great commandment : " Love your enemies and pray for those who persecute you."†   It is not enough to bring the gift to the altar, but it must be brought in a spirit of reconciliation with the " brother " who has " aught against " the worshipper.   There is no reconciliation with God to him who loves not his fellow-man.‡

Indeed, the prominence given to men's duties to one another in Jesus' exposition of righteousness both in the Sermon on the Mount and elsewhere may be regarded as a distinguishing and original feature of his teaching.   In answering the scribe who asked him which was the greatest commandment, he mentions not one commandment but two, and does not appear to subordinate that of love to man to the former, but to place the two upon an equal footing as " like " to each other. §   In this answer he not

* *Nam scelus intra se tacitum qui cogitat ullum,*
  Facti crimen habet—
For he who meditates any secret wickedness within himself incurs the guilt of the deed, Juv. Sat. xiii. 209.

† The commandment to hate one's enemies is not contained in Lev. xix. 18, and seems rather to be foisted upon the law by an inference from its spirit than anywhere found in it.   That the law commanded hatred of an enemy is said by Meyer to be " a false imputation."   Accords with this great injunction have been observed in Pindar, Pyth. ix. 95; Sophocles, Antig. 523; M. Antonin. vii. 70.

‡ See 1 John iv. 20: " For he that loveth not his brother whom he hath seen," etc.

§ Mark xii. 28–31; Matt. xxii. 34–40.

only goes beyond the question, but beyond the law itself which did not place the two commandments in such a relation. Besides there is implied in his answer that these two commandments are not first and greatest in the sense of standing at the head of a series, but that in them are included the whole law and all the admonitions of the prophets. But the most striking, the profoundest, and most original feature of Jesus' teaching of righteousness towards man appears in the point of view from which he regards and presents it. The reason why men should practise love and helpfulness toward one another, the motive which should prompt a benevolent disposition and activity, is the paternal love of God for men. Because God loves men, He takes pleasure in their love of one another, which must be cherished by them if they would be true children of the heavenly Father. Helpfulness, mercy, and forgiveness are not to be extended merely to those who practise them, but to those who may not render like services in return, and even to strangers, foreigners, and enemies.* That he who expects the divine clemency must show mercy toward his fellow-man is taught in the parable of the servant who having been forgiven a debt proceeded to exact payment of an obligation due him from a fellow-servant. The condemnation of the master falls upon him. Gratitude towards the forgiving master should have prompted in him like sentiments and deeds of mercy. Likeness to God is the supreme requirement that is made of man. It were certainly an error to seek to establish the originality of Jesus and his progress beyond the teaching of the Old Testament by appealing to his extension of the doctrine of kindness beyond the national limits and the giving to it of a universal applica-

* Matt. v. 43–48.

tion. For the duty of kindness to strangers and even enemies is by no means foreign to Old-Testament morals*; and the principles of general benevolence had been enforced by heathen philosophers before his time, so that the doctrine of love toward all men was previous to his promulgation of it the common property of the noblest thinkers. The peculiar, the original contribution which Jesus made to this department of ethics consists in the setting in which he placed the duty of universal love, or perhaps better, in the foundation on which he established it, when he gave it a religious significance and sanction by enjoining it as a duty for men on the ground of the divine love toward them, a duty the discharge of which makes them the spiritual children of their Father in heaven. In this apprehension of man's relation to his fellow-man there is neither any place for a prayer to God for revenge on one's enemies, like that of the imprecatory Psalms, nor for bitter feelings of vengeance in the heart. The vast difference between the desire to heap coals of fire on the head of an enemy, that is, to bring the blush of shame to his face, and the consciousness that if we fail in love and kindness toward him we have ourselves been unfaithful to a great obligation, and have not the spirit of our Father in us, indicates the immense advance which Jesus made in the conception and founding of the duty of man's love to his fellow-man.

The fact of this religious grounding of righteousness toward men naturally leads to the consideration of the religious aspect of Jesus' conception of righteousness in general, or to his doctrine of righteousness toward God. For if

---

* See Ex. xxiii. 4 f, 19 f ; Lev. xix. 9 f, 18, 33 f ; Deut. x. 18, xv. 7–11. xxiv. 17 f ; Ps. vii. 5, xli. 2 ; Job xxxi. 1–22, 29–32 ; Prov. xx. 22, xxiv. 29, xxv. 21 f ; Isa. lviii. 6 f ; Zech. vii. 9 f.

his teaching regarding men's duty to one another did not end
with the Golden Rule and with moral precepts in general,
neither did he limit righteousness to human relations considered under a moral-religious aspect. In a word, he did
not teach and exemplify morals only, but religion also.
He nowhere formulates the principle that morality cannot
attain the greatest strength, permanence, and fruitfulness
without religious sanction, conviction, and fervor; but
this principle is implied in his teaching and illustrated in
his life. His own trust in God was unconditioned, and
sometimes assumed paradoxical and extravagant expressions. His spiritual life was lived in an atmosphere of
prayer. To the storm-tossed disciples he puts the reproving questions: "Why are ye so fearful? How is it that
ye have not faith?" To the anxious ruler of the synagogue
he exclaims: "Fear not, only believe." He assures his
disciples with sublime confidence in God that "all things
whatever ye pray for and ask, believe that ye have obtained, and ye shall have them." * He does not transcend,
but he interprets, the law when he declares that its
"weightier matters" are "justice, mercy, and faith."†
The right attitude toward the "glad tidings" of the
kingdom is to "repent and believe."‡ The trust in God
which he enjoins is, indeed, in the spirit of the Old Testament, which abounds, particularly in the Psalms, in
similar expressions, but it receives through him a new
interpretation by reason of his conception of the Deity.
In his truly original apprehension of religion the old,
haunting "spirit of bondage" is banished, and no longer
does a tone of anxious legalism and of a hesitating, un-
quiet fear color the communion of the soul with God.

* Mark iv. 40, vi. 36, xi. 23.　　　† Matt. xxiii. 23.
‡ Mark i. 15.

The Father is no remote and awful Majesty, and the worshipper is not tortured with the fear that He will "turn from " him. Rather He is the all-pervading, benignant Presence who clothes the lilies, notes the fall of the sparrow, and numbers the hairs of His children's heads. The child's trust in Him may include in its simple petition the material gift of needful bread and the spiritual consummation of His kingdom on the earth. Between the Father who is so near and the child who is so dependent and needy there exists in the religion of Jesus the most intimate relation. There is no place for a mediator. The son who returns penitent from prodigality and riot falls into the open arms of the Father who goes forth to meet him. This great idea of God as Father involved a new conception of righteousness and religion to which the intervention of priest and sacrificial atonement is unknown—a conception to which Hebraism did not quite attain, and which Paul unhappily missed. Here is no righteousness "by faith," nor through saying "Lord, Lord," but he alone is "accounted " righteous who does the will of the Father in heaven.* The demand is great, and is nothing short of imitating the divine perfections, becoming perfect as the Father is perfect, but nothing is said of the impossibility of such an achievement. Man is to cast himself upon God in trust and love, to hear the words of Jesus and do them, to pray for forgiveness of his trespasses, and to follow the Master bearing his yoke and burden. Little account appears to be made of a righteousness without flaws, and nothing is intimated of "imputing righteousness without works," † but great stress is laid upon the disposition, the direction of the will to right doing, great sympathy is shown for the weak, the fallen,

* Matt. vii. 21-27.   † Rom. iv. 6.

the lost,* great joy is expressed over the return of a sinner to righteousness,† he who holds the creed of love to God and man is declared to be "not far from the kingdom of God,"‡ and the penitent publican who with downcast eyes smites his breast and confesses his sins is held up as the type of man for whom there is hope. No beatitude is pronounced upon those who may have become righteous by a perfect fulfilment of the law, nor upon any who by a divine decree may have been "declared" righteous on account of "faith," for such a righteousness is unknown to the original gospel, but they are called blessed who are conscious of their spiritual poverty, and they who hunger and thirst after righteousness are promised fulness of spiritual life.

4.—CONDITIONS OF ENTERING THE KINGDOM OF GOD.

From the times of the prophets the idea of a moral-religious renewal had been connected with the appearance of the Messianic kingdom, and John the Baptizer took up the refrain of his predecessors so far at least as the moral aspect of the renewal was concerned.§ A continuation of the prophetic message it was, too, when both John and Jesus announced repentance as a condition of enjoying the privileges of the kingdom of God. In the teaching of Jesus this word‖ implies a radical change of mind, disposition, purpose, the abandonment of a sinful life and obedience to the will of God. Besides this moral transformation he sought also to bring about a change of mind, of understanding, respecting the nature of the

---

* Matt. xviii., 11 ; Mark xiv., 38. ‡ Mark xii. 34.

† Luke xv. 32. § Matt. iii. 2 ; Luke iii. 11–14.

‖ μετάνοια, Matt. ix. 13.

kingdom as not temporal, but spiritual; in respect to worship, as not outward, but of the heart; and in respect to the place which material possessions and worldly rank and power should hold in the thought and life of men. In connection with repentance he placed the forgiveness or remission of sins,* but affixed to this the condition that the subjects of it must cherish a forgiving disposition toward their fellow-men.† Faith is commended ‡ and enjoined § as an attitude of mind favorable to a right life, and it is mentioned as a condition of receiving certain benefits from the healing power of Jesus and of performing great works,‖ but no doctrine concerning it is formulated. Faith in God occupies the foremost place, and faith in Jesus, or belief in his healing powers, and in the "glad tidings" is also required. Closely related to this appears to be the requirement of a child-like disposition, without which it is expressly declared that no one shall enter into the kingdom of God.¶ Little children, who could give nothing, but were in need of much, who set up no claims and pretensions, but were impressible and receptive, not only called forth the love and the blessing of Jesus, but were regarded by him as having the disposition which in men was required for entering the kingdom of God. Not self-sufficiency, consciousness of merit, and pride of knowledge, but receptivity, and the sense of need and dependence, constitute the disposition of the true disciple. Nothing appears to be more characteristic of the spirit of Jesus than his sympathy with the weak, the dependent, the needy,—those to whom much might be

---

* ἄφεσις τῶν ἁμαρτιῶν.   † Matt. vi. 12, 14, 15.
‡ Matt. viii. 10.   § Mark i. 15, xi. 22.
‖ Matt. ix. 22 ; Mark v. 34 ; Luke vii. 50, viii. 48, xvii. 6.
¶ Mark x. 14.

given and forgiven. Hence the blessing upon "the poor," or as one of the evangelists has it, "the poor in spirit," upon those whose sense of spiritual need is expressed by the words "hunger and thirst after righteousness," and upon those who weep, and those who are hated.* Had not the kingdom of heaven come that the hungry might be fed, the poor have the Gospel preached to them, those who longed for righteousness satisfied with the bread of life, the weeping be made to rejoice, and the mourners be comforted? Not, indeed, as one of the old prophets risen from the dead, but in the spirit of the great writer of the second Isaiah did the Prophet of this new kingdom of God associate with publicans and sinners, and proclaim himself the Saviour of those who needed a physician, come to seek and reclaim the lost.† But while the kingdom of God is not to be earned by a perfect righteousness; while the poor and the weak are received into it with a divine welcome; and while sinners are sought out to partake of its abundant hospitalities; there is still no abatement of the requirement not only of repentance but also of earnest striving. The kingdom is, indeed, a free gift, but it must be sought with strong desire and resolute will. It is not to be passively accepted, but rather "suffers violence," and "the violent seize upon it."‡ If those who will not accept its invita-

---

* Luke vi. 20–22 ; Matt. v. 3–6. It was "the poor" who according to the Old-Testament promise were to be blessed in the happy future time, and the third evangelist gives the beatitude accordingly (vi. 20, *cf.* iv. 18, vii. 22). Did he derive it from a text antecedent to that of the first Gospel? (See Feine, Eine vorkan. Ueberlieferung des Lukas, 1891, p. 113.) The first evangelist adds "in spirit," referring to those who as to their inner life ($\pi\nu\epsilon\acute{\nu}\mu\alpha\tau\iota$) are in a condition of poverty. This is also an Old-Testament conception. See Ps. cxxxi. 1 ; Is. lxvi. 2.

† Luke iv. 16–18 ; Mark ii. 16, 17.   ‡ Matt. xi. 12.

tion are excluded,* no less is he shut out in the darkness who by leaving off the wedding-garment fails to fulfil its conditions.†

These conditions appear in the culmination of their absoluteness and severity in the teaching regarding renunciation for the sake of the kingdom of God. The great requirement of righteousness, the service of God and man, takes unconditional precedence, and whatever is inconsistent with it must be renounced. The less must be sacrificed to the greater, the material to the spiritual interests. Whoever tries to save and serve both will lose all. But he who will lose his life for Jesus' sake and the gospel's will save it.‡ The entrance to life is through a " narrow door " § which is found only by the few who are willing to abandon the broad and easy way of self-indulgence and submit to the hardship and renunciation required by the law of unselfish service. A man cannot serve two masters, ‖ and the righteousness which claims the whole man for the will of God excludes devotion to earthly goods for their own sake. He who will attain it must be ready to stake all lesser values on the one supreme achievement, as the merchant in the parable " sold all that he had'" in order to buy the " one pearl of great price." ¶ The principle of renunciation receives its most uncompromising and harshest expression in the passage in the third Gospel which represents Jesus as turning to a multitude who were going with him and declaring the condition of discipleship to be that one must hate one's father and mother and wife and children and brothers and sisters, yea, and one's own life also, and

---

* Luke xiv. 16–24.   † Matt. xxii. 11.
‡ Mark viii. 35.   § Matt. vii. 13 f.
‖ Luke xvi. 13.   ¶ Matt. xiii. 44–46.

that all that one hath must be forsaken.*   He who would
be his disciple must be willing to bear his " cross " and
come after him.   The terrible significance of this word
" cross " in that time, when it was used as an instrument
of the most cruel death, indicates the extreme act of
renunciation which is here implied.   Milder than this
demand, yet conceived in the same spirit, is the requirement contained in the other two synoptics to pluck out
an eye or cut off a hand or a foot if either prevent one
from entering into life, rather than having all one's
members to be cast into gehenna.†   Of the rich young
man who would " inherit everlasting life," and had kept
all the commandments, the requirement is made to sell
all that he had and give to the poor, in order to supply
the one thing lacking.‡   To one who offered to follow
him, Jesus intimated in most pathetic terms that his
followers might envy the foxes and the birds, which had
their lodging-places, while he " had not where to lay his
head."   To another, summoned to discipleship, who would
first bury his father, the harsh answer is made : " Let the
dead bury their own dead, but go thou and carry the
tidings of the kingdom of God."   Not even a farewell to
the loved ones is permitted, but " no one that looketh
back after putting his hand to the plow is fit for the
kingdom of God." §

The difficulties which some of these passages present are
evident at a glance, and the efforts which commentators
have made to soften their harshness show the necessity
which is felt of reconciling them in some way with modern
sentiments and with other teachings of Jesus.   The

* Luke xiv. 25, 33.   † Matt. v. 29, 30 ; Mark ix. 43–48.
‡ Matt. xix. 16–23 ; Mark x. 17–23 ; Luke xix. 18–23.
§ Matt. viii. 19–22 ; Luke ix. 57–62.

requirement to hate one's nearest kindred in order to become a disciple is revolting to the most sacred feelings of the human heart, and the judgment rejects it in the teaching of one in whose instructions love of all men, the honoring of parents, and the sacredness of the ties of family held a conspicuous place.* The asceticism implied in contempt of one's own life is incompatible with a teaching which demands all the powers of man for the service of God in a kingdom of righteousness whose course and development were to be in human society.† The attempts which have been made to break the natural force of these demands are for the most part unwarrantable exegetical expedients. It is maintained, for example, that " hate " is not used in its ordinary sense, but means " the direction of the will to the separation from others as the opposite of natural love "; that these words were not spoken with reference to a time like ours when the doctrines of Jesus have won a wide recognition and dominion in the world, but at a time when it was necessary to stake all that a man had for the sake of the Gospel; and that it was the method of Jesus to state his requirements with the utmost clearness and brevity.‡ The fact is not without importance that Luke alone has the harsh demand to hate one's dearest kindred. In the first Gospel words bearing a resemblance to these demand that one should not love father or mother " more " than Jesus,§ and in themselves they present no difficulty, since they are in accordance with the general teaching of Jesus

* Mark vii. 10 f, x. 1–12 ; Matt. v. 31 f.

† Matt. xi. 19; Mark ii. 18 f.

‡ Wendt, Die Lehre Jesu, ii. pp. 383–386. Meyer, however, does not approve of the softening of μισεῖ in the passage in question. Commentar, 5te, Ausg. i. 2, p. 464. So also Grimm-Wilke, Clavis N. T. *sub voce.*

§ Matt. x. 37.

that spiritual aims and interests should be regarded as supreme whenever a choice is to be made between them and any temporal concerns whatever. They express, then, a universal truth which is applicable to an age of peace as well as to an age of conflict. The words in Luke, however, appear to be rather an intensified expression of this thought than a genuine saying of Jesus, who never required of his immediate disciples the breaking of sacred ties of kindred, and to whose whole teaching hatred in any form is opposed. Wendt's remark that they have especially a temporal application suggests the thought that they may be the vehement and extravagant expression of the feelings prevalent in a later period of storm and stress.

The requirement of the rich young man to sell all that he had and give to the poor as a condition of inheriting everlasting life has the peculiarity that in some cases more is needful than to keep the commandments. Similar instances of special requirements in particular cases appear to be those of the man who was not permitted to return to bury his father and of him who was forbidden to take leave of his family. Assuming that these are words of Jesus (and there appears to be no good reason for doubting their genuineness), we are not warranted in concluding from them that the general conditions of discipleship were equally severe and harsh. We do not find that Peter was required to give up his house, although he was an immediate follower of the Master who had not where to lay his head. In the case of the rich young man there may have been especial reasons for requiring the sacrifice of his possessions, for according to one of the accounts it appears that, whether from a consciousness of moral deficiency, or from what he saw in the searching look of the Master, he asked : " What lack I yet ?" The demand of

Jesus was doubtless better fitted to his need than to his inclination. The rich enter with difficulty the kingdom of the spiritual life. That it were better for one not to turn back among the spiritually dead mourners to assist in burying the dead, and for another not to take the risk of a farewell to those whom he loved, may fairly be presumed, just as in some it might have been commendable to follow the example of Jesus and not marry, " for the kingdom of heaven's sake." *

5.—GOD AS THE FATHER.

That the Jewish literature antecedent to Jesus furnished substantially the basis of his teaching concerning God has already been pointed out. But as his conception of righteousness was a new creation of an old idea, so it is with his doctrine of God. The Old-Testament idea is retained, and the manner of expressing it is not new. God is Creator, King, Lord of heaven and earth. He has His throne in the heavens, where the angels behold His face, and the earth is His footstool. † The God of Jesus is no impersonal abstraction, but a personality possessing qualities similar to those of men. He has a spirit, acts according to what seems good to Him, that is, thinks, has a will, and is good. ‡ His providence is over all, even to the birds and the grass and the lilies, but particularly over man, the crown of His creation, the immortal, capable of evil and good, and having light within himself. § To him God is merciful and kind, shows His goodness even to the sinner to

* Matt. xix. 12.
† Matt. xi. 25, v. 34–35, xxiii. 22, xviii. 10.
‡ Matt. x. 20, xvi. 23, xix. 17, xxvi. 39.
§ Matt. vi. 22, 26, 28, x. 28.

whom He gives the sun and the rain, hears prayer, observes the servant, forgives, and like a good shepherd will not let His lost sheep go, but rejoices more over one astray found than over ninety and nine in the fold. * The crown of all His attributes, or rather the essence of His nature, as Jesus represents Him is His Fatherhood. The repetition, the fond dwelling upon the word Father, shows its importance, its preciousness, in the thought and the heart of Jesus. To him it is not a figure, but represents a divine reality. It does not stand for a shadow of a human relation, but for a fact above and before all. God is the Father who is in heaven,† Father absolutely. The advance of the thought of Jesus beyond the average Jewish conception is apparent in the extension of his idea of God as Father so as to include all men in the divine family as subjects of the paternal interest and love. Not only did he teach his disciples to pray to God as their Father, but he calls Him "your Father" in addressing the people, ‡ and teaches that as such He cares for all and even gives His holy Spirit to all who ask Him. § With a wonderful tenderness he includes "the little ones" within the scope of the Father's solicitude, whose will it is that not one of them should perish. A general fatherhood is implied in a passage which defines a special sonship, as when he enjoins upon his hearers to love their enemies, that they

* Matt. v. 45, vi. 14, vii. 7, xviii. 12.

† ὁ πατὴρ ὑμῶν ὁ ἐν τοῖς οὐρανοῖς, *i. e.*, distinguished from and above earthly fathers. It is remarkable that except Mark xi. 25, Matthew alone has this full expression and the two other synoptists appear purposely to avoid it, using sometimes simply πατήρ, as is the case with Luke even in the Lord's Prayer. This fact presents a strange problem. See Holsten in Zeitschr. für wissenschaftl. Theologie, 1890, pp. 129 f.

‡ Matt. v. 45, 48, vi. 1, 4, 6, 18, 32.

§ Matt. vi. 31 f ; Luke xi. 13.

may " become " sons, that is, moral-spiritual imitators of their Father, whose sons they of course already are as objects of His interest and love.*   That Jesus' universal conception of the Fatherhood of God made an ineffaceable impression upon the tradition of his teachings is shown in the fact that in the Jewish first Gospel the collection of scattered sayings of his composing the Sermon on the Mount represents not the relation of Jahveh to Israel, but of the Father in heaven to mankind.   This denationalizing transformation of the Jahveh-idea, like that of the Jewish conception of righteousness, of the kingdom of God, and of the Messiah, is a striking evidence of the greatness and originality of Jesus, in whose thought the national gave place to the universally human.

The conception of the Fatherhood of God as it was held in the thought of Jesus resulted in the removal of the contradictions which inhered in the Jewish idea of Jahveh, and hence in its transformation into a purer and nobler type.   Jahveh was on the one hand a consuming fire, a jealous God, who " consumed " men by His " anger," and " troubled " them by His " wrath," and who " set their iniquities before Him," their " secret sins in the light of His countenance," so that " all their days were passed away in His wrath." †   On the other hand He is represented as " merciful and gracious, long-suffering and abundant in goodness," and it is said that He " does not deal with us according to our sins, nor reward us according to our iniquities." ‡   His anger was for the heathen and the wicked Jews, and his mercy for the theocratic and faithful of the chosen people.   Only a few of the loftier

* Matt. v. 44, 45.
† Ex. xxxiv. 14 ; Deut. iv. 24 ; Ps. xc. 7–9.
‡ Ex. xxxiv. 6 ; Ps. ciii. 10.

spirits among the prophets and psalmists saw and declared this merciful and paternal aspect of the divine nature, while the average religious consciousness of the people was darkened and troubled with " a fearful looking-for of judgment." In the teaching of Jesus the contradiction in question is resolved by a bold stroke of religious genius. Banished from the heavens is the jealous God (θεὸς ζηλωτής), and in His place is enthroned the Saviour-God (θεὸς σωτήρ), the Father of love and mercy. This endearing paternal appellation is constantly on the lips of Jesus instead of the stately " Lord," and words expressive of servitude, fear, and wrath, he rarely or never uses.* Not alone does the Father's love dispense pity and forgiveness to the children, but surpassing the conception of a psalmist who sang of its paternal bestowal upon those that " fear Him," it is in the thought of Jesus a seeking love, poured out upon the wandering and lost, and satisfied only with their recovery. † Well does the originality of this beautiful conception justify the saying of Jesus: " No one knoweth the Father but the Son, and he to whom it is, the will of the Son to reveal Him." ‡

The teaching of Jesus concerning the Father is, moreover, by no means a speculative abstraction, but a fruitful practical principle which is brought by him into the most important relations to human conduct. As authoritative requirement on the one hand and devoted obedience on the other express the normal relation of father and chil-

* He uses κύριος, " Lord," several times in quotations from the Old Testament, δοῦλος, " servant," in reference to the relation of man to God rarely (see Matt. xviii. 23–34, xxi. 33–43), and δουλεύειν, " to serve," only once (Matt. vi. 24), while φόβος, " fear," and ὀργή, " wrath," he never employs. Quite in the spirit of Jesus Paul says: " Ye did not receive the spirit of bondage so as to be again in fear," Rom. viii. 15.

† Matt. xviii. 12 f.   ‡ Matt, xi. 27.

6

·dren, so in the thought of Jesus the divine will is the law which man is required to observe. While the relation of man to God in respect to obligation is sometimes represented as analogous to that of servant to master, and the idea of reward is recognized, the highest, the one unique conception of this relation, is that of imitation of the spirit of the Father by men without consideration of reward, but only that they may become true children of God. This method of spiritual training by aspiration and inspiration is the practical outcome of Jesus' doctrine of the Fatherhood of God, and may be regarded as one of the most distinctive and important of his contributions to morality and religion. How he conceived the efforts of man for union and harmony with the Father to be met and responded to on the divine side is most beautifully and effectively set forth in the parable of the Prodigal Son.*   The main thought, the real purpose, of this parable is evidently to represent the paternal disposition of God toward man as a sinner, when penitent he desires to return to Him.   In opposition to the legalistic idea, according to which righteousness alone would win the divine favor and reward, and all sin must be treated with exact penalty and without forgiving grace, he shows by a beautiful touch of nature how the paternal love breaks through all the barriers which the child's transgression had erected, and rushes toward the returning wretched penitent with abundant gifts and overflowing joy. For the father it is a sufficient answer to the unsympathetic complaints of the elder son, who in the parable represents the legalistic point of view, to say : " It is meet that we should make merry and be glad ; for this thy brother was dead, and is alive again ; he was lost, and is found."   Of this parable

<hr>

* Luke xv. 11–32.

from the point of view of its ethical value it should be said that it is encouraging to sinners, but not to sin. The young man, who had consumed his substance in riotous living, stranded at length upon a land smitten with famine, and reduced to the degraded position of a swineherd, presents a terrible picture of the natural consequences of transgression which follow with remorseless certainty unchecked by any pitying hand. But that this inevitable condition is not final, that it is not without hope, that out of the lowest depths the penitent sinner may retrace his shameful way, is shown by the teaching that he still has a longing for his lost estate and the power to will the good, and that at the end of the homeward journey is the father, who will see him afar off, and go forth with open arms to meet him. The religious aspect of Jesus' doctrine of the Fatherhood of God finds its highest expression in this picture of a father yearning for his long-lost son, and joyfully preparing royal hospitalities on his return ; because of the love, hope, aspiration, and devotion which are implied in the heart of the absent prodigal in the supreme moment when he sets his face homeward. It is characteristic of the religion of Jesus that by its teaching of the Father it encourages the wayward and fallen in the hour of shame and weakness with the assurance of waiting love and forgiveness. Not less important, moreover, is the moral aspect of this paternal idea in the corollary of the brotherhood of man. As children of God men are all brothers, and the relation of mutual love and kindness is plainly expressed as a duty even to enemies, on the ground that God is " kind to the unthankful and the evil." It is, accordingly, characteristic of this moral teaching that the practice of brotherhood is not coldly enjoined as a duty, and enforced by the authority of God, but is presented to men as a principle which has not alone the divine sanction but also the divine example for its support.   Thus by Fatherhood in heaven and Brotherhood on the earth the celestial and terrestial realms, which in the common apprehension are widely separated, are united in one great economy in which love is the universal principle.   Morality, therefore, becomes a religion, not as an "enthusiasm of humanity," but as an aspiration after godlikeness.   In view of these facts it is not too much to say that under the idea of God as Father Jesus has presented morality and religion in a completeness and elevation never before attained, in a beauty and spiritual power than which it seems impossible for the human mind to conceive a greater and more effective.

6.—JESUS' ATTITUDE TOWARD THE OLD TESTAMENT.

How Jesus in his teaching of righteousness, of the kingdom of God, and of morals and religion in general, proceeded upon the recognition of the sacred Scriptures of his nation, but transformed and exalted them, has already been shown in several instances.   There remain, however, to be considered a few passages in which his relation to the Old Testament is particularly indicated.   The importance of the subject to an understanding of the spirit and method of the teaching of Jesus warrants a separate treatment in a small space at least.   It is to be noted in the first place that in many cases he speaks like a Jew of his time in appealing to the Old Testament as an authority.   He recognizes the validity of "the commandments of God" when he charges the Pharisees with laying them aside in order to keep their tradition, by which they "make void the word of God.*   He recog-

* Mark vii. 7-17.

nizes "the weightier matters of the law" as binding in reproving the scribes and Pharisees for omitting them.* In answering certain Sadducees regarding the resurrection he appeals somewhat vaguely to "the book of Moses," employing, indeed, a very peculiar method of argumentation.† To the important question, "Which is the great commandment of the law?" he replies by quotations from the Pentateuch, and when asked by the rich young man the way to everlasting life, he refers him to the Decalogue.‡ In the parable of the Rich Man and Lazarus, it is implied that hearing Moses and the prophets would save the brothers of the former from his fate in Hades.§ He defends himself against the charge of violating the sabbath by an appeal to David's example and "the law," and strengthens his argument by a quotation from Hosea.‖ There are several other passages of similar import which might be quoted.

On the other hand, Jesus often employs words which indicate a direct or indirect deviation of his teaching from that of the Old Testament, and in some instances he places himself in pointed opposition to the teachings which had been given to those "of old time." Although in the matter of violating the sabbath he appeals, as already remarked, to the Scriptures, he yet lays down a general rule regarding the purpose of this day which goes far beyond the question of disregarding the letter of the sabbath-law in exceptional cases, and maintains the right of private judgment as to how the day shall be observed in the interest of man. With the bold declaration that "The Son of Man is lord also of the sabbath," he

* Matt. xxiii. 23.   † Mark xii. 24–27.
‡ Matt. xii. 28–31 ; Mark x. 19.   § Luke xvi. 29.
‖ Matt. xii. 3–8.

declines for himself and his disciples subjection to the requirements for the observance of the day sanctioned by the Old-Testament legislation.* He invalidates in principle that part of the ancient code which relates to defilement from external contact by the declaration that "Nothing that entereth into a man from without can defile him." † With regard to divorce he says that the Mosaic permission of it was given on account of the hardness of men's hearts, and thus accords to the law only a transient and temporary value, as not consistent with the real will of God in respect to marriage. ‡ He gives a new reading to the law against adultery, and puts into it a meaning which was not contemplated in the original, or rather supplements it by a new injunction; § and as to the law of retaliation, he unqualifiedly abrogates it, and sets over against it a rule of non-resistance which is expressed in the most extreme terms. ‖ Besides, it is evident that he conceived the prophetic promises of the future and of the kingdom of God in an entirely different way from that of the Old-Testament writers, and that he completely transformed the Messiah-idea of the prophets.

The recognition of and appeal to the law and the depreciation and rejection of it, which appear in the passages just quoted, present a difficulty similar to that contained in the celebrated section of the first Gospel, in which Jesus appears to speak from a point of view of extreme legalism in immediate connection with sayings expressing great freedom and boldness in dealing with the law.¶ The words are: "Think not that I came to destroy the law

---

* Mark ii. 23–28.
‡ Mark x. 2–10.
‖ Matt. v. 38–43.

† Mark vii. 15.
§ Matt. v. 27, 28.
¶ Matt. v. 17–20.

or the prophets: I came not to destroy, but to fulfil. For truly do I say to you, Not till heaven and earth pass away shall one jot or one tittle pass from the law, till all be fulfilled. Whoever shall break one of these least commandments, and shall teach men so, will be called the least in the kingdom of heaven ; but whoever shall do and teach them, he will be called great in the kingdom of heaven. For I say to you, Unless your righteousness shall exceed that of the scribes and Pharisees, ye will not enter the kingdom of heaven." The proper interpretation of this passage in its connection will perhaps solve the difficulty presented by the apparently contradictory passages in question. The question on which the exegesis of the passage depends is, What did Jesus mean by saying that he came to "fulfil" * the law and the prophets? This word may mean in reference to a promise or a prophecy the accomplishment of it by the actual production of the thing promised. But that this cannot be the meaning here is evident from the connection, in which the discourse is of righteousness and not at all of Jesus' fulfilment of prophecy. There are two strong objections to giving to "fulfil" the sense "to cause God's will as made known in the law to be obeyed as it should be " : † first, that since "law" in the passage must mean the whole law, that is, the ceremonial as well as the moral, Jesus is made by this interpretation to declare in flagrant contradiction to the spirit of his teachings that he came to further the observance of the former ; and second, that the antithesis of the two clauses is not preserved, for the word translated "to destroy" ‡ must mean not "to violate," the opposite of

* πληρῶσαι.
† Grimm-Wilke's, Clavis N. T. *sub voce* πληρόω.
‡ *Καταλῦσαι.*

" obey," but " to abrogate," declare or make void.   This is the function of one who has legislative authority.   If, then, we understand "fulfil" in a sense which makes it a proper antithesis to " abrogate," the interpretation results which gives to the passage the meaning: " I came not to invalidate, but to establish and complete the law and the prophets as teachers of righteousness." * Such may very well have been the words of one who impressed the people as speaking with authority, and they are consistent with Jesus' general attitude toward the law in the apparently contradictory passages previously referred to.   In fact, the contradiction which they seem to present disappears in the light of this attitude of freedom and authority toward the Old Testament, assumed by one who was great enough to recognize and accept what was of permanent value in this record and to complete its teachings by adding new precepts and transforming old ideas by fresh interpretations. His fulfilment of the law and the prophets, then, was their completion by establishing and supplementing their fundamental principles—the perfect development of their ideal reality out of the positive form in which it was historically contained and limited. † With the intellectual greatness and spiritual freedom which are capable of assuming such an attitude of independence and supremacy toward the law are entirely incompatible the sayings that " not one jot [the smallest Hebrew letter] or tittle [the hook by which nearly similar Hebrew letters are distinguished from one another] shall pass from the law until all be fulfilled," and that rank in the kingdom of

---

* For other New-Testament usage of πληροῖν in the sense of " fill out," "complete," see Luke vii. 1 ; John xv. 11 ; Acts xii. 25, xiv. 26 ; 2 Cor. x. 6 ; 1 Thess. ii. 16 ; 2 Thess. i. 11 ; Phil. ii. 2.

† Meyer, Commentar, i. 2, p. 149. So substantially Wendt, Immer, Reuss, Baur, Keim, and many others.

heaven is to be determined by the observance or non-observance of "the least" of the commandments of the law. For these words cannot be otherwise fairly interpreted than as including the ceremonial prescripts ; and since it is altogether contrary to the spirit and aim of Jesus to confirm and give permanence to these, it is highly probable that the sayings in question received in the tradition a more Jewish-legalistic expression than he himself could have intended.

This view of Jesus' relation to the Old Testament appears to be confirmed by his answer to a question regarding the fasting of his disciples put to him according to the first Gospel by John's disciples and according to the third by the Pharisees. After giving a qualified recognition of fasting as an expression of sadness, he says : " No one putteth a patch of undressed cloth on an old garment ; for the piece that fitteth in teareth away from the garment, and a worse rent is made. Nor do men put new wine into old skins, else the skins burst, and the wine runneth out, and the skins are spoilt. But they put new wine into new skins, and both are preserved together." * This is a most decided expression in parabolic form of the incompatibility of the spirit of the new doctrine with that of the old, or at least with the old forms. He who attempts to fit the Christian idea of life and duty with the observance of the requirements of the law as to fasting, etc., will come into discord with himself ; " there will be an ever enlarging rent in his religious consciousness ; he cannot retain the old, because the new rejects it." If the spirit of the new teaching be put into a vessel of the old, it will break the vessel, and go to waste. Hence it must create a new form for itself. Let this last statement be duly emphasized. There

* Matt. ix. 16–18 ; Mark ii. 14–22 ; Luke v. 27–29.

was to be no harsh rupture with the old ideas and forms, no violent separation from the venerated historical faith. The new spirit has eternal youth, and can await the processes of evolution to get itself a new tabernacle. Accordingly, Jesus himself with the sublime patience of genius continued to put the new wine into the old skins, inasmuch as he did not radically break with traditional and legalistic Judaism. Wishing to preserve the substantial contents of the law, whatever was permanent and valid in it, he was great enough to know that he could not do this without respecting to some extent the ancient forms. Yet he clearly perceived the fundamental opposition of the new and the old, and foresaw that the vigorous spirit of the one would soon shatter the frail form of the other, and make for itself " nobler mansions " for the new ages to come.

7.—JESUS' TEACHING REGARDING HIMSELF.

That Jesus did not regard a doctrine of his person as a matter of paramount importance is evident from the fact that the historical sources of his teaching, the synoptical Gospels, do not contain any explicit formulation of it by himself. According to their story of his life he is so much occupied with the preaching of righteousness and the kingdom of God and with his mission of helpfulness to men, that an express teaching as to his nature and origin would have the appearance of turning aside from a direct course, and give the impression of incongruity. It is, accordingly, no easy task to determine from scattered intimations and from the various epithets which he applies to himself precisely what teaching respecting his person he intended to convey. The problem is connected with the question whether at different periods of his ministry he held different views of his nature and mission ; and this is again rendered difficult by uncertainty as to the correct chronological arrangement of the materials of the history in the synoptical Gospels. If we regard Mark's Gospel as containing the most correct chronology, and relegate some of the sayings and events recorded in the first Gospel to a later time than is there given to them, it will appear that it was not until near the end of his ministry that Jesus made any express declaration to his disciples of the nature of his mission. It is, of course, an entirely different question how early he became conscious of the real character of his work ; and still another question, on which everything depends with which this discussion is concerned, whether he regarded himself at any time as anything more than a teacher of righteousness and a herald of the kingdom of God. The absence of assumptions of superiority and exceptional rank certainly characterizes one phase of his teaching regarding himself. He lays no claim to a divine origin or nature, or to an extraordinary birth. He applies to himself an adage respecting prophets,* calls himself expressly a teacher,† and rejects the epithet " good " as belonging only to God.‡ The popular opinions respecting his person prior to the scene at Cæsarea Philippi indicate that he had neither claimed to be more than a man nor made upon the people the impression of

---

* Luke iv. 24.   † Matt. xxiii. 8.

‡ Mark x. 18, " Why callest thou me good ? " In the first Gospel Jesus is represented as saying : " Why askest thou me concerning that which is good ? " But here the question of the young man is also different : " What good thing shall I do ? " Yet why the fact that God alone is good should be alleged as a reason why this question should not be asked Jesus is not apparent. Mark's account appears to be the more correct, and Luke's agrees with it.

a superhuman being.   For it appears that he was regarded as John the Baptizer, Elijah, Jeremiah, or some other one of the prophets,* or in other words, as a forerunner of the Messiah.   Another aspect of his teaching concerning himself, however, which is different from this, though not incompatible with it, appears in the titles which he assumed, "Christ," "Son of God," and "Son of Man."

With regard to the title "Son of God," it would appear that Jesus did not think that a doctrine of his divine sonship was of sufficient importance to require at his hands a precise definition of it.   We can accordingly only infer the meaning which he intended to convey by the words which he employed to express his relation to the Father.   For the most part when he addresses God as the Father, or as his Father, or speaks of Him in this relation, there is nothing in the form of words or in the connection which appears to indicate that he thought of his sonship as different in principle from that of other men.†   He teaches his disciples to call upon God in prayer by the name of Father, as he himself was accustomed to address Him, blesses the peace-makers as "sons of God," and exhorts men to love their enemies that they may become sons of their Father who is in heaven.‡   It is doubtful, however, whether this view of the matter contains a complete account of Jesus' consciousness of his

---

* Matt. xvi. 13.

† Matt. vii. 21, x. 32, 33, xi. 25, xii. 50, xvi. 17 ; Mark xiv. 36 ; Luke xxiii. 46, etc.   The expression, "My Father who is in heaven," ὁ πατήρ μου ὁ ἐν τοῖς οὐρανοῖς, is peculiar to Matthew, and is generally used by Jesus when he is speaking of God to others, while in addressing Him he usually employs the simple term, "Father."   Holsten has made an elaborate study of the phrase, ὁ πατήρ μου, etc., in Zeitschr. für wissenschaftl. Theol., 1890, pp. 129–180.

‡ Matt. v. 9, 44, 45.

relation to God as Son. For he sometimes speaks of himself as "the Son," as if he were conscious of a sonship in a peculiar and eminent sense. In the parable of the husbandmen he evidently intends to represent his mission to the Jewish people as that of the "one beloved Son," who was rejected and slain.* A consciousness of preëminence appears also to find expression in the declaration that "no one knoweth the Son but the Father, nor doth anyone know the Father but the Son, and he to whom it is the will of the Son to reveal Him.† An exceptional relation of Jesus to God, at least in the degree of knowledge and communion, appears to be expressed in these words, and the conviction that he had a special mission to men could alone inspire the invitation which follows to those who labor and are heavy laden. This view appears to be the only conclusion of a fair interpretation of these words and others of similar import. Precisely what Jesus meant by this preëminent sonship it may be impossible to determine; but from his teaching respecting the spiritual sonship of those who love their fellow-men the inference appears to be legitimate that he regarded himself as "the Son" by preëminence, as knowing the Father and especially qualified to reveal Him to men, because, having fulfilled in the highest degree the conditions of this sonship, he was conscious of a spiritual affinity and communion with God

---

* Mark xii. 1–12.

† Matt., xi. 27. *Cf.* Luke x. 17–20. It is doubtful whether the original text is preserved in the Gospels, since Justin Martyr and Irenæus were acquainted with a reading which makes Jesus say : "No one knoweth the Father but the Son, nor the Son but the Father, and they to whom the Son may reveal him." Justin, Apol. i. 63, Dial. 100; Iren. Hæres. ii. 6, 1. See Hilgenfild, Theol. Jahrb, 1853, p. 215, Zeitschr. für wissenschaftl. Theol., 1867, p. 406 ; Keim. Gesch. Jesu, ii. p. 379.

which could belong to none who had not attained to his religious experience. His eminence above other "sons of God" would thus appear to be determined by degrees of spiritual endowment or development. This conclusion is supported by his own teaching regarding sonship, while the opinion that he had in mind a metaphysical sonship, that is, a divine nature, or a superhuman generation, is wholly without support either in the passages in question or in other teachings recorded by the synoptists. His consciousness of illumination and endowment from on high and of complete spiritual fellowship with the Father could find no more appropriate expression than the term "Son of God."

The title "Son of God" was, however, a Messianic designation both before and at the time of Jesus, and a consideration of his relation to it in this sense is necessary to a full and fair discussion of the subject. The term in its Old-Testament usage originated in the idea of the theocracy. Both the people and their king were called the son and first-born of God. Nathan is represented as speaking the word of Jahveh in reference to the seed of David: "I will be his father and he shall be my son. If he commit iniquity I will chasten him with the rod of men," etc.* In the second Psalm Jahveh is made to say to the anointed king: "Thou art my son, this day have I begotten thee."† As the Messiah-idea was developed out of the theocratic conception, it was natural that the term "Son of God" should become a Messianic title and acquire a signification synonymous with "Son of David," "Christ," (anointed, or king,) and "Messiah." There are several passages in the Gospels which show that it had

* 2 Sam. vii. 14.
† Verses 7, 12.   See also Ps. lxxxix. 27.

this meaning at the time of Jesus.* That this was not, however, the direct designation of the Messiah at that time, giving prominence to those characteristics of him on which the Jews laid the chief stress, and that the popular titles were " Anointed " ($X\rho\iota\sigma\tau\acute{o}s$), " King of Israel," and "Son of David," appears evident from the frequent recurrence of these terms in the Gospels and contemporaneous writings.† But however the Jews of his time may have regarded this appellation, there can be no doubt that Jesus attached to it primarily the idea of spiritual likeness to and fellowship with God, the Father. If he accepted it as a Messianic designation at all, it was in the sense of a transformed Messiahship, according to which the Messiah was not the Son of David and a temporal ruler, but the Son of God and a religious teacher and Saviour. He must have thought himself not to be the Son of God because he was the Messiah, but to be the Messiah because he was the Son of God. This complete reversal of the ideas of his time is a striking evidence of his originality and his religious genius. Whether or no he believed himself to be a descendant of David " according to the flesh," he never appealed to such a descent as evidence of Messiahship. On the contrary, after the multitude had hailed him as the son of David on occasion of his entry into Jerusalem he repudiated this relationship as belonging to the Messiah by an argument which, though it may seem strange to one who holds the modern ideas of interpretation, was doubtless convincing to the Jews. How,

* Mark xiv. 61 ; Matt. xvi. 16 ; John xi. 27, xx. 31.

† Mark x. 47, xi. 10, xv. 2, 18, 26, 32 ; Matt. ii. 2 ; John i. 49. Ps. Sol. xvii. 5, 23. 4 Esdras xii. 32. For the designation of the Messiah as Son of God there are to be quoted, Enoch cv. 2 ; 4 Esdras vii. 28, xiii. 32, 37, 52, xiv. 9. See Schürer, Gesch. des jud. Volkes, ii. p. 443.

he asks, can the Christ be David's son, since David calls
him lord ? *

That Jesus believed himself to have a Messianic mission
to his nation in this transformed meaning of the Messiah.
ship appears to be the only legitimate conclusion from
the scene at Cæsarea Philippi, where he accepted Peter's
declaration that he was "the Christ, the Son of the living
God." †   If we accept the chronology according to which
he does not appear before this time to have declared him.
self explicitly in a Messianic character, there would seem
to be in his proclamation of the kingdom of God, the Mes.
sianic kingdom, as already come, and in his assumptions of
spiritual authority, the expression of a consciousness of
leadership and preëminence which may be supposed to
have ripened even early in his ministry into a conviction
that his mission was Messianic in the sense in which in
accordance with his religious genius he interpreted this
conception.   The scene at Cæsarea Philippi is so well
authenticated, so firmly planted in the tradition of Jesus
that its rejection seems to be in the highest degree arbi.
trary. ‡   Whether the record of the first or of the second
Gospel be taken as the more correct, it is difficult to deny
that something of the nature of a Messianic declaration
to his disciples happened there without adopting a
method of interpreting the Gospels which would tend to
invalidate them altogether. §   Other serious objections
lie against the theory of Havet and Martineau that not
only this scene but the application of the Messianic title

---

* Mark xii. 36, 37.   † Matt. xvi. 16.

‡ On the contrary, see Martineau, The Seat of Authority in Religion, 1890,
Book iv. chap. ii

§ Mark's account is the simpler of the two, and probably the older. Chap.
viii. 27 f. *Cf.* Matt. xvi. 13–21. Luke does not locate the scene at Cæsare;
Philippi, but "in a private place" where Jesus was praying, chap. ix. 18 f.

to Jesus was an afterthought of his followers. For if
Jesus set up no claim to the Messiahship in any sense, it
is a difficult problem to account for the Messianic features
of his tradition as it has taken form in the Gospels. It
were surely a surprising and audacious invention which
should by an afterthought transform the Galilean carpenter's son, the preacher of righteousness and the healer of
the sick, who had been ignominiously put to death at the
instigation of the Jewish authorities, into the son of David,
the Messianic king of Israel. If he was, like John the
Baptizer, only a preacher of repentance and a prophet of
the coming kingdom, if in fact he was *not* " greater " than
this one, from what materials could an afterthought have
created the glorious figure of the Messiah? The Messianic traits of the Gospels require for their explanation
the hypothesis of the consciousness on the part of Jesus
of a Messianic mission, even though in a transformed
sense, and of the expression of this consciousness at Cæsarea Philippi or elsewhere, even though the expression
were misunderstood and interpreted in the sense of the
popular Messianism. The evangelists bear unconscious
testimony to his Messianic character when they record
his proclamation of the kingdom as already come, and
there is a consistency in their narratives when they report
his acceptance of Peter's confession as an open expression
of veiled implications which the disciples themselves had
not understood, because they were unable to comprehend
the Messiahship in the spiritual sense in which he apprehended it. Against this " slowness of heart " on the part
of his disciples his entire sincerity and lucidity of expression were ineffectual. One can readily sympathize with
those who think that in clearing Jesus of all Messianic
claims they set him free from the charge of insincerity.

7

But insincerity, double-dealing, and "accommodation" there are not in the case as a possible charge against him. He repeatedly declared and taught his disciples to preach that the kingdom had already come, and there had been no pomp and show of temporal power ; and immediately after the great scene at Cæsarea Philippi he began to speak of his humiliation, and rebuked Peter for his inability to comprehend a suffering Messiah. In fact, there is reason for believing that in the consciousness of Jesus the Messiahship was associated with the lowly " Servant of Jahveh " of the second Isaiah, the teacher who should "bring forth judgment to the nations," and to whom belonged no temporal dominion.   One has only to recall the scene in the synagogue at Nazareth * and the total impression of his life and work of service and ministration to find a confirmation of this view.†

But by whatever title he called himself or wished to be called of men, whether Servant of Jahveh, Servant of Man, or Son of God, Jesus never claimed divine rank, and did not fail to recognize his lowliness and dependence.   While in his spiritual fellowship with God, in his sonship, he doubtless recognized the source of his power and the true ground of his Messianic calling, he did not regard this moral preëminence as annulling the difference of nature which distinguished him as a finite creature from the Creator, his Father.   In the consciousness of sonship was implied subordination to the Father.   In his worship, in his cry for deliverance in Gethsemane, in his religious experience and example which cannot be removed from the story of his life without defacing it beyond recognition, are implied dependence, insufficiency in himself, faith, reverence, and love toward God—traits of humanness which

* Luke iv. 16–28.   † See Matt. xx. 28.

constitute the beauty of his character. In claiming to be Messiah, too, even in his exalted conception of Messiah-ship, he could not have thought of himself as other than a human personality, since according to the prophets the Christ was to be a man. His modification of the traditional Messianic idea consisted only in transforming the human king and Son of David into a human teacher and Saviour, the Son of God. In his spiritual endowments and his power over demoniacs he saw no occasion for self-exal-tation, but rather for giving glory to God, by whom all things had been delivered to him, and through whom he was able to master the evil spirits. * He declared, indeed, that the achievement of such mighty works as he performed lay within the power of other men through faith and prayer. † Though conscious that he was led by the divine love, and supported by the divine power which might through prayer be brought to his rescue with more than twelve legions of angels, ‡ he submitted his will to that of his Father in a sublime renunciation in which the strength of a great soul is seen to overcome through faith the infir-mities of human weakness and doubt. §

If, then, while conscious that as the greatest of the sons of God he had a Messianic office, Jesus recognized his dependence and limitation as a man, and accepted as the type of his mission and his fortune the Servant of Jahveh who in a lowly estate rendered his service of love to man, he may well be supposed to have found in the designation "Son of Man" a most appropriate title for himself. He alone employs it to designate himself, and he uses it with such frequency that it may be regarded a favorite term with him. He did not, however, originate it, for it is

* Luke x. 21 f, xi. 20. † Matt. xxi. 21 ; Mark ix. 23, 29.
‡ Matt. xxvi. 53. § Mark xiv. 36.

found in the Old Testament, where it is employed sometimes, in the poetic parallelism, of man as a member of the
human species, particularly when human lowliness and
weakness are emphasized,* and once when the people of
the Most High to whom God will accord an eternal kingdom are seen by the writer in the form of a Son of Man in
distinction from the world-kingdoms which had appeared
in the forms of beasts.† The writer of this passage does
not appear to have had a personal Messiah in mind whom
he designated as the Son of man, and the words have a
Messianic significance only in the general sense that they
relate to the national political prosperity and dominion.
But it cannot be denied that they are suggestive of a
personal Messiah under the name Son of Man, and it is
not improbable that in some circles of Jewish thought this
term may have come to have a Messianic meaning prior
to the time of Jesus, although this opinion cannot be
unquestionably established by the use of the term in the
book of Enoch, since the section in which it is employed
may be of Christian origin.‡ There can be little doubt,
however, that the term in question is not represented in
the synoptical Gospels as a current and popular designation of the Messiah, and that Jesus in his use of it did not
give to his hearers generally the impression that he was
that expected person. His use of it prior to the scene at
Cæsarea Philippi does not appear to have given this impression even to his disciples. His celebrated question on

---

* Num. xxiii. 19 ;   Ps. viii. 3 ;   Job xxv. 6 ;   Isa. li. 12 ;   Ez. ii. 13, and
frequently elsewhere ; Dan. viii. 17.

† Dan. vii. 13.

‡ See Dillmann, Das Buch Henoch, etc., 1853 ; Hilgenfeld, Die jüdische
Apokalyptik, 1857 ; Weisse, Die Evangelienfrage, 1856 ; Holsten, in Zeitsch. für wissenschaftl. Theol., 1891, pp. 46–55.

this occasion cannot be understood as meaning: " Who do men say that I, the Messiah, am?" but rather: " Who do men say that I, who call myself the Son of Man, am?" Besides he could not have declared Peter's confession that he was the Messiah to be given by divine illumination, if he had supposed that in the mind of this disciple the Son of Man and the Messiah were synonymous terms. It is, indeed, not obvious how the expression could have come among the Jews to have a Messianic signification. The passage in Daniel does not directly convey it, and its use elsewhere in the Old Testament is rather suggestive of human dependence and weakness in contrast with the greatness and power of God than of such qualities as the Jews were accustomed to associate with their Messiah, even though they conceived of him as a man descended from David. The conjecture is not wholly without probability for its support that if Jesus did not introduce the Messianic signification of the term, his use of it caused this sense to be popularly attached to it when in the tradition of his life his Messianic character was made distinctively prominent. The term belongs to the Gospel-tradition, and does not appear in the Epistles.

At what time in the course of his ministry Jesus came to regard himself as the Messiah is altogether a matter of conjecture. But there are indications in the manner of his teaching regarding the kingdom of God and in his assumptions of authority and preëminence that he was clearly conscious of such a mission before the open acknowledgment of it at Cæsarea Philippi. His unwillingness to be openly proclaimed as the Christ must not be regarded as indicating either that he rejected the title or thought that it was one to be held as " a private prerogative." In view of the fact that in his own thought the

Messiahship was transformed into a spiritual office, the conjecture is not improbable that he wished to prepare the people for the reception of the new kingdom of God, the kingdom as he conceived it, before announcing himself as its king.   It is not altogether clear, besides, that he at first attached to the term Son of Man, a distinctively Messianic signification.   But the difficulty of this problem is apparent on account of its complication with the question of the chronology of the Gospels.   While in the accounts of the second coming, which doubtless give an apocalyptic coloring to Jesus' actual sayings regarding the future, there is evidently to be seen the influence of the passage in Daniel upon the representations of the writers, there is great probability that, from the manner in which he speaks of himself as the Son of Man in words which are undoubtedly genuine, his conception of the appellation was rather derived from that frequent Old-Testament usage in which this term represents human nature in its dependence and limitation.*   In the answer to the scribe who wished to follow him, the saying that " the foxes have holes, and the birds of the air have lodging-places, but the Son of Man hath not where to lay his head," †‌ there is no intimation that the appellation in question had in the mind of Jesus the exalted signification of Son of God or Messiah, or even of the " Archetypal Man," but it rather appears to designate him as the man, who wishes only to be man in the most genuine and widest sense of the conception, as one who thinks nothing to be remote from himself which belongs to a human existence, to the fortune of a human life, and who therefore regards it as

---

* The passages referred to on a preceding page are especially suggestive of this relation in contrast with the divine nature.

† Matt. viii. 20.

his peculiar calling to submit to all the sufferings and sacrifices incident to his position among men for the service of mankind.* In view of the fact that Jesus employs this term without any indication of its origin and with no explanation of its meaning to himself, it would appear that a higher and more emphatic sense could only be read into it in this passage with its connection. A similar conception of the Son of Man appears to be expressed in the passage which follows the admonition to his disciples not to aspire after positions of authority, but to regard the place of a servant as the highest : "As the Son of Man came not to be served, but to serve, and to give his life a ransom for many."† A fortune in which service rendered to the benighted and wandering and suffering undergone at the hands of unfeeling and unappreciative men, predominate, is described in the words : "The Son of Man came to seek and to save that which was lost"; "So also is the Son of Man to suffer by them."‡ In such a use of this designation no reference to a Messianic dignity is necessarily contained, and none could be conveyed to the disciples or to other hearers. A participation in the ordinary conditions of human life is indicated in the saying : "The Son of Man came eating and drinking," etc., and a subordination to God is implied in the declaration regarding forgiveness for words spoken against the Son of Man as opposed to the unpardonable blasphemy against the Holy Spirit.§

* Baur, Zeitschr. für wissenschaftl. Theol., 1860, p. 280.

† Matt. xx. 28.   ‡ Luke xix. 10 ; Matt. xvii. 12.

§ Matt. xii. 32. To charge that the cure of demoniacs, which Jesus claimed to effect "by the finger of God," was effected through Beelzebub, was unpardonable "in this age or in the age to come," that is, in the pre-Messianic or in the Messianic age. It is doubtful that Jesus spoke these words; for all reference by him to a Messianic age still to come is irreconcil-

On the other hand there are several passages besides the apocalyptic sayings in which Jesus appears as the Son of Man to assume an exceptional rank and dignity, and to employ expressions regarding himself which could not but lead his disciples to think of him as occupying a peculiar and eminent position in the kingdom of God. In the explanation of the parable of the sower, the sower of the good seed is said to be the Son of Man.* As this is a parable of the kingdom, the position which Jesus assigns to himself as the representative of the celestial powers of good against the arch enemy, the Devil, in a great contest of the ages, is clearly one of high rank. When the Pharisees charged his disciples with breaking the sabbath by plucking and eating the ears of grain as they passed through the fields, he replied that in the temple the priests profane the sabbath and are blameless, and declared that something greater than the temple was there among them, closing with the announcement that the Son of Man is lord of the sabbath.† To certain scribes who denounced him as a blasphemer because he had declared forgiveness of sins to a paralytic he answered that the Son of Man had power on earth to forgive sins. ‡ In reporting this event the first evangelist remarks that the people glorified God who had given such power to men, that is, had raised up one man furnished with such a divine power.

The meaning of the term in question in the mind of Jesus has been regarded as involving one of the most difficult problems in New-Testament theology, and the

able with his belief in his Messiahship, in the spiritual kingdom and its spiritual king as already come.

* Matt. xiii. 37.   † Matt. xii. 1–9.

. ‡ Matt. ix. 1–8; Mark ii. 1–13.

paradoxical use of it in the passages just quoted to express now lowliness, now exaltation, is not an unimportant factor in the difficulty. The apparent disinclination of Jesus to define his nature and rank is, of course, another, and this might seem to enjoin the student of his teachings not to inquire too curiously into a matter to which he evidently attached little importance. One might well heed this implied injunction, were not the inquiry necessary in order to correct many tenacious and widespread errors. It is evident, then, in view of the foregoing considerations, that Jesus' employment of the term Son of Man as a designation of himself can only be understood in connection with his peculiar apprehension of the Messiahship, that is, with the transformed sense in which he appropriated this ancient Jewish title. Had he wished to declare himself as the Jewish Messiah, there was no lack of terms at his disposal which could not have been of doubtful import to his disciples and to the people. Instead of employing any of these he chose as his favorite and almost exclusive self-designation a term which had at the best a veiled and obscure signification, and which was by no means a current and popular expression for the Messiah. This he evidently did not use as an equivalent for the first personal pronoun, as if he could have said without incongruity: " If the Son of Man send them away fasting to their houses, they will faint on the road," etc., but only when he attached a special significance to it as a designation of himself. Precisely what this special significance was is the problem to be solved. The opinion that he intended by the expression to designate only his lowly position and fortune as a man is hardly tenable in view of his use of it in connection with the assumption of exceptional dignity and authority, as in some of the passages already quoted. Out of a combination of the two sets of passages, however, appears to come a solution of the apparent paradox which they contain and of the problem itself. For while to Jesus himself the popular designation of Messiah was not the Son of Man, but the Son of God, he employs the former expression in several passages in which it appears to have a Messianic import. But this Messianic import was not a traditional one, according to which the Messiah was to be a temporal ruler, but the ancient idea transformed, spiritualized, and raised to its world-historical significance. As the Messiah in this sense, then, Jesus regarded himself as a man sharing the common fortunes of his kind ; and as a man of exceptional spiritual endowments, charged with a great spiritual mission, and living in intimate communion with God, he did not hesitate to accept the appellation, Son of God. As Son of Man and Son of God he accepted the Messianic office, and in the former term he included the spiritual elevation which the latter expressed together with the human lowliness which was the obvious implication of the former.

The use by Jesus of a Messianic designation, which did not reveal him as Messiah, evidently presents a difficulty. How could he employ a term which he understood as a Messianic appellation, but which no one besides so understood, prior to the proclamation of himself as Christ at Cæsarea Philippi? This difficulty has led Brückner and Baldensperger to assume that the chronology of Matthew and Mark is incorrect, and that Jesus really prior to the event at Cæsarea Philippi preached a Messiahless kingdom of God, representing himself as only the herald of the kingdom and not its king. This conclusion appears unnecessarily to discredit the records, although it has been reached after the publication of learned treatises on the subject by several of the ablest masters.* Perhaps a solution of this problem may be found in the exalted spiritual sense in which Jesus regarded himself as Messiah. Not wishing to declare himself openly as the Christ in the Jewish sense of the term which was contrary to his conception of his mission, he employed as fitting to this conception the expression Son of Man, and used it as a veiling and problematical designation which was to serve until his spiritual idea of the kingdom of God and of himself as the Messiah should be in a measure prepared for and established. Whether the designation was original with him, or was suggested by the passage in Daniel or by other passages in the Old Testament, must remain a matter of conjecture. It should be observed, however, that in the passage in Daniel the representative of the kingdom of God was designated by a term which emphasized human qualities, and suggested both the dependence and the weakness of human nature and the victory with which it should ultimately be crowned. It is evident that this idea has an affinity with Jesus' conception of the Messianic kingdom as a spiritual and temporal economy which was to engage upon the earth in a successful conflict with the powers of evil. In the term Son of Man as employed in the Old Testament Jesus appears, then, to have found an idea to which he could attach his teaching regarding the Messiah and his kingdom, but in taking his departure from it he gave it, by a spiritual and original interpretation, a meaning which was strange and surprising to his countrymen. In the term Son of Man as applied to himself he included the idea of his participation in human nature, and indicated the

* Notably by Baur, Hilgenfeld, and Holtzmann.

lowliness of the external appearance and earthly fortune
of one who also bore the dignity and glory of the Messianic rank.   This idea appears to lie at the basis of his
declaration regarding the sabbath.   For if the sabbath
was made for man, then man may assume the right to determine how it shall be used for his purposes and his well-
being, and the Son of Man may well assert that he is lord
of the sabbath, and, as the Messianic representative of
God and of mankind, has the authority to decide how it
shall be appropriated to divine and human uses.   It is,
indeed, just this assumption of authority as the Son of
Man for the sake of mankind which distinguishes this
new-born Messiahship.   Precisely the qualities it is which
have constituted for ages the strength and greatness of
Christian character that Jesus unites in this transfigured
and spiritualized Messiah, lowliness and spiritual elevation, the love which extends a hand for the service of man
and the faith which reaches up to the Eternal, the Son of
Man and the Son of God united and constituting a personality which spends itself in helpfulness and renews
itself by worship—such is the new Messiah of world-historical significance and world-transforming power.*

* Among the most important discussions of the title " Son of Man " the
student may consult Reuss, La Théologie chrétienne au Siècle apostolique,
i. pp. 227 ff ; Baur, Neutestamentl. Theol. pp. 75 ff, and Zeitsch. für wissenschaftl. Theol. 1860, pp. 274 ff ; Immer, Neutestamentl. Theol. 1877,
pp. 105 ff ; Weizsäcker, Untersuch. über die evangel. Gesch. pp. 426 ff ;
Keim, Gesch. Jesu, ii. pp. 64 ff, and Der geschichtliche Christus, pp. 100 ff ;
Schenkel, Bibel-Lexicon, iv., article " Menschensohn"; Colani, Jésus-Christ
et les Croyances messianiques, etc., 2 ed. pp. 74 ff ; Beyschlag, Neutestamentl. Christol. pp. 9 ff ; Wittichen, Die Idee des Menschen, pp. 96 ff ;
Hilgenfeld, in Zeitschr. für wiss. Theol. 1863, pp. 327 ff ; Holtzmann, *ib.*,
1865, pp. 212 ff ; Hausrath, Neutestamentl. Zeitgesch., i. pp 420 ff ; Martineau, Seat of Authority, etc., Book iv. chap. ii ; Wendt, Die Lehre Jesu,
ii. pp. 44 ff ; Weisse, Die Evangelienfrage, pp. 196 ff ; Holsten, Zeitschr.

8.—THE SAYINGS OF JESUS CONCERNING HIS DEATH.

The questions whether Jesus foresaw and foretold his death by violence, and whether he attached any doctrinal significance to his passion, present grave difficulties to the student of the Gospels. The sayings which relate to the former of these questions naturally fall into two classes: those which contain only intimations of his suffering or death, and those in which his passion is announced explicitly and in detail. Intimations only are contained in the sayings that the disciples would fast when the bridegroom should be taken away from them; that the Son of Man must suffer at the hands of those who had "done what they would" with John the Baptizer; that the sons of Zebedee knew not what they asked, but would, indeed, drink of his cup; that the woman who poured the ointment upon his body did it to prepare him for burial; that he had a baptism to be baptized with, and that his soul was troubled until it be accomplished; and that he must go on day by day, for it could not be that a prophet should perish out of Jerusalem.* On the other hand there are several sayings in which Jesus is represented as explicitly foretelling his passion and giving details of it to the effect that he would be delivered up to the chief priests and scribes, who would condemn him to death, and hand him over to the gentiles to mock and scourge and crucify, and that on the third day he would rise from the dead.† If, now, it be assumed that the writers of the Gospels have correctly reported the sayings of Jesus

für wiss. Theol. 1891, pp. 1–80 ; Brückner, Jahrb. für Prot. Theol. 1886, pp. 254 ff ; Baldensperger, Das Selbstbewusstsein Jesu, etc., 2te Ausg. pp. 169 ff ; Stap, Études sur les Origines du Christianisme, 3 ed. pp. 322 ff.

* Matt. ix. 15, xvii. 12, xx. 22, xxvi. 12 ; Luke xii. 49, xiii. 33.

† Matt. xvi. 21, xvii. 22, xx. 17.

in which he foretells his passion and resurrection with such detail and particularity, it is necessary to assume also a supernatural foreknowledge of these events on his part, since by no natural combination could the place and the special features of the proceedings be foreknown. But this assumption of a supernatural prescience encounters a very grave difficulty in the circumstance that the narratives represent Jesus as appealing to the prophecies of the Old Testament in confirmation of his predictions regarding his passion. Since, now, these predictions and this appeal to prophecy are in immediate connection, it would be altogether arbitrary and unwarrantable to maintain that the former were upon the basis of superhuman insight, and that the latter was upon the basis of ordinary human knowledge ; that is, that in predicting the details of his passion he was divinely illuminated, while in interpreting the prophecies he proceeded as a Jew of his time would proceed. But it has been shown by a process of the most thorough and learned grammatical and historical interpretation of the Old-Testament passages in question that in none of them is there any reference to the passion of Jesus or to his resurrection. The application which Jesus is reported to have made of them cannot, then, have been made by superhuman knowledge, and there remains no support for the hypothesis of a miraculous foreknowledge of the particulars of his passion, since both operations must stand or fall together. Again, the supposition that Jesus foretold the circumstances of his passion with such detail as the evangelists represent encounters a still greater difficulty in the repeated statements in the Gospels that the disciples knew nothing of his approaching death, and in their conduct after his crucifixion. If he made such explicit statements regarding his death as he is reported to have made, it is incredible that they should not have understood him, and that his fate upon Calvary should have fallen upon them as a blow for which they were entirely unprepared, destroying their hopes in him as the one who "was to redeem Israel," that is, as the Messiah. They could neither have become familiar by unmistakable teachings * with the idea of a suffering Messiah, nor have been instructed, as the Gospels indicate that they were, that a violent death of the Christ was predetermined in the divine counsels and foreshadowed in the Old-Testament prophecies.

The conclusion to which these considerations appear, then, to point is that the explicit and detailed announcements of his death and resurrection which Jesus is represented in the Gopels as having made received their present form in the tradition of his life in the light of the events in question. The intimations of his passion, however, which are contained in the passages previously quoted, are not subject to the difficulties which render those particular predictions improbable, and are, indeed, explicable in accordance with the idea of the Messiahship which he entertained, and with the actual situation in which he was placed. Since in Jesus' conception of the kingdom of God renunciation and service, self-sacrifice and the depreciation of earthly goods and honors were required of its members, and since he as its head declared himself to have come not to be served, but to serve, he may very well be supposed to have anticipated from the beginning that his work could be completed only through trial and suffering. The fate of some of the prophets and of John the Baptizer may have occasioned the presentiments which are expressed in the intimations in

* "And he told them this *plainly*" (παρρασία), Mark viii. 32.

question.   From the time when he began to entertain the new idea of his Messiahship there could have been no necessity of an adjustment in his mind between the office of the Christ and his own sacrifice of himself for his cause.   As no kingly Son of David, but as the humble Son of Man, he saw in his life of homeless wandering, of kindly services of healing and helpfulness, in the endurance of the espionage and suspicion, the scorn and rejection of those in authority, not a fortune which was incompatible with his Messiahship, but its essential and glorious fulfilment.

The general character and tendency of Jesus' sayings regarding his sufferings and sacrifices indicate that he looked upon them as incidental to the service which belonged to his mission to mankind, and as necessary under the existing conditions to the establishment of his cause.   It does not appear from the general scope of his teaching that he attached to them any doctrinal significance.   Accordingly, those passages appear surprising and incongruous, in which he is represented as speaking of his death as a "ransom," and of his blood as shed "for the remission of sins."   After having said to the sons of Zebedee that they should, indeed, drink of his cup, he indicates to the disciples that among them rank should be determined by the degree of service, even as the Son of Man came not to be served, but to serve.   So far his words appear to be in entire accord with the occasion and with all his teaching, but the evangelist makes him add the surprising words: "And to give his life a ransom for many." *   It should be observed in the first place that the saying of Jesus as called forth by the occasion appears to be complete without these words, and that they as a

* Matt. xx. 28, λύτρον άντι πολλῶν.

doctrinal statement implying a somewhat developed theory of an atonement are unfitting to the connection in which he is discoursing of humility and of the high rank which should be given to those who best served others. But they appear most incongruous when regarded in rela- tion to his general teaching concerning the consequences of sin and the attainment of righteousness. In no other place is there even an intimation of a substitution of the sufferings and death of Jesus by which men should be relieved as by a " ransom." Rather the burden of his teaching is that men should repent and put themselves into right relations to God by obedience and by seeking His kingdom and His righteousness. In the Sermon on the Mount blessings are pronounced on those who hunger and thirst after righteousness, who make peace, who are persecuted for righteousness' sake, who are pure in heart; and there is nowhere in it an intimation that the divine favor is to be obtained in any other way than by love to God and man, that is, by the practice of morality and re- ligion. Man is represented in the teaching of Jesus as in immediate relations with the Father. The latter needs no propitiation, and for the former no sacrifice is required but that of his selfish passions. The man who would save his life must lose it. No other life is offered up as a substitute for his. They who labor and are heavy laden are, indeed, invited to come to Jesus, but not that he may bear their burdens for them. If any one will come after him, let him take up his own cross and follow. In Golgotha there is no substitution. Each soul must pass through it following the great Leader. This is the teach- ing fitted to produce the heroic character of which Jesus himself was the noblest type, and capable of nurturing a church which through conflict and martyrdom should conquer the world. It was quite in accordance with all his teaching, with his conception of his mission and of himself as the Son of Man, that Jesus gave up his life as the supreme act of renunciation for the sake of fidelity to himself and his cause ; and the power of his death, of his cross, is manifested, not in those who would fain grasp a crown on the " merits " of his sacrifice, but in the heroes who, nurtured in his spirit, have dared or died for conscience and the truth—in a Luther, a Huss, a Savonarola, and the great army of martyrs.

The saying, then, in which Jesus is made to speak of his life as a ransom must either be an addition to the discourse in which it occurs, reflecting the ideas of a later time, or it does not give in the Greek rendering an accurate reproduction of his words. The idea conveyed in the Greek Gospel is so incongruous with the teaching of Jesus regarding God and man, sin and the recovery from it, that to establish it as his would require evidence that no mistakes occurred in transmitting the tradition of his sayings, that the compiler of the first Gospel was incapable of error, and that the text of his writing was preserved uncorrupted down to the time when express witnesses for this passage can be found. A similar difficulty is presented in the passage in which Jesus is represented as saying on the occasion of his last meal with his disciples that the cup was his blood of the covenant shed for many for the remission of sins.* The variations of the three synoptical narratives and the new reading, to be considered further on, in the first and second, furnish indications of a solution of the difficulty. In the first place, it is worthy of note that the second and third Gospels do not

---

* Matt. xxvi. 28, εἰς ἄφεσιν ἁμαρτιῶν. *Cf.* Mark xiv. 24; Luke xxii. 20.

contain the words of the first : " For the remission of sins." They are also wanting in two quotations in Justin Martyr.* They are, besides, altogether incongruous with the teachings of Jesus, according to which the righteousness which consists in the fulfilment of the law is declared to be the condition of entering the kingdom of heaven. In the parable of the Prodigal Son reconciliation with the Father is represented as immediate, and hence without the intervention of an atonement. It is conditioned solely on repentance and return. In view of these considerations the words in question must be regarded as a later addition to the first Gospel, and as representing a theological conception of the significance of the death of Jesus which he could not have entertained. The omission of " new " before " covenant," according to the latest reading in the first and second Gospels, makes it appear questionable whether Jesus taught that by his blood a " new covenant," was confirmed, by which the relation of the sinner to God elsewhere defined in his teachings was altered. The idea of a covenant of " grace " is that of Paul and Luke, but is incongruous with the point of view of the first two evangelists. It is not improbable that the words " new covenant " found their way into Luke's Gospel under the influence of Paul, and that the conception of the establishment of a covenant of blood which is indicated in the first two Gospels without the word " new " may have had the same source. The incompatibility of the idea of a sacrificial atonement with the general scope and intention of the teaching of Jesus respecting the relation of man to God is so manifest that these words cannot but be regarded with suspicion. To what extent the Pauline

* Apol. i. 66, Dial. 70.

conception affected the representation of the first two Gospels is a matter of conjecture, but there is no doubt that the idea of the intention of the last supper which has prevailed in Christendom is that of Paul and Luke, and not that of the writers of Matthew and Mark. For, according to these latter, it does not appear that Jesus on the occasion of the supper thought of establishing a permanent rite or sacrament. It is only in the third Gospel that the words, " This do in remembrance of me," appear. Paul, indeed, writes that he had " received of the Lord," that is, Jesus, the account which he gives of the last supper ; * but this expression doubtless means that he had derived the information from the current tradition of the life of Jesus, and Paul's understanding of the intention of the last supper was that it was to be observed in remembrance of Jesus until his glorious appearance or the Parousia. † But this tradition appears to have been unknown to the writers of the first two Gospels. At least they give it no recognition, and since they wrote earlier than Luke, his account may show the natural traditional accretions of which the criticism of the Gospels detects many examples. The conjecture appears probable that the words, " Do this in remembrance of me," were not originally spoken by Jesus, but that in the celebration of the supper in the primitive church the presiding member of the community in distributing the elements may have exhorted the communicants to continue the repetition of the meal in remembrance of Jesus, and that from this primitive Christian ritual the words were added in the tradition to those actually spoken by Jesus. The doxology of the Lord's Prayer, " For thine

* 1 Cor. xi. 23 ff.
† ἄχρις οὗ ἄν ἔλθῃ, " until he come."

is the kingdom," etc., undoubtedly had a similar origin. In the latter case textual criticism is able to detect the origin of the added words, or at least to show that they are an addition. The fact that it cannot do this in the former case renders the addition of the doubtful words conjectural, but not improbable.

If, now, what has here been conjectured, and perhaps shown to be probable, corresponds with the facts in the case, it will result that at the last supper Jesus did not intend to establish a rite for the observance of future generations, did not attach the importance to the meal which has been accorded to it in the Church, and did not teach that a new covenant was established in his blood. On the occasion of the supper, when according to all the indications his life was in imminent peril, he may have spoken of the broken bread and the wine poured out as symbols of his body which was to be broken and of his blood which was to be shed, without attaching any doctrinal significance to them. If, moreover, he did not at the supper say that his blood was shed " for the remission of sins," and did not on another occasion speak of his death as a " ransom," then it will result that his sayings regarding his death were in entire agreement with the rest of his teachings, and that the doctrine of an atonement for sin, as it has commonly been taught in the Church, cannot be supported by his authority. It will not, however, result that the doctrine of the forgiveness of sin does not rest upon his teaching. For it is clearly implied in the Lord's Prayer, and the parable of the Prodigal Son presents a striking illustration of it. According to this parable, it does not appear, as has already been remarked, that any other atonement is required as the condition of forgiveness than the sinner may himself make by his remorse and repentance. Furthermore, it does not appear that forgiveness removes any of the natural consequences of transgression, except perhaps such as might result from an unforgiving rejection of the returning penitent. The parable leaves us in uncertainty as to the moral condition of the prodigal after his return, does not tell us whether he was happy or unhappy at the feast, and reveals nothing as to his future spiritual fortune.

9.—THE TEACHING OF JESUS REGARDING THE LIFE TO COME.

In entering upon the consideration of the subject of this section it is of the greatest importance to discriminate between explicit teachings of Jesus and his allusion to or acceptance of certain current beliefs of his time without developing them or giving importance to them by special sanction and enforcement. One attains this point of view only when one has arrived at a clear understanding of the scope of Jesus' actual teachings, and so far realized his position as to comprehend his idea of the work which he wished to accomplish. It is manifest at the outset that Jesus did not regard himself as possessing universal knowledge and as having the mission to instruct mankind on all matters of human interest and inquiry. He put forth no claims to so vast a mission, and modestly confined himself in his teaching within limits of which he appeared to have a very clear conception. Had his interpreters understood him in this respect the volume of so-called Christian theology would have been far smaller and its quality much better. Yet the difficulty of placing oneself at his point of view and perceiving the scope and intention of his mission is by no means insurmountable. One has only to observe the general trend of his sayings and to discriminate between those of them which are didactic and concern the main purpose clearly in view, and those which are incidental or contain only allusions to current opinions, to see that he was chiefly concerned with teaching men the nature of the kingdom of God and inducing them to become possessed of righteousness, in which he included all the great moral and religious virtues and achievements. While his aim was pre-eminently practical, it cannot be said that he had no theology, for his teaching concerning God was well-defined and prominent. His theology was not, however, speculatively held, but was definitely and persistently applied to the present life, as when he enjoined upon men the practice of kindness and forgiveness that they might be like their Father in heaven, and declared that love to God and men was the essential thing in the law and the prophets.

The distinction between the actually didactic sayings of Jesus and his acceptance and appropriation of current opinions may be seen by contrasting the former with his attitude and procedure with regard to the popular angelology and demonology of his time. With respect to the existence and nature of angels and demons he teaches nothing, but accepts what was currently believed. Leaving out of consideration the apocalyptic passages in which angels are spoken of as executing the Messianic judgment at the coming of the Son of Man in glory, we find in undoubtedly genuine sayings of Jesus these celestial beings of the Jewish mythology distinctly recognized as residents of heaven who surround the Deity.* They are mentioned on occasion of the argument with Sadducees concerning the resurrection with an intimation that they are not sensuously constituted like human beings,† and in another

---

* Luke xii. 9.   In the parallel, Matt. x. 33, reference to angels is omitted.
† Matt. xxii. 30 ; Luke xx. 36.

place guardian angels are recognized,* whether in accordance with the Jewish doctrine that every man has a guardian angel from birth, or with the belief which has incidental expression in the Old Testament that such spirits watch over the pious, is not certain.† As in the current Jewish mythology there was a realm of evil spirits with Satan at their head over against the realm of good spirits or angels, so Jesus recognizes the kingdom of Satan and the subordinate demons as powers hostile to the welfare of man.‡ Accordingly he says to Peter, "Get thee behind me, Satan! thou art my stumbling-block," § thus declaring that in that disciple's spirit of opposition to his mission he recognized a likeness to the great Adversary of men. At the last supper he is said to have remarked to Peter that Satan had asked for him that he might sift him as wheat.‖ In accordance with the current idea that diseases were caused by the evil powers, which is expressed in the remark of the third evangelist that a certain woman "had had a spirit of infirmity eighteen years," ¶ we find that Jesus proceeds with entire *naïveté* upon the theory of demoniacal possession, and frequently speaks of the cure of a class of ailments, of whose exact nature we have not a precise knowledge, as the casting out of demons.** He declares that the woman who was "bent together, and wholly unable to lift herself up," had been

---

* Matt. xviii. 10.

† See Von Cölln, Biblische Theologie, ii. p. 67, and Meyer, Commentar *in loc.*

‡ Mark iii. 23 ff.

§ Matt. xvi. 23 ; Mark viii. 33. Luke omits Peter's protest and the rebuke administered to him, chap. ix. 18 ff.

‖ Luke xxii. 31.　　　　　　　　　　¶ Luke xiii. 11.

** Mark i. 23 ff, 34, iii. 11 f, 15, 22 ff, v. 2-5, vi. 7, ix. 17 f, 22 ff ; Luke x. 17-20, xi. 14 f, xiii. 32.

"bound by Satan eighteen years," and he speaks of and treats persons known as demoniacs precisely from the point of view of his age and of the exorcists who, it appears, cured or professed to cure them. The attempt to remove the difficulty which appears to some people to lie in Jesus' acceptance of the demonology of his time by assuming him to have spoken of it figuratively is opposed to a sound interpretation of words which are so precise and direct as those in question. It is impossible to conceive that any one should speak otherwise than he did who without a didactic purpose should adopt the popular opinion. The interpretation which seeks to remove the difficulty by the supposition that in using the language in question Jesus adapted himself to the current opinions, knowing them to be erroneous and not wishing to correct them, is altogether unsound and baseless. For to say nothing of the tacit deception on the part of Jesus which is implied in it, the doctrine that Jesus was better informed than his contemporaries of the nature of the diseases in question is entirely *à priori*, since it rests upon a theory of his knowledge which we have no means of establishing. Both these expedients are rationalistic and altogether opposed to the critical point of view. They can be adopted only by one who at the cost of the perversion of the plain meaning of words is determined to make the records accord with a preconceived theory of the person of Jesus.

Now the sayings of Jesus regarding the condition and fortune of men after death can only be correctly interpreted when the current opinions in his time on the subject are taken into account, and a discrimination is made between what is didactic in his words and what is a mere reference to or appropriation of these opinions without a didactic purpose. That the Jews of the time of Jesus, with the possible exception of the Sadducees,* believed in the immortality of the soul is established by contemporary testimony as well as by the writings of the New Testament. According to the doctrine of the Pharisees the souls of men pass immediately after death into sheol or hades which is divided into two parts, paradise and gehenna, a place of reward and a place of punishment. Yet it is no real, vigorous life which is lived in this subterranean paradise, and a return to the upper world, or the resurrection, is the sole condition of entering upon the full enjoyment of existence. It is difficult to determine precisely how the doctine of the resurrection was conceived by the Pharisaic party at the time of Jesus. If the Sadducees who interrogated Jesus regarding it represented it correctly, it would appear that the Pharisees believed in a resurrection of the physical body with its original organs and passions. Yet in an address of Josephus to an imprisoned companion to restrain him from suicide the belief is expressed that the souls of those who "depart out of this life according to the law of nature * * * are again sent in the revolution of the ages into pure bodies."† The question, who according to the belief of the Pharisees were to have a part in the resurrection, is involved in obscurity. Were the pious Israelites only to be raised, or the good and the bad Israelities, or all men? According to Josephus, this fortune was to be that of the good alone, presumably of the

---

* The Sadducees denied the resurrection, but it is not certain that they did not believe in the continued existence of the soul in sheol, in accordance with the old Hebrew doctrine. See Hase, Dogmatik, 2te Ausg., p. 117, and Zeller, in Theol. Jahrb., 1847, p. 391.

† ἁγνοῖς σώμασιν. B. J. iii., 8, 5.

Jewish people. The Pharisees, he says, believe that souls have an immortal vigor, and that under the earth, (*i. e.,* in sheol) there will be rewards and punishments according as they have lived virtuously or viciously ; that the latter are assigned to an everlasting prison,* but that for the former there is power to revive and live again. † On the contrary the doctrine of the resurrection of both the righteous and the unrighteous is said in Acts to have been the doctrine, or at least the " hope," of the " sect " to which Paul had belonged, that is, the Pharisees ; ‡ and in the fourth Gospel a twofold resurrection is declared, that of those who have done good, and that of those who have done evil, the one to " life," the other to " condemnation." § . But in our first three Gospels there is no intimation that the doctrine of a resurrection of the unrighteous was held by the Pharisees. Rather if Jesus be allowed to have represented the Pharisaic belief, and is correctiy reported by Luke, the resurrection would appear to be only for those who should have been accounted worthy to obtain it.‖ Although the Jewish literature of the two centuries before the time of Jesus contains intimations of a resurrection of good and bad men, ¶ evidence that this belief was entertained by the Pharisees in the first century of our era appears to be wanting. In fact there were two doctrines held on this subject, for the second book of Maccabees, written about a century before Christ, appears to teach that it was believed that

* εἰργμὸν ἀΐδιον.
† ῥαστώνην τοῦ ἀναβιοῦν, "a facility of return to life," Ant. xviii. 1, 3.
‡ Acts xxiv. 15.
§ John v. 28, 29.
‖ Luke xx. 35. The first two Gospels do not report these words.
¶ See the Enoch-Parables, li. ·

Jews alone would be raised. *   The book of Daniel represents that " many " would be raised, " some to everlasting
life and some to shame and everlasting contempt." †   But
this resurrection was doubtless regarded as confined to
the Jewish people, and does not necessarily include all
of them.   The doctrines of the resurrection and the
judgment appear to have been gradually developed, and
it is difficult to determine precisely in what form they were
generally entertained at a particular historic period.   On
the whole there seems to be no good reason for rejecting
the very direct and definite testimony of Josephus previously quoted, to the effect that the Pharisees believed
that the righteous only could hope for deliverance from
the gloomy realm of sheol, while the wicked would be
detained there in an " everlasting prison."   The opinion
appears to be well grounded that the doctrine of a general
resurrection "did not establish itself till toward the end
of the first century, when Christianity had with some
definiteness separated from Judaism," and that " the
restoration to bodily life is generally treated in the New
Testament as a reward of Christian faith," while " for
unbelievers there . was no risen Redeemer, no definite
centre of activity in the coming life." ‡

The student of the Jewish doctrine of the resurrection
must be on his guard against imposing upon it the modern
Christian conceptions of the present life and the life to
come.   In other words, the Jewish doctrine must be regarded as connected with the national Messianic expectations.   While the Messiah was originally conceived as
merely a temporal ruler descended from David and having no connection with a judgment and resurrection, we

* Chap. vi. 9, 14, 23.   † Chap. xii. 2.
‡ Toy, Judaism and Christianity, p. 394.

find that shortly before or after the time of Jesus the author of the Enoch-Parables represents him as clothed with the functions of a judge. To what extent this idea prevailed among the Pharisees in Jesus' time it is impossible to determine; but its presence is plainly indicated in the apocalyptic accounts of the second coming in the synoptic Gospels, and in Paul's conception of this event. Here we find that the resurrection and judgment did not in the Jewish thought involve a change of worlds, as the doctrine is held by Christians at the present time. Rather in accordance with ideas expressed in the apocryphal literature of the century or two preceding the time of Jesus, the resurrection and judgment are connected with a change of earthly relations only. Although in the accounts of the coming of the Son of Man in the first three Gospels there is no mention of a resurrection, yet the scene is earthly. Paul conceived this coming as attended with a resurrection of "the dead in Christ," a "change" of the physical organism of the Christians then living, and an ascent to "meet the Lord in the air," after which they were to be "forever" with him.* His thought of a renovated earth at the coming of Christ appears to be a reproduction of an idea expressed in earlier Jewish literature.† In this conception of a Messianic crisis as it existed in pre-Christian and early Christian thought is seen the significance of the terms, "this age," and "the age to come," the former of which was employed to designate the pre-Messianic, and the latter the Messianic time, or "the kingdom of God." The translation of the Greek word for "age" (αἰών) by "world" has contributed to a misunderstanding of the

---

* 1 Cor. xv. 51 ff, 1 Thess. iv. 13–18.

† Rom. viii. 20–23; *cf.* Is. lxvi. 17; 2 Pet. iii. 13.

Jewish conception of the two great world-periods which were conceived to be separated by the advent of the Messiah, and strengthened the tendency to read modern Christian ideas of the life to come into many New-Testament passages. When after the crucifixion it appeared that Jesus had not realized the Messianic expectations, the truly Messianic age, "the age to come," was regarded as still in the future to be ushered in by his second advent. Attention to this fact will remove obscurity from many texts in the Gospels and Epistles. It was, however, natural and inevitable that these national Messianic limitations should in the course of time fall away, and that with a more developed conception of the life to come its scene should be transferred from the earth to the heavenly regions. This idea would naturally be connected with the earlier one of a resurrection of the saints to share in the joys of the earthly reign of the Messiah by the notion of a second resurrection, that of the wicked, and perhaps a general judgment, by which the scene of earthly life would be brought to a close. Hence there is an intimation of a second resurrection in the words of Paul, "The dead in Christ shall rise first," and in the Apocalypse a judgment is mentioned as occurring after the millennial reign of the saints.* It is not probable, however, that this more developed view of the future was entertained by the Pharisees of the time of Jesus.

There remains now to be considered what relation Jesus held to the beliefs of his time concerning the life to come, and to what extent he may be regarded as teaching a doctrine respecting it. From the foregoing review of contemporary Jewish opinion it is evident that he found already existing a definite doctrine of the immortality of

* Chap. xx.

the soul and of the resurrection of the body, which was doubtless held subject to certain limitations imposed by the national Messianic expectations. That he surpassed these limitations so far as the locality of the life to come is concerned, and did not conceive of it as an earthly state under the Messianic reign, appears probable from such sayings as: " Lay up for yourselves treasures in heaven "; " Great is your reward in heaven "; " Rejoice that your names are written in heaven." * This point of view is the only one that was consistent with his conception of his Messiahship and the kingdom of God as spiritual and already existing. If he employed the language which is attributed to him by the synoptists respecting the coming of the Messiah with the clouds of heaven to sit on an earthly throne of judgment, he must have entertained the popular Jewish belief that the Messianic future was a temporal condition. For these apocalyptical passages unquestionably indicate a descent of the Son of Man to the earth within the life-time of the then existing generation to "sit upon the throne of his glory " as a judge of the nations. They are in accord with the Jewish idea of the Messiah's earthly reign, and give expression to such hopes as his followers may very likely have cherished, who as Jews conceived of the life to come only in connection with the national Messianism. His spiritual conception of the future existence of the soul in a heavenly state renders it very probable that he did not employ the language in question.

The sayings of Jesus regarding the resurrection are so fragmentary and obscure that no complete doctrine can be derived from them. In answering the question of certain Sadducees concerning, as is probable, the Phari-

* Matt. v. 12, vi. 20 ; Luke x. 20.

saic teaching on the subject he expresses himself very positively and didactically with reference to two points, the immortality of the soul and the nature of the body in the resurrection-state. In the third Gospel he is represented as implying that the resurrection is a reward of merit which only those shall obtain who "have been accounted worthy" of it. These "will be sons of God, for they are sons of the resurrection," and "cannot die any more." The first two Gospels omit these words and report him to have said only that those who are raised do not marry, but "are as the angels in heaven." * In another passage in the third Gospel two resurrections are implied, in accordance with the view which is expressed in Paul's words, "The dead in Christ shall rise first," where Jesus is reported to have spoken of a recompense to be had "at the resurrection of the righteous." One can hardly refrain from raising the question whether there be not grounds for a critical doubt of the genuineness of the words: "They who have been accounted worthy to obtain that world and the resurrection from the dead," and, "Thou shalt be recompensed at the resurrection of the righteous." They are akin to the Pauline view in implying two resurrections; they are not found in the other two Gospels ; and there is a hint of the resurrection as belonging to the Messianic time conceived as in the future (also a Pauline idea) in the words, "to obtain that world," which in the original mean "to obtain that age," † that is, the age to come, or that of the Messiah. If Jesus regarded the Messianic age as that in which he lived, and the kingdom of God as already come with him, he cannot consistently have spoken in this way of the

* Matt. xxii. 30–33 ; Mark. xii. 24–27 ; Luke xx. 34–39.
† *Τοῦ αἰῶνος ἐκείνου τυχεῖν.*

resurrection, and his teaching of a reward in heaven is incompatible with the teaching of a recompense in the Messianic age which was temporal and earthly. If, now, this critical doubt should be found to be tenable, and if Jesus' only words concerning the resurrection were to the effect that they who are raised will not marry, but will be as the angels in heaven, and that they cannot die any more, then we have as positive teachings on the subject: 1. That there is a resurrection; 2. That in the resurrection-state the earthly bodily conditions are absent, and the raised are as the angels in heaven; 3. That the resurrected cannot die any more. It is evident that much is wanting here to a complete doctrine of the resurrection. For it is not stated who are to be raised, whether all men or a part of mankind, and there is no indication of the time when the resurrection is to take place, and whether it means an immediate entrance of the soul upon spiritual conditions at death, or its union with an angelic body after an indefinite tarrying in hades. To one who should wish to found a complete doctrine of the resurrection on the sayings of Jesus respecting it these omissions would be embarrassing, as would also the vague reference to the Jewish mythology in the saying that the resurrected are "as the angels," since we know nothing of the angelic nature and modes of existence. It is evident, then, that Jesus did not intend in the sayings in question to formulate a complete and explicit doctrine of the resurrection, but that his purpose was in the main to correct the crude and materialistic ideas of the Jews regarding the life to come. If the incompleteness of his teaching on this subject was intentional, as we may very well believe that it was without deciding whether it resulted from reserve or a want of knowledge, the conclusion does not appear

9

improbable that he did not think that his great cause of righteousness and the kingdom of God would be promoted among men by such definite information as might furnish a basis for a dogmatic thesis on the resurrection.

With regard to a state of existence intermediate between death and the resurrection Jesus appears to have adopted the popular Jewish conception of sheol, hades, or the underworld, as a place of reward and punishment prior to the resurrection. In the parable of the rich man and Lazarus which appears to be intended to teach that the judgment of God upon men does not always accord with that of their fellow-men upon the earth,* it is represented that Lazarus was at his death carried by angels to Abraham's bosom, that is, to a place of honor in the underworld, while the rich man after he had died was in torment there. These two places in hades, which it appears were separated by a great gulf, are evidently the paradise and the gehenna of the Jewish mythology. It is not known, however, that according to the Jewish conception of the underworld the inhabitants of the two regions could see and converse with one another; and we may regard this episode in the parable as introduced by poetic license, so to speak, in order to carry out the purpose of the teaching, which was not to formulate a doctrine in regard to the underworld. The popular mythology appears to have been adopted and adapted to the didactic end in view. Luke also reports that on the cross Jesus said to the " penitent " malefactor, so-called : " This day shalt thou be with me in paradise." In view of these facts it is certainly unwarrantable to say that Jesus did not accept the current Jewish idea of the underworld as the abode of souls immediately after death. If he spoke these

* Luke xvi. 19–31 ; *cf.* verse 15.

words to the malefactor, he must have believed that he would himself descend into that region. Yet one may accept this conclusion while holding that definite disclosures as to an intermediate state constituted no part of his real teaching. The traditional conceptions of the people among whom he was reared were a part of his mental furnishing, and he could not but employ them in adapting his teaching to the comprehension of his hearers. But not to deny, even apparently to accept as realities, Satan, demons, angels, paradise, hades, gehenna, and a resurrection out of the underworld, does not constitute these things a part of his teaching, does not make them real, does not warrant us in constructing dogmas upon them. Had he taught among the Greeks, and used their hades as a vehicle of his ideas or an illustration of his teaching, it would not follow thence that the Greek hades was anything but a mythological conception. Somewhere the line must be drawn between the things which he knew and was inspired to teach and the things of which he was not informed and felt no call to teach. The dogmatist and the rationalist, twin brothers, will each draw this line where it suits his prepossession or his caprice. The critic must draw it according to the facts, that is, as he is taught by the record to draw it. Now the record clearly teaches him that there are certain great ideas which constituted the substance of the teaching of Jesus, on which he laid the stress of his ministry, on which he heroically staked its fortune and his life—the fatherhood of God and the brotherhood of men ; the spiritual kingdom of heaven and himself its king; immortality, righteousness, justice, mercy, love to God and man—principles fundamental in the moral and spiritual orders of human existence and essential to human salvation. The record also teaches with equal

clearness that on certain other matters he placed no
emphasis, that in fact he thought them to be unessential,
such as the mythological ideas of his times, good and evil
spirits, details of the resurrection, arcana of the underworld, particulars of the life to come, and that he employed
them as subordinate and subsidiary to his great aim to
bring men into accord with one another and with God.
How to make a right discrimination between these two
groups of ideas is a great lesson ; and although the dogmatic theologian does not look into it, it is the first lesson
that the interpreter of the great Teacher should learn.

That Jesus had a vivid conception of the enormity of
sin and of the terrible punishment which it entails is evident from the language whether literal or figurative in
which he speaks of it. To derive from his words, however, an explicit and detailed doctrine concerning the
fate of the wicked after death is very difficult if not
impossible. His sayings in regard to the judgment, for
example, are involved in great obscurity. The words
ascribed to him respecting the coming of the Son of Man
to a judgment on the earth within the life-time of the
generation then living, including the celebrated discourse
in the twenty-fifth chapter of the first Gospel, cannot even
if they are genuine, concern the final destiny of mankind
at large. But apart from the fact that they have never
been fulfilled, they are, as has already been pointed out,
so entirely incompatible with his idea of the kingdom of
God and his Messiahship, that their spuriousness may be
regarded as scarcely questionable. Other sayings respecting "the judgment" and "the day of judgment"* are
too vague to serve as the basis of any other doctrine than
that a judgment of some kind awaits all unrighteousness.

* Matt. v. 22, x. 15, xi. 24, xii. 36, 41, 42.

It is evident that his conception of the divine judgment transcended the popular Jewish belief which connected it with the reign of the Messiah, but his precise view of it is indeterminable. His very definite reference to gehenna, the Jewish place of punishment in the underworld, in connection with the penalty of sin presents no little difficulty. In the first place it is not clear, as has already been shown, whether or no he held the popular Jewish belief that the wicked would have no resurrection, but would remain in the "everlasting prison" in sheol. One passage appears to indicate the contrary in which he speaks of fearing God who has power to destroy both soul and body in gehenna.* Since the soul was not supposed to be connected with the body after death until the resurrection, the possible punishment here referred to could not be inflicted upon the unresurrected occupant of gehenna. The futility, however, of attempting to found a doctrine upon this vague and isolated passage is manifest. More precise are other references to gehenna, such as: "Whoever shall say, Fool! shall be in danger of the gehenna of fire"; "It is better for thee that one of thy members should perish than that thy whole body should go away into gehenna." † This appears to be a distinctive adoption by Jesus of the Jewish belief in the underworld-punishment of the wicked, since he cannot be supposed to have declared that there was "danger" of something which he did not believe to exist. The question, however, arises whether he adopted the belief

* Matt. x. 28.

† Matt. v. 22, 29, 30; Mark ix. 43-48. Mark intensifies the saying by adding: "Where their worm dieth not, and the fire is not quenched," in imitation of Isa. lxvi. 24. What Jesus actually said is of course indeterminable.

in whole or only in part.   No means exist for answering this question categorically, but important results must follow from any conjectural answer to it.   If we suppose him to have adopted it in whole and to have intended his adoption of it as a doctrine regarding destiny, then it follows that he actually taught that there is a realm called sheol under the surface of the earth to which the souls of the dead descend; that this is divided into two parts, paradise and gehenna; and that in the latter is an " everlasting prison " in which the spirits of the wicked are confined, and from which there is no release, while from paradise the good will be resurrected at the coming of the Messiah.   Whoever is not willing to accept this mythology as the Christian doctrine of destiny must assume that Jesus adopted the Jewish belief on the subject only in part, or not at all in reality, but only employed the current terms in order to impress upon the popular understanding certain important spiritual principles.   What he was intent on teaching is that sin entails punishment, and he is not to be quoted as an authority on the topography of the underworld and the Jewish mythology in general.

From the spiritual character of his teachings in general the conclusion appears to be warranted that Jesus did not adopt and teach the Jewish belief as to the underworld in its literal import. No doubt he regarded the danger which he typified by " the fire of gehenna " as a very grave and very real danger; but it does not follow from this that the reality of the fire, or that of gehenna as an underworld-locality, was a capital point in his teaching. How long he conceived that the punishment which he referred to under the popular symbol of gehenna-fire would continue there are no data for determining.   His adoption of the terms for the didactic purpose in view does not imply his adoption of all that they signified to the popular imagination. It would appear, accordingly, that a resort to the analogy of his teaching is the only means of determining his views of the nature and duration of punishment. If, then, we accept Mark's report of his words in reference to the sin against the Holy Spirit* instead of the account in the first Gospel, he appears to have taught that there was one offence which might expose the offender to an indefinite continuance in sinning ($\alpha i\omega\nu i\sigma v$ $\dot{\alpha}\mu\alpha\rho\tau\dot{\eta}\mu\alpha\tau\sigma\varsigma$). But even if it were established that this æonian duration was conceived as endless, nothing but the possibility of such a state is here implied. In fact Jesus nowhere expressly affirms the endlessness of punishment. On the other hand he does not expressly declare that it is not endless, and that at some time all the consequences of sin will cease to exist. In fact, on the subject of destiny he maintained a remarkable reserve and reticence, as if he did not regard an explicit teaching on this subject as an essential part of his work. His great doctrine of the fatherhood of God does not appear to have been promulgated primarily with its relation to human destiny in view, but rather as an ethical-religious principle. The optimistic inference respecting the destiny of man which may legitimately be derived from it is, however, of great moral and religious importance. In the teaching of the father who goes out to meet the returning prodigal, placing no arbitrary limits of " probation " on his repentance, is conveyed a deathless hope for the fallen soul. More than a hope is expressed in the teaching of the good shepherd who goes forth and seeks for the be-

---

* Mark iii. 29. Here again the precise words of Jesus are indeterminable—a fact which should moderate the zeal of the theologian and the maker of systems.

nighted estray until the lost is found.   An assurance is here given that the unwearied divine love can never abandon its own.   While, then, the teaching of Jesus distinctly emphasizes the enormity of sin and the dire consequences of a wicked life, it does not furnish explicit dogmatic statements on which a complete doctrine of human destiny can be established.*   One who delights in

* Whether Jesus' view of the life to come was substantially that of the Pharisees of his time, and if it differed from theirs, how and to what extent, are problems difficult of solution.   If the synoptic apocalyptic sayings as to his second coming are rightly attributed to him, he must have held with the Jews that the Messiah's advent denoted " the end," and his reign the future, "eternal" condition of men, although from this point of view the omission of the resurrection is remarkable. In the Enoch-Parables (li. 1, 2,) a general resurrection is mentioned at the coming of Messiah, at which the righteous are to be "selected" for salvation.   If, however, the synoptic apocalypse is not to be ascribed to Jesus, the question arises whether or no he transcended in his conception of the future the Jewish Messianism, and thought of the life to come in accordance with the modern Christian idea.   While from the exegetical point of view such a rupture with the prevalent ideas of his time may appear improbable, and is in fact generally so regarded, his spiritual conception of his Messiahship, which did not admit at all of the materialistic apocalypse, may well be urged in favor of it.   One can hardly think of him in view of his evident conception of the kingdom of God as believing with the writer or writers of the Book of Enoch that the abode of the blessed in the future was to be Jerusalem, while the wicked would be consigned to an "accursed valley" (probably that of Hinnom) to enhance by the spectacle of their eternal misery the bliss of the saved.   (See Enoch xxvii. 3 ; lxii. 12 ; cviii. 14, 15.)

The Jewish literature of the time immediately antecedent and subsequent to Christ contains no intimation of a deliverance of the wicked from their penal doom.   In the synoptic apocalyptic eschatology the " Depart from me" appears in itself to be final.   To the foolish virgins the definitive answer is, " I know you not."   In the fourth Gospel those who have done evil come forth to " a resurrection of condemnation."   Yet the later Jewish theology taught a release of some from the torments of gehenna (Weber, § 74), and the Christian tradition of the preaching of Christ in the underworld is not without significance in this connection.   While Jesus gave no direct and definite expression to the " eternal hope," it is certainly unwarrantable to

constructing an eschatology will find scanty encouragement and meagre material in his words. He appeared to
think it of vastly greater moment that men should concern themselves with what is required for righteousness in
this world than with what the next world may have to
disclose—with justice, mercy, and love, rather than with
celestial or infernal arcana. Yet his knowledge of man
and his faith in God gave him a cheerful view of human
destiny. Preëminent among those sons of hope who
have been the immortal teachers of men, he was the divine
optimist.

maintain that he did not cherish it on the ground that it was not generally
entertained by the Jews of his time. The genius of the great Teacher cannot
be thus limited who so far transcended his age in spiritual insight and
humanity. In view of his great doctrine of the fatherhood of God, with
which the definitive exclusion of any repentant soul from the higher life by
divine decree is totally irreconcilable, and in the light of the passages
referred to in the text, there appears to be reason for believing that Jesus
could not have entertained the thought of the rejection of any returning
prodigal or of the final abandonment of any benighted estray. With his
faith in God, in man, and in his own cause, he could not have held any view
of human destiny which is incompatible with the consummation of everlasting
"joy in the presence of the angels of God." On the views of the Jews
as to the life to come the student may consult Schwally, Das Leben nach
dem Tode nach den Vorstellungen des alten Israel und des Judentums, ein-
shliesslich des Volksglaubeus im Zeitalter Christi, 1892, and Schürer, A
History of the Jewish People in the Time of Jesus Christ, New York, 1891, ii.
2, pp. 179–184.

CHAPTER II.

THE JEWISH-CHRISTIAN INTERPRETATION.

AMONG the interpretations of the gospel which criticism discerns in the New Testament that of the Jewish-Christian followers of Jesus naturally presents itself first for consideration, since it is that of the original Christian community, and may be regarded as representing more nearly than any other the impressions of the immediate disciples of the Master. Impressions, indeed, it is, rather than a definite system of belief, which we shall here have to deal with. For the Jewish-Christian tendency had no great champion in the character of a religious genius and literary master, like Paul and the author of the fourth Gospel, who was able to give it an intellectual expression and embodiment in a work of renown. Champions it must be conceded, however, to have had in the persons of those men whom Paul has immortalized under the title of Pillar-Apostles, Peter, James the brother of Jesus,* and John. These stood at the head of the Jewish-Christian Church in Jerusalem, and regarded themselves as charged with the ministry " to the circumcised." † The interpretation of Christianity which prevailed there was strictly Judaistic. The Jewish believer in Jesus stood forth, indeed, from his fellow-countrymen distinguished by his acceptance of the Nazarene as the

---

* Mark. vi. 3 ; Gal. i. 19, ii. 9, 12.　　　　　　　† Gal. ii. 9.

Messiah, but it was not in his thought to separate himself in any other respect from his people and their law and customs. He was still a worshipper in the temple and a zealot for the law.* As a believer in the ancient covenant of Jahveh and His people he looked for the fulfilment of the promises made through the prophets that from Zion should the law of God go forth and the word of God from Jerusalem. But to him the acceptance of the Messiah by men of other nationalities and their admission into the Christian community implied their submission to the Jewish rite of circumcision. The account in the tenth chapter of Acts of a vision of Peter and his baptism of gentiles without circumcision cannot be regarded as historical in the light of subsequent events. That the "pillars" of the Church in Jerusalem adhered to the strictly Jewish-Christian view in reference to the admission of gentiles is evident from the facts that Paul thought that the matter at issue between himself and the Jewish party must be adjusted with them "privately," else he "should run, or had run in vain," † and that the emissaries who at Antioch prevailed upon Peter no longer to eat with the gentile converts "came from James," and were undoubtedly carrying out the wishes of their superior.‡ It may be regarded as a fairly well-established

---

* Acts ii. 46, iii. 1, xxi. 20 f.　　　　　　† Gal. ii. 2.

‡ Gal. ii. 12. Lechler's ingenious attempt to show that the Jewish apostles were not a party to the conflict with Paul cannot be regarded as successful. Das apostol. u. nachapostol. Zeitalter, 3te Ausg. 1885, pp. 160 ff. See also: Zeller, Vorträge, etc., pp. 202 ff ; Pfleiderer, Das Urchristenthum, 1887, pp. 43 ff ; Immer, Neutest. Theol., pp. 177 ff ; Baur, Paulus, etc., 2te Ausg. i. pp. 119 ff ; Lipsius, Art. "Apostelconvent" in Schenkel's Bibel-Lexicon, i. p. 144 ; Holtzmann, Hand-Commentar, 1889, i. p. 367 ; Havet, Les Origines du Christianisme, iv. pp. 138 ff ; Hilgenfeld, Einleit. in das N. T., 1875, pp. 593 ff.

conclusion of criticism that a correct view of the attitude of the Jewish-Christian apostles toward the admission of the gentiles to the Church and toward the mission of Paul must be derived from the Pauline Epistles, and not from the book of Acts, the "tendency" of which to represent the original apostles as occupied with the gentile mission cannot well be denied.*

The beliefs of the Jewish Christians respecting the person of Christ, their Christology, may be substantially gathered from the first Gospel and the discourses ascribed to Peter in the Acts. While the latter are probably by no means verbatim reports, but rather compositions of the author of the book, they appear to rest upon an historical basis and to be in the main free from Pauline influence and dogmatic reflection. Peter, then, is reported to have said of Jesus that he was "a man approved of God to you by miracles and wonders and signs which God wrought by him"; that "by the hand of godless men" he had been crucified and slain; but that "God raised him up, having loosed the pains of death, because it was not possible that he should be held by it," and "exalted him by His right hand as a leader and Saviour to give repentance to Israel and forgiveness of sins." † Noteworthy here are the limitation of the office of Jesus as Saviour to "Israel," in accordance with the Jewish-Christian point of view, and the absence of all traces of the dogma of the expiatory or atoning effect of his death. As to this latter doctrine,

---

* See Schneckenburger, Zweck der Apostelgesch., 1841, pp. 61–151 ; Zeller, Apostelgesch., 1854, pp. 216 ff ; Martineau, Seat of Authority, etc., pp. 280 ff ; Weizsäcker, Das apostol. Zeitalter, 2te Ausg. 1890, pp. 42 ff ; Toy, Judaism and Christianity, pp. 366 ff ; Holtzmann, Hand-Commentar, i. pp. 317–322.

† Acts ii. 22–25, v. 31.

however, it should be said that while the distinctive foundation of it as a part of a dogmatic system was first made by Paul, it is probable that it was not long strange to Jewish-Christian thought. The attempt to reconcile the death of Jesus with his Messianic office would naturally lead men of Jewish race, to whom the idea of a sacrifice for sin was familiar, to the conclusion that he did not simply die as a malefactor, but, as the Son of God, gave his life for men. The occurrence of a connection of his death with the idea of a " ransom " and of his blood with " the remission of sins " in the synoptic tradition, which was essentially Jewish-Christian, appears to confirm this conclusion.* That Jesus was the Jewish Messiah, that is, the one foretold by the prophets, was a cardinal principle in the circle of ideas under consideration. This was not held as a self-evident article of faith but as a doctrine which required proof, since, in fact, nothing could be more incongruous with the Jewish conception of the Messiah than was the entire earthly fortune of Jesus. Accordingly, since no proof could be more effective for a Jew than that derived from his sacred books, passages were found in the Old Testament which, when treated by the methods of interpretation then in vogue, could easily be made to yield the desired confirmation. The predominant tendency to establish this doctrine distinguishes the first Gospel which shows an extensive perversion of Old-Testament texts in this interest,† and in the discourse of Peter in the Acts already referred to passages from Psalms xvi. and cx. are very arbitrarily forced into the service of the demonstration in

* See page 112.

† This subject is fully treated in the author's Gospel-Criticism and Historical Christianity, Chapters IX. and X.

question by a method which if admitted to be valid would put an end to the rational interpretation of ancient writings.*

The interest which was felt among the primitive Christians in the Messiahship of Jesus is apparent in the accounts of his wonderful birth of a virgin whose conception was from the Holy Ghost. From the Jewish point of view a genealogical table which should show his natural descent from David would appear to tend to establish his Messiahship. But such a table would be manifestly worthless from the Jewish genealogical point of view, if Joseph were not his father. The attempt to hold in thought and unite the two conceptions of a natural descent and a supernatural generation shows the *naïveté* and illogicalness of the primitive Christian intelligence. If, as is very probable, the former was the original idea, the fact that it was neutralized by the latter appears to indicate the strength of a tendency to idealize the Messiahship of Jesus. For a supernatural generation formed no part of the original idea of the Messiah who was to be a lineal descendant of David, and the genealogies show that this notion was probably not the primitive one among the Christians. But, as the anointed ($X\rho\iota\sigma\tau\acute{o}s$), he was doubtless conceived as in intimate relations with the divine Spirit which was supposed to have inspired the prophets, and which according to one tradition was given to him " without measure." That even from the Jewish-Christian point of view, however, the supernatural generation of Jesus was not thought to be essential to his Messiahship is evident from the later

* The original *intention* of the writers of these passages to apply them to the circumstances of their times is so obvious as not to require elucidation. To interpret a writing is to ascertain the intention of the writer.

history of the two sects into which the Jews who believed in him were divided on this question,* and from the oldest Gospel, that of Mark, which contains no account of the mysterious virgin-birth. It is also significant that there is no allusion to this event in the discourses of Peter, as reported in the Acts, and in the writings of Paul. The communication of the Spirit at the baptism appears to have satisfied the tradition as known to Mark, and from this point of view the supernatural generation would appear to be superfluous. It is probable, then, that the legend of the miraculous conception took its rise in the interest of intensifying the idea of Jesus' relation to the Spirit, and of giving it an expression which should be more radical and inward than that of the story of the baptism. That the two should be entertained and recorded together, although one of them renders the other superfluous, is not surprising when we consider the small part which reflection plays in the formation of traditions. It is probable that out of this tendency to exalt and legitimatize the Messianic office of Jesus proceeded the story of the temptation, which in the first and third Gospels has received a highly legendary form and coloring. As Messiah it was necessary that he should be shown at the outset to be superior in conflict to the great enemy Satan. Accordingly, he is no sooner furnished at the baptism with the Spirit than he is led into the wilderness to win over the power of evil the great victory which should be symbolical of the issue of his entire mission. That his whole career was conceived as a

---

* The Ebionites held that Jesus was the son of Joseph, and was endowed with the Spirit at the baptism, while the Nazarenes maintained the supernatural generation. See Baur, Vorlesungen über die christl. Dogmengesch., 1865, i. 1, p. 145.

struggle with Satan appears to be indicated in the re-mark with which the third evangelist concludes his account of the temptation, that the Devil departed from him " for a season."

Another doctrine which could be developed only in the Jewish-Christian consciousness was that of the second coming or Parousia of Jesus as the Messiah. As his death and burial without a resurrection would have been to Jewish believers the death and burial of his Messiah-ship, so without a second coming in glory and power he would be a Messiah without a kingdom. A Messiah who should be a great spiritual teacher and die for his convic-tions remained unintelligible to the Jewish mind, although the tradition clearly presents such a view as that of Jesus himself. A suffering and crucified Messiah could only be accepted after it had been shown by a rabbinical exegesis that what had happened to him had been intended in the divine counsel, and foretold by the prophets. Hence Peter declares in Acts that it was " by the settled purpose and foreknowledge of God " that Jesus had met his fate " at the hands of godless men," and Luke represents that after the resurrection, when Jesus met two disciples on the way to Emmaus, he made apparent to them that " the Christ should suffer these things, and enter into his glory " by an elucidation " beginning with Moses and all the prophets." * In this tradition is manifest the interest which was felt in establishing by the authority of Jesus himself the sort of exegesis which could make the Old Testament yield proofs of his Messiahship, just as in the fourth Gospel he is made to quote a passage from a Psalm to make it appear that the treachery of Judas was fore-told, if not predetermined.† The strength of this ten-

* Acts ii. 23 ; Luke xxiv. 26 f.   † John xiii. 18 f.

dency is shown by the fact that in the discourse ascribed
to Peter in the second chapter of Acts he does not appear
to be willing to leave the resurrection and ascension of
Jesus to rest upon the testimony of witnesses, but seeks
to support them by an unwarrantable exegesis of words
supposed to have been written by the " patriarch " and
" prophet " David.   The significance of this procedure is
manifest when we consider that the appeal to the Old
Testament shows the conviction that the resurrection and
ascension were a necessity from the Messiahship of Jesus,
and the fulfilment of a divine decree and foreordination.
Whatever may have been the relation of this apprehension
of these events to the production of a belief in them, it
was evidently thought to be necessary to a confirmation
of them to the minds of those at least who had no
other proof.*   A further advance in the idealization of
the Messiahship is indicated in the conception of an
exalted position held by Jesus after his ascension, all
power being given to him in heaven and on earth.†   Accordingly he is represented as standing on the right hand
of God, or sitting on the right hand of power.‡   These
conceptions were preliminary to that of a great concluding event which was to be a world-catastrophe.

---

* A discussion of the resurrection with the hypotheses of bodily resusci-
tation, spiritual manifestation, vision, etc., cannot be undertaken here.
Regarding the ascension, however, it may be remarked, that no definite
statement of it as a fact is given in the Gospels.   There is no intimation of it in the first two Gospels if we except the probably spurious
appendix to the second.   The first Gospel locates the last interview of Jesus
with his disciples in Galilee, while the third reports that he "parted"
from them at Bethany directly after the resurrection.   Only in Acts do we
find the story developed and a definite account given of an ascension in a
"cloud" after a forty days' sojourn on the earth.   Acts i. 3, 9.

† Matt. xxviii. 18.   ‡ Acts vii. 55 ; Matt. xxvi. 64.

10

In conceiving of a world-catastrophe, Jewish-Christian thought was consistent with itself. For that the Messianic kingdom was to be a world-kingdom was a Jewish conception which all the spiritual teaching of Jesus had not been able to overcome in the minds of his followers. Unless, then, all the Messianic hopes of his disciples were to perish forever at his death, unless they themselves were to have no part in the glorious kingdom, and were doomed to go down into sheol without seeing its advent, they must believe that he was presently to descend to the earth in person, and accomplish that work to which his former career was only a prelude closing with a tragedy. If the "age to come" were not a phantom or a dream; if all things were not to remain as they had been; if the bonds of oppression were ever to be loosed, and the righteous vindicated and avenged,—then must he whom they believed to be the Messiah really manifest himself as such, and establish his kingdom with becoming pomp and power. Only by this thought of the Parousia, the belief in which was universal and dominant among the early Christians, could the Messiahship of Jesus be reconciled in the minds of Jewish Christians with the termination of his earthly career, which they were able to regard only as an ignominy and a failure. No better illustration is furnished in early Christian literature of the transformation of the gospel effected by Jewish-Christian thought under the dominant influence of the Messianic idea than is presented in one of the discourses of Peter in Acts in which he exclaims: " Repent, therefore, and turn from your ways, that your sins may be blotted out, in order that the times of refreshing may come from the presence of the Lord, and that He may send forth Christ Jesus who was before appointed for you ; whom heaven, indeed, must receive until the times of a restoration of all things, of which God spake by the mouth of His holy prophets from the days of old." * Jesus had indeed preached repentance, but he declared at the same time that the kingdom of God had already come. To him there was no other palingenesis than that spiritual one which his teaching should effect, and he did not imagine that heaven must "receive" him until the time of an apocalyptic "restoration of all things." But to Jewish-Christian thought the past was stale and flat, a sad round of weariness and oppression ; and nothing short of apocalypses and a world-catastrophe, a descent of the Son of Man with the clouds, as he had been seen to go up, and a dramatic judgment of all nations before his "throne," could realize its Messianic dream.

The doctrine of the Holy Spirit as an active principle of the Christian life appears to have originated in the Jewish-Christian circle of thought. As it was by the Holy Spirit † that Jesus as Messiah was endowed or anointed, so this influence or charism was supposed to be effective in the disciples and early believers for the carrying on of his work. Accordingly, the promise of Jesus to his disciples is recorded that the Spirit of their Father will speak in them, ‡ and they are commanded to tarry in Jerusalem after the resurrection until they are endowed with power from on high.§ This promise is represented in the second chapter of Acts as having been fulfilled by a great outpouring of the Spirit on the day of Pentecost, in accordance, as was supposed, with a prophecy of Joel. The opinion hardly needs defence that the narrative in question is not to be regarded as historical in detail. The

<hr>

* Acts iii. 19–22. † πνεῦμα ἅγιον.
‡ Matt. x. 20. § Luke xxiv. 49 ; *cf.* Acts i. 5.

speaking with tongues* which is represented as one of the expressions of the Spirit, and evidently means according to the intention of the author the employment by the disciples of a large number of foreign languages without having learned them, has no subsequent confirmation, and was without doubt differently apprehended by Paul, as a phenomenon which came under his observation.† If, then, abstraction be made of all that is legendary in the narrative, the historical fact which is its basis will appear to be that the disciples believed themselves to be possessed of the same Spirit that qualified Jesus for his work. They believed that the Christian community, or Church, began to exist with the communication of this Spirit, and that this gift or charism did not concern them alone, but was bestowed upon all who became associated with them. It was supposed to be communicated at baptism into the name of Jesus upon repentance, and Peter is said to have declared to the " men of Judea and all who dwell at Jerusalem " that the promise was to them and to their children " and to all who dwell afar off."‡ Again it is related that although certain Samaritans had been baptized into the name of the Lord Jesus, the Holy Spirit had not yet fallen upon any of them, and that they received it only when Peter and John laid their hands upon them.§ On the contrary, it is recorded that in the case of Cornelius and the gentiles who with him were converted by the preaching of Peter the Spirit was poured out on them, and they spake with tongues, and that because of this they were directly baptized.‖ In the case of certain disciples of John who " did not even hear

* $\gamma\lambda\omega\sigma\sigma\alpha\iota\varsigma\ \lambda\alpha\lambda\epsilon\tilde{\iota}\nu$.　　　　† 1 Cor. xiv. 2 ; Rom. viii. 26.
‡ Acts ii. 39.　　　　　　　　§ Acts viii. 17.
‖ Acts x. 44–48.

whether there was a Holy Spirit," both baptism into the name of Jesus and the laying on of hands preceded the descent of the Spirit and the speaking with tongues.* While the external phenomena which are reported to have accompanied the endowment with the Spirit are involved in some obscurity which it would be foreign to the present purpose to attempt to clear up,† it should be observed that the conception of the Holy Spirit in the Jewish-Christian community does not appear to have involved the doctrine of the Trinity, which was of later origin.‡ In accordance with the thought of Jesus they regarded the Spirit as an expression of the activity of the one God, or as the Spirit of the Father.§ It may not be possible to determine precisely what powers the gift of the Spirit was conceived to bestow upon those who received it, but that it was regarded as a special charism qualifying the recipient to give infallible teaching either by the pen or by the spoken word, is nowhere implied. In fact, it does not appear to have been conceived as a gift bestowed exclusively on those who were appointed to teach, since all converts are represented to have received it. One can only speculate about the precise psychological fact which the accounts in Acts regarding

* Acts xix. 1–6.

† The student may consult Hilgenfeld, Die Glossolalie, etc., 1850; Zeller, Apostelgesch., pp. 110 ff; Meyer, Commentar, iii. pp. 51–60; Schenkel, Art. "Zungenreden" in Bibel-Lexicon, v. p. 732 ; Lechler, Das apostol. u. nach apostol. Zeitalter, pp. 23 ff : Weizsäcker, Das apostol. Zeitalter, 2te Ausg. pp. 589 ff.

‡ Lamson, The Church of the First Three Centuries, 1860. Of later origin also is probably the commandment (Matt. xxviii. 19) to baptize into the name of the Father, Son, and Holy Spirit, since the baptism of the apostolic age was into the name of Jesus. See Wittichen, Jahrb. für deutsche Theologie, vii. p. 336.

§ Matt. x. 20.

the bestowal of the Spirit endeavor to represent. Some other matters are also involved in obscurity. It is clear, however, that the early Christians experienced a spiritual quickening which they believed to come directly from God, that they held Jesus to be the Messiah, and preached repentance and baptism into his name together with brotherly love.

CHAPTER III.

JEWISH-CHRISTIAN interpretations and apocalyptic were fortunately a transient phase of the historical development of the gospel of Jesus. Within the circle of the original apostles the word of the great Teacher, which was essentially a message to mankind, could not have had an apprehension and exposition adapted to the requirements of a universal religion. Among them was no man of a religious genius and spiritual greatness equal to the emergency which was produced by the question whether Christianity should become a world-religion or remain the tenet of a Jewish sect. They were essentially Messianists (if the word may be allowed), and would have stood " gazing up into heaven " to discern the signs of the Messiah's coming, until weary of the fruitless waiting they would have abandoned the cause of him whose kingdom did not come, and have left the teachings of Jesus to the fortunes of the flood of rabbinical maxims. Their propaganda, which was nothing if not Messianic, would soon have come to an end, when men who asked for the signs of the Messiah's advent should receive the despairing answer that a day of the Lord was as a thousand years,* and the propagandists unable to endure the reproach of a king so tardy would have been absorbed by the powerful Judaism about them

* 2 Peter iii. 8.

or scattered by reason of its calamities to the four quarters of the globe. The critical alternative, then, with which the gospel was confronted shortly after the death of Jesus, was to remain in the custody of the Jewish apostles and perish, or to be set free and exposed to the perils of liberty. In its liberation it must run the risk of transformation. For it could be set free only by being apprehended afresh and embodied in a new system of thought. That this system of thought could under the circumstances only be Jewish, and the result of the transformation a more or less modified Judaism, is evident. For no gentile thinker was likely to be interested in a religion which was based upon Jewish Messianism, and required circumcision as a condition of admission to its communion. It was only a Jew, then, of intellectual greatness, breadth, and culture enough to enable him to overcome the prejudices of his race, and of spiritual insight, feeling, and personal power adequate to the great emergency, who could set the gospel free from the fetters in which it had been bound by a provincial Jewish Christianity, and give it a philosophical interpretation and dogmatic expression, which should make it in his exposition of it for many ages the religion of the most enlightened nations of the world. This procedure would appear, indeed, to be only the substitution of one Jewish interpretation for another; but it would mark no little advance, for it would be the substitution of a cosmopolitan Jewish interpretation for a provincial Jewish one. It would be too much to expect that the new creation should have in it nothing of the old system. Just as the transformed Christianity of the Reformation was not free from some deposit of Romanism, so it might well be expected that the new·Christianity of the gentile period would not be without traits which would betray its origin. Neither was final. Both were transformations waiting to be themselves transformed in the course of the endless development of the eternal principles of the gospel of Jesus.

I.—OUT OF JUDAISM INTO CHRISTIANITY.

Details of the early years of Paul's life, of his education, and of the formative influences under which he grew up are almost entirely wanting. The authority of Acts should doubtless be accepted for Tarsus in Cilicia as his birthplace notwithstanding Jerome's opinion to the contrary.* That he was born of Hebrew parents and educated as a Jew we know from his own testimony.† This training in a Jewish home may be regarded as excluding any considerable influence from the Grecian literature and philosophy which were cultivated in no small degree in Tarsus.‡ The opinion that he was especially qualified to be the apostle to the gentiles by familiarity with Greek thought is not as well sustained by indications in his writings as has been supposed. The address at Athens can hardly be cited for the quotation from Aratus, since it can by no means be regarded as an accurate report; and the quotation from Epimenides in the Epistle to Titus cannot be taken into account in view of the probable spuriousness of that writing. The maxim which appears to be quoted from the Thais of Menander:§ " Evil communications corrupt good manners," is quoted without regard to the metre, and does not necessarily imply acquaintance with the works of this poet, since it was very likely a current proverb. If Paul had had any acquaint-

---

* Acts ix. 11, xxi. 39, xxii. 3 ; Jerome, Vir. illust., i. 172.
† 2 Cor. xi. 22 ; Phil. iii. 5.   ‡ Strabo, xiv. 4.
§ 1 Cor. xv. 33.

ance with Greek literature and philosophy, it is very improbable that, so much given to quoting as he was, he would not have betrayed it by occasional reference and illustration. His testimony already referred to proves him to have been no Hellenist, but a Hebrew of the Hebrews. He wrote Greek with difficulty,* and his tolerable acquaintance with the language appears rather to have been derived from intercourse with Greeks than from literature or the grammarians, since his style shows some striking Hebraisms apart from many minor offences of the kind.

Since acquaintance with the Old-Testament Scriptures was an important part of a Jewish education, we are not surprised to find in the Epistles of Paul evidences of great familiarity with these writings. As the Jews of the New-Testament times, however, spoke the Aramaic dialect, and could not readily use the Old Testament in the original text, we find that Paul in common with the writers of the Gospels and Josephus made the greater part of his citations from the Septuagint translation, which he sometimes followed where it was incorrect, and again improved by an independent rendering.† His citations show a wide acquaintance with the historical, prophetic, and poetic books of the Old Testament and with known and unknown apocryphal writings.‡ In particular does he appear to have made a liberal use of the book of Wisdom, in which occur the teachings that death came into the world on account of sin, and that the righteous Israelites shall judge the heathen in the day of the Messiah,§ to-

* Gal. vi. 11.

† 2 Cor. iv. 13 ; 1 Cor. xiv. 21 ; Gal. iii. 11 ; Rom. ix. 17.

‡ See Meyer on 1 Cor. ii. 9 (Commentar, v. p. 63) and Rückert and Ewald on 1 Cor. ix. 10.

§ Wisdom, ii. 24, iii. 8, v. 17, xv. 7.

gether with other doctrines and some illustrations which appear in his writings. The student who passes from the study of the rabbinical literature to that of the Epistles of Paul not only finds sayings which remind him of the apothegms in which that literature abounds, but often recognizes in the apostle's treatment of the Old-Testament Scriptures the rabbinical point of view and exegetical artifices. These traits do not appear in his pages as if sought with labor, but rather as the result of early impressions and fixed modes of thought, as the natural expression, in fact, of one " to the manner born." The strange notion that the women ought to have their heads covered in the Christian assemblies " on account of the angels "* must be referred to a Jewish origin, whether we regard it as a reminiscence of the Jewish idea that angels were present in the worshipping assemblies,† or trace it to the narrative in the book of Enoch concerning the sin of the angels with the daughters of men.‡ In saying that Isaac was "persecuted" by Ishmael he does not follow the account in Genesis but a tradition recorded in the book of Jubilees. The idea that "Satan transforms himself into an angel of light "§ does not appear to have any other source than the rabbinical doctrine that temptations of the Devil came to men in the forms of angels. Accordingly, the " angel " who is reported to have wrestled with Jacob was supposed to be Satan in disguise. This

* 1 Cor. xi. 10, $\delta\iota\dot{\alpha}$ $\tauο\grave{\upsilon}s$ $\dot{\alpha}\gamma\gamma\acute{\epsilon}\lambda\upsilon s$; *cf.* Targum on Gen. vi. 2.

† See the Septuagint version of Ps. cxxxviii. 1 and Tobit xii. 12.

‡ Enoch v.f.; *cf.* Hilgenfeld, Zeitschr. für wissenschaftl. Theol., 1864, p. 183. Meyer adopts the former view, and designates the latter as the reading of a fleshly meaning into the passage (fleischerne Eindeutung), asking with amusing *naïveté* whether there were not matrons and old women among those who were warned ! Commentar, v. p. 305.

§ 2 Cor. xi. 14.

thought doubtless lay in the apostle's mind, and was assumed to be familiar to his Jewish-Christian readers.   The
fancy that the rock from which Moses is reputed miracu-
lously to have obtained water was no natural rock, but the
Messiah who in this disguise followed the children of Israel
in their wanderings was a current rabbinical tradition.*

Not only was Paul's doctrine that the Old-Testament
Scripture is the infallibly inspired word of God that of the
Jews of his time, but his interpretation of it was conformed
to the current rabbinical method, which applied to the
text violent exegetical pressure and unlimited allegorizing.
Accordingly he finds a prophecy of Christ in the promise
to Abraham, because it was made to the " offspring " of
the latter, and not to his " offsprings." †   The injunction
in the law not to muzzle the ox that treadeth out the corn
he allegorizes and applies as if the intention of the writer
had been to teach that the apostles should have the support of the congregations to which they ministered.   It
was written, he maintains, on the missionaries' account,
since God does not care for oxen.‡   The story of the two
wives of Abraham, Sarah and Hagar, was " written alle-
gorically " of the heavenly Jerusalem which is free and the
mother of the Christians and of the earthly Jerusalem
which is in bondage with her children ; and he establishes
this interpretation by a quotation from Isaiah.§   Akin to
the allegorical interpretation is the typological which finds
in an historical event or a word a type or an example

---

* 1 Cor. x. 4 ; Onkelos in Num. xxi. 18–20.   To hold with Meyer (Commentar, v. p. 265) that Paul did not adopt this idea from the rabbinical lore,
but originated it, is to concede at least the influence upon his mind of the
rabbinical method of treating Scripture.

† Gal. iii. 16 ; *cf.* Gen. xiii. 15.

‡ 1 Cor. ix. 9.   A more humane view is expressed even in Jonah iv. 11.

§ Gal. iv. 21.

which was written as an " ensample " for a situation or a person in some future time. In the use of this method Paul almost equals Philo in ingenuity and invention. The patriarchs, Moses, the children of Israel in the desert, are regarded as types of the Christian community. As, if the type be once allowed, the caprice of the interpreter may apply it indefinitely, so Paul finds in the veil upon the face of Moses two types, one of the vanishing glory of the old Covenant, and one of the cover which was upon the hearts of the Jews in the reading of the Old Testament, and which prevented them from finding in it the Christology which he read into it. * A theory of the Scriptures which makes them lend themselves so readily to the ends of argumentation has its perils, not the least of which is that of a too frequent resort to it. Accordingly, every admirer of the genius of Paul must regret to find him so often prejudicing his cause by inept appeals to passages in the Old Testament, as if such an authority were alone adequate, and reason futile.

Paul first appears in Christian story in Jerusalem on the occasion of the stoning of Stephen.† The open confession of Jesus and the bold denunciation of the Jews as murderers by this Hellenistic Jewish Christian seem to have excited the indignation of Paul, then " a young man," and full of zeal for the law and the traditions of his nation, and he appears to have been thought to be a suitable agent of further persecution of the hated sect. Having set out for Damascus on his cruel mission, he reached that city a changed man by reason of an experience which was second only to the mission of Jesus himself in importance for the cause of Christianity. There is no record of the details of this event which can lay claim to strictly historical

---

* 2 Cor. iii. 13 ff.   † Acts vii. 58.

credibility, since the accounts of it in Acts do not agree among themselves, and are not at first hand.* From Paul's references to it in his Epistles † it does not appear that he attached great importance to any external circumstances which may have accompanied it. He declares here that he had seen Jesus the Lord, and that it had pleased God to reveal His Son in him. ‡ It is upon this experience, in whatever way referred to, that he grounds his claims to apostolical rank and dignity. Had he not seen Jesus as well as the other apostles? If the Lord appeared to them after his resurrection, did he not also finally appear to him as " to one born out of due time "? God, indeed, revealed His Son in him that he "might publish the glad tidings of him among the gentiles." Believing himself called to the Master's work, he appears to connect this call with a mysterious experience which he does not definitely locate or define. We can only conjecture what he means by the declaration that he had seen Jesus. That a bodily manifestation to the physical vision is intended is by no means certain, and can scarcely be said to be probable. Even in the accounts in Acts it is not recorded that any form was visible, but only a bright light. However real, objectively real, the manifestation may have been thought by him to be, he cannot have regarded the experience as the seeing of a bodily personality, for every materialistic construction of the event is excluded by the words : " to reveal His Son *in* me," which may be cited as his own interpretation of it. Of similar import are the words concerning the light which God had commanded to shine in his heart to give the light of the knowledge of the

---

* Chapp. ix. xxii. xxvi. † 1 Cor. ix. 1, xv. 8 ; Gal. i. 13–16.

‡ οὐχὶ Ἰησοῦν τὸν κυριον ἑόρακα; ὤφθη κἀμοί; ἀποκαλύψαι υἱὸν αὐτοῦ ἐν ἐμοί.

glory of God in the face of Christ.* In accord with this view is his doctrine of the spiritual resurrection-body made in the likeness of the glorious body of Christ, since flesh and blood cannot inherit the kingdom of God.† That he conceived of such a heavenly body as visible to eyes of flesh is in the highest degree improbable.

Other experiences of Paul recorded by himself throw light upon the one in question, and tend to confirm the opinion that this " heavenly vision " was an inward experience. With an apology for an apparent boasting he writes in detail of "visions and revelations of the Lord" which he had had, and which appear to relate to realities conceived by him to be no less vivid and objective than that experienced at his conversion. " Whether in the body or out of the body," he knows not, he was " caught up into the third heaven, into paradise," and "heard unspeakable words." ‡ Likewise the journey to Jerusalem undertaken in order to confer with the original apostles was made in accordance with a "revelation,"§ and it is recorded in Acts that he had a vision which determined him to go to Macedonia, " concluding that the Lord had called him to publish the glad tidings to them." ‖ These facts appear to indicate that Paul had a constitutional tendency to visions, or at least that they were the form which the apprehension of certain truths and the resolving of certain perplexities assumed in his consciousness. One can scarcely suppose that a man of his intellectual character could have taken so important a step as the going to Jerusalem to confer with the Jewish-Christian apostles or the mission to Macedonia without careful

* 2 Cor. iv. 6. 　　　　　† 1 Cor. xv. 44, 48 ; Phil. iii. 21.
‡ 2 Cor. xii. 1-6. 　　　　§ κατ' ἀποκάλυψιν, Gal. ii. 2.
‖ Chap. xvi. 9.

deliberation, or even that paradise and the "unspeakable words" heard in the vision of the third heaven had not occupied his thoughts. However strongly dogmatic considerations may predispose the student to seek an explanation of these visions by the hypothesis of supernatural intervention, he must concede that the presumption is in favor of their production by natural causes, and that unless these can be shown to be inadequate, resort to that hypothesis is unwarrantable. Now it is evident that our knowledge of the matter is so meagre that a dogmatic conclusion regarding it must be altogether preposterous and irrational. We can do nothing, then, but inquire into the psychological antecedents of these phenomena, and in particular of the event usually called the conversion of Paul, but designated by himself as the revelation of Christ in him. The intimate connection of the subject with Paul's relation to Christianity requires its consideration before we proceed to a study of his explicit teachings.

Psychological antecedents of this conversion of Paul from Judaism to Christianity there must be supposed to have been, unless in a manner most unscientific and most unpauline his faith in Jesus be regarded as produced without antecedent reflection, reason, and consideration of its grounds, but by the subjection of his mind to an external power. It is true that Paul says it pleased God to reveal His Son in him. But this omission to mention secondary causes, which was so natural to a Jew, should not influence our analysis. Among the most obvious antecedents of the change in question must certainly have been some knowledge of the point of view, opinions, and grounds of belief in Jesus, which were current among the Christians whom he was persecuting, since he can hardly be supposed not to have heard their defence. He must have known that they believed that Jesus was the expected Messiah, and that although he had been ignominiously put to death, he had been raised from the dead, and was expected to come in glory and establish his kingdom. Doubtless rumors of manifestations of the resurrected Jesus to Peter, to James, to the five hundred, had reached his ears; and although as a Jew he may very likely have scoffed at the idea of a crucified Messiah and at the attempts to prove from the Old Testament that the prophets had foretold such a Messiah, and have rejected as a dream or a fraud the story of the resurrection, yet he could not escape from these ideas, could not but reflect upon them, could not but recognize their power when he saw men ready to die for them. It is very probable also that in his zeal for the law and the traditions of Judaism, the impetuous spirit of Paul had undertaken more than he could well carry out, and that although in his fury he may have "breathed out threatenings and slaughter," his sensitive nature revolted at the distress and agony which his cruelty produced. Nothing is more natural than that a man of his conscientiousness and his tenderness of heart should have been tormented with doubts as to the rightness of his dreadful work, doubts as to whether he might not be contending against God. To such a man doubts of this kind could not but give rise to the most earnest and most torturing reflections. To reflect, to hesitate in the midst of his abominable inquisitions, or perhaps when they were about to be renewed, was to give place in his mind to all that he had learned of Jesus from the lips of his victims, to recollections of their heroism and faith, to all that they had adduced as reasons for their belief from the Scriptures, to relate these things with his convictions, his Messianic hopes, his doctrine of the divine foresight

and the sovereignty of the law, of righteousness, of atonement, and by means of his great logical power, insight,
and religious feeling, to struggle with the mighty problem until it should be solved.

The cross and the resurrection were the central difficulties of the problem as it lay in the mind of Paul. To him,
as a Jew, the cross was a "stumbling-block." How could
that one be the Messiah who instead of winning a crown
had in the judgment of his nation earned the cross? We
may conceive this difficulty to have been overcome in his
thought by reminiscences of passages from the Old Testament, particularly from the fifty-third of Isaiah, which
he had perhaps heard adduced by the Christians, and by
the presence of another problem in his mind, that of the
salvation of his nation, or their attainment of a righteousness worthy of the Messianic time. How far they were
from this achievement! Could the law be in fact fulfilled?
How should the warfare of the forces of good and evil in
himself and others ever be decided in the interest of righteousness? Whence should come deliverance from "the
body of this death"? How should this dread dualism be
solved? To conceive of the mission of the Messiah as
the bringing in of righteousness, which was an idea by no
means strange to Jewish thought, and of his death as the
abolition of that dualism by removing the curse of the
law—an idea which was also contained in the Jewish doctrine of atonement—this was to solve the chief problem,
that of a suffering Messiah, and to take away the offence
of the cross. But if Jesus had died in accordance with
the divine decree to accomplish this great work for his
nation, if in this sense he were indeed the Messiah, then
to the logic of Paul there could be no objection urged
against the declaration of the Christians that the crucified

had risen from the dead.   For though God might suffer him to be sacrificed and to "die for the nation," He could not abandon him to sheol. Raised he must be, and exalted to heaven, a being of light clothed with a "glorious body." *   Might not the testimony of the Christian martyrs and the dying vision of Stephen then represent a divine reality, since they confirmed so well the logical solution of the great problem of righteousness and the Messiahship? That Paul may have reasoned in some such way as this is more than probable from what we know of his intellectual character; and that such reasoning reënforced by the testimony, the devotion, and the heroism of the persecuted disciples of Jesus should result in his conviction that their cause was right, and that in opposing it he was contending against God, may be regarded as scarcely open to question.   If, then, we are not warranted by the analogy of experience in believing that Paul's transition from Judaism to Christianity was by a leap or by an external propulsion; if we are to suppose that his conversion was a product of which the factors were his antecedent beliefs as a Jew, a process of reasoning upon certain data, and the obtrusive fact of the life of Jesus, together with the testimony of his disciples; if we cannot, without disregarding the presumptions furnished by history and the nature of the human mind, assume that such an intelligence as his could devote itself with enthusiastic ardor to a cause without rational conviction of its truth; if in a word this great transformation was not effected by magic—then must we maintain that the revelation of the Son of God in him and his seeing of Jesus were a spiritual manifestation and vision which had definite and necessary psychological antecedents.

* σῶμα της δόξης, Phil. iii., 21.

His own statements regarding the event rather imply than exclude these antecedents; while the unhistorical accounts of it in Acts would naturally find no place for them.*

2.—THE POINT OF DEPARTURE.†

The Pauline gospel can be understood only when it is regarded as an independent system of thought, and not as a product of reflection on the teachings of Jesus. Records of the life of Jesus Paul did not possess, and although he occasionally shows points of contact with the tradition of his teaching, only two events of his earthly career appear to have impressed him deeply—the crucifixion and the resurrection.   To the original apostles, who cherished the

---

* The conversion of Paul does not appear inexplicable from a psychological point of view, when it is considered that Judaism contains theological ideas which to a logical mind facilitated the transition to Christianity. From Isaiah liii. the doctrine had been derived that the sufferings of the righteous have an atoning efficacy to compensate for the sins of the people, and that Paul combined this doctrine with the death of Jesus there can be little doubt.   The righteousness of the nation which was postulated by Pharisee-ism as a condition of the Messianic time, conceived to be near at hand, might well be supposed to be effected by a great atonement, if in view of the spiritual condition of the people there was any hope of its realization. Again, by means of the popular allegorical exegesis, with which Paul shows familiarity, it was easy to interpret many passages of the prophets and psalms as fulfilled in the passion of Jesus; a resurrection from the dead could not be obnoxious to a Pharisee, and the idea of a crucified and resurrected Messiah who should bring to the world a new righteousness might not only he easily reached by Paul from Jewish premises, but was actually held by him on scriptural grounds (1 Cor. xv. 3), as he interpreted Scripture.

† The following study of the Pauline apprehension of the gospel is based upon Romans, Galatians, 1 and 2 Corinthians, I Thessalonians, and Philippians. The genuineness of no one of these is open to serious doubt, although Baur contested that of 1 Thessalonians and Philippians. The subject cannot be discussed here, and no attempt is made to present a complete view of the Pauline theology.

tradition of the historical Christ, and expected him to come again in person to complete that Messianic work which had been interrupted by his death, * Jesus was the Jewish Messiah. A crucified Messiah was, indeed, to them a stumbling-block, but they got over it by connecting the Messiahship in a modified form with the more glorious second manifestation or Parousia. But Paul construed the Messiahship in an entirely different way, if, indeed, he may not be said to have abandoned it altogether. To him as a Jew the cross had, indeed, been a stumbling-block, as it remained to other Jews, but to him as a Christian it was no longer so, for he looked upon it as a symbol of the vanishing of the old dispensation and of the introduction of a new order of religious administration. In the death of Jesus he saw the abolition of the law and the dethroning of Judaism from its seat of spiritual empire. He who on the cross appeared to his panic-stricken followers as the perishing Jewish Messiah was to Paul a universal Messiah dying to Judaism that he might live to mankind. To him Jesus had "died for all, that they who live should no longer live to themselves but to him who died for their sakes and rose again." † No longer now does he know Christ "according to the flesh," that is, as the Jewish Messiah, for in his thought Jesus on the cross died to all the national, fleshly, sensuous limitations which in Judaism attached to the Messiah, and became the representative of a world-principle of life and "a quickening spirit."

Paul sets forth the point of view from which he regarded the gospel and the significance of the mission of Jesus, and gives undoubtedly at the same time a section of his spiritual biography, in the following words: " For the law of the Spirit of life set me free in Christ Jesus from the law

* Acts iii. 19 ff.   † 2 Cor. v. 15, 16.

of sin and death.   For what the law could not do, in that it was weak through the flesh, God had done who on account of sin sent His own Son in the likeness of sinful flesh, and passed sentence of condemnation on sin in the flesh; so that what is required by the law might be accomplished in us who walk not according to the flesh, but according to the Spirit."*   Thus in Jesus Christ he sees a governing principle of the Spirit of God which leads to everlasting life.   Christ himself is the Spirit, † and the consciousness of the Christian is in its essential nature the consciousness of possessing the Spirit of God or of Christ. The Christian believer has " received the Spirit." ‡   His consciousness is essentially spiritual, and is not one of bondage, but of liberty, is in fact one of sonship; being led by the Spirit of God " he is a son of God.§   The Spirit even " beareth witness " with his spirit that he is a child of God. ‖   The relation of this idea that in the mission of Jesus there came into the world a new and absolute principle of spiritual life to Paul's general view of the world and his philosophy of salvation is apparent.   It accords with the doctrine that the first man, Adam, in contradistinction to the second man, Christ, and to the Christian believer, was merely " a living soul"; that in the order of things that is first which is natural or animal, and afterwards the spiritual; that sin reigned from Adam to Christ; and that the natural man cannot possibly fulfil the spiritual law for want of the power to break the force of the flesh.

That this point of view was essentially Jewish is evident from the fact that it is dominated by the idea of the law

* Rom. viii. 2–5.   † 2 Cor. iii. 17.
‡ Gal. iii. 2, πνεῦμα.   § Rom. viii. 14.
‖ Rom. viii. 16.

and finds its illustrations only in Jewish mythology or history. It was, as we have seen, entertained in a rudimentary form and without philosophical development in the Jewish-Christian apostolical circles, so far as the communication of the Spirit to men upon belief and baptism is concerned. Here its Old-Testament source is indicated by an appeal to a prophecy of Joel. Paul may very likely have worked out the doctrine of the Spirit independently, influenced perhaps by the book of Wisdom, with which, as has been previously remarked, he appears to have been acquainted. Here the doctrine is taught that Wisdom or the Holy Spirit descends into the souls of men communicating knowledge and virtue and making them friends of God and prophets.* In receiving this doctrine into his system Paul identifies Jesus with the idea of Wisdom and the Spirit from above, and makes him the source of the divine power which he believed to be communicated to the Christians. We should, however, omit a very important factor in this conception if we did not take into account Paul's great religious nature, his sense of sin and of its power in human life, his high ideal of righteousness, and that revelation of the Son of God in him by which he saw at the moment of his transformation a way of escape from his bondage by faith and a dying to the law. How fundamental and important was the office of the Spirit in Paul's philosophy of the gospel appears in his repeated reference to its operations. Not only does he recognize this power in such subordinate manifestations as the speaking with tongues, or the ecstatic expression of feeling, and call those who were so affected among the Corinthians, spiritual men or " pneumatics," † but to him

* Wisdom, Chapp. vii. viii. ix.

† πνευματικός, 1 Cor. xiv. 37.

the Spirit is the supernatural divine power of life which, transcendent before Christ, has through him become immanent in the souls of believers, and produces in them illumination, knowledge of spiritual things, and ability to overcome the weakness of the flesh.*   " The things which eye hath not seen, and ear hath not heard," etc., "God has revealed to us by His Spirit."   All knowledge of divine things is attained by this instrumentality.   "We did not receive the spirit of the world, but the Spirit of God, that we might know the things that have been given us by the grace of God." †   This spirit is represented as taking up its abode in believers, for to the Corinthians Paul says : " Know ye not that ye are God's temple, and that the Spirit of God dwelleth in you?" ‡   Without this divine power no one is even able to make a confession of Jesus, for "No one can say, Jesus is Lord, but by the Holy Spirit." §   It is "with the Holy Spirit " that the second Epistle to the Corinthians is written.‖   The Spirit is not conceived by Paul as a third personality different from God and Christ, but rather as one with both, so that the distinction appears to vanish in his thought, and God's Spirit, Christ's Spirit, and Christ are different terms for the same conception.¶   In one passage " the Lord," that is, Christ, is distinctly declared to be "the Spirit." **

These are only a few of the many passages in Paul's writings in which his doctrine of the Spirit finds expres-

---

* So prominent a part does Paul assign to this divine power in believers that it has been contended that he did not recognize a $\pi\nu\epsilon\tilde{\upsilon}\mu\alpha$ as naturally belonging to man. See Holsten, Zum Evangelium des Paulus und des Petrus, 1868, pp. 384 ff, and *per contra* Pfleiderer, Zeitsch. für wissenschaftl. Theol. 1871, pp. 161 ff.

† 2 Cor. ii. 10, 11.   ‡ 1 Cor. iii. 16.

§ 1 Cor. xii. 3.   ‖ 2 Cor. iii. 3.

¶ Rom. viii. 9–11.   ** 2 Cor. iii. 17.

sion. As an absolute principle of the Christian life it was conceived as not only opposed to the flesh in the individual and an immanent source of spiritual quickening, but as marking the fundamental distinction between the temporal and fleshly "elements" of Judaism and the new, eternal Christian dispensation. The vanishing of Judaism, the death of Jesus to the law and to its fleshly Messiahship, the abolition of the law forever on the cross, the necessity that all men should also die to it, be baptized into the Spirit, and rise into newness of life—this was Paul's point of departure. The veil upon the face of Moses was a symbol that the Israelites did not behold "the end of that which was to be done away."* But whenever their heart turneth to the Lord, or Christ, the veil is taken away; and as the Lord is the Spirit, and where the Spirit of the Lord is there is liberty, the unveiled beholders of his glory "are changed into the same image from glory to glory, as by the Lord, the Spirit."† For them whatever was limiting and encumbering in Jewish legalism, whatever was severe and difficult in the attainment of Jewish righteousness, whatever was fleshly and transient in Jewish Messianism—all this was done away in the presence of the Spirit, the absolute principle of life and liberty. It does not belong to an historical study to investigate the validity of this Pauline doctrine of the Spirit, and determine whether it represents an objective reality, or is the expression of a subjective experience which is capable of a psychological explanation. It should be remarked, however, that it indicates a wide departure from the point of view of the original Church of the Jewish-Christian apostles. As to Judaism the Spirit was transcendent, and came into relation with men only occa-

* 2 Cor. iii. 13.   † 2 Cor. iii. 17, 13.

sionally, when it inspired the prophets, so to the Jewish-Christian believers it was manifested in certain signs on occasion of baptism or the laying on of hands by the apostles. They knew nothing of the speculative doctrine of the Spirit as an absolute principle of the Christian life in which was dissolved into types and " ensamples " all that they reverenced in their history and traditions, before which the majesty of the old law must bow, and by whose authority the good old way of the righteousness of the fathers and the prophets was declared impossible. More than a departure from the original gospel of Jesus is this Pauline speculative doctrine; it is a radical transformation of it. Jesus declared that he came not to destroy the law, but to fulfil it ; and while he doubtless expected that it would be outgrown so far as it was narrow and unspiritual, he said nothing of a metaphysical abolition of it by his death. In his teaching the religious life was not represented as being the result of a mystical indwelling or communication of the Spirit, but as being attained by repentance and obedience. 'His great precepts were to love God and men and to strive for righteousness and the kingdom of heaven. The Spirit as a supernatural influence in the religious life was foreign to his thought. On the contrary, he made his appeal to the natural intuitions and sentiments of men, and on these as capable and efficient he depended for the accomplishment of the spiritual ends which he had in view. To his great and lucid intelligence this Pauline speculative point of view would have been impossible, and to his feelings the Pauline " ecstatic speaking with tongues " and the idea of the Spirit making " intercession with groanings that cannot be uttered," would have been only less offensive than frequent scenes of the modern revival, where the cross is represented as a symbol of a vicarious sacrifice, and multitudes gather shaken with emotion and driven to the place by the instinct of personal safety.

3.—SIN AND THE FLESH.

In the teaching of Jesus there is only infrequent mention of sin in the concrete, and no doctrine of it in the abstract. But in the doctrinal system of Paul it occupies a very prominent position, and casts an ominous shadow upon human nature and human life as regarded from his point of view. His doctrine of sin shows the influence upon his thought of the Jewish theology in which he was reared, and may be regarded, since Jesus taught nothing respecting the origin and nature of sin, as a modification of the gospel through rabbinical speculation. The Jewish theology furnished both a natural and an historical explanation of the entrance of sin into the world. The former, which may be regarded as inclusive of the latter, proceeded upon the assumption of an impulse to evil (yeser ha-ra) residing in the human body and constantly striving against the inclination to good (yeser ha-tob) which existed in the soul. The evil impulse was so strong as generally to prevail, and its first historical success was gained in Eve and Adam through their temptation by Satan or "the old serpent."* There resulted from the fall of Adam a troop of natural evils, particularly physical death, which was ordained as a punishment, and such a moral deterioration that the will of man became subject to the control of the fleshly impulses, and was bent to the commission not only of sins of a sensuous nature, but also

* The Jewish theology must of course trace the origin of sin to God, since He created man with fleshly impulses—an act of which He repented. See Weber, System der altsynag. Theol., p. 214.

of spiritual transgressions. The inclination to good was so weakened that it was unable in general to offer a successful resistance to the lower nature, and the attainment of righteousness was rendered extremely difficult if not impossible, although by the observance of the law (Thora) the good impulses might be so strengthened as to make their victory possible. But such cases are exceptional, and the great majority of men are subject to the sway of their lower nature. Only actual transgressions were, however, regarded as sins, and no guilt attached to a man because of the natural impulse to wrong-doing. Accordingly, in the Jewish theology there was no doctrine of inherited or transmitted sinfulness, and all punishments were thought to be the results of individual offences. The penalty was inflicted rigorously "measure for measure," and "No death without sin" was an established maxim. The death of children was charged to the sins of their parents, while that of the righteous was a means of salvation, a deliverance out of the present evil world.

It accords with the philosophical point of view of Paul that he deals very largely with sin in the abstract. He conceives of it as a condition and a power. Jews and Greeks are subject to it; it has come into the world and dwells in man, working all manner of evil, deceiving, slaying, as if possessed of personality.* He draws a terrible picture of the condition of the heathen world under the power of sin, whom "God has given over in the lust of their hearts to impurity," and sees his own nation subject to the same malign influence.† Experience reveals the deplorable condition of the individual in whose members this fatal power works, mastering the inclination to good and the will which would obey the law, and bring-

* Rom. iii. 9, v. 12, vii. 9, 11, 17.   † Rom. i. ii.

ing him into a bondage against which he vainly strug-
gles.* As if Scripture could make more certain what
observation and experience have established, Paul com-
bines several passages from the Psalms to prove the
universality of sin,† which he regards as a "law" of the
members, a recognized principle in the economy of God,
who "delivered up all to disobedience," and whose revealed word "shut up all under sin."‡ Paul's explanation of this power of sin is essentially that of the Jewish
theologians. He finds two principal causes for it—the
transgression of Adam, and the nature of man as "flesh."
With regard to the former his fundamental proposition
is that "through one man sin entered into the world,
and through sin death, and thus death came through unto
all men, because all sinned."§ The doctrine of this
passage and its connection appears to be that through
the transgression of Adam sin came into the world as a
universal power to which all men were to such a degree
subjected that they became personally sinners; and that
physical death came into the world through sin, and that
all were subjected to it on account of the judgment
pronounced upon Adam, but only because all personally
sinned. Thus the dominion of death extended over all
men not only because of Adam's sin, but also because of
individual transgressions whereby the universal judgment
of death was made effective for each. The mediate
cause of death is the sin of Adam, its immediate cause
the sin of each individual. That this was actually the
state of things before the Mosaic law was given is shown

* Rom. vii. 7–25, vi. 17.   † Rom. iii. 10–19.
‡ Rom. vii. 23, xi. 32 ; Gal. iii. 22.
§ διὰ τῆς ἁμαρτίας ὁ θάνατος . . . . . ἐφ' ᾧ πάντες ἥμαρτον,
Rom. v. 12.

by the words: " For all the time before the law sin was
in the world; but sin is not set to one's account when
there is no law. Yet death reigned from Adam to
Moses even over those who had not sinned in the manner
in which Adam transgressed " (*i. e.*, by violating a positive commandment).* In other words, in the case of
those who had not sinned as Adam did, the actually
existing sin was punished by death in accordance with
the maxim that they who sin without a law will also
perish without a law—a doctrine which was fundamental
in the Jewish theology.† The death of innocent children
was doubtless not in Paul's mind, but the Jewish idea of
the solidarity of the family, according to which the sin
of the parents is visited upon the children, would have
furnished him with a solution of the problem. It should
be observed that according to the teaching of Paul it is
not sin which has " come through " to all men, but death,
which came with sin. Hence he cannot be said to have
taught the doctrine that the death of all, even of little
children, is a penalty of hereditary sin born in all, or immediately of Adam's sin. The dogma of original sin as
taught in the Church cannot legitimately be derived from
Paul's writings. He regarded sin and death, indeed, as
having become great powers in the world through Adam ;
but he knew of no guilt which was not through individual sinning, and his proposition concerning death as a
judgment upon sin is that it " came through unto all men
because all sinned," that is, that it is directly due to personal transgression, indirectly to Adam's.‡

* ἐπὶ τῷ ὁμοιώματι τῆς παραβάσεως Ἀδάμ, Rom. v. 13, 14.
† See Rom. ii. 12.
‡ That Paul regarded Adam as naturally mortal appears to be implied in
1 Cor. xv. 47.   The introduction of death by sin can then only be ex-

We should expect, then, that Paul would have a doctrine of the origin, seat, and development of sin in the individual. Such a doctrine which is implied in his teaching respecting the relation of Adam's transgression to the human race, and is to be expected from him by reason of his education in the Jewish theology, is actually contained in his conception of the flesh.* The exact determination of the meaning of this term in his thought is involved in difficulty. In accord with the Jewish theology it is evident that he recognized in human nature two impulses corresponding to its two sides, body and soul. He sees a schism in man arising from a twofold " law " or impulse, the one good, the other bad. The good impulse, which dwells in the " inner man," or the " mind," † is in sympathy with the law of God, but on account of the opposition of the " other law in the members " ‡ has not the power to fulfil it. This fleshly impulse is represented as natural to man, but as not resulting in sin until " the commandment came," for " without the law sin is dead." When the commandment is known the latent tendency to sin springs into activity with its train of lusts and passions, the rent in human nature is disclosed, the conflict of opposing im-

plained from Paul's point of view by supposing that Adam might have become immortal had he not sinned and hence been expelled from the garden and so prevented from eating of the tree of life. See Gen. iii. 22. The dependence of the whole discussion,upon Jewish legend and speculation is instructive. The Jewish theologians also held that Adam was mortal in the sense that he could sin, but that he brought death upon himself and his posterity by sinning. Had he not sinned he might, like Elijah, have escaped death. Jewish theology also attempted to solve the antinomy which is contained in the two propositions, that sin and guilt are not hereditary, but death, their penalty, is, since the whole race is mortal regardless of moral desert. See Weber, System der altsynagog. Theol., pp. 238–240.

   * σάρξ.   † ἔσω ἄνθρωπος, νοῦς.

‡ ἕτερος νόμος ἐν τοῖς μέλεσιν.

pulses begins, the peace of innocence in which the subject had " lived " is broken, and he has the bitter foretaste of death.   Sin comes to life and he dies.   Thence his better self is in bondage to the tyrannous power of sin ; he is " fleshly, a slave sold to sin," yet at the same time he distinguishes between his real, true self and this foreign and hostile power which rules in him, that is, in his flesh, so that it is no longer he that transgresses but sin which dwells in him.   The " inward man " takes delight in the law of God, but the other law which wars against the law of the mind ($νοῦς$) brings the man " into captivity " to the law of sin which is in his " members." *   These expressions throw some light upon the Pauline conception of the flesh, and appear to show that he saw in the natural man something more than he thought this term to cover. Since there is the " inward man," the $νοῦς$, which contends against the outward man, or the flesh, the mind striving in opposition to the sarkical or fleshly impulses, there would hardly appear to be grounds for affirming that Paul conceived of the flesh as the body, and of the latter as " composing the real, substantial essence of man." †   As the seat of sin and the cause of the infirmity by reason of which man is brought into bondage to it, he doubtless regarded it, but he distinguished it from the self, and represented it as the external, earthly side of man, the " members," whereby he is allied to the lower animals, and distinguished from God and heavenly creatures.   In this sense Paul frequently employs the term of the material of the earthly body, designating events, conditions, and rela-

---

* See Rom. vii. 7-25.

† So Baur, Neutestamentl. Theol., p. 143.   Holsten's view is essentially the same, who regards $σάρξ$ and $ἄνθρωπος$ as substantially synonymous in the Pauline teaching.   Zum Evangel. Paulus, etc., p. 393.

tions which refer to the body as " fleshly," " in the flesh," and " according to the flesh," * without regard to moral relations. The term is generally employed in the Old Testament to designate man as mortal, frail, and weak ; and as it is but a step from this idea to that of moral weakness as residing in his physical organism, we find in a single passage in the Psalms sin connected with the impure origin of the body in the natural act of generation. † But in general the Old Testament writers do not recognize the body as the seat of sin. In the later Jewish theology however, it was regarded not only as the ground of intellectual and moral weakness, but as the seat of sin, particularly in the sexual instinct. Paul shows points of contact with the Old-Testament conception and with that of the teaching in which he had been reared in such expressions as: " I conferred not with flesh and blood," " fleshly wisdom," " fleshly weapons," etc., ‡ and when he calls the Corinthians " fleshly " or " unspiritual " because of their party-strifes, indicating that they were merely natural men, or as he had just before called them, " psychical " men who were destitute of understanding for spiritual things,§ though not necessarily without that power of mind or reason ($\nu o\tilde{v}\varsigma$) which is indeed capable of perceiving and even taking delight in the law of God, but unable alone to fulfil it.

Paul's conception of the flesh was, then, substantially that of the Jewish theology and speculation, according to which there resides in the body an impulse to evil-doing (yeser ha-ra). The flesh was to him the seat of a power of sin, of a bad impulse opposed to the Spirit and to " the in-

* Rom. i. 3, ii. 28, ix. 3 ; 2 Cor. x. 3 ; Gal. ii. 20 ; Phil. i. 22, 24.
† Ps. li. 7.   ‡ Gal. i. 16 ; 2 Cor. i. 12, x. 3 f.
§ 1 Cor. ii. 14, iii. 1–4.
12

ward man," whose better knowledge and will it continually resisted and dominated. "The mind of the flesh is enmity against God; for it doth not submit itself to the law of God, neither, indeed, can it." It has desires against the Spirit, and renders its subjects unable to do the things which they would.* In spite of the intimate relation to the body which the flesh is represented as holding it does not appear that Paul identified it with the body † nor, indeed, with the natural man as a personality, although "according to the flesh" and "according to the [natural] man" are synonymous expressions.‡ The flesh produces not alone sins which may be regarded as originating in the body, for although offenses against chastity hold a prominent place in the catalogue of "the works of the flesh," there are mentioned also, idolatry, sorcery, hatreds, strife, rivalry, outbursts of wrath, cabals, divisions, factions, envyings, etc.§ It is but a step from the conception of the flesh as the seat of sin to an identification of it with sin itself, so that the expression "to walk in or according to the flesh" should be equivelant to, "to live in sin or according to the principle of sin." Paul appears, then, to have employed the term in three significations to denote: 1, simply the body without reference to moral relations; 2, the natural man in his sensuous nature and moral-religious weakness; 3, the natural man

* Rom. viii. 7; Gal. v.16.

† In Rom. vi. 6 the destruction of "the body of sin" is mentioned. This σῶμα τῆς ἁμαρτίας is probably not identical with σάρξ, but may be the body as the "organ" of sin, according to Tholuck, or as subject to, governed by, sin, according to Meyer.

‡ Baur appears to go too far in maintaining that the σάρξ is conceived of as so dominating the νοῦς that the latter was in Paul's thought only an "accident" of the former. Neutestamentl. Theol., p. 146.

§ Gal. v. 19 f.

as positively sinful. The words "to live in the flesh," and "to walk in the flesh," and "to walk according to the flesh," appear to have now one and now another of these meanings according to the connection.*

The preponderance of the idea of sin as a power and a principle in human nature in the thought of Paul throws somewhat into the background the conception of sin as an act and its relation as such to man's self-determination or freedom. In the gospel of Jesus, from which speculation was quite remote, the reverse is the case. We find, however, in Paul's writings no explanation of the origin of this power of evil which has its seat in the flesh. To say that it was inherited only removes the source farther back, for Paul evidently regarded the fleshly impulse as latent in Adam until the positive commandment awoke it. The impulses to wrong-doing, the lusts of the flesh, the passions, which bring forth the horrid brood of evil works, he must have thought to be natural to man and not the result of his free choice. The power of sin in the flesh did not spring from man's free personal acts of sin. Rather man as a fleshly creature is powerless under the might of sin in his members, sold to it, like a slave. He is unable to do the good, however much he may approve it with his "mind," and feel himself under obligations to obey the divine law. The flesh does not strive against the law, and bring about disobedience because man has decided by an act of free choice against the commandment of God, but because the impulse of the flesh is in itself toward evil and against God, and he who is under its power is not able to decide for the good and perform it. His sole hope of deliverance is in somewhat

* See 2 Cor. x. 3 ; Gal. ii. 20 ; Phil. i. 22 for the first sense ; Rom. viii. 4 for the last ; and 2 Cor. x. 2 f for a double sense.

which he has not in himself. Only the "law of the Spirit of life" can set him free in Christ Jesus from this tyrannous law of sin and death.* If, then, sin as a principle or a power is original and latent in human nature, only awaiting the emergence of the law to "seize the opportunity" and work all manner of sinful desire† ; if it thus existed in our first parents, and the "first man" was "of the earth, earthy," a "natural" man of flesh and blood which "cannot inherit the kingdom of God," so that it cannot be said that sin as an act of transgression wrought a change in human flesh in Adam or effects one in that of the individual sinner; if the body is in its nature a "body of sin" and a "body of death" to which the power of sin clings so persistently that even in those who as Christians have received the counteracting power of the Spirit it cannot be fully overcome—how can sin and death be said to have come into the world through Adam's transgression? To the first man, who in contrast with the second man, Christ, the life-giving spirit ‡ was not spiritual, but "animal" and of the "corruption" which does not "inherit incorruption," death cannot be regarded as incidental and dependent on an inward act, but must be natural and necessary. In direct opposition to this Paul teaches that death in the race and the individual is the result of a decree of God in punishment of sin, and hence is not a natural necessity, but a judicial dispensation called forth by the act of man. The Hellenistic doctrine that death is natural and necessary in the constitution of man and that of the Jewish theology that it is the consequence of sin appear to be united in the Pauline teaching without definite reconciliation. Again, Paul's teaching furnishes no answer to the ques-

* Rom. viii. 8.   † Rom. vii. 8.   ‡ 1 Cor. xv. 45, 46.

tion how sin can be said to have come into the world through Adam, since it resides as a principle in all men as naturally " fleshly," and in each only awaits the occasion furnished by the law " to come to life."   If it is not transmitted, and all men are subject to death only "inasmuch as all have sinned," the significance of Adam's causal relation to it as a world-power and a universal principle is not apparent.   Furthermore, if man was originally con-stituted by his Creator with a dominant power of sin in his members, if he is naturally so subject and enslaved to the flesh that in spite of all his knowledge and good-will he does what he would not,* the consistency of the judgment which pronounces a universal condemnation of death upon the race on account of sin is not obvious. Yet with all this teaching of the fatality of the flesh Paul appears to recognize a power of choice in man which may be appealed to, and censures the heathen because they "did not choose to retain God in their knowledge."†But this appears to have been written when he was not influenced by the exigencies of his theory that man cannot be saved without the righteousness of Christ.

<h3 style="text-align:center">4.—CHRISTOLOGY.</h3>

The Christology of Paul proceeds from the point of view from which his entire theology was developed, that Christianity was not a fulfilled Judaism, but a new and independent principle of life, a " new creation,"‡ related to Judaism as freedom to bondage, as the Spirit to the flesh. It is a transformation of the Christology of the original apostles and of the tradition of Jesus on which the synoptical Gospels are founded in that it throws into the back-

* Rom. vii. 19.   † Rom. i. 28.   ‡ καινὴ κτίσις.

ground the teaching and Messiahship of Jesus, and brings into the foreground his atoning sacrifice and a metaphysical conception of " the second Adam " and " the man from heaven," by which the ordinary Jewish Messianism was altogether transcended. Accordingly, Paul never applies to Christ the appellation, Son of Man, which was Jesus' favorite designation of himself. He does not appear to use the term Son of God in the Jewish-Messianic sense, but rather in order to indicate that Christ was of the essence of God in that he was " Spirit," " Spirit of holiness," and " life-giving Spirit," even "image of God." *   His conception of the nature of Christ was determined by his theory of the work of Christ. As the Saviour of men from sin he must have been without sin. †   Since he communicated the Spirit to men, he must have been of a

---

* Rom. i. 4; 1 Cor. xv. 45; 2 Cor. iii. 17; εἰκὼν τοῦ θεοῦ, 2 Cor. iv. 4. In the thought of Paul, Christ was not simply an exalted man, but rather a heavenly being subordinate to God. He was not God, but the Son, " the image of God," the divine glory shone in his face; and he must at last become subject to Him who put all things under him. (2 Cor. iv. 4, 6; 1 Cor. xv. 28). The first man, Adam, became a living soul, but the last Adam became (was created) a life-giving spirit; the first man is from the earth, the second man is from heaven (1 Cor. xv. 45, 46). From this point of view should probably be interpreted the difficult passage, Rom. i. 4, "appointed with power to be the Son of God according to the spirit of holiness by the resurrection of the dead." "According to the flesh," *i. e.*, in his earthly manifestation, he was of the seed of David, but according to the spirit of holiness, the spiritual side of his nature, the Spirit which he *was* (" the Lord is the Spirit ") he was set forth by the resurrection in his true nature as the Son of God, that is, assigned to his proper rank as " the second man from heaven," the originator and archetype of a new spiritual mankind. This Pauline conception appears to be closely related to the idea of the Jewish theology, doubtless familiar to the apostle, according to which the Messiah as Son of Man was kept in heaven until the time of his manifestation. *Cf.* Weizsäcker, Das apostol. Zeitalter, p. 124.

† 2 Cor. v. 21, τὸν μὴ γνόντα ἁμαρτίαν.

spiritual nature. If whatever Adam as the fleshly head of the race represented of corruption and sin, if whatever was thought to have come into the world through him, was counteracted in Christ, then must Christ have been a man of an essentially different kind. Over against the earthly man was " the man from heaven." If through the one came death through the other came the resurrection of the dead.* Since man, as the descendant of Adam who was only a " living soul," † a merely psychical man, could not by nature have the Spirit, he must be transformed according to the image of the spiritual Adam, and become a "new creation." Christ is revealed as the life-giving Spirit, which he was by creation, through his resurrection from the dead.‡ A new power of life is disclosed in him which man may appropriate by faith, and through it overcome the flesh which holds him in bondage, and from him begins a process of renewal which the Holy Spirit effects, transforming the sinful children of Adam into children of God, the fleshly men into spiritual men. In this Christology there is a transformation not only of the Old-Testament Jewish Messianism but of Jesus' teaching regarding himself. For the conception of Christ which it contains is equally remote from the second David, the victorious prince, the lion of the house of Judah, and from the suffering Son of Man, the spiritual teacher and prophet of

---

* 1 Cor. xv. 21, 47.

† $\psi v \chi \dot{\eta}\ \zeta \tilde{\omega} \sigma a$. In the Pauline anthropology a spiritual or pneumatic principle is accorded to man ; but in Adam and his natural descendants the psychical or sensuous is regarded as dominant, while in Christ, the second Adam, the spiritual predominates, so that it may be said of him that he is essentially $\pi v \varepsilon \tilde{v} \mu a$, and not merely $\pi v \varepsilon \tilde{v} \mu a$, but $\tau \dot{o}\ \pi v \varepsilon \tilde{v} \mu a$. " The Spirit " which through him is communicated to men should not be confounded with spirit as an element of human nature, the rational power, etc.

‡ 1 Cor. xv. 45 ; Rom. i. 4.

righteousness. The metaphysical second Adam, the man from heaven, neither ushers in an earthly kingdom at the head of armies nor brings a message of the kingdom of God, teaching men how to enter it by the attainment of a human righteousness.

While this conception of Christ as the man from heaven is unique in relation to the New-Testament circle of ideas, and was first introduced by Paul into Christian literature, it is doubtful that he originated it. The notion of an ideal man was entertained by Philo, and Plato is suggested where we read in this Alexandrian philosopher of a difference between man as created in time and man as found in the image of God before time was, the former, of body and soul, mortal, the latter, idea, pure form, incorporeal. Again he speaks explicitly of a " heavenly man," and an " earthly man." The Messianism of the Septuagint translators of the Bible shows itself in the connection of the idea of preëxistence with the person of Christ,* who is arbitrarily assumed by them to have been in the thought of the original writers. In the Enoch-Parables the Messiah is represented as being in the image of an ideal man and as preëxistent: " His appearance was that of a man, and full of grace was his countenance like a holy angel " ; " Before the stars of heaven were made was his name named in the presence of the Lord of spirits "; " And therefore was he chosen and hidden before Him before

* In Ps. lxxii. 5 it is said of the king :   " They shall fear thee as long as the sun and the moon endure," etc.   The Septuagint reads here as of a preexistent Messiah :   " He will live as long as the sun, and was *before* the moon."   In Ps. cx. it is said of the king :   " Thy people shall be willing in the day of thy power, in the beauty of holiness from the womb of the morning."   The Septuagint reads, " I brought thee [the Messiah] forth from the womb *before* the morning star."

the world was created," etc.* That Paul thought Christ as the man from heaven to have been a created being is evident from the connection in which he places his origin with that of the first man, Adam. The one as well as the other "became." † There is great probability that he also believed Christ to have existed as a celestial being prior to his appearance upon the earth and even to have taken part in the creation of the world. In connection with instructions regarding things offered in sacrifice to idols he says : "To us there is but one God, the Father, from whom are all things, and we to Him ; and one Lord Jesus Christ, through whom are all things, and we through him,"‡ Here it is certainly probable that the words "from whom are all things " and " through whom are all things " should be understood as conveying essentially the same idea both as to the extent of "all things " and as to the production of them, in the former case by a first cause and in the latter by an agent. It is extremely arbitrary to interpret "all things " as referring in the former clause to the universe, and in the latter to the economy of salvation, or to assume the idea of creation in the former, and that of government in the latter. Preëxistence is very clearly implied in the declarations that " God sent His Son in the likeness of sinful flesh," and that " When the fulness of time came God sent forth His Son, born of a woman." § For although the idea of a sending of Jesus and of prophets is expressed in the synoptic Gospels, to which the concep-

---

* Enoch xlvi. 1, xlviii. 3, 6. See Dillmann, Das Buch Henoch, p. 160. Toy's opinion that an ideal preëxistence may here be intended (Judaism and Christianity, p. 326) is not supported by Dillmann with whom Hausrath agrees.

† 1 Cor. xv. 45, ἐγένετο.

‡ 1 Cor. viii. 6.   § Rom. viii. 3 ; Gal. iv. 4.

tion of preëxistence is foreign,* yet the case is quite different here where the words "in the likeness of sinful flesh" and "born of a woman" evidently denote special and peculiar conditions, and imply that the writer thought of Christ as not originally connected with a body of flesh and as not necessarily existing only through a human birth.   In like manner the declaration that Christ in contrast with Adam, who was "of the earth, earthy," was the man "from heaven," † must mean either that his origin was from heaven in the sense that he was generated by the Spirit, or that he preëxisted in the celestial regions. But since the former idea is totally foreign to the Pauline Christology, the latter is probably conveyed in the expression.   The words: "For ye know the grace of our Lord Jesus Christ, that though he was rich yet for your sakes he became poor, that ye through his poverty might be rich," ‡ can only mean that for the sake of saving men he renounced the glory, dominion, and blessedness which in his preëxistent state he had with the Father, in order to enter upon the humiliation of his incarnation.   The interpretations, "although he might have been rich," and "although he is rich," are not only ungrammatical, but contrary to the connection, in which the apostle urges upon the Corinthians the practice of liberality in giving for the needs of others, and cites the example of Christ

---

* Mat. x. 40, xxiii. 34 ; Luke xx. 13.   The absence of the idea of the preëxistence of Christ from the Jewish-Christian tradition and from the synoptic Gospels which are based upon it may perhaps be explained by the fact that the early tradition was the *naïve* historical account of the life and teachings of Jesus colored chiefly by earthly Messianic expectations.   It was reserved for the speculative mind of Paul to introduce this idea from the Jewish thelogy and perhaps from Philo as a presumption necessary to his theory of redemption which required no less a personage than "the man from heaven."

† 1 Cor. xv. 47.   ‡ 2 Cor. viii. 9.

who, though he was rich, became poor. A similar thought of the renunciation of Christ is conveyed in the passage: "Let this mind be in you which was in Christ Jesus who, being in the form of God, did not regard it as a thing to be grasped at to be on an equality with God, but made himself of no consideration, taking the form of a servant, and becoming like men," etc.,* where the Philippians are exhorted to humility in imitation of Christ who, when he was in his preëxistent state in the form of God, that is, as a heavenly being, spirit, "the image of God,"† did not grasp at an equality with God, but humbled himself to the lowly position of a servant and to the death of the cross.

It is not clear how Paul conceived of the entrance of this supersensible, heavenly being into human conditions through generation. He says that Christ "was born of the seed of David according to the flesh."‡ So much may be regarded as conceded to Jewish Messianism. But he was only "appointed" to be the Son of God in the higher, transformed Pauline sense of Messiahship through his resurrection, whereby it was manifested that he was not subjected to death, but had in him the principle of life, the "life-giving Spirit" which could not be dominated as in the case of other men by the principle of sin in the flesh. The Pauline Christology appears to proceed from an idea of a twofold creation of man, suggested perhaps by the double account in Genesis, that of an "earthy" man, Adam, and that of a "heavenly" man, Christ, who remained in heaven, essentially Spirit and so God-allied, a being of light, reflecting the glory

---

* Phil. ii. 5–8. † 2 Cor. iv. 4.

‡ These words evidently exclude the supernatural generation as recorded by the first and third evangelists.

of God, until "the fulness of the time came," when he was "sent forth," "that we might be adopted as sons."* Christ was accordingly the spiritual or pneumatic man, the typical man, who represented in himself the perfection of human nature. In his earthly condition, united with the flesh, his original, preëxistent splendor as "Lord of glory" was not fully manifested, but he was "appointed with power," that is, manifested in his true nature by the resurrection, after which he returned to the heavenly regions in a "body of glory" to resume his former estate. The teaching that Christ was "sent" in the "likeness of sinful flesh"† appears to indicate that his earthly body was not his original corporeity corresponding to his original, heavenly manifestation, but one assumed for his entrance upon human conditions. Whether this "likeness"‡ was conceived by Paul as indicating that the flesh of Christ was tainted with sin like that of other men, or that, while like these in respect to material and form, he was unlike them in being free from sin, is a difficult and much-contested exegetical question. Since the word "likeness" may mean either similarity or equality, it is evident that by itself it can furnish no explanation of the thought of the apostle, for it is indeterminable whether likeness in all respects or only in some is intended. In the Pauline anthropology the flesh is by nature sinful, that is, it is the seat of impulses to sin. If, then, to be "in the likeness of sinful flesh" is to have the natural tendencies and impulses to sin, it can hardly be said that Christ "did not know sin."§ With a flesh in all respects like that of other men he must have known sin as impulse and temptation to wrong-doing, for not

---

* Gal. iv. 4.   † Rom. viii. 3.
‡ ὁμοίωμα.   § 2 Cor. v. 2L

actually to have transgressed can hardly be the meaning of the words, " did not know sin."   But if Paul intended to teach that Christ was as to his flesh in all respects like other men, it is difficult to see why he did not say simply " in sinful flesh " instead of " in the likeness of sinful flesh." On the other hand, if he meant that Christ was in some respects like other men as to his flesh, he used the word "likeness " in accordance with his usage of it elsewhere,* and taught here in accord with his Christology in general which recognizes in Christ no temptation to sin, no struggle with the flesh.   From the interpretation that the flesh of Christ was not thought to be like that of other men in all respects there is, however, the possible inference that his flesh was not conceived as real, but only as an "accident " of the Spirit which he essentially was.† But to this view is decidedly opposed the teaching that Christ was born of the seed of David according to the flesh.   The complete manhood implied in this expression is also with difficulty reconcilable with the idea that he did not possess the "sinful flesh " common to all men. The problem perhaps presents difficulties which cannot be entirely overcome by exegetical skill.   The preponder-

* Rom. i. 23, v. 14 ; Phil. ii. 7.

† This Docetic view has been maintained by Baur and Hilgenfeld as the Pauline idea of the flesh of Christ.   See Baur, Neutestamentl. Theol., pp. 189 f, and Hilgenfeld, Zeitschr. für wissenschaftl. Theol., 1871, pp. 182 ff. Although the extraordinary nature of the flesh of Jesus appears to imply the supernatural conception, there is no intimation of this idea in Paul's writings. It is in fact excluded by the teaching that Jesus was "born of the seed of David according to the flesh "—an expression which can only mean according to Jewish usage that his generation was through a male descendant of David.   *Cf.* Pfleiderer, Der Paulinismus, 2te Ausg., p. 133 ; Stevens, Pauline Theology, 1892, p. 212.   Paul does not solve the problem of sinlessness in a man naturally generated.   The sinlessness of some men was, however, maintained in the Jewish theology.   See Weber, System, etc., p. 224.

ance of probability appears, however, to be in favor of the conclusion that, if Paul was not writing carelessly, and chose the word "likeness" with intention, he meant to teach that the flesh of Christ was only partly similar to "sinful flesh," similar in that it was flesh, dissimilar in that it was not touched with sin.*

It is consistent with the importance which Paul assigns to Christ as the "man from heaven" and with the rank which he conceives him to have held in the scale of being, that in the Pauline Christology great significance should be attached to the work of Christ, or in other words, that salvation and the nature of Christ should be closely connected with each other. Since Paul practically disregarded the teaching and example of Christ, and constructed an original doctrine of his relation to men as Saviour as well as of his person, there remained as points of attachment for his system of thought only the two closing events of Jesus' earthly career, his death and resurrection. The significance which he attached to the former of these is shown by words which appear to identify Christianity with the cross, so that the teaching of it is the teaching of the cross, † and by his declaration that he was determined not to know anything save Jesus

* See Zeller, Zeitschr. für wissenschaftl. Theol., 1870, pp. 301 ff. A psychological problem is presented in the doctrine that Christ, the heavenly preëxistent man with a developed spirituality, became Jesus, the carpenter's son, and passed through the stages of human growth and education. Yet the fact undoubtedly is that Paul thought of Jesus as an earthly man and as identical with the man from heaven. He gives no intimation of the presence in his mind of the problem how the two personalities might be reconciled with each other, and if it ever occurred to him we do not know how he solved it or whether he attempted its solution at all. But he acknowledged that he knew only "in part " (1 Cor. xiii. 9), and raised many problems which he did not resolve.

† λόγος τοῦ σταυροῦ, 1 Cor. i. 17.

Christ and him crucified.* The significance which he attached to the death of Christ can only be understood in connection with his idea of the law. The cross and the law are antitheses in the doctrinal system of Paul. On the one hand, the law demands fulfilment, and on the other, man by reason of his weakness through the flesh is unable to render obedience, so that it is a fundamental principle in the Pauline theology that by the works of the law no man shall be justified.† " What the law could not do, in that it was weak through the flesh, God did, who on account of sin sent His own Son in the likeness of sinful flesh, and passed sentence of condemnation on sin in the flesh, so that what was required by the law might be accomplished in us." ‡ Reliance upon the works of the law is futile, and all who put their trust in their own obedience are self-deceived, for instead of a blessing they will reap a curse. The only way of deliverance is through a new order of things by which the old is done away. At the head of this new order is " the second Adam," " the man from heaven," who accomplishes for men what they could not do of themselves. He takes their place in relation to the law and the righteousness which it requires. He redeems them (buys them off) from the curse of the law by becoming a curse for them. § It is evident that this is the only logical conclusion from the Pauline conception of the law and of righteousness. The

---

* 2 Cor. ii. 2. The reference by Paul of the fact of the crucifixion to the tradition of Jesus in 1 Cor. xv. 3 (" that which I received ") should not be confounded, as it is by Weizsäcker (Das apostol. Zeitalter, p. 137), with a derivation of his *doctrine* of the death of Christ from the same source. The words " for our sins " (ὑπὲρ τῶν ἁμαρτιῶν ἡμῶν) are doubtless a Pauline interpretation added to the tradition.

† Rom. iii. 20.   ‡ Rom. viii. 3 f.

§ Gal. iii. 13, ἐξηγόρασεν ἡμᾶς ἐκ τῆς κατάρας τοῦ νόμου.

more the law and the ideal of righteousness are exalted in contrast with man's futile efforts to accomplish a perfect obedience, the greater is the necessity for a supernatural intervention. God may be merciful and forgiving, but the law stands in the way of the dispensation of His grace, for its requirements must be satisfied. Hence Paul does not conceive of the divine love as shown directly to men, but through Christ. It is commended to them in that while they were yet sinners Christ was sent to furnish a means of deliverance from the curse of the law, by receiving that curse in his own person. In the words, "Having become a curse for us" "for" is not to be understood in the sense of " for our benefit," or " for our sake," but " in our stead." * As the representative of the human race Christ is conceived by Paul to have taken upon himself the penalty which the guilt of men had incurred, and to have " bought them off" from the curse of the law, which was death, by himself dying for them. †

* $\dot{v}\pi\acute{e}\rho$, "for," does not necessarily contain the idea of representation, neither does it exclude it. The idea of one acting in the place of another is more accurately expressed by $\dot{\alpha}v\tau\acute{\iota}$. Since $\dot{v}\pi\acute{e}\rho$ is used by Paul of sins ($\dot{v}\pi\grave{e}\rho$ $\dot{\alpha}\mu\alpha\rho\tau\iota\tilde{\omega}v$) as well as of persons, it is perhaps correct to say with Meyer that it does not in itself convey the idea of substitution. But "since what is done for one's advantage frequently cannot be done without acting in one's stead, we easily understand how $\dot{v}\pi\acute{e}\rho$, like the Latin *pro* and our *for*, comes to signify ' in the place of.'" Grimm-Wilke's Clavis N. T., *sub voce*. Accordingly the baptism "for" the dead ($\dot{v}\pi\grave{e}\rho$ $\tau\tilde{\omega}v$ $v\epsilon\kappa\rho\tilde{\omega}v$) probably conveys the idea of baptism in their stead (1 Cor. xv. 29), and "that he may minister to me in your place" ($\dot{v}\pi\grave{e}\rho$ $\delta o\tilde{v}$) is evidently the sense in Philem. 13. Meyer, it should, however, be remarked, regards Paul's conception of Christ's sufferings as that of a *satisfactio vicaria*, since the latter's bloody death was thought by the former to be an atoning sacrifice, according to Rom. iii. 25. Commentar, 4te Aufl. iv. p. 190.

† *Cf.* Rom. iv. 25, v. 6, viii. 3 ; Gal. i. iv., iii. 13 ; Cor. xv. 3.

The question very naturally arises, how Paul conceived of the effect of Christ's death, how he thought Christ *could* die to the obligation of the law

This idea is clearly expressed in the words: " We thus judged, that if one died for all, then all died ; and he died for all, that they who live should no longer live to themselves," etc.*   If the words, " one died for all," mean that one died for the benefit of all, then it would not follow

for mankind. It is difficult, perhaps impossible, to penetrate into the apostle's thought so as to find a solution of this problem which may, indeed, not have lain in his mind at all.   His conception of the personality of Christ together with the Jewish doctrine of sacrifice may throw some light upon it. The resurrection proved to Paul that Jesus was the Messiah, and he conceived the Messiah to be the head and representative of the human race, and his death to be the fulfilment of a divine design of redemption. Now since death is the wages of sin, the *sinless* Messiah could not have died except to pay the penalty of the sins of others, to satisfy the law for them, to "buy them off," so as to free them from its curse. In the Jewish economy the sacrificial victim died in the place of the sinner, and averted his death. So righteousness and life are possible to sinners according to the Pauline-Christian idea only through the representative death of Christ as a sin-offering.   This objective revelation of grace is made subjectively available through faith. (See Holsten, Zum Evangel. d. Paulus u. d. Petrus, p. 251.)

The law had reference to sin, "came that the trespass might abound" (Rom. v. 20), and its chief significance related to the penalty. When this was paid he for whom it was paid was set free from the law, since it no longer had any claim upon him. Christ, as the representative of mankind, paid the penalty for all, satisfied the law, died to it, since it demanded death. He thus became "the end of the law" (Rom. x. 4), for in his death it was done away (2 Cor. iii. 13, 14). Men were "bought off" from its curse by his becoming "a curse" for them. The law did not excommunicate him, but he did *it* away by satisfying its claims "one for all." Accordingly, men through faith are "delivered" from it, "having died [in Christ's death] to that by which they were bound" (Rom. vii. 6). In Paul's thought the law had no saving efficacy. In the atonement of the saving person, Christ, the law is supplanted, and gives place for believers to a "new covenant," "the law of the spirit of life" being introduced by which men are "set free [through faith] from the law of sin and death" (Rom. viii. 2). Christ "was made a curse" because he received the penalty of the law. It was the *payment* by him, not the particular *manner* of his suffering, that sets free all who accept him by faith.

* 2 Cor. v. 14, 15, ὑπὲρ πάντων ἀπέθανεν.

13

that therefore all died, but that on account of the death of the one for them they would not need to die. But Paul's conclusion from the premise that one died for all is that therefore all died, and to him, " one for all," signified, one as the representative of all in the sense that his act or suffering is regarded as that of those whom he represents. Evidently the idea is not that all really died, but that in Christ as their representative are regarded as having died. The penalty of the law, death, having been paid by him who, as the second Adam, the spiritual head and representative of the race, suffered it on the cross, men may be regarded as in him dead to the law, set free from its curse. They " have been crucified with Christ.*   They are identified with him in his death.   He is " the end of the law " † to them, as he is the beginning of life to them.   The relation of Christ to mankind, then, is better expressed by representation or identification than by substitution. Because he was crucified for men, they are crucified with him ; because he lives they live, he in them, they in him.

The relation of Christ and men, though reciprocal, is not in Paul's thought that of equals, so that any man might be conceived as taking Christ's place in the plan of redemption.   The expression " The man Christ Jesus " evidently meant to him more than the mere humanity of Jesus.   Christ was without sin, and was therefore qualified as the spotless head of the race to bear in his death the curse of the law for all, having none to bear on his own account.   Therefore the apostle says: " Him who knew not sin God made to be sin for us, that we might become God's righteousness in him."‡   In his earthly existence this " second Adam," " the man from

* Gal. ii. 20.   † Rom. x. 4.   ‡ Gal. v. 21.

heaven," is conceived as so representing mankind under the conception of the solidarity of the race that in his death all died, just as by his obedience all may be made righteous. While the doctrine of the Jewish theology, that on account of the idea of the solidarity of the family and of the nation punishment and righteousness might be vicarious within the limits of either, doubtless lay at the bottom of this Pauline theory of atonement, Paul added to it a subjective element in making a personal solidarity with Christ the condition of appropriating the benefits accruing from his death. The divine love manifested in Christ must be responded to by a personal love and faith. Both the objective and the subjective aspects of the death of Christ, the fact and its appropriation by men in the interest of salvation, are expressed in the words: "For all have sinned and fail of obtaining the glory which cometh from God; being accepted as righteous freely by His grace, through the redemption which is in Christ Jesus, whom, in his blood, through faith, God hath set forth as a propitiatory sacrifice in order to manifest His righteousness on account of His passing by in His forbearance the sins committed in former times; in order to manifest His righteousness at the present time, so that He may be righteous and accept as righteous him who hath faith." * Here the death of Christ, his bearing

---

* Rom. iii. 23-27. One can hardly refrain from asking why, if the righteousness of God had been prejudiced by "forbearance" toward "the sins committed in former times," justice did not require that the omitted punishment for these sins be now inflicted upon the persons who committed them (supposing these offenders to be still in existence), since a former deficiency in the manifestation of the divine righteousness must, it appears, be somehow made up for?! This question Paul does not answer. A scheme of atonement was evidently more prominent in his thought than the requirements of justice.

the curse of the law, is represented on the one hand as a means of manifesting the righteousness of God, which might appear to have been invalidated by His failure to administer due punishment for the sins of the pre-Christian times, and on the other as a means of redemption for all who through faith will appropriate it. The use of the term " propitiatory sacrifice " or " means of propitiation " * as some choose to call it, raises a question of some difficulty. Who or what was to be propitiated? What was the obstacle to be removed? If we say that the law was satisfied and the righteousness of God vindicated by the sacrifice of Christ, whereby a penalty was paid which had not been inflicted on those who had deserved it, we appear to lay too much stress upon abstractions. What is this law which can be satisfied, and this righteousness which can be vindicated, apart from God? It would appear to be necessary to clear ideas on the subject to say that a satisfaction of the law and of the divine righteousness must be a satisfaction rendered to God, and that if Christ was "set forth as a means of propitiation," a change is implied in the attitude of God. This view appears to be supported by the words : " Much more, then, being now accepted as righteous through his blood, we shall be saved through him from the wrath [of God]. For if while enemies we were reconciled to God by the death of His Son, much more having been reconciled shall we be saved by his life." † The deliverance of " enemies " from the peril of the wrath of God, which must be supposed to be directed against them, can scarcely

* ἱλαστήριον. The meaning "propitiatory sacrifice" or "means of propitiation" may be regarded as a fairly well established conclusion of exegesis.

† Rom. v. 9–11.

be conceived as effected merely by a change of disposition
on their part. The attitude of the subject of the wrath
must be supposed to be changed in order that its objects
may be secure. This change Paul conceived to have been
brought about by the death of Christ which was propitiatory in the sense that it satisfied God in respect to His
law and His righteousness. The penalty of the law, in
paying which themselves men would have perished, having
been paid by the great head of the race, those who were
formerly enemies may be " accepted as righteous through
his blood." They are thus brought into a condition of
reconciliation with God, and since the still living Christ is
conceived as active in the interest of salvation in his state
of exaltation, they may "be saved by his life." The
reconciliation is effected by the removal of the human
guilt, which occasions the judgment of the divine wrath,
through Christ's satisfaction of the law. That this was
the apostle's point of view is evident from his declaration
that in Christ God was reconciling the world to Himself
in that He did not reckon to them their trespasses.* Paul'
did not attempt a formal reconciliation of the love and
wrath of God. He laid, however, the chief stress upon

---

* 2 Cor. v. 19. How Christ *could* effect man's redemption by standing
in his place as the representative of the race, and suffering the consequences
of human guilt ; how the righteousness of God could be vindicated by the
pains of a guiltless sufferer ; how in accordance with natural law any one
can atone for an offender's sin except the offender himself ; and how the
procedure in question is reconcilable with divine justice and with the historical method of man's education and discipline through suffering for his
errors and transgressions—these problems are not solved by Paul. It is
doubtful that they admit of solution upon his premises. They indicate the
weak points in his theology, and perhaps account in part for its early and
late decline. It contains many " stumbling-blocks " to every one who cannot think the thoughts of a Jew, and has been made acceptable to modern
thought only by a rationalizing of its distinctive tenets.

the former, and appeared to conceive of it as original in the divine nature and not as resulting from the atonement. But that nothing might be done to the prejudice of God's righteousness or His law, the divine love was supposed to reach man only on condition that his guilt had been removed through a representative propitiation. Man is the object of the love of God, not directly as in the teaching of Jesus, but indirectly through the great atonement which, indeed, was instituted by love as a means through which love itself might become effective. Hence Paul says that God commendeth His love to us in that while we were yet sinners Christ died for us.*

Paul, however, regarded the death of Christ under another aspect than the one just considered, and saw in it a means of the moral-religious renewal of believers through their mystical union with the head of the race in his crucifixion and resurrection.† The death of Christ was an "act of righteousness" through which "all obtain the gift of righteousness unto life." ‡ Jesus Christ was made to us wisdom, and righteousness, and sanctification, and redemption." § He "gave himself for our sins, that he might deliver us from the present evil world." ‖ Paul reminds the Romans that in having been baptized into Christ they were baptized into his death. Thus were

---

* Rom. v. 8.

† This is regarded by some interpreters of Paul as the chief if not the sole point of view from which he contemplated the death of Christ. Weizsäcker appears to hold the former view (Das apostal. Zeitalter) and Matthew Arnold the latter (St. Paul and Protestantism). Neither of these opinions can, however, be sustained without more or less rationalizing in the interpretation of Paul's words. Rightly regarded this second aspect under which Paul views the death of Christ is the logical sequence of the former. The apostle was not a nineteenth century liberal Christian, that he should have found the idea of propitiation offensive.

‡ Rom. v. 18.   § 1 Cor. i. 30.   ‖ Gal. i. 4.

they " buried " with him, that as he was raised from the
dead, they might also " walk in newness of life." Having
been made completely like him in his death, they will be
made like him in his resurrection also. As he died to sin,
but lives to God, so they should regard themselves as
dead to sin, but alive to God through him. * The significance of this dying of Christ and of men in him as the
representative of the race is set forth in the general proposition that " He that has died has been set free from
sin," † that is, legally he is released from all its claims
and consequences. " Sin reigned in death," ‡ and he who
with death has received " the wages of sin " is henceforth
set free from its dominion. This doctrine of the Jewish
theology is applied by Paul to Christ and the believers in
him, in order to show that the former by his death as
the representative of the race had borne the curse of sin,
and once for all satisfied its claims and broken its power,
and that the latter dying with him, their head, were with
him free from sin, victorious, subject no longer to its
dominion, no longer " debtors to the flesh." § The bondage to sin in which mankind had been held since Adam,
and in which they were not only a prey to death, but
subjects of the fleshly impulses and of a will powerless for
good, having been broken by the great sacrifice, those
who through baptism had entered into the fellowship of
Christ's death, and been " buried with him," were free
now both from the guilt of sin and its penalty which is
death,‖ and from slavery to it, which is moral and spirit-

---

* Rom. vi. 5-11.

† Rom. vi. 7.

‡ Rom. v. 21.   § Rom. viii. 12.

‖ Not that they would never die, but that death could have no power
over them, since if the spirit of Christ dwelt in them, He who raised up
Christ from the dead would give life to their mortal bodies. Rom. viii. 11.

ual incapability.   In the atonement believers were morally quickened and invigorated.   Through Christ's death and their appropriation of it in baptism there has been effected a transformation of their life, and they are now able to comply with the moral requirements, they are " alive from the dead," and having been made free from sin they may be the bondmen of righteousness.*   The bondage of the law is also broken ; for "the law has dominion over a man only as long as he lives."   Christ was " under" it while he lived in the flesh, but its claim was extinguished in his death.   Now since in the death of one for all, all died, Paul says to his brethren that they were also " slain to the law through the body of Christ," that they " might be connected with another, even with him who was raised from the dead," that they " might bear fruit to God." †

The resurrection is inseparably connected with the death of Christ in the doctrinal system of Paul, and is a factor of the greatest importance in his conception of salvation.   The revelation of the resurrected Son of God in him was the great fact of his experience from an apprehension of which his conversion proceeded.   This view denotes one of the distinctive differences between his apprehension of Christianity and that of the original apostles, and shows one of the aspects of the transformation of the gospel which his original genius effected. They proceeded from what they had known of Jesus as a teacher.   He took his departure from the dead and resurrected Lord of glory, and refused to know anything of a Christ "according to the flesh."   Not as a Jewish teacher or a Jewish Messiah did he conceive of Christ, but as the archetypal spiritual man who in dying and rising from the dead died and rose for Gentiles as well as

* Rom. viii. 13, 18.   † Rom. vii 4.

for Jews. If to Paul the whole earthly mission of Christ finds its significance and its culmination in the death on the cross, an act of "obedience" through which "many will be made righteous" and by which "sentence of condemnation was pronounced on sin in the flesh," * it is through his resurrection that his work receives its authentication and the divine seal. Without the resurrection and the life of exaltation which followed it, all that preceded it would have been without power and significance. He "was delivered up on account of our trespasses, and raised from the dead that we might be accepted as righteous." † If in his death we are regarded as having died with him, in his life we are to live with him, ‡ since believers have in his resurrection not only an assurance of their own, § but also the earnest of a life in the Spirit in this present time effected through his new life, so that they live not of themselves, but by reason of the glorified Christ's living in them, ‖ and by the reception of the Holy Spirit ¶ which he has and communicates to them. Through his resurrection he is appointed "with power" to be the Son of God, and exalted to be the "Lord both of the dead and the living" that to him "every knee should bow of those who are in heaven and those on the earth and those under the earth."** He has become the Lord who is the Spirit, "the Lord of glory" whose body is a heavenly effulgence, a "body of glory."†† Death has no longer dominion over him, having died to sin he lives henceforth to God and for His glory, and shall reign until he has put all enemies

---

* Rom. v. 19, viii. 3.   † Rom. iv. 25.

‡ Rom. vi. 4–7 ; Gal. ii. 20.   § 1 Cor. xv. 12 ff.

‖ Gal. ii. 20.   ¶ Rom. viii. 19 ; 1 Cor. xii. 3.

** Rom. i. 4, xiv. 9 ; Phil. ii. 9 ff.

†† 1 Cor. ii. 8 ; 2 Cor. iii. 17 ; Phil. iii. 21.

under his feet, death last of all.* To Paul the resurrection of Christ was the ground of men's faith in his saving work. Hence he says: " If Christ hath not risen your faith is vain ; ye are yet in your sins," † that is, without his resurrection his death were unavailing for atonement and justification, and those who have believed in him have cherished a faith which is to no purpose. ‡ If he were abandoned of God in his death, then was his death no atoning sacrifice for sin. They did not in fact die to sin and the flesh in him, if he were not raised and they with him to " newness of life." Thus the resurrection of Christ is conceived as supplementing, completing, and rendering effective his death to sin. It was for the sake of man's justification on condition of man's faith in the atoning significance of his death, and this faith is possible only on the ground of his resurrection. But Paul sees a further efficiency in the resurrection, for he conceives the hope of salvation to rest not alone in what Christ wrought for men in his death and resurrection as isolated and temporary facts, but also in the assurance that the resurrected one still lives in his heavenly state, and, as the Lord who

---

* Rom. vi. 10; 1 Cor. xv. 25 ; Phil ii. 11. With all the exaltation of Christ to a position of dominion and glory Paul clearly denotes the distinction between him and the Deity.   An agent of God, a subordinate, he will finally, when all things have been put under him, become subject to Him who subdued all things to him, "that God may be all in all," 1 Cor. xv. 28. The words : ὁ ὤν ἐπὶ πάντων θεὸς εὐλογητός (Rom. ix. 5) may in themselves be referred to God or to Christ, and may if separated from the preceding words, be read, " He who is over all, God, be blessed," etc., or if taken in immediate connection with the preceding words (Was the Christ), " who is over all, God, blessed," etc. The analogy of the Pauline doctrine must furnish the decision. But Paul nowhere calls Christ God in any sense. Tischendorf places a period between these words and the foregoing, and thus makes them an ascription of praise to God.

† 1 Cor. xv. 17.   ‡ πίστις ματαία.

is the Spirit, "life-giving Spirit," dwells in the believers
as an animating principle, so that as a community they
may be regarded as the "body" of Christ, and as individual "members" of Christ.   In their life in him they are
connected with the Father whose love is assured to them
in and through him who is at the right hand of God
making "intercession" for them.*   Accordingly, believers
may hope that, as Christ was the "first-fruits of them that
have fallen asleep," those of them who had died will be
raised at his coming again, those of them who remain
alive will be changed, and all, bearing the image of his
glorious body, will in fellowship with him enter into a
state of final blessedness. †

5.—JUSTIFICATION BY FAITH.

The justification of man or his acceptance as righteous
according to the divine standard, that is, by a judgment
of God, is the practical end of the Pauline theology.   In
this result the work of Christ through his death and resurrection finds its temporal culmination.   The question how
that union of man with God which is expressed by the
term sonship, or adoption as son, and a mark of which is
the indwelling in him of the Spirit of God, is brought

* Rom. viii. 34–39 ; 1 Cor. vi. 15, xii. 27. "Who also intercedeth for
us" (ὃς καὶ ἐντυγχάνει ὑπὲρ ἡμῶν), Rom. viii. 34. In the idea of intercession appear to be implied the necessity and the possibility of favorably
influencing the Deity in the interest of men. Intercession is ascribed to
"the Spirit" also in verses 26 and 27. See besides Heb. vii. 25, "Who
ever liveth to make intercession for them," and 1 John ii. 1, "We have an
advocate with the Father " (παράκλητον πρὸς τὸν πατέρα). The doctrine of propitiation is doubtless related to this idea. Yet no attempt is
made by Paul or by the two other writers to reconcile the fatherhood of God
with the doctrine that He should need to be interceded with for His children.

† 1 Cor. xv. 22, 51 ; 1 Thess. iv. 13–18.

about, is answered negatively by Paul in the fundamental proposition of his system, that " by the works of the law no man is justified," or "accepted as righteous."* His theological doctrine has its roots in the conception of righteousness which he derived from the Jewish religion ; but in the function assigned to faith it stands in fundamental opposition to that conception as it was understood by the Jewish teachers in general and by Jesus himself, so that he may be said to have transformed the religion of his nation and the gospel of his Master by a bold and radical innovation. This innovation did not consist, indeed, so much in giving a new meaning to righteousness considered with reference to the divine judgment as in a new conception of the way in which it may be acquired. By righteousness † the apostle means the right, the adequate relation of man to God. While it is a subjective condition, that is, a state of the man who holds this relation, it is regarded as proceeding from God, and hence is defined as the righteousness of God. ‡   The Jewish conception of the righteousness acceptable to God, that is, attainable by the works of the law,§ was declared by Paul to be impossible, not, indeed, by reason of any imperfection in the

* ὁ ἄνθροπος οὐ δικαιοῦται ἐξ ἔργων νόμου.

† δικαιοσύνη.

‡ δικαιοσύνη θεοῦ, ἡ τοῦ θεοῦ δικαιοσύνη, Rom. i. 17, iii. 21, x. 3. See Meyer on Rom. i. 17, Commentar, 4te Aufl. iv. p. 56 f. Baur who in his Paulus and his Neutestamentl. Theol. held the genitive θεοῦ to be objective and the phrase to have the sense, "righteousness determined with reference to God," appears to have abandoned this opinion in Theol. Jahrb., 1857, p. 64, under the influence of Holsten's interpretation. See Holsten, Zum Evangel. des Paulus, etc., p. 408.

§ By the law (νόμος) Paul evidently meant the Mosaic law. This was identical in his thought with the moral law, and he accordingly does not regard the heathen as ἄνομοι, or without a law, but as a law to themselves, having what the law required written in their hearts. Rom. ii. 14, 15.

law itself, which he pronounces " holy, right, and good," *
but, as has already been shown, because of the weakness
of the flesh. Paul accordingly knows no righteousness
but that through faith. For him the gospel is to every
believer, Jew and Greek, the power of God unto salvation ;
for therein is revealed the righteousness which is of God
from faith to faith,† that is, a righteousness whose essential
principle, whose beginning and end are faith. The pri-
mary meaning of this word faith,‡ which holds so important a place in the Pauline system of salvation, is confidence
in the revelations, the message, and the promises of God,
like that of Abraham. It is a confidence in Him who
raised Christ from the dead in order that believers might
be accepted as righteous.§ If sometimes Paul speaks of
it as a merely intellectual conviction of a fact, as, for example, that God raised Christ from the dead, he does not
stop at this point, but introduces a religious element of
trust and an affection of the heart. It is not enough to
acknowledge with the mouth that Jesus is Lord, but one
must believe in the heart or with the entire devotion of
the inmost being ; and he expressly says that " with the
heart man believeth so as to obtain righteousness." ‖ While
the believer is conceived as in part passive, as acted upon
by the word of gospel-truth, " a demonstration of the Spirit
and of power," and illuminated by a light from God which
shines in the heart, and " laid hold of by Christ," ¶ yet
faith is essentially an act implying freedom, " obedience
from the heart," subjection to the divine plan of justification, a laying hold of Christ, and an appropriation of the
benefits which accrue from his sacrifice.* This act is not

* Rom. vii. 12.   § Rom. iv. 24.
† Rom. i. 16, 17.   ‖ Rom. x. 9, 10.
‡ πίστις.   ¶ 2 Cor. iv. 6 , Phil. iii. 12.
** Rom. i. 5, vi. 7, x. 3 ; Phil. iii. 12.

regarded, however, as belonging to the class of good works by which righteousness could be earned. It is not a performance by which righteousness could be acquired, and to which merit attached as to "works of the law," but rather a condition of being accepted as righteous without boasting, a humble, trusting self-surrender to the divine will as revealing itself in grace through the gospel of reconciliation. *   Man is powerless to achieve righteousness under the law by his own act, and can only with profound humility cast himself upon the grace of God, and accept His free gift, thankful with an answering love for the sacrifice which has purchased it for him on the cross.†

Since, then, there is no ground for a man's boasting in any achievement of his own in respect to righteousness, and all his "glory" should be in the cross of Christ, ‡ faith in Christ has in the system of Paul a distinctive and prominent place. Hence if righteousness is from God it is "through faith in Jesus Christ"; the life of the believer is lived through faith in Christ ; if a blessing was promised, it was through faith in Jesus ; if believers are sons of God, they are such through faith in His great Son ; and if a man have righteousness, it is not his own, no impossible righteousness of the law, but that which "is through faith in Christ," that "which is from God upon faith." §   While Jesus generally spoke of faith in himself as a belief in his healing powers, ‖ and the original apostles cherished a faith in him which was connected with an eschatological hope of his second coming, the faith of Paul in Christ was a new conception of his original genius

* Rom. iii. 27, iv. 4, x. 4–10 ; Phil. iii. 4.
† Gal. ii. 20 f, iii. 22 ff ; Phil. iii. 18 ff.   ‡ Gal. vi. 14.
§ Rom. iii. 22 ; Gal. ii. 16, 20, 26 ; Phil. iii. 9.
‖ See, however, a Pauline trait in Luke vii. 50.

which had the power to transform all that it touched. His faith in Christ was not a belief in him as a teacher and an exemplar, for of these aspects of his life Paul took no account, but a feeling of grateful and loving identification, of mystical union and fellowship with him in his death and resurrection. Having died with Christ, the believer is regarded as belonging in this union with Christ to him alone. Dead to sin in this union, he no longer belongs to the law ; the old relation of bondage is dissolved, and a new one of liberty is formed in the death of Christ. He was slain to the law through the body of Christ that he might be connected with another, even with him who was raised from the dead.* There is no more for him the fruitless struggle for an impossible righteousness with its alternations of hope and despair, but in the consciousness of freedom and the joy of reconciliation with God he feels himself to be a " new creation." Having " put on the Lord Jesus Christ," he has taken into his heart with love the ideal, and realizes the power, of the life of the sonship of God. This beautiful mysticism is expressed in the fine words: " I have been crucified with Christ, and no longer do I live, but Christ liveth in me, and the life which I now live in the flesh I live in faith in the Son of God who loved me, and gave himself for me." † His life in faith in Christ and Christ's living in him are doubtless to Paul two expressions for the same idea, his idea of what faith in Christ was in his experience—a mystical fellowship with him, a loving devotion in a unity of life with him. To have faith in Christ is to be in him. He is a Christian who is " in Christ," or who has Christ living in him. Hence the injunction: " Try yourselves, whether ye are in the faith," and the question: " Know ye not

* Rom. vii. 4.   † Gal. ii. 20.

your own selves that Christ Jesus is in you?"*   Faith in Christ is union with him, membership: "He that is connected with the Lord is one spirit with him."†

This union and fellowship with Christ through faith are regarded by Paul as bringing the believer into the relation of sonship with God—the hignest relation that man can attain.   Accordingly the apostle says: "Ye are all sons of God through faith in Jesus Christ, for as many of you as were baptized into Christ did put on Christ."‡   Having the spirit of Christ, he is conscious of the spirit of adoption as a son of God.§ Set free from the curse of the law, he is no longer a "bond-servant," but a son, and if a son, then an heir.‖ But the theological genius of Paul required a formula for this spiritual condition, and he found it in the Jewish theology and the terminology of the Septuagint.   A divine declaration or act of judgment is assumed to be pronounced in order to set the seal of God upon this new creation and give it recognition and validity before the court of heaven.   The condition is said accordingly to be one of "justification," and the subject is supposed to be "accepted as righteous" or "justified,"¶ that is, acquitted or declared to be just. That the meaning is not "to make or render righteous" is evident from the fact that the term is applied to God in the words: "That Thou mayst be justified in Thy words," etc.,** that is, be acknowledged as just in Thy judgments.   This is also the sense in the passage in which the term is used of those who by reason of obedience are already righteous: "The doers of the law will be accounted righteous."†† The application of the term

---

* 2 Cor. xiii. 5.   † 1 Cor. vi. 17.   ‡ Gal. iii. 26.
§ πνεῦμα υἱοθεσίας, Rom. viii. 15.   ‖ Gal. iv. 7.
¶ δικαίωσις, δικαιοῦσθαι.   ** Rom. iii. 4.
†† δικαιωθήσονται, Rom. ii. 13.

to believers is shown by the formulas, "accept as righteous," "faith is accounted as righteousness," and, "not
to charge with sin." * It is evident that the ground on
which the judgment of justification rests is not contained
in the word itself, since it is applied to the case of one
who has fulfilled the law and to that of one who has only
faith to plead. To Paul the former sort of righteousness,
though an abstract possibility, had no existence in fact on
account of the fleshly nature of man which held him in
bondage to sin. Accordingly, he recognized no justification on the ground of merit acquired by keeping the law,
but laid the whole stress upon that which by the grace of
God was a free gift.† The basis of his doctrine of justification was, then, in his doctrine of salvation, as is evident from the words: "I do not set aside the grace of
God ; for if righteousness come through the law then did
Christ die for naught." ‡ To him the death of Christ
were futile if it was not an act of divine grace which
opened to man a new way of righteousness without reference to the works of the law. The divine act or decree
of justification rests primarily upon the free mercy of God,
since the promised salvation is bestowed not for merit,
but despite the guilt of man, as a gift of grace.§ Secondarily, justification is grounded "objectively in the atoning death of Christ and subjectively in the faith of man." ‖
Because the curse of the law was borne in the great sacrifice on the cross, God may declare the sinner free of
guilt without prejudice to His own righteousness. Since
he that has died is freed from sin, the sin of the world
was atoned for in the death of the representative of man-

* δικαιοῦντα, λογιζεται πίστις εἰς δικαιοσύνην, Rom. iv. 4, 5.
† Rom. iii. 24, iv. 4.   ‡ Gal. ii. 21.
§ Gal. iii.; Rom. iv., v. 15–21, xi. 30 ff.
‖ Rom. v. 1, 9.

14

kind, the man from heaven, and the justification of the individual is nothing else than the appropriation by each of that universal judgment of justification which was conditionally declared for every one. The condition is the acceptance through faith of that general atonement for himself, being " made completely like him [Christ] in his death " and " in his resurrection also." *

In this doctrine there is manifestly not merely a bare "imputation" of the "merits" of Christ or of his righteousness to the sinner. It is only by a perversion of Paul's teaching that this idea has been derived from it. The believer is not " accepted as righteous " only on account of the merits or the righteousness of Christ, but also by reason of the faith with which he has personally accepted the atonement. This faith is not, however, conceived, as has already been remarked, to be of the nature of an act of obedience to the law to which merit attaches in the sense in which it is applied to " works," else justification through faith would not be an act of grace, "a free gift," but a judgment pronounced in accordance with desert, which would have no connection with the atoning work of Christt. It might, indeed, appear on a superficial view that if " faith is accounted as righteousness " a man would be regarded as having something which he does not really have, and that there would be an incongruity between the subject of whom righteousness is affirmed and the predicate, righteous, as if one should say, " James, a wicked man, is accounted righteous because of his faith." The moral-religious consciousness could not but take offence at this as a fictitious sort of righteousness. But in his conception of justification by faith Paul did not abandon the moral idea that lay at the basis of the righteousness

* 2 Cor. v. 15; Rom. vi. 5; Phil. iii. 10.

which is " accounted as a matter of debt." *   On the contrary he was much in earnest about the moral factor in his theory of justification by faith, and having abandoned the law of works, he introduced as an essential factor another " law," that of " the Spirit of life." †   " The law of the Spirit of life set me free," he says, " in Christ Jesus from the law of sin and death." ‡   The Spirit is the determining principle of life for the believer in Christ, since as such he can have in him alone his spiritual life.   The Spirit is, indeed, received by the preaching of faith,§ but faith becomes for the believer a living reality in the possession of the Spirit by which the process of justification is alone completed.   God who is " the justifier of him who had faith " does not then, according to Paul, " account " as an imaginary righteousness the faith of the " ungodly " man, and arbitrarily " declare " him to be righteous while in fact he remains what he was before, but the justification is a real one, because in " the law of the spirit of life," in the Spirit as a principle actually working in him, he is in truth put into a relation with God which corresponds with the moral ideal.   He has been " clothed with the Lord Jesus Christ."   Unable to attain a righteousness of his own, that is, to earn it by the works of the moral law, he has had bestowed upon him " the righteousness which is from God " ‖ as a gracious gift from the Source of life.

It cannot but be conceded that Paul's statement of his doctrine of justification by faith is in a high degree extreme and abstract.   It appears to proceed from the point of view

---

* κατὰ ὀφείλημα, Rom. iv. 4.
† νόμος τοῦ πνεύματος ζωῆς.
‡ Rom. viii. 2.   § Gal. iii. 2.
‖ δικαιοσύνη θεοῦ as opposed to one's own (ἰδία) righteousness.

of the opposition of Judaism and his apprehension of Christianity, and it is not surprising that his successors in the Christian Church during the first two centuries do not appear to have sympathized warmly with his radical apprehension of the matter. That a mediating tendency early manifested itself only shows the natural reaction of the human mind against extreme positions vehemently maintained. The Epistle of James is manifestly an attempt to soften the harshness of the Pauline doctrine if not to substitute another in its place, and it is worthy of note that even those early writings which show a favorable disposition towards Paul's views, as the first Epistle of Peter and Hebrews, seek to avoid the contested word " justify," and emphasize the virtuous life and moral perfection. The Pauline doctrine of justification does not besides appear to be recognized in the Johannine writings.* It may be questioned whether Paul is just to Judaism on the one hand and to Christianity on the other when he distinguishes them so sharply as representing exclusively the former righteousness by the works of the law and the latter righteousness by faith, and whether he correctly sets forth the religion of the Old Testament and the religion of Jesus, or presents a one-sided apprehension of both. Since he does not profess to have had a knowledge of the teachings of Jesus in detail, it is not to be wondered at if he has not correctly represented them. But it cannot but be surprising that he represents the law as having for its sole function to punish and condemn. Reading Paul's arraignment of the law, one would think that under the Old-Testament economy the attainment of righteousness

---

* In 1 John ii. 29 and iii. 10 the *doing* of righteousness is expressly emphasized: πᾶς ὁ ποιῶν τὴν δικαιοσύνην ἐξ αὐτοῦ γεγέννηται; and πᾶς ὁ μὴ ποιῶν δικαιοσύνην οὐκ ἔστιν ἐκ τοῦ θεοῦ.

was not possible, that man was doomed to a fruitless struggle with the flesh, and that he was helpless under the condemnation of the law, groping in the darkness of despair without a gleam of grace. Yet it may very well be questioned whether in fact there have been two great world-periods, in one of which under the "first-man" all men were hopelessly under the curse of the law, despite their good will and good works, and in the other are "accepted as righteous" through faith by reason of the obedience of "the man from heaven." Who would undertake to maintain with the Old Testament before him that its moral law was given on the presumption that obedience to it was impossible and righteousness a fiction, that its religion was a bare legalism which took no account of man's incomplete obedience, did not recognize the virtue of a good will and a right disposition, and had no place for mercy and forgiveness? On the contrary, according to its teaching, the divine requirements are satisfied if a man "do justly and love mercy and walk humbly with his God," and the divine helpfulness stoops to "create" in men a "new heart" and a "right spirit." The idea that the divine forgiveness and grace and the communication of the divine Spirit to men are conditioned on "the obedience of one man" appears to be an addition made by Paul to the Old-Testament religion—an addition which became a logical necessity from his too abstract conception of the law. On the other hand, his conception of faith has a certain hardness and inflexibility, which are apparent when an application of it is made to actual life. He appears himself sometimes to have lost sight of it, and thus to have left a problem which is not easily solved. We seem to hear words conceived in the spirit of the ancient lawgivers and prophets in the declaration that

God "will render to every man according to his works"; that "tribulation and distress will be upon every soul of man whose works are evil," but "glory, honor, and peace upon every man whose works are good"; that "the doers of the law will be accounted righteous"; and that "we must all be made manifest before the judgment-seat of Christ, that each one may receive the things done in his body."* These words appear to have been written by Paul in entire unconsciousness of any conflict between them and his doctrine of faith. But if the possession or the absence of faith determines a man's righteousness or unrighteousness in the divine judgment, and men are to be judged according to their "works," how can faith be regarded otherwise than as a "work." If only the "doers" of the law are to be accounted righteous, then must not the act of faith be a doing of the law, and does not the law stand after all? Again, it has been said that the Pauline doctrine of faith does not meet all the requirements of practical life, since it fails to answer the question how the believer's transgressions subsequent to his acceptance as righteous through faith are to be disposed of. It is evident that Paul in elaborating his doctrine of righteousness by faith did not have these questions in mind, but was thinking only of the opposition of Judaism and a conception of Christianity founded on the death and resurrection of Christ. He had no occasion to attempt the reconciliation of positions which did not perhaps appear incongruous to him in whom "the two souls, that of a Pharisee and that of an apostle, struggled with each other."

It fares no better so far as logical consistency is concerned with the relation of faith and predestination. The

* Rom. ii. 5–11; 2 Cor. v. 10. See also 1 Cor. iii. 13, 14, ix. 17 ; Gal. vi. 7.

whole doctrine of faith rests upon the presumption of man's free choice and self-determination, so that whoever will may appropriate the free gift offered in the atonement of Christ. Yet in the ninth chapter of Romans Paul lays down the doctrine that God without regard to man's act and by a pure purpose of election chose Jacob and rejected Esau " before the children were born or had done anything good or evil, to the end that His purpose, according to election, might stand, not depending on works, but on the will of Him who calleth "; and then he proceeds to prove from the Old Testament that God's compassion depends on His own will, man's act being of no importance in the case, since " it dependeth not on him who willeth nor on him who runneth, but on God who showeth mercy."*   Accordingly, Pharaoh was raised up for the "very purpose" that God might " show forth His power in him"; and the apostle draws thence the conclusion that God " hath mercy on whom He will, and hardeneth whom He will, " and has " the right, " like the potter, " to make of the same lump of clay one vessel for an honorable use and another for a dishonorable. "†   The question, however, how God can require a man to be other than he is, since it is impossible that he should be other than God has predetermined him to be, is excluded by Paul as an impertinence of human reason.   If God has made of the Jew a " vessel of wrath, " to make known His power, let the Jew not question the Almighty, but be thankful that, a vessel " fitted for destruction, " he has been " endured with patience " so long.   Yet with the most illogical *naïveté* he declares in the same chapter that

* Rom. ix. 11–17.

† This comparison was perhaps suggested by a passage in the book of Wisdom, xv. 7.

Israel did not attain to a law of righteousness " because they did not *strive* for it by faith," and in the following chapter he lays down in absolute terms the law of liberty to the effect that " every one that believeth may obtain righteousness." It is evident, however, that Paul did not intend to establish an argument for predestination in reference to men in general, but that in the exigency of his polemic against the claims of the Jews to be the chosen people of God he gave excessive prominence to the doctrine of the divine sovereignty only to return immediately to his great principle of faith, leaving the two propositions over against each other without metaphysical reconciliation.*

6.—THE FUTURE.

Paul did not conceive the work of Christ to be consummated in the temporal deliverance of believers from the bondage of sin and the bestowal upon them of the divine righteousness through faith. The economy of Christian redemption, whose head was the man from heaven triumphant over the grave, included a victory won from the powers of the underworld, the subjection of the " enemies " of the Christ, and an unbroken union of believers with him. It was a cardinal principle in the Pauline theology that they who had received the Spirit had in this endowment an earnest of the " redemption " of their " bodies," since, " if Jesus died and rose again, then will God through Jesus bring again with him those

---

* Philo also held that men's virtues are a gift of God, forbade them to ascribe goodness to themselves, and wrote of a "grace" which chose its instruments from birth ; yet it seems not to have occurred to him to renounce the doctrine of moral accountability. See Zeller, Phil. der Griechen, iii. p. 651, Theol. Jahrb., 1854, pp. 259 ff.

who have fallen asleep."* The beginning of the great consummation was the second coming of Christ from heaven in person for the establishment of his kingdom. When he should "descend" "with a loud summons, with the voice of an archangel, and with the trump of God," "the dead in Christ" would rise first. Then those who should be living, among whom Paul evidently expected to be himself when he wrote 1 Corinthians and 1 Thessalonians, would be "changed," that is, their earthly, material bodies would be transformed into a higher order of corporeity corresponding to the resurrection body, which would be conformed to the glorious body of Christ.† Of

---

* Rom. viii. 11, 23 ; 1 Thess. iv. 14.

† 1 Cor. xv. 51 ff ; 1 Thess. iv. 13 ff ; Phil. iii. 21. It is not entirely clear what relation Paul conceived the new spiritual body to hold to the body of flesh, and how and when believers were to be clothed with this garment of "glory." The indispensable condition of its bestowal appears to be the possession of the Spirit, or the indwelling of Christ, according to Rom. viii. 10 f. Here he tells the believers that if Christ be in them, their bodies though dead (subject to death), will receive life through Him who raised Jesus from the dead, on account of the indwelling of His Spirit, or, according to another reading, through His Spirit dwelling in them. Although a special exercise of the divine power as in the resurrection of Jesus appears to be implied here, this passage may perhaps be interpreted without violence so as to bring it into accord with 1 Cor. xv. 35 ff, where the new body is represented as being formed from the old, as the stalk grows from the grain which, sown in the ground, "dies" as a condition of being "brought to life." In the latter passage the indwelling of Christ is evidently implied as the condition on which the personality survives the death of the body. But elsewhere Paul speaks of the new body as a "building provided by God, a house not made with hands, everlasting in the heavens," and of "longing to be clothed upon with our habitation which is from heaven" (2 Cor. v. 1-3). He who should be thus "clothed upon" would not be found "naked," *i. e.*, would not be a bodiless spirit in the underworld. When Paul wrote this passage he was probably thinking of a transformation of the earthly body into "the body of glory" without the intervention of death, like that which the believers who should survive the

an intermediate state Paul formulated no doctrine, although such a state is evidently implied, in accordance with the current Jewish belief, in the resurrection at the Parousia of those who had " fallen asleep."   Those would not, of course, descend to the underworld who survived the coming of Christ in glory.   There are, however, indications in later Epistles that he held the doctrine of an immediate entrance at death upon the heavenly life, and perhaps thought that he would not live until the time of the Parousia.   He speaks of the celestial body as a " house not made with hands, everlasting, in the heavens," of longing " to be clothed upon with our habitation which is from heaven," and of being well " pleased rather to be absent from the body and to be at home with the Lord." *   Again he writes to the Philippians of his " desire to depart and to be with Christ." †   This idea of " being at home with the Lord," or Christ, immediately after death evidently excludes a tarrying of the spirit in the underworld and a resurrection.   Hence the agreement of this phase of the apostle's eschatology with the earlier one is hardly to be maintained, unless with Meyer we assume that he had in mind in the passages in question only himself and his possible death by martyrdom, in which case he might have believed, in accordance with a notion of his age in reference to martyrs, that he would pass im-

Parousia would experience (1 Cor. xv. 52).   The thought is in accord with a spiritual Hellenism rather than with Jewish apocalyptic, and in expressing it Paul laid the foundation for a hope of believers in the future which was independent of the second advent and a resurrection.   He separated Christianity from Judaism and gave it to the world.   He attempted no reconciliation of the two points of view, and thus set an example which his interpreters will do well to follow.

* 2 Cor. v. 1–9.

† Phil. i. 23.

mediately into the heavenly state. This assumption is, however, entirely gratuitous. It is evident in any case that the resurrection out of an intermediate state has scarcely standing in the Pauline system, and may be regarded as hardly more than an empty term. Since the dead are raised "incorruptible," it is not the old body which comes up, and the uniting of souls which are called from hades with a spiritual body is a resurrection only in the sense that the immortal part is supposed to rise out of the underworld. The supposition does not seem improbable, then, that Paul, having abandoned the materialistic Jewish doctrine of the resurrection of the body, was led at length by the force of his logic to abandon the idea of the underworld in connection with a resurrection and to hold that immediately after death the believer's soul is "clothed upon" with the new habitation which is "everlasting, in the heavens," although at one time he evidently believed in a rising of the "dead in Christ" at the Parousia, in the sense probably that they would then first be united with the spiritual heavenly body.

This spiritual view of the resurrection,* which stands in such striking contrast with the popular Jewish materialism, has important consequences in relation to the extent of the great transformation of the dead and the living at the Parousia. If the question, who of the dead and the living were believed by Paul to be destined to receive the spirit-

---

* It has been said, however, that Paul does not always maintain the purely spiritual view, but sometimes approaches a lower, venal apprehension of the relation of the resurrection to conduct. Why should we expose ourselves to perils, why fight with beasts at Ephesus, if there is no resurrection ? he asks. If the dead rise not, let us eat and drink, for to-morrow we die, 1 Cor. xv. 30–33. But see Rom. xii. 1 ; 2 Cor. v. 14, 15 ; Gal. ii. 20. The Jewish and Christian points of view thus sometimes appear in an opposition which he did not take the trouble to reconcile.

ual heavenly body at the second coming of Christ, that is, to be endowed with the incorruptible or immortal life, be answered in logical accordance with one of the fundamental principles of his teaching, the answer must unquestionably be that this boon was conceived to be reserved for believers only.   For it is incontestable that Paul regarded the Spirit as the principle not alone of the ethical-religious life, but also of the life from the dead.   Even if Christ be in you, he says to the Romans, the body is dead, that is subject to death, because of sin ; but if the Spirit of Him who raised up Christ from the dead dwell in you, He who raised up Christ from the dead will also give life to your mortal bodies. *   Accordingly, the assurance that believers will be "clothed upon" with the spiritual heavenly body, and that for them mortality will be "swallowed up by life" is found in their possession of the Spirit which is given them as a pledge † of this consummation.   Paul's application to Christ of the Hellenistic idea of the arche-typal spiritual man or the man from heaven is of import-ance in this relation.   As through the first or earthy man came death, so through the second or spiritual man came the resurrection of the dead ; and "if by one trespass death reigned through one man, much more will they who receive the abundance of grace and of the gift of righteous-ness reign in life through the one man, Christ Jesus."‡ Here the reception of grace and righteousness, that is, the entrance into the condition of belief in Christ, is repre-sented as the condition of sharing in the Messianic reign, of becoming "heirs" with Christ ; and since flesh and blood could not "inherit" this kingdom, the transforma-

* Rom. viii. 10 f.
† *ἀρραβών*, 2 Cor. v. 4, 5.
‡ 1 Cor. xv. 20 ; Rom. v. 17.

tion or clothing upon with spiritual bodies at the Parousia is to be the happy fortune of those who living or dead had previously become " members " of the resurrected spiritual head of mankind.   For Paul Christ was " the first fruits " of the resurrection, the first in " order " in this great spiritual transformation and victory over death.   Next in order were to be those who should be Christ's at his coming, that is, the Christians.*   It is evident that Paul's argument does not proceed from the resurrection of Christ as a man like other men to the conclusion that because he, one merely human being, was raised from the dead, therefore all men will be raised, or that all are naturally immortal.   A conception so tame could have found no place in his mystical thought.   Rather since through their connection with the first or earthy man death came upon all men only in that all sinned, so through the second or spiritual man life comes through to all only in that they believe, and those alone have the " pledge " of the resurrection who are " in Christ," that is, are joined with him by faith in a mystical union.

That such was Paul's thought regarding the extent of the transformation of the living and dead at the Parousia cannot be successfully disputed. 'The dead " in Christ," those who are "Christ's," will at his coming be called forth from the realms of death and clothed upon with spiritual incorruptible bodies.   As to the living there is no general statement, but he evidently intended to include only believers in the number of those who should be transformed.   " We who are living, we who are left, shall be changed " can only refer to the living Christians.   Nothing could be more incongruous with Paul's whole system of thought than the supposition that the dead believers would

* 1 Cor. xv. 23 ; *cf.* Gal. v. 24 ; 1 Thess. iv. 16.

be raised at the Parousia, and all living men, good, bad, and indifferent, be "changed" suddenly, arbitrarily, into the spiritual and bodily likeness of Christ. This would have been unthinkable to Paul, because to him the indwelling of the Spirit was the pledge of the bodily transformation into an incorruptible state, and the Spirit was given only to those who had accepted Christ by faith. The question, what he thought was to become of the innumerable dead who had not believed in Christ and of the millions of living unbelievers, is not easily answered. The declaration that, "As in Adam all die, so also in Christ will all be made alive," * does not assert a universal resurrection ; for it is made in connection with the Parousia at which, as has been shown, only all who were "in Christ" were to be raised. The second "all" is accordingly limited to believers, just as in the words: "As, then, through one trespass all men have come under condemnation, so through one act of righteousness all obtain the gift of righteousness unto life," the "all" in the second clause includes only those who should believe. † That Paul had taught the Corinthians in accordance with this interpretation appears to be evident from the custom of baptizing for the dead, which he mentions if not with approval at least without disapproval.‡ It is evident that dead relatives or friends who had departed without faith in Christ would not be baptized through the baptism and confession of the living unless it was believed that their resurrection could thereby be secured. "If the dead rise not," asks Paul, "what are they doing who are baptized for the dead?"

* 1 Cor. xv. 22.

† This conclusion is supported by most of the great exegetes. See, however, Meyer *in loc.*

‡ 1 Cor. xv. 29.

This certainly does not mean, " if all the dead rise not,"
but " if the dead in Christ rise not," for if all were
expected to rise, baptism for the dead would be superfluous.   It appears to be in accord with a fundamental
idea of Paul's that the life in the flesh, the life without the
Spirit that quickeneth even the mortal body, excludes
from the resurrection, and has as its end " destruction,"
or " perishing."   The opposite of " perish " is to be raised,
as is evident from the saying that if there be no resurrection then they who have fallen asleep in Christ are
" perished," * and that " we are the odor of death to those
who are perishing."†   They that " live according to the
flesh are sure to die," yet since believers also die there
must be something more than the natural death of the
body implied in the dying of unbelievers, namely, that
that they will not " live " again, as will those who " by the
Spirit make an end of the deeds of the body."   The
" end " of the " enemies of the cross of Christ " is
" destruction." ‡   The day of the Lord, or the Parousia,
cometh as a thief in the night, and upon those who are
saying, Peace and safety, " doth sudden destruction come,
and they shall not escape."§   Throughout the Pauline
theology there is manifest the dualism of flesh, sin, death
or destruction, and the Spirit, justification, life or resurrection.   The antithesis of life, everlasting life,‖ in which
is included the clothing upon with the incorruptible body,
is death, or hopeless tarrying in the realm of the dead.
It is manifest that a resurrection of those who were not
" in Christ " to a judgment of condemnation or to ever-

* 1 Cor. xv. 18, ἀπώλοντο.
† 2 Cor. ii. 15.
‡ Phil. iii. 19, ἀπώλεια.   § 1 Thess. v. 2, 3.
‖ ζωή, ζωὴ αἰώνιος.

lasting punishment is entirely incongruous with this point of view, since for these Paul knows of no resurrection at all.*

While this view appears to be consistent with itself throughout and with the general trend of Paul's teaching, indications have been pointed out in his Epistles of eschatological ideas more akin to Judaism. He does not, indeed, expressly say that those not " in Christ " will be raised, but a resurrection of unbelievers appears to be implied in the words : " The dead in Christ will rise first," and " the last enemy, death, shall be destroyed." There are clear declarations of a judgment, of " the day of the Lord," of " the judgment-seat of Christ " and of God, and of a " day when God shall judge the secrets of men by

* The outcome of the work of Christ at the Parousia would, however, by no means be meagre according to this conception, for Paul believed in the coming in of "the fulness of the gentiles " and the saving of "all Israel " before that event.   See Rom. xi. 25 f.

While a resurrection of unbelievers is nowhere explicitly affirmed by Paul, and is excluded by his fundamental principle that the possession of the Spirit is the pledge of life from the dead, it appears to be implied in the declaration concerning the day of wrath when God "will render to every one according to his works," and of the day when "God will judge the secrets of men by Jesus Christ " (Rom. ii. 5, 6, 16).   The reference in these passages to the Parousia can hardly be denied. · A universal judgment is also the natural inference from the remark that " the holy will judge the world " (1 Cor. vi. 2).   But it is evident that this language of Jewish apocalypse is no more reconcilable with the teaching that Paul had most at heart than the doctrine of a renovated creation and a reign of Christ till all enemies should be put under his feet, is reconcilable with the ascent of the resurrected and living saints at the Parousia with bodies of glory to meet the descending Lord in the air, and be "forever" with him.   The harmonists who think they can reconcile Paul with himself and find in his teaching a "system" of theology have no difficulty, of course, in showing that to "render to every man according to his works" is compatible with the doctrines of grace and justification by faith.

Jesus Christ." * He also speaks of a " reign " of Christ until all enemies are put under his feet, and of the " creation " as promised a deliverance " from the bondage of corruption into the freedom of the glory of the children of God." † To the believers in Corinth he promises the exalted function of judges of the world and even of angels.‡ " The holy " will sit with Christ at the Parousia on the judgment-seat. All this has an apocalyptic-millenarian aspect which is hardly reconcilable with the spiritual-mystic conception of eschatology previously considered. It has well been asked why a judgment should be thought necessary for the resurrected " dead in Christ " who had already been " accepted as righteous," or for the believers living at the Parousia, who were to be " changed in the twinkling of an eye " into the likeness of Christ's body of glory, why, in fact, these should have to " appear before the judgment-seat of Christ " who were deemed qualified to sit with him in judgment upon the world and even the angels. The deliverance of the groaning creation appears to imply a reign of Christ upon the earth and perhaps a subjection there of his " enemies," in which case some light might be thrown upon the question previously raised regarding the destiny of the unbelievers who should be living at the Parousia, if we knew what was meant by the putting under the feet of Christ. But in the graphic apocalyptic account of the Parousia in 1 Thessalonians the resurrected are represented as ascending to meet the coming Lord " in the air "—a statement which certainly does not imply either a reign upon the earth or a judgment. The incompatibility of ideas is still further apparent when we attempt to reconcile

* 1 Cor. viii. 13 ; 2 Cor. i. 14, v. 10 ; Rom. ii. 16, xiv. 10, etc.

† 1 Cor. xv. 25 ; Rom. viii. 21.   ‡ 1 Cor. vi. 2, 3.

15

either a judgment of the believers or their ascent to meet Christ in the air with the doctrine that immediately at death they were " at home with the Lord," and already clothed with the spiritual body " from heaven." Finally " the end " is not defined with a dogmatic clearness. Christ, having reigned until all his enemies are under his feet, will deliver up his kingdom to the Father, that God may be all in all, that is, all " in Christ and in whatever his kingdom may contain." If this kingdom is supposed to be a transformed humanity, we have here a doctrine of the restoration of mankind, which we might believe to be taught if it were not for the repeated declaration that destruction and perishing are the fate of those who have lived according to the flesh, and if there were an intimation that Christ during his " reign," the duration of which is undetermined, were to be engaged in the conversion of the living unbelievers. But we are told only of his enemies being put under his feet, an expression which implies Messianic conquest rather than evangelization, and in the Pauline teaching there is no resurrection to life for unbelievers. Paul's teaching regarding " the end " can, however, have no importance for us apart from the interest which attaches to it as a phase of the history of doctrines; for to him the final consummation was near at hand.* The voice of an archangel and the trump of God which he conceived to be about to sound were not for the millions who have since " fallen asleep," and the horoscope of destiny was not cast by him for the ages yet to be. His eschatology contains different and irreconcilable ideas, some of which appear to have been held in successive periods of his life, and others at the same time, without

* Rom. xiv. 12 ; Phil. iv. 5 ; 1 Cor. vii. 29.

any attempt to bring them into the unity of a system of thought. If that phase of it which has exerted the greatest influence was that which he was most in earnest about, there can be no doubt that he expressed his deepest conviction not when he wrote after the manner of a Jewish apocalyptist concerning a descent of Christ to the earth with " the trump of God," of the rising of the dead, of a renovated creation, of a judgment-seat, of a Messianic reign, and of a subjection of the Messiah's enemies, but when as a spiritual Hellenist he wrote of the mystic union with Christ by which the soul was inwardly transfigured and clothed upon at death with the habitation from heaven, emerging from the bondage to the clogging flesh to be in joyous freedom "at home with the Lord."* It is evident that, destitute of this spiritual conception and employing only the weapons of Jewish materialism, he could not have advanced his cause with those at Corinth who doubted that there is a resurrection, and that had he not been in touch with Hellenistic ideas he could never have con-ceived and carried out the great apostleship to the gentiles. The doctrine that the deliverance of the souls of believers from the dreary realm of the underworld and their real entrance upon the immortal life began only with the second coming of Christ furnished a doubtful consola-tion at the best, which would have been neutralized by the despair of an indefinite waiting for the ever-postponed Parousia. The advance, then, of Paul's thought beyond this Jewish conception not only shows the greatness of his mind, but denotes the ascendancy of his influence in the gentile world, and reveals him as the cosmopolitan

---

* The idea that the fleshly body is a burden to the soul is expressed in the Hellenistic book of Wisdom, ix. 15.   See 2 Cor. v. 2.

teacher who delivered the gospel of Jesus from the peril of asphyxiation in the atmosphere of provincial narrowness, and established it as a universal historical power.

It is evident from the foregoing considerations that what is called Paulinism is not so much a system as a combination of theological and religious ideas without strictly logical connection, which may be regarded as a transformation of Christianity rather than an interpretation of it, since they are not concerned with an exposition of the teachings of Jesus, but with a metaphysical and mystical construction of his death and resurrection with relation to the problem of salvation. In the exigencies of controversy the apostle appears to have assumed extreme positions which are not easily reconcilable with one another, as when he emphasizes human responsibility and declares men " inexcusable " for not living righteously, and again represents the inward man as powerless for good under the dominion of the flesh, and in bondage to sin ; and when he makes justification by faith depend on the sacrifice of Christ, and yet presents Abraham as an example of the attainment of righteousness by faith without the intervention of Christ, thus apparently making the essential superfluous. His great merit was that he delivered Christianity from the shackles of Judaism, and rendered it possible that the gospel of Jesus should become a world-religion. His thought, then, marks a transition, and perhaps necessarily had two sides, the one turning toward the Judaism from which it was seeking to free itself, and the other toward the Hellenism which it was striving to win. The latter aspect of his thought together with the great Jewish monotheistic doctrine survived, and accomplished the work for which it was fitted.

His idealism, spirituality, and mysticism commended
themselves to gentile thought, and transformed Hellenistic philosophy into religion. His Jewish apocalyptics,
the Parousia, the trumpet which should call up the dead,
also had their day, and still perform a ministry to those
who will have no religion which is not a poorly-disguised
materialism. The Christology which he placed in the
foreground of his teaching, a conception of " the second
Adam " and the " man from heaven," is so metaphysical
and so foreign to the simplicity of Jesus that it is not
likely to hold a permanent place in religious thought.
The acceptance of men as righteous by faith is too extreme and abstract a doctrine to find general favor without important modifications; but the spiritual principle
of dying to sin and living again in union with God and
Christ embodies a universal truth which is confirmed by
the deepest human experience, and it is likely to be permanent with or without the mystical application which
his Christology gives to it.*

That the attempt of Paul to give to Christianity at
the same time a Jewish and a Hellenistic interpretation
resulted in a transformation of it has already been pointed
out. This transformation appears especially in his Christology and his doctrine of redemption. Jesus did not
represent himself as the preëxistent second Adam and
the man from heaven, nor did he teach that he came to

---

* Matthew Arnold appears to accept this doctrine in its mystical aspect.
Yet Goethe, whom he quotes as a " witness " to it, omits the mysticism :

> " Stirb und werde !
> Denn so lang du das nicht hast,
> Bist du nur ein trüber Gast
> Auf der dunkeln Erde——

" Die and re-exist ! for so long as this is not accomplished, thou art but a
troubled guest upon an earth of gloom."

bear the curse of the law in his death. He knew of no righteousness which was reckoned to men on account of faith, but only of one which, like that taught by the prophets, was gained by an obedience sanctified by love to God. He would bring men into that immediate communion with the Father in which he found strength and peace, and whereby they in subjection to the divine will should be transformed and quickened ; but he knew of no mediator and intercessor and no magical new creation. But however much the great apostle may have contributed to a doctrinal transformation of Christianity, it should not be overlooked that his life and character were a noble exemplification of its spirit, and will survive as a helpful influence and an inspiration to mankind, whatever may be the fortune of his doctrinal teachings. With all his reliance upon faith he was a man of action, and displayed unwearied zeal in the cause of the gospel, a missionary of the noblest type. He was a vigorous champion of reason and intellectual liberty and of the freedom of the spirit, despite his bondage as a Jew to the letter of the sacred books of his race. A man of the deepest piety, he was conscious of his dependence upon God, of his inability apart from the Spirit and the indwelling Christ, and though self-reliant and bold, even vehement and intolerant toward the narrowness which would defeat his ends, he was of all men the most affected with a sense of his unworthiness. His gratitude to God was as abundant as his aspiration for perfect fellowship with Him was earnest and ardent. In nothing did he more eminently manifest the spirit of his Master than in his self-sacrificing devotion to the welfare of mankind, which is especially touching in his affectionate interest in his " brethren according to the flesh," for whose conversion he toiled, and hoped against hope. In his immortal hymn to Love * the poetic genius of his nation found its latest inspired and classical expression. †

* 1 Cor. xiii.

† On the Pauline teaching the student may consult : Immer, Theol. des N. T., pp. 205–356 ; Weiss, Bibl. Theol. des N. T., 3te Ausg., §§ 58–87 (Eng Trans., i. pp. 292 to end); Pfleiderer, Das Urchristenthum, pp. 153–280 ; Der Paulinismus, 2te Aufl. ; Baur, Paulus, 2te Ausg. ii. pp. 123–315, and Neutestamentl. Theol., pp. 128–207 ; Weizsäcker, Das apostol. Zeitalter, pp. 106–139 ; Lechler, Das apostol. u. nachapostol. Zeitalter, 3te Ausg., pp. 269–387 ; Von Cölln, Bibl. Theol., ii. pp. 167–338 ; Hausrath, Neutestamentl. Zeitgesch., ii. pp. 439–499 ; Holsten, Zum Evangelium des Paulus u. des Petrus, *passim ;* Holtzmann, Judenthum u. Christenthum, pp. 553 ff ; Pfleiderer, The Influence of the Apostle Paul on the Development of Christianity (The Hibbert Lectures, 1885); Matthew Arnold, St. Paul and Protestantism ; Toy, Judaism and Christianity (see " Paul " in Index of Subjects) ; Reuss, La Théologie Chrétienne au Siècle Apostolique, ii. pp. 14–242 ; Martineau, The Seat of Authority in Religion, Book iv. chap. ii. §§ 2, 3, chap. iii. §§ 2, 3 ; Stevens, The Pauline Theology, 1892 ; Beyschlag, Neutestamentliche Theologie, 1892, ii. pp. 1–252 ; Coquerel, First Historical Transformations of Christianity, 1867, pp. 111 f ; Crooker, Different New Testament Views of Jesus, 1890, pp. 32 f.

CHAPTER IV.

THE DEUTERO-PAULINE INTERPRETATIONS.

PAULINISM does not appear to have met immediately with a general acceptance in the Church in the form in which it was conceived and presented by its great and original author. With other times came new exigencies and the necessity of new adjustments of Christianity to them, and this bold transformation of the gospel of Jesus was destined itself to be transformed by its friends, and adapted to the changing needs of the believers in an age teeming with novel ideas and daring speculations. It might be expected that the result would show a softening of some of the harder lines of Paulinism and the prominence in Christian thought of conceptions whose descent could not be traced directly from the great apostle. If Paul "planted" in Hellenistic soil, and the Alexandrian Apollos "watered," it may very well have turned out that "the increase" was a crop of ideas and speculations related both to the Synagogue and to the philosophy of Philo. By reason of its origin, its birth out of the throes of a Hebrew soul struggling for freedom from Jewish legalism, Paulinism contained ideas which could be appreciated only by minds familiar with the school of thought in which the apostle had been trained. Adapted to the reconciling of Jews with Christianity by removing the "offence" of the cross, these ideas of the opposition of the law and the gospel, of a representative propitiation, of the abolition of the curse of the law, and of a righteousness which was "accounted" to men through faith, could not be understood by gentiles, and very soon fell into disuse, among those who had no interest in and no comprehension of the original Pauline contest against Judaism. On the contrary, certain of Paul's ideas which had an affinity for gentile thought were appropriated by thinkers who were favorable to Paulinism in general, and adapted in connection with current speculations to the exigencies of post-apostolic times. The New-Testament literature which represents this modified Paulinism has received from criticism the designation Deutero-Pauline, and may be regarded as embracing the Epistles to the Hebrews, Colossians, and Ephesians, and the first Epistle of Peter.

I.—THE EPISTLE TO THE HEBREWS.

The first of these Epistles, which is evidently the work of a Pauline Christian favorably disposed to the Alexandrian thought, was probably written in the last quarter of the first century for the purpose of strengthening the wavering faith of certain Jewish Christians.* In order to counteract an assumed tendency on the part of the per-

---

* The date, authorship, and address of the Epistle to the Hebrews are indeterminable. It was probably written between A.D. 80 and 90, and addressed to Roman Christians. That Paul was not its author has long been held by the critical school, and is now generally conceded. The limits of this work require the acceptance of the conclusions of criticism with regard to the various New Testament writings without a discussion of their grounds. The critical school is, however, divided on the question of the date of the Epistle. But the date is not a matter of great importance. Hilgenfeld, followed by Davidson, places the composition shortly before A. D. 70. See, however, Holtzmann in Schenkel's Bibel Lexicon, ii. p. 623. Volkmar dates it at 116-118.

sons addressed to go back to their former Jewish belief, the writer makes it his chief object to show the superiority of Christianity to Judaism. Over against the changing, sinful priesthood of Judaism, and its frequent sacrifices in an earthly sanctuary, which serve only for outward purification, he places Christ conceived as a great high priest whose one sacrifice has effected salvation forever, he having entered "into a sanctuary not made with hands," "into heaven itself, now to appear in the presence of God in our behalf."* The contact of the writer with the idealism of the Alexandrian philosophy is indicated in his conception of archetype and copy, reality and shadow, applied to the heavenly and earthly sanctuaries. As a high priest "who sat down on the right hand of the throne of the Majesty in the heavens," Christ is a minister of "the true tabernacle," while those priests "who offer the gifts according to the law" "serve the mere delineation and shadow of the heavenly things."† The Christology of Paul denotes, as has been shown, a wide departure from the teaching of Jesus regarding his person, and that of this writer is a marked deviation from Paulinism in this regard. As Paul knew nothing of Jesus as "the apostle and high-priest of our confession,"‡ so the author of Hebrews appears not to know anything of him as "the second Adam" and "the man from heaven." In the Pauline doctrine of the work of Christ the stress is laid upon his death and resurrection, while in Hebrews the chief prominence is given to his heavenly function as

* Heb. ix. 24.

† Heb. viii. 5, ὑπόδειγμα καὶ σκιὰ τῶν ἐπουρανίων; ix. 23, ἀντίτυπα τῶν ἀληθινῶν. See book of Wisdom ix. 8, where the temple is spoken of as a μίμημα σκηνῆς ἁγίας ην προητοίμασας ἀπ' ἀρχης, "a copy of the holy tent which Thou didst prepare from the beginning."

‡ Heb. iii. 1.

high-priest and intercessor. Although the writer does not designate Christ as the Logos, he ascribes to him some of the functions which Philo attributes to this agent, and there can be little doubt that the form in which his Christology is presented shows the influence of the Alexandrian speculator. While he does not appear to have advanced so far in the understanding and development of the Alexandrian gnosis as the author of the fourth Gospel he shows more points of contact with it than Paul, and may be regarded as in this respect holding an intermediate position between these two great writers.

The importance which the writer of this Epistle attached to his doctrine of the person of Christ is apparent in the Christological propositions which he lays down at the outset as the basis of his argument. There are to be observed here as in Paul's writings the absence of a distinctive treatment of the teachings of Jesus and a tendency to an idealizing exaltation of his person and office, in which the historical Jesus, the teacher, the preacher of righteousness, the Son of Man, and the prophet of the kingdom of God, disappears from view to give place to the Son of God, the high-priest, and the heavenly intercessor in behalf of the faithful. When the writer calls Christ the Son of God, it is evident that he neither employs the term in the Jewish-Messianic sense, nor in the Pauline sense, but to designate him as the appointed "heir of all things," the agent of the creation, a "brightness" from the "glory" of God, and "an image of His being," who "upholds all things by the word of his power."* The ideas of the preëxistence of Christ and of his agency in the creation are Pauline, but other attributes and functions ascribed to him transcend Paulinism and

* Heb. i. 2, 3.

betray an Alexandrian origin. The word employed to express the idea of a brightness or reflection of the divine glory is an Alexandrian term * which is found in the book of Wisdom and in Philo, and only here occurs in the New Testament. In the expression "the image of His being," † that is, His person, is contained the idea that the nature of the Father is impressed upon the Son so that the latter is, so to speak, a copy of the former. Finally, as the writer had conceived of Jesus as an agent in the creation of the worlds, he continues the sketch of his greatness by representing him as seated at the right hand of the Majesty on high and upholding all things by the word of his power, thus ascribing to him the functions of a universal Providence, just as Philo regarded the Logos as " the bond of all things," who " holds together and administers the universe." ‡ Having shown the superiority of Christ over the prophets as mediators of the Old-Testament revelation, the writer proceeds to demonstrate his preëminence over the angels who were regarded by the Jews as also agents in the communication of the divine word to men. If this argument is directed, as some suppose, against a tendency in his readers to put Christ, angels, and the spiritual powers on an equal footing and so to degrade Christianity to a level with Essenene and

* ἀπαύγασμα. Meyer finds in this term the three ideas of independent existence, of origin, and of similarity, *i. e.*, existence apart from God, origin from Him, and a nature similar to His. Commentar *in loc*. So in the book of Wisdom the personified wisdom of God is called " the brightness of the everlasting light," ἀπαύγ ασμα φωτὸς αἰδίου, vii. 26.

† χαρακτήρ. In Philo the Logos is said to be the image of God, and the rational soul is compared to a coin stamped with the seal of God, the impress (χαρακτήρ) of which is the everlasting Logos. *Cf*. Col. i. 15, εἰκὼν τοῦ θεοῦ ἀοράτου, " image of the invisible God."

‡ *Quis rer. div. hær.* 44 ; *Vita Mos.* iii.14.

other mystic spirit-cults, it would appear to be made conclusive by the citation from a Psalm in which the writer makes God himself address the Son as " God." * So Philo designates the Logos as "the second God," although regarding him [it] as subordinate to and dependent on the Supreme Being. †

Philo's speculative idea that the Logos dwelt in the great Jewish teachers, and was represented by the high-priest, is, however, surpassed by the thought of the Christian Alexandrian who wrote this Epistle that, "we see him who was made a little lower than the angels, Jesus, on account of the suffering of death crowned with glory and honor, that by the grace of God he might taste death for every one." ‡ The advance of Christianity beyond Alexandrian speculation is here indicated in the religious aspect which the incarnation is made to assume. The Son of God becoming human and making a sacrifice once for all in behalf of mankind, brings man to God, and so unites the upper and nether worlds, the world of ideas and the world of sense, between which philosophy had been able to effect only a metaphysical reconciliation. It is not clear how the writer conceived the entrance of this exalted preëxistent being, the image of the divine personality, upon a human life to have been effected. In one place he says : " It is well known that our Lord sprang out of Judah," § an expression which clearly implies a natural birth of human parents. On the other hand he represents Christ's prototype as Melchisedek who was

---

* Heb. i. 8. But of the Son [He said] thy throne, O God, is for ever and ever, Ps. xlv. 6. The application of the passage from the Psalm to Christ is a perversion of its original sense.

† See Drummond, Philo Judæus, 1888, ii. pp. 195 ff.

‡ Heb. ii. 9. § Heb. vii. 14.

"without father, without mother, without record of descent, having neither beginning of days nor end of life." *
It is difficult to draw another conclusion from this than that he intended to attribute a similar origin to Christ, for there does not appear to be any other reason for his going out of his way to say that of Melchisedek which is not contained in the mention of him in Genesis. † He appears also to imply a supernatural intervention in bringing Christ into the world when he misinterprets a passage from a Psalm so as to make Christ say in it: "A body didst thou prepare for me." ‡   He could hardly have had recourse to this passage if he had had in mind only the natural human body. Pfleiderer calls attention to the denial in the nearly contemporaneous Epistle of Barnabas of the doctrine that Jesus was the son of man, and concludes that the Docetic Christology of Gnosticism, which maintained that Christ's body was not a real one of flesh and blood, was then well under way, but not yet accounted a heresy.   In any case there appear to be in the Epistle two hypotheses of Christ's entrance into human life which the writer has left without formal reconciliation.   The Christology of the Epistle appears to contain other incongruities in that it represents Christ who was the "image"

---

* Heb. vii. 3.

† Meyer's opinion that the writer meant simply to say that no genealogy of Melchisedek is given in the Bible flattens the whole passage, and makes this reference to the descent of the prince of Salem unmeaning.

‡ Ps. xl. 6.   The reference of the passage to Christ is easily explained by the writer's allegorizing tendency in accordance with his Alexandrian education ; but his rendering of the original : " Thou hast opened my ears " by : " A body didst Thou prepare for me," can be explained only by supposing him to have followed blindly the incorrect Septuagint version.   For an explanation of the error in the Septuagint see De Wette, Commentar über die Psalmen, p. 249, and Meyer on Heb. x. 5.

of God as being tempted " in all points as we are," as being
" perfected through suffering," and as " learning obedience
by what he suffered." He by whom the worlds were
made, the sustainer of all things, second apparently only
to the Deity in glory, is said to be " crowned with glory
and honor *on account of the suffering of death*." * To the
thought of this writer as well as to Paul's two currents
appear to have contributed, the one bearing Hellenistic
idealism and speculation, and the other the materials of
history and tradition. Neither writer attempted an adjustment of the two deposits to each other.

The Epistle has not the appearance of having been
written with especial reference to the Pauline apprehension of Christianity, and many of the ideas which were
prominent in the apostle's thought do not seem to have
been in the writer's mind. The principal points of contact
with Paulinism are the teachings that all things are from
God and to Him; † that Christ was the image of God,
and that all things were made by him; ‡ that Christ
humbled himself and was exalted; § that death was overcome by Christ; ‖ that Christ suffered for sinners; ¶ and
that Christ acts as an intercessor before the Father.**

---

* Heb. ii. 9 f, iv. 15, v. 8 f. The idea that Christ's temptation and sufferings were a means of his moral development does not appear elsewhere
in the New Testament. The writer doubtless wishes to present Christ to
his readers as an example of constancy under persecution. The doctrine is
manifestly unpauline, and the writer does not appear to have thought of the
difficulty of reconciling the conception of a preexistent Christ crowned with
the glory of a divine nature with that of an afflicted human being attaining
perfection and honor through obedience and pain.

† Heb. ii. 10; Rom. xi. 36; 1 Cor. viii. 6.

‡ Heb. i. 1–3; 2 Cor. iv. 4; 1 Cor. viii. 6.

§ Heb. i. 4; Phil. ii. 8, 9.   ‖ Heb. ii. 14; 1 Cor. xv. 54–57.

¶ Heb. ix. 26–28, x. 12; Rom. vi. 9, 10.

** Heb. vii. 25; Rom. viii. 34.

These Pauline ideas cannot, indeed, be said to be incidental to the controlling purpose of the author, but his controlling purpose is so different from that of Paul that his employment of them cannot be regarded as unqualifiedly Pauline. The fundamental distinction between this and the Pauline Epistles lies in the apprehension of the relation of Judaism and Christianity. To Paul Judaism was preëminently a law which was to be fulfilled, while to the writer of Hebrews it is a body of ritual arrangements intended to effect communication between Israel and God and culminating in the priesthood. In the priesthood and not in the law consist its importance and whatever permanence it had. In the priesthood too is the point of contact and union of Judaism and Christianity. For the work of Christ is viewed under the conception of a priesthood, and the new religion which he brought is a new institution of atonement surpassing that of Judaism and put into effect by a high-priest infinitely superior to his predecessors under the old dispensation. These represented a transient institution, an economy which was only a shadow of that which was to come. He has his prototype in Melchisedek, is "a priest forever," and having entered into the heavenly sanctuary, has effected an everlasting atonement. The means by which he becomes the chief of redemption are his suffering and death. He assumed flesh and blood "that through death he might bring to naught him who had the power of death, that is, the Devil, and might deliver those who, through fear of death, were all their life-time subject to bondage." * Accordingly God "prepared a body" for him, that by the sacrifice of it he might do away with the ancient offerings of beasts, and effect our sanctification. †

* Heb. ii. 14, 15.   † Heb. x. 5–10.

The difference between this point of view and that of
Paul is manifest. He, indeed, conceived the death of
Christ to be the great factor in redemption, but to him
Christ was the "man from heaven" who as a representative of the human race passively received the curse of the
law in his death, and so fulfilled the law for all. Of this
doctrine there is no trace in our Epistle. The writer of it
regards Christ not as the passive representative sufferer,
but as the active high-priest who brings his holy life to
God in obedience and patience as a precious offering, and
by this ethical act of sacrifice operates upon our hearts
for their purification and perfection, and opens to us
admittance to the heavenly sanctuary, to complete communion with God. The high-priest of the old dispensation was required to enter "once every year" into the
holy of holies with the blood of beasts, in order by the
sprinkling of blood to remove the guilt of the people and
restore the broken covenant with God. But the fact that
this act of atonement must be forever repeated proved
that the means was inadequate and ineffective for the
purifying of the worshipper. Hence there was need of a
better sacrifice and a greater high-priest. This high-priest
is Christ, the heavenly Son of God, whom in the type
Melchisedek God appointed before the institution of the
Levitical priesthood as the everlasting high-priest of the
new dispensation.* It was not necessary for him, like
the human high-priests, to offer a sacrifice for his own
sins, for although he shared in our weaknesses and liabil-
ity to temptation, yet as the superhuman Son of God he

---

* Heb. ix. 7, 9, 13 ; x. 1, 4. "Once every year," Philo is charged with
this technical error. Did the writer of the Epistle derive it from him ? The
high-priest entered the holy of holies on one day in the year twice according
to Levit. xvi. 12–16, according to the Talmud several times.

was unstained by sin, and hence could offer a better sacrifice than the Levitical priests. "For if the blood of goats and bulls, and the ashes of a heifer sprinkling those who have been defiled, sanctify to the purifying of the flesh, how much more shall the blood of Christ, who by his everlasting spirit offered himself without spot to God, purify your conscience from dead works for the worship of the living God!"* Thus while Paul's point of departure for his doctrine of atonement was the theory of propitiation and satisfaction which was held by the Jewish theologians, the author of Hebrews proceeds from the Old-Testament sacrificial ritual regarded as a symbolical prototype of the higher ethical-religious sacrifice of Christ. Paul's arraignment of Judaism was from his point of view directed against the law as "weak through the flesh," and ineffectual for righteousness. The author of this Epistle also has his charge against Judaism, but from his point of view the charge rests against the sacrificial system, and he declares that "it is impossible that the blood of bulls and goats should take away sins." † Remaining then, in a closer contact with Judaism than Paul's sharp antagonism to the law permitted him to maintain, he conceives of a better purification than the Levitical annual cleansing in which "there is a remembrance of sins every year." ‡ Christ with his own blood has entered once for all into the true sanctuary of heaven, and effected an everlasting salvation, the real putting away of sins, "perfecting by one offering forever those who are sanctified," so that the ancient word of prophecy is fulfilled : " I will put my laws into their hearts, and in their minds I will write them, and their sins and iniquities I will remember no more." For "where there is remission of sins there is no longer

* Heb. x. 14.   † Heb. x. 4.   ‡ Heb. x. 3.

offering for sin." * The great sacrifice on the cross is
regarded as removing the consciousness of guilt in men
which separates them from God and putting them into
that condition of holiness which corresponds to Christ's
own perfection. This work of the great high-priest,
begun on earth, is continued in heaven, where he has
entered into the celestial sanctuary and still makes intercession. Thus in this Epistle the death of Christ is
conceived as effecting essentially the same result as in the
teaching of Paul. But while Paul saw in the sacrifice on
the cross the satisfaction of the law or of the divine righteousness, this writer entirely ignores that fundamental
idea of the apostle's and regards the great offering from
an ethical point of view as immediately related to the
consciousness of men and bringing about purification
from sin as a moral-religious result. † We find here too
the unpauline idea of a completion of the work of Christ
in the upper, heavenly sanctuary, and miss the great
Pauline doctrines of the agency of the Spirit, and of the

* Heb. x. 17, 18.

† The doctrine that we are reconciled to God by the death of Christ is,
indeed, expressed in the Epistle, and the writer approaches very near the
Pauline thought of a representative suffering of the legal penalty when he
applies as types to the death of Christ the Old-Testament sacrifices of atonement which probably rest upon the idea of substitutional offering. Hence,
Christ is called a merciful and faithful high-priest to make atonement for
the sins of the people (ii. 17) and the mediator of a new covenant by whose
death is secured "redemption from the transgressions under the first covenant" (ix. 15), since "without the shedding of blood there is no remission "
(ix. 22). Jesus indeed "tasted death for every one" (ii. 9) ; but instead of
the Pauline ideas expressed in Rom. iii. 25 and Gal. iii. 13 concerning his
suffering to manifest the righteousness of God and bear the curse of the law,
it is said that the object of his death was to "take away sin," and to be
himself made perfect through suffering, together with the quite incongruous
remark that the testator must die in order to put the covenant in force.

dying with Christ and the rising with him to newness of life.

Instead of accepting the Pauline doctrine that the death of Christ removed the curse of the law, the writer of Hebrews conceives of the effect of the sacrifice on the cross as a " bringing to naught of him who had the power of death, that is, the Devil." *   To Paul death came into the world through sin, and in his theology the Devil has no conspicuous place.   The introduction of Satan as the personal representative of the power of death in this Epistle appears to indicate the beginning of the development of the Christian mythology in which the Prince of the realm of evil was supposed to have certain rights over the souls of men by reason of Adam's transgressions.   For the Pauline teaching that death as the penalty of sin was overcome by the sacrifice of Christ, who in his person as a representative of the human race suffered it for all men, this writer substitutes the mythological conception of the overthrow of the Devil, who as the original author of sin is regarded as the King of death. †   The writer does not appear to have been favorably inclined towards the Pauline metaphysical abstractions, among which was the idea of the law as a power whose demands God must recognize and satisfy.   Accordingly we may suppose that the simple, concrete personality of Satan commended itself to him as the representative of death who was " set at nought" by the great sacrifice of Christ which was conceived as breaking his power, since it was a means of snatching men from the grasp of death by freeing them

* Heb. ii. 14, διάβολος.

† There is perhaps here a trace of the influence of the book of Wisdom upon the writer. See Wisdom ii. 24: " By the envy of the Devil [διαβόλου] came death into the world, and those experience it who belong to him."

from sin. This *naïve* popular mythology, whose origin is easily traced, may very well have satisfied an age which was not capable of comprehending, much less of attaining to, the "monstrous moral enormity" of the mediæval theology which regarded the justice of God as requiring satisfaction and finding it in the sacrifice of Christ—a doctrine which "mingles its fierce lights of expiation and its massive shadows of despair with the whole theology of Christendom."

Another important deviation of the doctrine of this Epistle from the Pauline thought appears in its teaching regarding faith. Faith is assigned, indeed, no unimportant part in the Christian life; it is necessary for those who hear the word in order to "profit"; it is a profession to be "held fast"; it is a "foundation" to be laid.* But we find nothing here of Paul's apprehension of it as a mystic union with Christ whereby his death and resurrection are inwardly appropriated. The great Pauline opposition of faith and works is here retired into the background, and instead of justification by faith without works, we read of Christ as an *example* who "learned obedience by what he suffered, and, being perfected, became the author of everlasting salvation *to all who obey him.*" † Unlike Paul the author does not emphasize faith in Christ, but his conception of it is vague and general, and corresponds with the conception of Philo as an ideal disposition of the emotions in opposition to the sensuous, fleshly tendency, in particular as confidence in God's promises and support. Christ is rather the prototype than the object of faith, and as he "for the joy that was set before him endured the cross, despising the shame," so we ought to "run with perseverance the race

* Heb. iv. 2, vi. 1, x. 23.   † Heb v. 9.

that is set before us, looking to him as the author and perfecter of our faith," * that is, as Jesus by his example has given us a demonstration of faith even to his death on the cross, so we ought to make that virtue ours "with perseverance." This is quite unpauline; but the writer indicates another departure from his great predecessor in teaching that faith is to be directed to the possessions of the unseen future world. It is sententiously declared to be "the assurance of things hoped for, a conviction of things not seen." † It is the conviction of the reality of the upper world, the assurance that what is hoped for in respect to the promised reconciliation with God and participation in the glory of Christ will surely be realized. As it was remarked in the foregoing chapter, the Pauline terminology regarding justification by faith is avoided, and instead of the Pauline "to be justified," and "to be accounted righteous through faith," we have here "to have the testimony that he pleased God," "to obtain a good report through faith," ‡ and even the expression, "*wrought* righteousness through faith." § Evidently righteousness is not conceived by this writer as by Paul to be a gift of God received by faith, whereby the believer is liberated from the curse of the law by reason of the atoning, propitiatory death of Christ, but as a pious disposition which is confirmed by obedience in action and suffering, and constitutes the essence of faith itself. The tendency of the writer is indicated by the use which he makes of a catchword of Paul's taken from Habakkuk ii. 4: "The just shall live by his faith." Paul renders

* Heb. xii. 2.   † Heb. xi. 1.

‡ Heb. xi. 4, 5, 39, μαρτυρεῖσθαι δίκαιον εἶναι, μαρτυρεῖσθαι διὰ πίστεως.

§ Heb. xi. 33, ἐργάζεσθαι διὰ πίστεως δικαιοσύνην.

this: "The just by faith shall live," that is, he who is righteous through faith shall have part in the Messianic life at the Parousia. But our writer understands the words in their original import: "The righteous man will preserve his life as a result of his faith," his trusting endurance, which is the opposite of "drawing back." * There could be no place, then, in our writer's thought for the Pauline opposites, faith and works, faith and the law; for a faith which, like that conceived by him, is the direction of the human will. in conformity with the will of God, includes in itself works, or the fulfilment of the moral law. While for Paul the essence of faith was a religious receptivity, a devotion of the life to Christ, and a mystic union with him, for the writer of Hebrews it is, in part, a hope in the promised possessions of the future world, and in part a moral power of obedience, patience, and endurance, which constitute the disposition acceptable to God.

The Epistle is poor in eschatological features. The writer does not employ apocalyptical imagery, and says nothing of a scenic general judgment and a millennial reign of Christ. "The resurrection of the dead" and "everlasting judgment" are mentioned among those "first principles" which he admonishes his readers to leave, as apparently unimportant, that they may "press on to perfection." † That Christ is to come again appears to be a doctrine accepted by his readers. He exhorts them that they excite to love and good works, not forsaking the assembling of themselves together; "and so much the more, as ye see the day [of the Parousia] approaching." ‡ Mention of the judgment and the sec-

---

* Gal. iii. 11.; Heb. x. 38. See Meyer on the passages.
† Heb. vi. 2.   ‡ Heb. x. 24, 25.

ond appearance of Christ is vague and evidently incidental, as in the words: "As it is appointed unto men once to die, but after this the judgment; so also Christ having been once offered up to bear the sins of many will appear the second time without sin for the salvation of those who are waiting for him."* Since "those who are waiting for him" can only be the believers, the fortune of unbelievers at the Parousia is left undetermined. This is, however, in accordance with the vagueness of the author's eschatology in general. It is evident that he attached small importance to such matters as "baptism" "resurrection," and "judgment," which to him were elementary † in comparison with his doctrine of the perfect, heavenly priesthood of Christ. With respect to the lapse of believers the doctrine of Paul receives a very emphatic supplement. For those who "willingly sin" after they have "received the knowledge of the truth, there no longer remaineth a sacrifice for sin, but a certain fearful looking-for of judgment," etc. ‡ These may abandon hope, "For it is impossible that those who have once been enlightened and have tasted the heavenly gift, etc., and have fallen away should be again renewed to repentance, since they crucify to themselves the Son of God afresh and put him to open shame."§ While the saying regarding the sin against the Holy Ghost has some analogy with this, nowhere else in the New Testament is the hopelessness of the condition of believers who may have fallen· from their allegiance so definitely and unqualifiedly set forth. That this dogmatic assertion is not in accord with the case of Peter, with the spirit of Jesus, with any known psychological principles, and with the

* Heb. ix. 27, 28.   † ὁ τῆς ἀρχῆς λόγος.
‡ Heb. x. 26, 27.   § Heb. vi. 4–6.

facts of experience, could not have affected the tone of this writer, who perhaps thought that severity and an awful warning were the only means of obviating an impending lapse of his readers.

2.—THE EPISTLE TO THE COLOSSIANS.

The Epistle to the Colossians is an important document of the deutero-Pauline literature, and may be discussed as to its doctrinal contents independently of the question whether it contains a genuine Pauline nucleus. It was occasioned apparently by the appearance among the believers in Colossæ of certain phases of belief which were a departure from the true Christian doctrine, but the exact nature of which it is not easy to determine. Perhaps the tendencies which the Epistle combats denoted the beginnings of the Gnosticism which later played so important a part in Christian history. That the persons addressed were gentile Christians appears probable from several allusions, particularly from the words: "And to you who were dead in your trespasses and the uncircumcision of your flesh hath He given life together with him [Christ], having forgiven us all our trespasses."* Over against the erroneous doctrines of his readers the writer of the Epistle sets the, to him, true idea of Christ's person and the Christian knowledge which is better than the false gnosis to which they were inclined. As in the Epistle to the Hebrews so here this Christological doctrine is laid down at the outset and made fundamental to the main purpose which is to combat the erroneous views held by the persons addressed. The Christology is also a further development of that of Hebrews, whose writer the author follows in the appre-

* Col. ii. 13. *Cf.* i. 13, 21.

hension of the relation of Judaism and Christianity not, indeed, precisely as type and antitype, but as unreal and unessential and real and essential, as shadow and substance. From the point of view of the absoluteness of Christianity he proceeds to the establishment of the absoluteness of the person of Christ. Like the author of the former Epistle he avoids the application of the term Logos to Christ, and although his Christology shows resemblances to that of Paul in some points, yet on the whole it goes beyond the apostle's, and applies to Christ predicates which in Philo are applied to the Logos. It is a step nearer than the Christology of Hebrews to the more developed Logos-idea of the fourth Gospel, yet it keeps close to Paul in representing Christ as in intimate connection with the world. When the author calls Christ "the image of the invisible God," and "the first-born of the whole creation,"* we are reminded of the Pauline expressions, "the image of God," and "the first-born among many brethren";† but the epithet "invisible" suggests Philo's idea of the Logos as the revelator or visible copy of the hidden God, and the term "first-born of the whole creation" reminds us of his doctrine that the Logos was in distinction from the world the first-born Son of God. But the writer carries still further his exaltation and idealization of Christ in the words: "For in him were created all things, those in the heavens and those on the earth, the visible and the invisible, whether thrones or dominions or principalities or powers, all things have been created through him and for him ; and he is beyond all things, and in him all things subsist."‡ This surpasses

* Col. i. 15.   † 2 Cor. iv. 4 ; Rom. viii. 29.
‡ Col. i. 16, 17. "In him," v. 16 ; *ἐν αὐτῷ* is equivalent to *δἰ αὐτοῦ* with the additional shade of meaning that the things created by him have their ground in him—that is, "in him all things subsist," v. 17.

the Pauline teaching that Christ was the agent of creation through whom all things were made, since he here becomes the end of creation " for " whom all things were made and the indwelling cosmic principle in whom all things subsist, the bond and supporter of the universe. This doctrine is as remote from the Pauline conception of Christ as " the man from heaven," as it is akin to Philo's teaching that the cosmos was " founded in the divine Logos," that the Logos is " the bond of all things " and " holds and binds all the parts together and prevents their dissolution," and that it is the principle sustaining and directing the totality of existence.*

Thence the author proceeds to set forth the office of Christ with reference to the work of redemption in terms corresponding to the exalted rank already assigned him. He is the head of the church, since he is the beginning, that he may be in all things preëminent; " for God was pleased that in him all the fulness should dwell, and by him to reconcile all things to Himself, having made peace through the blood of his cross, by him, I say, whether the things on earth or those in the heavens." † This denotes an advance in the exaltation of Christ beyond Paul and the author of Hebrews, neither of whom conceived that in him " dwelt all the fulness of the Godhead bodily." ‡ The heavenly or archetypal " man " of Paul might, indeed, be conceived to be " the image of God," but not the embodiment of " all the fulness of the Godhead." We are rather here again reminded of Philo, who conceived the Logos as the " place " or essence of the divine energies, whom " God himself has *filled* entirely with immaterial

* κόσμος . . . . ἰδρυθεὶς ἐν τῷ θείῳ λόγῳ; λόγος . . . . δεσμὸς ὢν τῶν ἁπάντων; συνέχει [λόγος] τὰ μέρη πάντα, etc., Pfleiderer.

† Col. i. 18–20.

‡ Col. ii. 9, πᾶν τὸ πλήρωμα θεότητος σωματικῶς.

powers." *   It may be left undecided whether "the fulness of the Godhead" is conceived to have dwelt in Christ necessarily and from the beginning, or from the time of his resurrection and exaltation, but there can be little doubt from the abrupt way in which the writer introduces the word *pleroma*,† fulness, in the declaration in question that the term was known by him to be current among his readers, and accordingly that he knew them to be influenced by Gnostic speculations, and wished to counteract these by teaching that all the primal powers which the Gnostics assumed in the *pleroma* dwelt *bodily* in Christ, since in him was the *pleroma of the Godhead*. Since the use of this term cannot be shown among the Jewish Theosophists, the Gnosticism which the writer had in view must have been later than the time of Paul. Whether the Gnostic *pleroma* was supposed to be in discord and to need reconciliation or no may not be clear, but it is evident that a new and unpauline idea of the extent of Christ's reconciling function is here advanced by this writer when he includes in it " the things in the heavens." According to Paul the work of Christ was limited to the human race, of which as " the man from heaven " he was conceived to be the head and atoning representative. There appears furthermore to be an allusion to the Gnostic idea of the distinction of the world of spirit and the world of matter, in the declaration that in Christ were created "the things visible and invisible "; and the " dominions, principalities, and powers " which are said to have been created in him were according to Irenæus and Epiphanius current Gnostic terms.‡   To declare that all these things were created

* See Drummond, Philo Judæus, ii. p. 162.

† πλήρωμα, a Gnostic term employed to express the totality of the primal powers or æons included in the divine Being.

‡ Iren., Adv. Hæres., i. 24, 1 ; Epiph., Hæres., xxiii. 1.

in Christ, that he is "before" them all, and that they all "subsist" in him is the author's way of overcoming the Gnostic tendencies of his readers. Especially effective in this regard must have appeared to him the declaration that on the cross Christ "having disarmed principalities and powers [orders of spiritual beings according to the Gnostics] made a public show of them, and led them captive in triumph." * This conception taken in connection with the declaration that in the death of Christ "the hand-writing in ordinances which was against us He hath taken out of the way, nailing it to the cross," is significant as well for what it expresses as for what it omits. We do not find here the genuinely Pauline idea of the death of Christ as a representative satisfaction of the law rendered to the divine justice; but rather as in Hebrews it is taught that in his death Christ "brought to naught him who had the power of death, that is, the Devil," so here he is represented as robbing the spirits of evil of their power, supposed to be represented by a bond of the law which they held against sinful men and leading them captive in triumph, having "nailed to the cross," that is, annulled in his death, their claim to the souls of men. Evidently the abstract "curse of the law" was not easily understood by the gentile Christians, and so in place of the original Pauline doctrine of atonement there may very likely have been developed the conception of a conflict of Christ with demonic powers, and their overthrow by virtue of his great sacrifice. All this is evidently far removed from Paul's great mystic doctrine of an appropriation of the sacrifice of Christ by faith. There appears also to be an attempt on the part of the writer of this

---

* Col. ii. 15. Paul has, indeed, in Rom. viii. 38, ἀρχαί and δυνάμεις, but nowhere such a Christology as appears in this Epistle.

Epistle to apply the Gospel to the exigencies of the
Church at Colossæ, by exalting Christianity to the chief
place among "mysteries."[*]   A secret mystery-worship
may have been one of the erroneous tendencies which he
wished to counteract, as well as the inclination to worship
angels and put Christ on an equality with celestial spiritual beings.   We find here also another doctrine which is
hardly reconcilable with the genuine Pauline teaching.
To Paul the sacrifice of Christ was an all-sufficient act of
atonement, and he could not without the greatest incongruity have spoken of filling up in his sufferings in the
flesh that which is wanting of the afflictions of Christ on
behalf of the Church.[†]   In combating the false gnosis of
his readers, the author appears to have made their ideas
to some extent his own without a conscious acceptance of
their errors.   His teaching concerning the reconciliation
of "the things in heaven" through Christ shows the impression which Gnostic ideas had made upon him.   In his
doctrine of redemption there are other traits which do
not belong to the Pauline interpretation of Christianity,
especially in the passage: "Who rescued us from the
empire of darkness, and transferred us into the kingdom
of His beloved Son, in whom we have our redemption,
the forgiveness of our sins."[‡]   "The empire of darkness"
doubtless refers to the non-Christian world as supposed to
be ruled by demons[§] from whose sway Gnosticism would
deliver men by means of ascetic practices.   This is quite
remote from the Pauline redemption from the curse of the

---

[*] Col. i. 27; ii. 2; iv. 3. Paul, indeed, speaks ἐν μυστηρίῳ to the
"perfect," but to this writer the Gospel is altogether a "mystery."

[†] Col. i. 24.   [‡] Col. i. 13.

[§] See Eph. ii. 2, "According to the course of this world, according to the
prince of the powers of the air," etc.

law, from death, and from the wrath of God. As in the Epistle to the Hebrews, so here redemption is regarded as consisting in the forgiveness of sins, while the Pauline representative atonement and the righteousness "accounted" by reason of faith disappear from view. But the forgiveness of sins is an idea which has no distinct expression in Paul's Epistles. There is, however, in this Epistle a point of contact with Paul which is wanting in Hebrews in the doctrine of being buried with Christ in baptism and rising with him from the dead.*

3.—THE EPISTLE TO THE EPHESIANS.

The Epistle to the Ephesians shows so marked a dependence on that to the Colossians that the opinion that it is a working over of the latter appears to be well supported. It was evidently written to counteract certain tendencies which indicate the beginnings of Gnostic errors which were probably different in detail from those combated in the former Epistle. There appears to be indicated a tendency to heathen libertinism, to a depreciation of Judaism, and to mystery-worship, to counteract which the writer lays stress upon the moral requirements of Christianity not without a predilection for certain Jewish points of view. Judaism appears to be brought into closer relations with Christianity than is consistent with the original Pauline view of the matter, when the gentiles addressed are said to have been formerly "without Christ." since they were "aliens from the commonwealth of Israel and strangers to the covenants of the promise." Unpauline too is the idea that Christ in his death "broke down the middle wall of partition between" Jews and gentiles,† not less than the

* Col. ii. 12.　　　　　　　† Eph. ii. 12–15.

expression, "God of our Lord Jesus Christ." In the Christology of the Epistle is observable a tendency toward the monotheistic point of view in the avoidance of the doctrine of Colossians that Christ had a part in the creation of the world, although expression is given to the idea that in him all things subsist. The mediation of Christ has relation to the Christian economy, but antedates his earthly manifestation, so that we have our "inheritance" in him "the Beloved," "being predestinated according to the purpose of Him who worketh all things after the counsel of His own will." * While Christ is here as in Colossians regarded as the reconciler of "things in heaven," but not as disarming principalities and powers and leading them captive in triumph, he is said to have been exalted after his resurrection, and "seated at the right hand of God in the heavenly regions far above all rule and authority and power and dominion and every name that is named not only in this world but also in that which is to come." † After the manner of Paul the author indeed regards salvation as "by grace" and as "the gift of God," but the Pauline conceptions of justification by faith and of the opposition of faith and works are foreign to him. As a Hellenistic thinker he could not entertain these Jewish ideas and that of a representative atonement. He accordingly says nothing of Christ's death as a bearing of the curse of the law, but rather sees in it an offering acceptable to God for the sake of the Church. The effect of Christ's ethical act of sacrifice is the purifying dedication of the Church to a nuptial union with him through the forgiveness of sins. Having been dead in trespasses, believers are made alive with him. The expressions employed in describing this result, "dead in trespasses,"

* Eph. i. 6, 11. † Eph. i. 20 f.

" made alive in Christ," " forgiveness of sins," "to be brought near," belong to the later Paulinism of Hebrews and Colossians and not to the genuine Epistles of the apostle (Heb. vi. 1, vii. 19, ix. 22, x. 18; Col. i. 14, ii. 13). Here as in Colossians are wanting the specifically Pauline expressions "to declare righteous," and "righteousness of God." The disappearance of some of the phases of the Pauline thought, among which may be noted that of "accounting" one righteous through faith, is as striking as is the prominence given to others which were naturally more akin to Hellenistic modes of thinking, such as being "raised up with him," "life with Christ," etc., as well as to the unpauline idea of the forgiveness of sins.

In the Christology of Colossians the emphasis is laid upon Christ as the "fulness of the Godhead" and the . reconciler of the things in heaven and the things on the earth. But in Ephesians the mission of Christ is conceived with especial reference to the establishment of a united Church by a reconciliation of Jews and Gentiles, the partition wall between which two parties he is said to have removed by his death.* In the former Epistle Christo-

---

* Eph. ii. 14. The opinion appears to be well grounded which regards the Christology of this writer as a development of that of Paul. The idea of preëxistence is common to both, but Paul had no conception of a preëxistent Christ *in* whom were included by a divine predestination all who should belong to him, so that he becomes an ideal representative of the Church, the personified idea of Christendom in whom believers were chosen ",before the foundation of the world" (i. 4–14). The Christology of the Epistle indicates a tendency toward the more developed Johannine conceptions, particularly in the teaching that Christ "descended" to the earth, and that "he who descended is the same as he who ascended" (iv. 9 f, *cf.* John iii. 13). The ascending of Christ "in order that he may fill all things" reminds us of Colossians. In fact, the Christology of the two Epistles is substantially the same, but while in Colossians the prevailing interest in the exaltation of Christ is directed against an unchristian worship of angels, in Ephesians the

17

logical speculation reached its height in the conception of Christ as the *pleroma* of Deity, while in the latter the Church as the body of Christ is his "fulness," "the *pleroma* of him [Christ] who filled all with all." *   The idea of the Church as the mystical "body of Christ," which is contained in the two Epistles,† is not Pauline, but was probably suggested by the words of Paul that " Christ is the head of the man," and that "we though many form one body in Christ." ‡   But Christ is not here conceived as one member of the body, or the head, but the Spirit which animates the body, for Paul evidently did not think of the man, as the body of Christ, of the wife as the body of the man, and of Christ as the body of God. But the writer of Ephesians appears to draw such a conclusion from the conception of Christ as the head of the Church, or Christ and the Church as constituting an organic unity, when he enjoins upon husbands the love of their wives as their own bodies. §   The Church as the " fulness" of Christ or the realization of his nature in a human expression is regarded in its growth as " the building up of his body."   All the members animated by the " head," " well put together and compacted," " grow up in all things unto him." ‖   There appears thus to be attached to the

motive is to bring him as a cosmic principle into the closest possible relation to the Church. He gave himself up for the Church, and in his preëxistent state forsook his Father for its sake (v. 31, 32).

* Eph. i. 23, iv. 13.   This was evidently written with reference to the Gnostic idea of the $\pi\lambda\eta\rho\omega\mu\alpha$, " the filled," a term employed for the supersensible world as opposed to the material world or the $\kappa\acute{\epsilon}\nu\omega\mu\alpha$, " the empty."   It is probable that the writer thought that he was refuting Gnosticism on its own grounds and with its own terminology when he declared Christ to be the one who "*filleth* all with all."

† Col. i. 18, 24 ; Eph. i. 23, iv. 12, 16, v. 23.

‡ 1 Cor. xi. 3 ; Rom. xii. 5. *Cf.* 1 Cor. xii. 27.

§ Eph. v. 28,   ‖ Eph. iv. 12, 15, 16.   *Cf.* Col. ii. 19.

pleroma the idea of an increase whose result is that "we all attain to the unity of the faith and the knowledge [*epignosis*] of the Son of God, to a full-grown man, to the measure of the stature of the *fulness* of Christ." * "The building up of the body of Christ" is said to be effected by the agency of apostles, prophets, evangelists, pastors, and teachers, to each one of whom is given grace according to the measure of the gift of Christ who when he ascended on high "gave gifts to men." † In this teaching of the gift of "the Spirit of wisdom and revelation" by which "the eyes of the mind are enlightened" there is evidently an approximation to the later doctrine of the fourth Gospel regarding the Holy Spirit, which is there conceived as sent by Christ for the further illumination of his followers. ‡

The Epistle has a mythology well developed in the direction of demonology. The readers are admonished to put on the whole armor of God that they may be able to stand against the wiles of the Devil; for the conflict which is to be waged is not against flesh and blood, but against the Evil One who shoots "fiery darts" and against a whole hierarchy of demons who are named according to their supposed classes as "principalities, powers, and world-rulers of this darkness," "spiritual hosts of evil in the heavenly regions." § On the contrary the absence

---

* Eph. iv. 13, *Cf.* Col. ii. 19, αὔξησις τοῦ θεοῦ, "increase wrought by God."

† Eph. iv. 7, 11.

‡ Eph. i. 17, 18, iii. 5, iv. 11. *Cf.* John xiv. 16, xv. 26, xvi. 7.

§ Eph. vi. 10, 14. Here not only the phraseology but the whole conception of the Christian conflict is different from Paul's. He wrote, indeed, of "the God of this world" who darkens the understandings of believers (2 Cor. iv. 4) but conceived that the conflict of the Christian was against the flesh, not against "principalities and powers" and "the spiritual hosts of

from the Epistle of all eschatological features is remarkable. There is no mention of the great Pauline doctrine of the second appearance of Christ and no intimation as to the conclusion of the work of the Saviour, which appears to be conceived by the writer with almost exclusive reference to the exigencies of his time, which were "the building up" of a united Church of Jewish and gentile Christians and the reconciliation of opposing parties in Christ the Head.

4.—THE FIRST EPISTLE OF PETER.

The writing traditionally designated as the First Epistle of Peter and addressed "to the strangers scattered through Pontus, Galatia, Cappadocia, Asia, and Bithynia, chosen according to the foreknowledge of God," etc., is an exhortation to patience under suffering and to a life worthy the Christian name, which probably dates from the end of the first century or the beginning of the second. It shows approximations to the Johannine teaching and an acquaintance with and dependence on the Pauline Epistles, and on Hebrews, the Epistle of James,

evil in the heavenly regions." Such a conflict is not even mentioned in Colossians, the writer of which regards the hostile powers of the invisible world as overcome in Christ's death on the cross, and led away in triumph. A further development in this direction appears in the fourth Gospel, where together with the higher significance of the person of Christ a more concrete and distinctive expression is given to that of his great adversary, the Devil, the opponent of God and of Christ. There the large number of evil spirits, which the writer of Ephesians employed to enhance the supernatural power of the Evil One, disappears, the wickedness and hatred of the great Archon of this world are emphasized, and bad men are represented as composing his host (John xii. 31, xiv. 30, xvi. 11). With relation to the development of doctrine on this subject the Epistle occupies a middle position between the Pauline and the Johannine views. *Cf.* Köstlin, Lehrbegriff des Evan. u. der Briefe Johann., p. 375, and Pfleiderer, Der Paulinismus, 2te Aufl. p. 460.

and perhaps Ephesians. It reveals nothing of any peculiarities which may be supposed to have belonged to Peter, but rather agrees so much with the teaching and diction of Paul that it can only be regarded as one of the developments to which the great impulse which proceeded from him gave rise. It is not, however, a thorough-going representative of Paulinism, and is not distinctively concerned with the great controversies which Paul started. Rather it shows how half a century after the time of the great apostle his ideas were modified and adapted to later exigencies and modes of thinking. The accords which the Epistle shows with the Pauline writings accordingly indicate a contact with his general religious and ethical ideas rather than with his distinctive doctrines.* The writer says, indeed, to his gentile readers that they have been saved from their former mode of life "by the precious blood of Christ as of a lamb without blemish and' without spot." † Christ suffered for us, *leaving us an ex ample* that we should follow his steps.‡ The purpose of his sacrifice was to bring us to God.§ It is evident that

---

*Compare 1 Peter i. 5 with Gal. iii. 23 ; 1 Peter ii. 6, 7 with Rom. ix. 33 ; 1 Peter ii. 13, 14 with Rom. xiii. 1–4 ; 1 Peter iv. 10, 11 with Rom. xii. 6, 7 ; 1 Peter v. 1 with Rom. viii. 18 ; 1 Peter iii. 8 with Rom. vi. 10.

† See John i. 29 ; Heb. ix, 14.

‡ 1 Peter ii. 21. The words: "Who himself bore our sins in his own body upon the cross" ($\dot{\epsilon}\pi\grave{\iota}$ $\tau\grave{o}$ $\xi\acute{v}\lambda o\nu$, "carried them up to the cross ") rather implies a taking away of our sins than the Pauline representative atonement, the bearing of the curse of the law. This idea of purification through the death of Christ is clearly expressed in the words which follow : " In order that having become alienated from our sins [$\dot{\alpha}\pi o\gamma\epsilon\nu\acute{o}\mu\epsilon\nu o\iota$, having died to them] we may live to righteousness." A similar ethical-practical result of the death of Christ is expressed in i. 18 : " Not with perishable things, silver or gold, but with the precious blood of Christ, were ye redeemed *from your vain manner of life* received by tradition from your fathers."

§ 1 Peter iii. 18.

the moral influence of the death of Christ is the predominant thought of the writer, and that the Pauline idea of a representative atonement for sin, of Christ's bearing the curse of the law, and of justification by faith were absent from his mind. Faith, indeed, has no subordinate place in the Epistle, but it serves a practical and hortatory rather than a dogmatic end, and the readers are exhorted to remain firm in it, opposing the adversary, the Devil. The conception of faith, as Pfleiderer remarks, is not the genuine Páuline one, but that of Hebrews and the I Epistle of Clement. Its object is not Christ as the historical Saviour from sin, but Christ as the glorified one, now indeed invisible, but soon to be revealed in order then to bring deliverance. The Pauline idea that he that hath died has been justified (set free) from sin assumes here the expression: " He that hath suffered in the flesh hath ceased from sin," * thus receiving the moral application that the desire for sin ceases in the sufferings of the flesh. Salvation is apprehended as an appropriation of the disposition of Christ and a following of him in patience under suffering and persecution. His death serves us as an " example," and by his resurrection and exaltation to " glory " we learn that our " faith and hope are in God." Baptism is the antitype of the Noachian deluge, and is regarded as saving the believers, not after the mystic conception of Paul as a symbol of dying with Christ and being raised with him to a new life, but as having the moral significance of the earnest seeking for a good conscience, by the resurrection of Jesus Christ which is conceived apart from all mysticism as the motive for this moral covenant with God. †

The writer of this Epistle shows a tendency to find in

* I Peter iv. I.   † I Peter iii. 21, 22.

the Old Testament, like the author of Hebrews, models and types for Christians and Christian institutions,* and surpasses Paul and the latter writer in his view of prophecy, assuming that not merely the Holy Spirit but the spirit of Christ dwelt in and spoke through the prophets, declaring " beforehand the sufferings to come upon Christ and the glories which were to follow." † An exaltation of Christianity consistent with itself throughout is apparent in various parts of the Epistle. To believers " is the honor," and their joy is " full of glory "; they are called out of darkness into a " wonderful light "; they are born of imperishable seed " through the word of God which liveth and abideth "; on them " resteth the spirit of glory and of God." ‡ Whether on account of the writer's purpose to adjust differences and establish harmony in the churches or for some other reason the Epistle contains no definite Christology. The spirit of Christ in the prophets "testified of the glories which were to follow," that is, perhaps, his resurrection and exaltation " on the right hand of God, having gone into heaven, angels and authorities and powers being made subject to him." § The Epistle has no distinctive eschatology, and contains only incidental recognition of the popular expectation of the early second coming of Christ. The readers are admonished to see to it that " the proof of their faith may be found unto praise and glory and honor at the manifestation of Jesus Christ," and to be sober and hope for the grace that is to be brought to them at that time.

* 1 Peter iii. 5, 6, 20 f.

† 1 Peter i. 10, 11. *Cf.* John xii. 37–41 ; Heb. viii. 8–12.

‡ 1 Peter ii. 7, i. 8, ii. 9, i. 23, iv. 14. *Cf.* John xvii. 22, i. 5.

§ 1 Peter iii. 22 ; *cf.* Col. ii. 10 ; Eph. i. 20 f. 1 Peter iv. 11 ; *cf.* Heb. xiii. 21.

"When the chief Shepherd shall appear" they "will receive the crown of glory that fadeth not away." * The writer appears to express more definitely than Paul the doctrine of a general resurrection and judgment at the Parousia in the words: "Who shall give account to him who is ready to judge the living and the dead." † The bold innovation upon Pauline and all other antecedent Christian teaching is ventured in giving place to the tradition that Christ went in the spirit "and preached to the spirits in prison who were disobedient in times past when the long-suffering of God waited in the days of Noah," ‡ and in the more general teaching that "the Gospel was preached to the dead that they might indeed be judged according to men in the flesh, but might live according to God in the spirit." § The doctrine of the descent of Christ to the underworld, probably between his death and resurrection, and of his ministry to sinful spirits there, is no doubt unequivocally expressed here, and all attempts to give another meaning than this to the words in question are grounded upon a faulty exegesis. Other mythological features are less developed in this Epistle than in Ephesians. The "adversary, the Devil," is, however, distinctly recognized, and compared to "a roaring lion" who "walketh about seeking whom he may devour." ‖

It is characteristic of the deutero-Pauline literature of

---

* 1 Peter i. 7, 13, v. 4.　　　　　　　　† 1 Peter iv. 5.

‡ 1 Peter iii. 19 f. Baur's interpretation of this passage by referring "the spirits in prison" to the angels who were supposed to have sinned (2 Peter ii. 4) does not appear to be well sustained. Theol. Jahrb. 1856, p. 254 f. and Neutest. Theol., p. 291. See also Spitta, Christi Predigt an die Geister, and von Soden on the passage in question in Holtzmann's Hand-Commentar.

§ 1 Peter iv. 6.　　　　　　　　‖ 1 Peter v. 8.

the New Testament that it shows a more decided influence of the Alexandrian speculations than appears in the Epistles of Paul and the effects of contact with Gnostic ideas in their origin. Greek thought here manifests itself in the beginning of the conquest which it was destined to win. The exaltation of the person of Christ is carried to the extent that a cosmic position is assigned to him. He is regarded not only as the medium of the creation of the world, but as a cosmic world-spirit in whom all things subsist, and his work as Saviour includes not mankind alone but the universe of spiritual existences. His victory is over principalities and powers whom he leads captive in triumph, and through him is revealed to the spiritual entities " in the heavenly regions " " the manifold wisdom of God according to His purpose for ages." He was not one of the Gnostic æons, but the *pleroma* of the Godhead dwelt in him bodily. It corresponds with his exalted position that he should have been not merely the preacher of the Gospel to men, but to the dead in the underworld, that his conquest of the powers of evil might include the gloomy realm of hades, when he should have " ascended on high, and led captivity captive." The dualistic antithesis of heaven and earth, the Son's kingdom of light and Satan's kingdom of darkness, appears in these writings prior to its more definite expression in the fourth Gospel. The Gnostic conception of God as absolutely removed from the world is avoided, and the Father is the Creator through the medium of the Son, below whom, however, are powers akin to the Alexandrian orders of demons and the angels of the early Syrian Gnosticism, who have apparently some claim upon mankind which is annulled through Christ, being " nailed to the cross." The death of Christ has its significance rather with reference to the claims of these world-powers than, as with Paul, with regard to God and the demands of His righteousness, and in relation to men directly is conceived as a moral influence and example.*

* On the subjects treated of in this chapter the student may consult: Hilgenfeld, Einleit. in das N. T., 1875, pp. 352–390, 618–641, 659–680 ; Holtzmann, Einleit. in das N. T., 2te Ausg. 1886, pp. 276–296, 326–345, 514–524 ; Davidson, Introduction, 1868, i. pp. 168–194, 216–279, 372–440; Bleek, Der Brief an die Hebräer, etc., 1828–1840 ; Riehm, Der Lehrbegr. des Hebräerbr., etc., 1858–9; Wieseler, Untersuch über den Hebräerbr., etc., 1861 ; Baur, Neutest. Theol., pp. 230–265, 287–297 ; and Paulus 2te Ausg. ii. pp. 3–49 ; Pfleiderer, Der Paulinismus, 2te Ausg.,.ii. Th. chap. 2. Urchristenthum, pp. 620–684 ; Köstlin, Lehrbegr. des Evangel. u. der Briefe Johannis, 1843, pp. 352–365, 472–481; Weizsäcker, Apostol. Zeitalter, 2te Ausg. pp. 488 ff, 560 ff ; Holtzmann, Ephes. u. Kol. Briefe, 1872, pp. 206–241; Meyer's Comm. on Col. and Eph., and Meyer-Huther on 1 Peter ; Salmon, Introd. to N. T., 5th ed., on the Epistles in question ; Lightfoot on Col. and Ellicott on Col. and Eph. ; Weiss, Bibl. Theol. of N. T., Eng. Transl., i. pp. 204–221, ii. pp. 75–118, 166–229 ; Toy, Judaism and Christianity, pp. 118, 119, 430 ; Schwegler, Das nachapostol. Zeitalter, 1846, ii. pp. 1–28, 304–344.

CHAPTER V.

THE JOHANNINE TRANSFORMATION.

ALEXANDRIAN speculation had already about one hundred years before the composition of the fourth Gospel by its doctrine of the Logos prepared the way for the Christology which constitutes a distinctive feature of the apprehension of Christianity which is called Johannine. Johannine is, however, a conventional designation, and is used as such by those who do not believe that the great writing which contains this interpretation of the gospel of Jesus proceeded from the apostle John, the son of Zebedee.* The internal character of the fourth Gospel shows that it was written with a doctrinal rather than an historical purpose, and reveals an author whose point of view and culture were fundamentally different from those of the original apostles of Jesus. The influence of Alexandrian thought is much more distinctively apparent here than in the Pauline and deutero-Pauline writings, not only in the application of the Logos-idea, but also in the conception of the relation of God to the world; so that there appears to be ground for affirming that this Gospel could not have been written independently of the works of Philo, and good reasons for believing moreover that its author was well

* For a discussion of the authorship and date of the fourth Gospel the reader is referred to the author's Gospel-Criticism and Historical Christianity, Chapter vii. and the literature of the subject therein mentioned.

in touch with the characteristic ideas of this Jewish-Greek speculator. It will not be possible within the limits proposed for this work to enter into a detailed discussion of the opinions of Philo which are related to the doctrines of the fourth Gospel. Reference can only be made to them as occasion may require.* Suffice it to remark here that fundamental characteristics common both to Philo and this Gospel are a dualistic conception which places God and the world in distinctive contrast, and the theory of a mediation of the two opposites through a divine messenger and interpreter, the heavenly Logos. The Johannine doctrine of the Logos requires explanation, since it cannot be supposed to have sprung into existence without a cause. Indeed, the form in which it is presented in the prologue to the Gospel presupposes that the author assumed it to be already known to his readers. The theory that it was an esoteric teaching of Jesus first made known by the disciple John, the assumed author of the Gospel, can only be maintained by cutting off the synoptic tradition, to which it is unknown, from all connection with an apostolical source. The doctrine of the Logos who in the beginning was God and with God, through whom the world was made, who as the only-begotten Son is a being partaking of the divine essence, and who as a mediator between God and the troubled cosmos comes to his own, and flashes as a light upon the insensate darkness, finds a natural and historical connection only with the philosophy

* The student who is interested in studying the speculations of Philo in detail will naturally consult his complete works either in the original or in the English translation (Bohn's Library) and the expositions of his opinions by Gfrörer, Philo und die Alexandrinische Theosophie, etc., 1831, Dähne, Geschichtliche Darstellung der judisch-alexandr. Religions-Philosophie, 1834, Réville, La doctrine du Logos dans Philon., etc., and Drummond, Philo Judæus and the Alexand. Philosophy, 1888.

of Philo. With the Word of God in the Old Testament these ideas can have only a forced and artificial connection; and if the sources of much that is contained in Paulinism and deutero-Paulinism must be sought elsewhere than in its pages, one will certainly search them in vain for the historical antecedents of the Johannine conception of the Logos. Philo did not, indeed, connect the Logos with the Messiah, if he ascribed to this agent in fact any real personality at all (a question which we must leave to be settled by his commentators), and it may be doubted whether he could have united the functions of the two consistently with the Jewish Messiah-idea. The fourth evangelist, however, in combining the ideal principle of the Logos with the historical personality of Jesus of Nazareth gave to the Philonic mediating agent, the Logos, a definite form and a religious character which the Alexandrian speculation was in the nature of the case unable to compass.

The tendency of the Christology of the New Testament to exalt and idealize the person of Christ reaches its highest point in the fourth Gospel. The synoptic evangelists contented themselves with a supernatural birth, a descent of the Holy Spirit at the baptism, and an apocalyptic coming with the clouds to judgment. Paul conceived of him as the preëxistent "man from heaven," the archetypal "second Adam," the Spirit. In the deutero-Pauline Epistles he becomes the agent of creation, the great highpriest, the brightness of the divine glory, the image of the person of God, the sustainer of all things, and the victor who leads captive the principalities and powers of evil in triumph in his train. The doctrine of the fourth Gospel is an advance beyond the antecedent views, and may be regarded as a development of them. Here the historical Jesus is represented as the divine Logos who was in the beginning with God, and was God, by whom the world was made, who became flesh and took up a temporary abode among men to reveal the Father and return to His bosom whence he came forth. The writer's doctrine of the person of Christ and his purpose to exalt him to the highest eminence short of an equality with the Deity are evident in the declaration that "the Logos was God."* In this expression God is evidently the predicate, and the meaning can only be that the Logos was a being who, though not identical with the Supreme Being, yet partook of His nature and essence. In the conception of the Logos and in the terms employed of him there appear to be implied on the one hand his separate personal existence, and on the other a most intimate connection with the Deity and even a movement toward unity with Him. † The genesis of the Logos-idea is undoubtedly to be found in the thought, which is not, indeed, foreign to the Old Testament, that God does not immediately reveal Himself, but is in His essence invisible and incapable of direct manifestation.   Under the influence of Platonic and Stoic

---

* θεὸς ἦν ὁ λόγος, John i. 1. Philo also called the Logos God, a second God, and distinguished him from the Supreme Being by omitting the article before θεός as applied to him (θεός, instead of ὁ θεός).

† The expression of the relation of the Logos to God which is contained in the original cannot well be rendered in an English translation. The words "with God" and "in the bosom of the Father" (John i. 1, 18) are expressed in the Greek in a manner intended to convey "ideal annexation," "always turning toward," "moving toward the heart of God and seeking to remove in unity with Him all that separates and distinguishes from God." The structure is that of prepositions with verbs of rest which are more frequently employed with verbs of motion, πρὸς τὸν θεόν, εἰς τὸν κόλπον, etc. "Difference in unity and unity in difference" appears to be a happy expression of the relation implied in the terms employed. See Winer, Gram. of N. T.; Grimm-Wilke's Clavis N. T.; and Baur, N. T. Theol. on the passages.

speculations, this idea became prominent in the Jewish-Alexandrian philosophy of Philo, in which the Logos is the epitome of all the divine powers. Proceeding forth from his immanence in God,* in which condition he is conceived as containing the archetypal world in himself, the Platonic real world, the world-ideal, he becomes the sum-total of the relations of God to the world,† to whom are ascribed creation, the communication of power and endowment, light, life, and wisdom, so that he is not essentially different from the divine Spirit in qualities and the effects which he produces, though in fact only the manifestation of Deity. Accordingly, he is the image of God, the oldest and first-born son of God, the possessor of all the fulness of Deity, the mediator between God and the world. If it be conceded, as it probably must be, that unless in the Christian consciousness of his time Christ had already been exalted to the eminence of a divine being, it would not have occurred to the author of the fourth Gospel to apply to him the current Logos-idea of the age, it is evident that he could not have given more effective expression to the estimation in which he was held than by applying to him this Philonic designation, which may have been suggested by the fact that the Christian doctrine was called the word (logos) of God. In the meaning of Logos the idea of "word" or organ of revelation is fundamental, since logos is reason only so far as "thought is conceived as also a speaking or expression." It has been shown that in the conceptions which we find in the prologue to the Gospel, Logos, life, light, fulness, grace, truth,‡ there are analogies with Gnostic ideas and

* As the "inward Logos," λόγος ἐνδιάθετος.
† As the "uttered Logos," λόγος προφορικός.
‡ λόγος, ζωή, φῶς, πλήρωμα, χάρις, ἀλήθεια.

in particular with the doctrine of the æons, and that there is some ground for the theory that the exalted and purely spiritual apprehension of Christianity, and the dualism of God and the world, light and darkness, etc., which finds frequent expression in the Gospel, indicate the influence upon the writer of Gnosticism in its earlier stages at least. But it should be noted that the author is silent regarding a proceeding of the Logos from God, his emanation or generation with which Gnosticism and Christian theology zealously occupied themselves. Apart from calling him the only-begotten Son he appears intentionally to avoid all speculations of this sort, and to assume a dependence of the Logos upon the Father without entering into metaphysical inquiries regarding its nature.

The Johannine doctrine of the nature of God and of His relation to the world constitutes an important feature of the fourth Gospel. The basis of this theology is monotheism, and God is recognized, as in Philo and the Old Testament, as the highest Being, God in the absolute sense, "the only true God." * The fundamental and most distinctive doctrine concerning God is contained in the words ascribed to Jesus in his conversation with the Samaritan woman : "God is Spirit, and they who worship must worship in spirit and in truth." Related to this doctrine is the teaching of the prologue that " No one hath ever seen God ; the only-begotten Son who is in the bosom of the Father, he hath made Him known." † So clear and definite an expression of the spirituality of God is found in no antecedent writing of the New Testament. Not only are all corporeal predicates of Deity excluded,

* John xvii. 3. v. 44 ; *cf.* I John v. 20, and Philo's τὸ γενικώτατον, " the most generic thing."
† John iv. 24, i. 18.

but it is implied in the emphatic declaration of the spirituality of His nature that all spatial limitations of His
worship, as Jerusalem and Gerizim, are incompatible with
it. From this point of view it is held that spirit cannot
be regarded as one of the predicates of the Deity, as
if one should speak of the spirit of God, but that Spirit
and God are identical terms, and that in His absolute
essence He is Spirit. As Spirit, God is the antithesis of
" the flesh " ; * He is the truth by preëminence, and nothing has validity and permanence which does not come
from him. His word is truth, and they who do the truth
perform works which are wrought in Him. † He is also the
living One who has life in Himself and communicates it
to the Son ; ‡ as such he is not, however, the eternal
repose of the Gnostics but rather the Philonic ever-active,
absolute source of energy. As He "worketh hitherto,"
and no Sabbath-rest is known to Him, so the Son may
work on all days. § He is the original source of all creative, sustaining, saving activity, and the Son who, like the
Philonic Logos, is His manifestation and agent, does
nothing but what he sees the Father do and is commis-
sioned by Him to execute. ‖ While the attributes
ascribed to God in the fourth Gospel are also ascribed to
Him in the Alexandrian philosophy, the doctrine that He
is Spirit was unknown to the latter.

In the Johannine doctrine of the relation of God to
men His love is assigned a prominent place, as in the
synoptic record. Philo had previously dwelt with considerable fulness upon this quality of the divine nature.

---

* John i. 13, vi. 63.
† John xvii. 17, iii. 21, 33, viii. 26 ; *cf.* 1 John i. 5, "God is light," etc.
‡ John v. 26, vi. 57.
§ John v. 17.   ‖ John v. 19, 30.
18

He even includes external nature among the recipients of
the prodigal goodness of God which is manifested in the
rain poured into the sea and in the fountains which are
made to gush forth in desert places.   In His munificence
God bestows good things upon all, even upon the imper-
fect, that He may provoke them to the pursuit of virtue,
and shows pity toward the unworthy.   "He not only
pities after He has judged, but judges after He has pitied ;
for with Him pity is older than judgment."   He made
the world not for Himself, for before the creation He was
sufficient unto Himself, but because He was "good and
bountiful." *   Without stint there are awarded to those
who are worthy "the abundant riches of the graces † of
God " which "issue from ever-flowing fountains, peren-
nial, unceasing, and without intermission."   The fondness
with which Philo dwells upon this quality of the divine
nature is indicated by the numerous predicates which he
applies to it.   God is munificent, giver of wealth, kind,
and lover of man, benevolent, propitious. ‡   Were it not
for the love of God all men would perish.   All the good
things which they possess, virtue, piety, good-will, righteousness, faith, etc., are His gifts, and it is the greatest
sin for man to attribute any good to himself.   So great,
indeed, is the prodigality of the divine beneficence that
it is necessary that it be restricted by the limited capacity
of its recipients ; for the created, being too weak to receive its vastness, would faint unless the lot of each were
measured out in due proportion.   As in Philo, so in the
Johannine thought, love is the predominant motive of
the divine activity.   It is eternal in the divine nature, and

* ἀγαθὸς καὶ φιλόδωρος.

† χάριτες, graces or favors.

‡ χρηστός, φιλάνθρωπος, εὐμενής, etc.

God loved the Son before the foundation of the world.*
The direct declaration that " God is love " is not, indeed,
contained in the Gospel, but this teaching of the first
Epistle of John is perhaps implied in it, if it be compatible
with this doctrine that a class of men should be designated as the special objects of His love. We do not find
in this Gospel such expressions of the impartial goodness
and love of God as that " He maketh His sun to rise on
the evil and on the good," and the teaching that men
ought to love their enemies that they " may become sons
of their Father who is in heaven," the " merciful " One
who " is kind to the unthankful and the evil." † The
writer shows no predilection for dwelling on the goodness
and mercy of God, and in this respect he is not to be
compared with some of the prophets and psalmists and
even with Philo. God's love of the world and His good-
will and beneficent purpose toward all men in the mission
of Christ are declared in the words : " God so loved the
world that He gave the only-begotten Son, that every one
who believeth on him may not perish, but may have everlasting life. For God sent not the Son into the world to
condemn the world, but that through him the world
might be saved." ‡ Yet notwithstanding this declaration
of the universal divine good-will it must be conceded
that the author of the Gospel did not escape the influence
of the Gnostic dualism of his age, that he never loses
sight of the two realms of light and darkness which
stand in eternal opposition to each other, and that he
frequently represents the children of light as the special
if not the sole objects of God's love, while he conceives

* John xvii. 24 ; yet a special reason for the Father's love of him is given
in another place, x. 17.

† Matt. v. 45 ; Luke vi. 35.   ‡ John iii. 16, 17.

the unbelieving children of darkness to be in a condition which is little short of hopeless. Love of Christ and belief in him on the part of men are represented as the condition of the bestowal of God's love upon them. "He that loveth me will be loved of my Father"; "If any one love me he will keep my word; and my Father will love him."* These fortunate ones "were" God's, and He "gave" them to Christ. They are not of the hostile and darkened "world," but "believed," and are made the sole subjects of the prayer of the departing Christ, who is "glorified in them."†

In the terms of this prayer it appears to be indicated that there is a class of men who are the especial objects of the divine interest and of the regard of Jesus, those whom God has "given" to him and those who "may believe through their word." The petition for these is that they may be kept from the Evil One, and that they may be made perfect in one, so that "the world" may know that Christ is the sent of God who loves them as him.‡ On these falls the light of hope and of celestial favor. The unbelievers appear, however, to be left in the shadow of seclusion and disfavor. Jesus is made to say expressly that he does not pray for "the world," presumably because they who are represented by this term, the children of darkness and unbelief, are not objects of the Father's love, since it definitively declared that he who does "not believe in the Son shall not see life, but the wrath of God *abideth* on him." § This must be regarded as one of the hard sayings of this "spiritual" Gospel, and it reminds one much rather of the vehement Baptizer, the

---

* John xiv. 21, 23, *cf.* xvii. 23, 26.
† John xvii. 6, 9, 10, 16.
‡ John xvii. 20, 21.   § John iii. 36.

fiery Revelator, and the impetuous Paul, than of the Jesus of the synoptists, even when pronouncing the seven woes. This peculiarly Johannine idea that those who " were " God's, from what antecedent time-limit does not appear, the believers in Jesus and those who should be their followers, are the especial objects of the divine love, stands in immediate connection with the doctrine of judgment which is set forth in this Gospel. One has only to read it superficially to see that the predominant principle of discrimination between men is not character, but belief or unbelief in Christ. He that believeth shall not perish, but hath eternal life, shall never thirst, shall not die, though dead shall live, shall do greater works than Christ himself performed ; while he that believeth not abideth in darkness, and is the object of the divine " wrath." * The chief object of the mission of Christ is that men may believe, and the Gospel is declared to have been written expressly for this purpose. † We miss here the emphasis upon conduct which we find in the Sermon on the Mount and in such words as : " He that heareth my words and doeth them, I will tell you to whom he is like," etc. Again, we find in this Gospel no trace of the deutero-Pauline doctrine that all men are " by nature children of wrath," ‡ and the Pauline teaching that " the law worketh wrath " § upon the whole race as fleshly and unable to fulfil it does not appear to have been accepted by the writer. Rather does he seem inclined toward the Pauline doctrine of predestination which, as has been shown, the Apostle did not reconcile with his fundamental propositions, for those who in this Gospel are said to be " of

* John vi. 35, 47, v. 24, xi. 25, 26, xii. 46, xiv. 12.
† John vi. 29, xi. 15, xiv. 29, xvii. 21, xx. 31.
‡ Eph. ii. 3.   § Rom. iv. 15.

God," " of the truth," who by a natural impulse inborn in the children of light or by a divine determination (" drawn " by the Father) come in faith to Christ, suggest Paul's "vessels of mercy which God had prepared before for His glory." *   Accordingly, judgment in the Old-Testament sense, one may even say in the sense of the apocalyptical eschatology of the synoptists, is unknown to the Johannine theology. It is expressly declared that " the Father judgeth no man, but hath committed all judgment unto the Son," † and yet he " came not to judge the world," ‡ for he that believes is not condemned, and the unbeliever " is condemned already." § The believers " were " God's, and as to them there is required only " the realization of the relation in which they always stood to God," which is effected by the revelation of the truth in Christ for which they who love the light have a natural affinity. Hence Christ is made to say that he judges no man, and that he was not sent into the world in order to judge it ; ‖ and the conception of judgment which the writer evidently represents is that of a process inwardly effected, a " crisis " determined by the attitude of men toward Christ and the " light," without an external decree or an apocalyptic assize. This " crisis " or separation between those who love the " light " and those who love " darkness," the children of God and the children of " the world," which is hostile to Him according to the dualistic conception of the writer of the Gospel, is, so to speak, automatically carried on by the natural gravitation of the two classes without the interference of God or Christ. The " word " which Christ has " spoken " will judge at the last day.¶

* John xviii. 37, vi. 44 ; Rom. ix. 23.   † John v. 22.
‡ John xii. 47.   § John iii. 18.
‖ John viii. 15, iii. 17.   ¶ John xii. 48.

The dualism of the author of the fourth Gospel culminates in the conception of a personal power of evil. This conception was not, however, original with him. As the intensity of his idea of the hostility of the children of darkness was due to the opposition which in his time the non-Christian world manifested toward Christianity, and as Hellenism furnished him with a philosophical basis for dualism, so Judaism, Hellenism, and antecedent Christian thought, supplied a well-developed doctrine of Satan. In the book of Wisdom it is taught that by the envy of the Devil sin came into the world; in the synoptic Gospels Jesus begins his career by a victory over him, and throughout his ministry contends with and subjugates demonic powers; Paul represents Satan as an adversary whose "devices" he knew;* and in the deutero-Pauline literature is developed, as we have seen, a hierarchy of evil powers. In the Johannine thought Satan plays a conspicuous part as a power at the head of all the forces of evil and directly opposed to God, Christ, and all that is good. He is "the prince of this world" (Paul had already named him "the God of this world"), the Devil,† "the Evil One."‡ He was "a murderer from the beginning"; "he abideth not in the truth, because there is no truth in him"; "when he speaketh a lie, he speaketh from his own nature, for he is a liar and the father of it."§ The hatred of and opposition to Christ manifested by the Jews are chargeable to him as their source, for these enemies of Jesus who are filled with animosity toward him, and are ready to slay him, are declared to be "the children of the Devil." But his opposition is destined to failure. He fights a losing battle. He is doomed to be "cast out," to

---

* 2 Cor. ii. 11, iv. 4, xi. 3, 14, xii. 7.

† *ὁ διάβολος.* ‡ *ὁ πονηρός.*

§ John viii. 44 ; *cf.* Wisdom ii. 24.

be "judged," and to be overthrown.* The sphere of his
activity is different in the fourth Gospel from that which
is assigned to him in the synoptics. In the latter, as in
Paul, he exercises a malign influence upon the bodies of
men ; but in the former his realm is conceived as spiritual
and ethical. Hence in the Johannine record no demoniacs
appear, and Satan rules not over orders of demons and the
powers of the air, as in the deutero-Pauline literature, but
in the souls of the children of darkness. From this teaching
of the overthrow of Satan it is evident that the Johannine
dualism is not carried to the point of conceiving him to
be the peer of God. But although a subordinate being
who is unable to stand against the powers of good represented by the Logos, he is not regarded as created. At
least no explicit declaration is made concerning his origin.
Was he perhaps conceived as uncreated, eternal, like the
darkness to which he is allied, that in the Hebrew cosmogony was present before the foundation of the world?
That he was not thought to have been originally good,
an archangel who fell from a high estate to become the
prince of darkness, appears to be implied in the remark
that he was a murderer "from the beginning." It can
hardly be reconciled with the point of view of the writer
of the Gospel that he should have regarded the personifi-
cation of evil as a creation of God, a part of the "world"
which was made through the agency of the good Logos.
Did he adopt the Gnostic view according to which the
Demiurge (the inferior God, the Jaldabaoth, the creator
of the world, the God of the Jews) was the father of the
serpent ?† Words in viii. 44 may with great plausibility
be interpreted as favorable to this view, for they are capa-

---

* John xii. 31, xvi. 11 ; *cf.* 1 John iii. 8.
† Iren. Adv. Haer., i. 30, 8 ; Epiph. Haer., xxxvii. 4.

ble of being rendered : "A liar is also his father." * But the words do not require this rendering, and the connection favors the ordinary interpretation: "He is a liar and the father of it," though Meyer renders them : "He is a liar and the father of him [the liar]." It is very improbable, besides, that the author of the Gospel could have conceived of a Demiurge, or a creative god, subordinate to the Deity, since to him the Logos is the former of the world. Avoiding all metaphysical inquiries as to the origin of evil, he seems to have contented himself with referring its manifestations in the darkened world to an uncreated power.

The more sharply the transcendent God and the world under its "prince," the personified power of evil, were contrasted, the greater was the need of a mediator between them, an organ of revelation, through whom those who were to be saved might be rescued from the dominion of Satan and the realm of darkness. As in Philo, so in the Johannine thought, this mediator is the God-allied Logos who by nature stands in immediate connection with the supreme Being, is in fact divine, and as such called God. He condescends, however, from his high estate to come into relations with men in order to give to as many as would receive him power to become children of God. † Without entering into metaphysical speculations as to the mode of his origin, the writer of the Gospel contents him-

---

* Ψεύστης ἐστὶν καὶ ὁ πατὴρ αὐτοῦ. It is noteworthy that Hilgenfeld so interpreted these words in Das Evangel. und die Briefe Johannis, 1849, in Die Evangelien, etc, 1854, and in Einleit. in das. N. T., 1875. But it has not fallen under the notice of the writer that this scholar has been followed in his interpretation of the passage by any authorities. He also reads, ἐκ τοῦ πατρὸς τοῦ διαβόλου ἐστέ in the same verse, "Ye are of the father of the Devil."

† John i. 12.

self, and we may suppose satisfied his contemporary readers, with the teaching that the Logos was " the only-begotten Son," * and that his manifested " glory " was as
that of " an only-begotten of a father." †   In this sonship
is implied a community of essence with the Father, and
it is evident that " the Son of God " in the fourth Gospel
represents a conception essentially different from that
contained in the term in the synoptics.   The Christian
consciousness of the age in which the Gospel was written
required an exaltation of Christ not inferior certainly to
that which had been accomplished in the deutero-Pauline
literature, and could apparently be satisfied with nothing
short of conferring upon him all the glory and divinity
that could be bestowed in consistency with the monotheistic doctrine, which must of course be kept intact.
The declaration that the Logos was " in the beginning
with God " indicates an intention of the writer to avoid
all perplexing questions regarding the time and the manner of the generation implied in sonship, and in the idea
of Son as well as in the teaching that he " was God " he
conveys the doctrine of an essential identity of essence
with God, unity and likeness with Him, which are emphatically expressed in the declaration that he who has seen the
Son has seen the Father. ‡   That the unity of the Father
and the Logos is conceived as one which is not incompatible with difference of personality and independence
of the individual self-consciousness is evident from the
words said to be spoken of the disciples: " That they all
may be one, as Thou Father art in me and I in thee."§
As one with the Father, the Son is not only called God,
but is represented as receiving adoration as " Lord and

* μονογενὴς υἱός, John i. 18.   † John i. 14.
‡ John xii. 45, xiv. 9, *cf.* x. 30, 38.   § John xvii. 21.

God." * It is evident, however, that this dignity is conceived to belong to him only as Son, since absolute existence is plainly ascribed to the "only true God" alone. The Son is, indeed, "the truth and the life," but not absolutely such. He is "the way" by which men may come to the Father, and only through him can they come. † As God, though not "the only true God," divine qualities are ascribed to him, and he is ranked with the Deity as an object of faith. "Everything that the Father hath is mine," he is made to say. "As the Father hath life in Himself, so did He give to the Son also to have life in himself." ‡ He is represented as having supernatural knowledge, as knowing all things, heavenly as well as earthly, the human heart, and God Himself, as annihilating space with his far-seeing vision, and penetrating into the distant future with prophetic foresight.§ He is able to disclose the hidden things of God and of the celestial realm, for he speaks as one knowing from what he has seen and heard.‖ Not only does the Father show him all things that He does, but whatever the Father does that does the Son in like manner. ¶ As the organ of almighty energy, he is endowed with the most marvellous miraculous powers, and easily performs works which surpass all the wonders of the earlier evangelic tradition. Yet with all this godlikeness of endowment he is in all things dependent on and subordinate to the Father, unable to do anything of himself, and speaking only the words which are given to him from above. The Father is "greater" than he. **

* John xx. 28.   † John xiv. 6.
‡ John xiv. 1, xvi. 15, v. 21, 26.
§ John vi. 64. xvi. 4, 30, xvii. 25, i. 18, 48, ii. 25, iii. 12, 31, x. 15, vii, 29.
‖ John iii. ii. 32, vi. 46, viii. 40.   ¶ John v. 19, 20.
** John v. 19, xiv. 16, 28.

His oneness with God is manifested in the complete sub-ordination of his will to that of his Father, which with unselfish devotion he seeks to do for the divine glory. To do the will of Him who sent him, this is the food which his disciples knew not of.*

While the Johannine Logos-idea was probably derived from Philo, as has already been remarked, the relation of the two conceptions is not by any means such that the one covers the other. Rather they differ in that the Alexandrian is metaphysical and vague, and the Johannine is religious and concrete. The fact is significant that the author of the fourth Gospel applies the term Logos to Christ only twice, once in speaking of his preëxistence, and again in mentioning his incarnation. This is done, too, in the prologue, where he was writing independently of the evangelic tradition, and could express without restraint his individual views. Throughout the rest of the Gospel, however, other than metaphysical and specu-lative interests become dominant, and with all the in-fluence of a dualistic conception approaching Gnosticism, he comes under the sway of the personal Jesus as reve-lator, teacher, Saviour, and Son of Man.† In Philo the Logos has a place in a highly speculative system, if, in-deed, the thought of the Alexandrian may properly be said to constitute a system, while in the fourth Gospel the metaphysical Logos appears only in the prologue to an ideal life of Jesus at the basis of which lies the conception of the oneness of the Son with the Father. Accordingly, despite the abstract terms "life" and "light" which are applied to him, the Logos of the Gospel becomes a con-crete personality who, though not at all conceived as having an earthly, temporal development like the Jesus

* John iv. 34, xiv. 13.   † John i. 51, iii. 13, v. 27.

of the synoptists, is yet a human type of piety and filial submission to the divine will. Apart from the idea of the Logos as participating in the creation, as God, and in the beginning with God, the metaphysical coloring of the Philonic thought is here wanting, and the Logos appears as a representative of personal religion, of a divine-human sonship, and of a mystical-ethical relationship to the Father. He has a personal mission to men, that as many as believe on him may become children of light. He is "the way, the truth, and the life," the source of divine illumination and truth to men among whom he appears, heaven-descended, for a brief time as a teacher and guide. But remote as the Christ of the fourth Gospel is on the metaphysical side from the Logos of Philo, he is not less far removed on the historical side from the Jesus of the synoptists. These writers, who based their works upon the recollections of eye-witnesses and the Palestinian tradition, could have found no suggestion of the super-human heavenly Logos in their materials or in their environment. For the genesis of this Johannine conception there was needed the whole antecedent development of the idealizing of the person of Christ—the ideal man from heaven conceived by Paul, who did not proceed upon a personal knowledge of the historical Jesus, and the deutero-Pauline enhancement of this doctrine, together with the Logos-speculations of the Alexandrian philosophy. The Johannine idea of Jesus is a riddle in relation to the synoptic conception of him only to those who refuse to regard both doctrines historically.

That the preëxistence of the Logos is fundamental in the Johannine Christology has already been intimated. Not only is this doctrine laid down in the speculative prologue to the Gospel in the propositions that he was

" in the beginning with God," and was God, and that the world had its becoming through him, but the writer puts into the mouth of Jesus himself the most unequivocal declarations of a celestial existence prior to his appearance in the flesh. He is made to say that he " came down from heaven," and to speak of ascending " where he was before." He who came from heaven speaks not of earthly things, but of what " he hath seen and heard." * Is he charged with making himself greater than Abraham? His answer is: " Before Abraham was I am." †   That he should have been conceived as inactive in his preëxistent state and without interest in the work which in the flesh he was to accomplish is *à priori* improbable. He is, indeed, expressly said to have had a part in the formation of the world. While it is not implied that, according to the doctrine of Hebrews, he upheld all things by the word of his power, it is more than implied that before entering upon his work in the world as the incarnate Son he was active in reference to the foreordained economy of salvation. The idea that the Christian economy was foreseen and prepared before the creation of the world was already current long before the composition of the fourth Gospel. The kingdom was prepared " before the foundation of the world "; the " mystery " of the Gospel was hidden for generations, and " for eternal ages unrevealed "; the Christian believers were " chosen " in Christ before the creation ; and the proclamation of the gospel was a making known to " the principalities and powers in the heavenly

* John iii. 13, 32, vi. 62.

† John viii. 58.   The use of the verbs of existence here is striking : " Before Abraham became or was born [γενέσθαι] I am [εἰμί]." In εἰμί is expressed being in itself, and the idea of becoming is perhaps excluded. That is, Jesus according to his divine essence was before time and without a becoming such as may be predicated of men.

regions the manifold wisdom of God according to His purpose for ages." * Accordingly, the author of the fourth Gospel regards the preëxistent activity of the Logos as dating from the very beginning of the creation. It would be arbitrary to suppose that man was not included in the world (cosmos) which "became" through the agency of the Logos, and to assume that the human race was thought to be for ages without his influence. Indeed, the evangelist expressly asserts that "life" was in the Logos, and that "the life was the light of men." Furthermore, this "light" which he was from the beginning "hath been shining in the darkness, and the darkness received it not." † The ethical-religious illumination which proceeds from him is conceived to have shone in pre-Christian times, for he is the true light which lighteth every man that cometh into the world, ‡ so that every one may if he will become a child of the light. Since the Logos is the organ of divine revelation, he is conceived to have been active in this capacity in pre-Christian times, as Philo and the Alexandrian translators of the Old Testament regarded the Theophanies of Hebrew story as manifestations of Deity through him or simply as Logophanies. From the same point of view the author of Hebrews represents the preëxistent Christ as speaking through the prophets and psalmists with reference to his

---

* Matt. xxv. 34 ; Rom. xvi. 25 ; Eph. i. 4, iii. 9 ; Col. i. 26 ; 1 Peter i. 20.

† John i. 4, 5. The present tense, $\varphi\alpha\acute{\iota}\nu\epsilon\iota$, signifies "shines from the beginning until now without interruption." See Meyer. The conception is that of a supernatural, heavenly $\varphi\tilde{\omega}\varsigma$ which manifested itself through revelation and prophecy.

‡ This is the interpretation favored by most exegetes, and there does not appear to be sufficient reason for following with Noyes the rendering of Hilgenfeld, Ewald, and others : " The true light which lighteth every man was coming into the world." See Meyer *in loc.*

earthly mission, and reveals the Alexandrian influence not only in this conception but also in the allegorizing of the Old Testament with which he seeks to establish it.*

There can be no doubt that at the time of the composition of the fourth Gospel the tendency to Christianize the Old Testament by an allegorical interpretation which read into it prophecies of the circumstances attending the mission of Christ was in full force. In adopting this idea and method the evangelist followed the example of preceding writers, as may be seen in the first Gospel, the Epistles of Paul, Hebrews, Barnabas, and other writings. This appropriation and Christianizing of the Old Testament as the revealed word of God answered an urgent need of the Church in the second century, and we accordingly find that the writer of this Gospel in common with his contemporaries saw its chief significance in the supposed testimony which it could be made by the current methods of interpretation to bear to Christ. Consistently with this point of view it is declared that Moses wrote of Christ,† while in apparent inconsistency with it an unconcealed hostility to the Jews leads the writer to depreciate the law and the entire Old Testament and to put into the mouth of Jesus the harsh declaration that all the teachers who had preceded him were thieves and robbers.‡ Not only is Moses expressly contrasted to his disadvantage with Christ, but the events at Cana and the pool of Bethesda are perhaps allegorical representations of the inadequacy of the ancient economy. When he makes Jesus denounce the Jews as the children of the Devil, the author is thought to follow the writer of Barnabas who attributed their fleshliness to the influence of demons, although he

---

* Heb. ii. 12, 13. x. 5–9. † John v. 46.
‡ John viii. 44, i. 17, v. 39, x. 8.

avoids the Gnostic dualism which the latter approached, and maintains the connection of the Jewish and Christian economies. Perhaps the inconsistency which appears in the appeal to Old-Testament prophecy and the depreciation of Judaism and its great law-giver may be explained by the theory that "the prophets, so far as they correctly foretold the Christian economy, were thought to be the organs of revelation through whom the preëxistent Logos expressed himself," while the Jewish religion in general as mere "law" and rite was regarded as of little worth. At any rate the idea of the preëxistent activity of the Logos was not unknown to the writer, and doubtless finds expression in the words: "I have other sheep which are not of this fold," * in which Jesus is made to assume that the light which had from the beginning shone from the Logos upon the darkness of the world had been effectual among the heathen, so that there were some of them who were children of light, who belonged already inwardly to the fold of the good Shepherd, and needed only to be "gathered together." † The revelation of the Logos through the prophets is distinctively expressed in connection with a quotation from Isaiah concerning the hardening of the people's hearts toward Jesus in the words: "These things said Isaiah because he saw his glory, and spake of him." ‡ This conception is in accordance with the fundamental idea of the fourth Gospel, with that which constitutes its distinctive doctrinal character, viz., that the Logos was preëxistent and immanent in God, that he hypostatically proceeded forth from Him for the act of creation, and then was active as a creative, life-giving, illuminating personal power, effecting in essen-

---

* John x. 16. † John i. 5–9 ; xi. 52.
‡ John xii. 41.
19

tial godlikeness God's revelation of Himself in the spiritual realm, and finally completing that revelation in the man Jesus Christ. All the revelations preceding his earthly manifestation are, however, conceived as only the twilight in contrast with the dawn. "The sombre nocturnal heavens of the old covenant are sown with lights which shine only as reflections of the dawning daylight of the New Testament. Moses and the prophets are only moon and stars whose borrowed light testifies of the existence of the still invisible Sun, before whose effulgence they must finally pale and be extinguished. The last witness is the briefly-shining morning-star which announces the approaching sunrise, and which must decrease as the splendors of the Sun increase." *

If, then, the revelation of the Logos in his earthly manifestation was thought to be more glorious than that effected by his preëxistent activity, we should expect to find that his entrance upon human relations was not regarded as a descent from his heavenly dignity. In fact the author of the fourth Gospel does not, like Paul, speak of Christ's mission in the flesh as an humiliation. The declaration that the Logos became flesh, which is a capital proposition of the Johannine doctrine, does not at all imply the assumption by him of a complete human nature. Although the word flesh is sometimes employed in the New Testament by synecdoche for the entire man, and again to designate the natural in man as opposed to the spiritual, it is usually applied to human nature to distinguish it as essentially a bodily organism. To become flesh, then, can neither mean to become carnal, nor to become wholly man, but only to assume a fleshly body. It is true that in the fourth Gospel Jesus is made to speak

* John iii. 30, 31, v. 35.

of laying down his life for men, * but that the animal life-principle is here intended is evident from the use of the same term in Peter's declaration: " I will lay down my life for thee." † The ascription to Jesus of affections of the soul or spirit does not necessarily imply the conception by the evangelist of a human soul as the subject of the trouble or emotion. On the contrary, the divine Logos as the organ of revelation may very well have been supposed to be so related to human nature as a mediator as to be capable of such affections of the soul as are attributed to him. ‡ The manner in which the evangelist speaks in the prologue of the two manifestations of the Logos, the pre-existent and the earthly, implies rather a continuity of the activities of an identical personality than a becoming man in the sense of assuming a human soul. The incarnation can hardly be said to be conceived as denoting a division of the work of the Logos into two distinct periods. It is the same subject that was the light of the world shining upon its darkness from the beginning, and in the flesh continuing his revealing and life-giving activity. The *Logos* became flesh, and took up a temporary abode as in a tent § among men. The incarnation of the Logos appears, then, to have been conceived not as an assumption by him of a human nature in its entirety, but as an accident of the personality of the preëxistent divine Son who in the flesh remained essentially the same being as before. There are traits of the fourth Gospel which appear to be traceable to this point of view. In the original tradition on which the synoptic Gospels are founded Jesus is represented as a man, and his endowment for his mission

---

* John x. 11, 15, 17.   The word here employed for life is ψυχή.
† John xiii. 37.   ‡ John xi. 33, xii. 27, xiii. 21.
§ ἐσκήνωσεν.

is consummated in the descent of the Holy Spirit at the baptism. A later tradition added a supernatural generation. In this Gospel, however, the account of the baptism is omitted, although a descent of the Spirit is mentioned, not as an endowment of the divine Logos, but as a sign to John that he might be able to recognize him as the Son of God.* A supernatural generation could find no place in a narrative which proceeds upon the assumption that the Christ whose earthly history is recorded was the preëxistent divine being who was .with God in the beginning, and was God. As the Logos he was regarded as already abundantly endowed, and the process in question would naturally be thought to be superfluous. In accordance with this idea of the divine nature of Christ the story of the temptation is omitted. The prince of this world has nothing in him, and it would be incongruous to suppose that the great Logos could be tempted, as well as that a forty-days' fasting and struggle in the wilderness could be a fitting preparation for his ministry. The Johannine Christ has no awful agony in Gethsemane, and to forebodings of suffering and death he gives no expression. On the cross he utters no heart-broken cry of a human soul which feels itself abandoned of heaven, but majestically exclaims, "It is finished," and dies like a god.

The employment of the term "Son of Man" in this Gospel is not opposed to but rather illustrative of the point of view in question. The use of the term in several instances by the writer is probably due to the influence of the synoptic tradition of which he could not have been independent.† But the expression is not used as in the

---

* John i. 33.

† The principal passages are : i. 52, iii. 14, v. 27, vi. 27, 53, xii. 23, 34, and xiii. 31.

synoptics in frequent connection with the lowly estate of a wandering teacher who "has not where to lay his head." The idea of a participation in human nature of the one who bears the name is not conveyed by the relations in which it stands; for although the writer undertook to construct a history of Jesus, he never loses sight of the dominant dogmatic purpose of his work which is definitely set forth in the prologue. The Son of Man is represented to Nathaniel as one on whom he shall see angels descending from the opened heavens, that is as the organ of revelation, the Logos, who effects as a mediåtor communication between the upper and nether realms. To Nicodemus the Son of Man is represented as the one who "came down from heaven." As the celestial preëxistent being he "is in heaven,"* that is, "he maintains even in his earthly estate as the incarnate Logos the continuity of his consciousness of God," and is able as no one else to give report of "heavenly things." Whatever may be the meaning of the much-disputed passage: " And He gave him authority to execute judgment because he is a son of man," † the entire connection in which the words stand indicates a purpose to exalt Jesus in accordance with the dogmatic aim of the Gospel. He is the Son, the Son of God, to whom belongs the honor which men give to the Father, and at the sound of whose voice the dead will come forth from their graves. ‡ The most that can be said of the term in this connection is that it designates the Logos, a human phenomenon in the capacity of judge, as the representative of the hidden God who "judges no man," or in other words, the relative humanity of him

* John iii. 13.
† John v. 27, "a son of a man," the usual article is omitted.
‡ John v. 23, 28, 29.

who is the Son of God—a conception whose Philonic origin is evident. The words: "Truly, truly do I say to you, unless ye eat the flesh of the Son of Man and drink his blood ye have no life in you," * stand in connection with the declaration that Christ is "the living bread which came down from heaven," and the term Son of Man is employed with a doctrinal significance similar to that conveyed in the latter words which accord with the point of view of the prologue. The heaven-descended one gives the true bread, and they who appropriate him in faith will háve eternal life. †

The words already quoted from the Gospel in the discussion of its doctrine of the preëxistence of the Logos confirm the view here presented of the continuity of his existence and nature in the heavenly and earthly abodes. He who was upon the earth as Jesus is conceived as the one who was before in heaven, and "came down" thence. There is no intimation, either in the words which express the individual reflections of the evangelist, or in those put into the mouth of Christ, that the writer thought of the doctrine that the Jesus of history was the preëxistent Logos united with a human spirit. The expression, "the Logos became flesh," simply means that he who was "with God" and "was God" assumed a human body. It is evident that in the study of the doctrines of this Gospel one cannot without great arbitrariness distinguish between the reflections of the evangelist and the words which he puts into the mouth of Christ. The latter have the appearance of being free compositions of the writer, since the extended and involved discourses which are attributed

* John vi. 53.

† Meyer regards the words "of the Son of Man," as equivalent to $\dot{\epsilon}\mu o\tilde{v}$, " of me."

to Jesus cannot have been transmitted by tradition like the pithy, aphoristic sayings recorded by the synoptists. The entire work bears the impress of one mind, and the discourses have been happily characterized as variations on the theme contained in the prologue. The problem how the divine, preëxistent Logos assumed a human body is not solved by the fourth evangelist. It does not even appear to have been thought of by him. Two representations of Jesus, that of the prologue and that of the synoptic tradition, stand side by side throughout the Gospel without an attempt to reconcile them, one may even say without a conceivable reconciliation. With the utmost *naïveté* Jesus is said to have been in " glory " with the Father " before the world was," to have " come down from heaven," * and yet to have had a mother and brothers, even Joseph as father. † The Logos become flesh is identified with the historical Jesus of Nazareth, ‡ and made to appear as a human personality after the manner of the synoptic tradition with respect at least to his descent from earthly parents, without, however, any intimation of a supernatural generation. While this incongruity does not admit of solution, it may perhaps be explained in its genesis as the inevitable result of an attempt to unite in one representation the historical Jesus with the Philonic conception of the heavenly Logos from a point of view which borders very closely on the Gnostic doctrine of Christ as actual personality composed of the man Jesus of Nazareth and the heavenly æon united with him at the baptism. Yet the predominance of the idea that he was the Logos in the flesh is apparent

* John xvii. 5, vi. 38.
† John ii. 1 f., 12, vi. 42, vii. 3, 5, xix. 25, 26.
‡ John i. 46.

even when the writer approaches most nearly to the
representation of him as a human personality. For in
connection with the passages in which the writer makes
him speak of his dependence upon the Father appears
the declaration that the Father is greater than he, * from
which it is evident that his dependence upon God is not
that of a man. The writer could not have made him say
that God is greater than a man, but the intention is obvious to teach that Christ notwithstanding his oneness with
God stood in a relation of subordination to Him. †

The Johannine doctrine of salvation constitutes a
striking feature of this type of New-Testament teaching.
In its fundamental characteristics it is related to the dualistic conception of the opposition of light and darkness,
and consists in the overcoming of the latter through the
self-revelation of the Logos. The Logos is the light
which from the beginning illuminates every man that
comes into the world, and on his part the manifestation
of himself is a saving efficacy. On the part of men it is
faith in him who has come as a light into the world which
saves them from the realm of darkness, for whoever believes does not " remain in the darkness." ‡ As many as
believe in him become sons of God, have eternal life, and
do not come into judgment.§ Now, since the degree of
faith depends upon the intensity with which its object is
presented, a vivid manifestation and a persistent " glorify-

* John xiv. 28 ; *cf.* iv. 34, v. 30, viii. 29, xv. 10, xvii. 4.

† The doctrine maintained by Baur that the writer of the fourth Gospel
intended to represent the flesh of Christ as not that of a human body "in its
true and full sense," in other words, that he held the Docetic conception of
the body of Christ as apparent only but not real, is hardly defensible. It
rests upon such passages as vii. 10, viii. 59, x. 39, vi. 16, all of which admit
of satisfactory explanation without this hypothesis.

‡ John vii. 46.   § John v. 24, vi. 47.

ing " of Christ might be expected to form a prominent feature of this soteriology. In fact we find that the exaltation of his person is a leading object of the Gospel, that all that relates to salvation is intimately connected with him whose word is a fountain of " living water," and that the greatest emphasis is laid upon the necessity of " receiving " him into the consciousness of the believer, the appropriation of him as " the bread of life." They who will be saved must, however, carry on a continuous conflict with the unbelieving world which will hate them as it hated the Son of God. Corresponding to the great antithesis of light and darkness is the antithesis of belief and unbelief, and only in so far as the light flashing upon the darkness illuminates the souls which are susceptible to it, and causes them to " come to " it, is the dominion of unbelief and of the prince of this world overcome.

So far as the teachings of Jesus are regarded as one of the principal means of accomplishing his saving work, they have according to the point of view of this Gospel a distinctive reference to his person, the absolute significance of which is the prominent theme of his discourses. This significance does not, however, lie as with Paul chiefly in the closing acts of his career, but in his revelation of the truth, especially as to the Father's will and love. The doctrine laid down in the discourse addressed to Nicodemus that unless a man be " born from above " he cannot enter the kingdom of heaven serves to introduce and emphasize the teaching that such " heavenly things " are to be known through the testimony of the Son of Man " who came down from heaven," and testifies that which he has seen.* The teaching communicated to the woman of Samaria reaches its culmination in the exaltation of the person of

* John iii. 11, 13.

Jesus as the one able to supply the "living water" which will be to him who drinks of it "a well of water springing up into everlasting life."* In the extended discourse in the fifth chapter Jesus is not only charged by the Jews with making himself equal with God, but proceeds to furnish at least the appearance of a justification of the charge by identifying his "raising up the dead " and "giving life " with the divine activities, and by claiming such honor as men accord to the Father. Hearing him and believing in God are declared to be the two apparently equally important conditions of attaining everlasting life.† The spiritually dead will hear in the hour that is coming and now is the voice of the Son of God, and they who hear, that is, shall have given attention, will live. The qualification for this mighty work is declared to reside in the life which the Son has in himself, as God has life in Himself. Yet the hearers are told not to marvel at this, for the marvellous performance is to be the calling forth into life of all the bodily dead ; " The hour is coming in which all that are in the tombs will hear his voice, and will come forth, they who have done good to a resurrection of life, and they who have done evil to a resurrection of condemnation."‡ This general conception is further elaborated in what follows, and Jesus is shown to be not only the life-giving principle, but the nourishment and support of all spiritual life under the figure of " the true bread from heaven " which Moses did not give. To come to him is never to hunger and to believe in him is never to thirst. In his personality as the Logos become flesh there are for those who will feed upon him spiritual health, nourishment, and life. The bread which he will give for the life of the world is his flesh ; for he is not

* John iv. 14.   † John v. 23 f.   ‡ John v. 28, 29.

merely the Logos but, as the Saviour of men, the Logos in the flesh, so that what he is to them as the bread of life is designated as flesh, and even as flesh and blood. He who eats his flesh and drinks his blood has everlasting life, and he will raise him up at the last day. In his manifestation in human flesh he is solely and absolutely the life of the world. He who will receive him as such by faith, that is, will eat his flesh and drink his blood, will dwell in Christ, and Christ will dwell in him. His oneness with God, that absolute glorification of his person which is a distinguishing feature of this Gospel, is indicated in the bold saying: "As I live by reason of the Father, so he that eateth me shall live by reason of me." The divine life-principle is identical in both, "and this is the will of the Father that every one that looketh on the Son and believeth in him shall have everlasting life." * In the development and application of the conception of "light" which the evangelist makes fundamental in his doctrine of the nature and mission of Christ the emphasis is not laid so much upon the teachings us upon the personality of the Logos. While in the synoptic Gospels the doctrines and the example of Jesus are placed in the foreground, we find here the obtrusive purpose to give prominence to his personality. He himself is the light of the world, and he who follows him will not walk in darkness, but will have the light of life. As long as he is in the world he is the light of the world.† Even the so-called "new" commandment that the disciples should love one another is brought into relation to his person. They are commanded to love one another as he had loved them, he who gave them an example of self-devotion in the act of washing their feet,—an act whose significance

* John vi. 34–58   † John viii. 12, ix. 4.

was immeasurably great by reason of the greatness of the condescension of the doer,—he who gave his flesh as the bread of life for the world in a love than which no man has a greater.* The authority with which he commands rests upon the importance of his person. Well may his followers do what he bids and does who is in such a relation to God that his love for them is comparable to that of the Father for him. †

In accordance with the doctrine that belief in Christ is essential to salvation, his works as well as his teachings are exhibited for the purpose of glorifying his person. As proofs of what he is his works are called "signs," ‡ or revelations of his divine nature and glory ; and since he can do nothing but what he sees the Father do, all his works have a supernatural character. They are the expression of his divine nature, are such as no one has ever done, are works in fact which the Father accomplishes through him, and are evidences of his supernatural mission, for the sake of which those must believe who will not believe on account of his words. § The unbelief of the Jews is declared to be especially censurable because of the signs which he had shown them,‖ and the miracles are said to be done for the manifestation of his glory and that of the Father. ¶ In the case of a healing performed on the Sabbath he is not only made to say that he is on an equal footing with God, in that like Him he works regardless of days, but the explicit declaration is put into his mouth that he has a better testimony than that of John, for : " The works which the Father hath given me to perform, the works

---

* John xiii. 34, 4–16, xv. 13.
† John xv. 9.　　　　　　　　　　　　　　　‡ σημεῖα.
§ John v. 17 f., xiv. 10, xv. 24, x. 38.
‖ John x. 32, xii. 37.　　　　　　　　　　¶ John ii. 11, xi. 4, 40.

themselves which I do, bear witness of me that the Father hath sent me." *   In the account of the feeding of the five thousand nothing is said of Jesus' "compassion " for the multitudes, † for the Logos of this Gospel is not represented, like the Jesus of the synoptics, as having the sentiment of pity, but the sign is brought into connection with a doctrine of the person of Christ as " the bread of God," " coming down from heaven and giving life to the world." ‡ The account of the marvellous cure of a man born blind is introduced with the announcement of the remarkable teleological declaration that he was so born in order that " the works of God might be made manifest in him," and the performance of this " sign " is made the occasion of repeating the statement of the favorite doctrine of the writer that Jesus is " the light of the world." § The greatest of all the signs that Jesus is reported in this record to have wrought, the raising of Lazarus, is said to have been done for the purpose of causing the disciples and " the multitude standing around " to " believe," and is recorded in order to introduce a new doctrine of his person.   He was glad that he was not present with Lazarus during his illness, that the disciples may believe, and at the grave he prays in order that the multitude may believe, when they shall see the prayer answered, that he was sent of God ; and the doctrine that the Logos is life and by his power is able to overcome death is expressed in the words :   " I am the resurrection and the life ; he that believeth in me, though he have died will live, and whoever liveth and believeth in me will never die."   Thus the principal signs reported in this Gospel serve to glorify Christ and to set forth from different points of view the greatness and

---

* John v. 36.   † Matt. xiv. 14 ; Mark vi. 34.
‡ John vii. 32.   § John ix. 5, *cf.* i. 4, viii. 12.

divine significance of his person in such a manner as to produce in men that faith in him which is the indispensable condition of their salvation. It is a total misapprehension of the point of view of the writer of this Gospel to suppose that he records the wonderful works of Christ either as deeds of benevolence or simply as historical facts. They are intended as evidences of his divine mission and authority, proofs that the Father sent him, and reasons why men should believe in him and be saved.

As the death of Jesus was the culmination of his earthly career, so the exaltation of his person and the manifestation of his power and saving efficacy are represented in this Gospel as reaching in this event their highest point. In view of the approaching tragedy Jesus is made to exclaim : " Father, the hour is come ; glorify Thy Son, that Thy Son may also glorify Thee."* In being "lifted up " † Jesus is represented as not merely raised upon the cross, but as attaining the acme of his spiritual elevation and attractive power. He is accordingly made to say that " as Moses lifted up the serpent in the wilderness, so must the Son of Man be lifted up, that every one who believeth in him may have everlasting life." Exalted as a spectacle to mankind in this supreme glorification, he will draw all men unto him. ‡ Instead of being an hour of humiliation and ignominy the hour of his death is that in which the Son of Man is to be "glorified." From this event dates the highest fruitfulness of his mission, for "unless a grain of wheat fall into the ground and die, itself abideth alone ; but if it die it beareth much fruit." § The powers of darkness which had arrayed themselves against him during his life, and opposed him as " the light of men," gather in the

* John xvii. 1, .*cf* xii. 28.　　　　　　† ὑψοῦσθαι.
‡ John iii. 14, xii. 32.　　　　　　§ John xii. 23, 24.

last hours to effect his defeat. The Devil enters into Judas,* and the Jews who are "the children of the Devil" plot his downfall. But in the approaching tragedy which his terrestrial and infernal enemies think will be the consummation of his overthrow he sees the discomfiture of the former and the dethronement of the latter. "Now," he exclaims, "is the judgment of this world; now will the prince of this world be cast out."† As the more he becomes an object of faith to men, the more does the power of the Evil One diminish, so in this act of spiritual exaltation in which he gives his flesh as "the bread of life" for the world he sees the beginning of the downfall of Satan and of an ever-widening sway of the dominion of his own truth and spirit, which will be consummated only when "all men" shall have been "drawn" to him.

As the Johannine Christ, the Logos who was with God "in the beginning," and "was God," is essentially a different conception from that of the Pauline second Adam and the man from heaven, so his work in the world and his relation to men as Saviour stand in fundamental contrast to the doctrine of salvation elaborated by Paul. Not inconsistent with this is, however, the fact that the fourth Gospel shows the influence of the Pauline thought. But Paulinism, as a whole, does not constitute its point of view. To one who had left Judaism and the law so far behind him as this writer had it is evident that a doctrine which was so much occupied with and determined by them as was Paul's could have only a slight importance. That he accepted, however, the Pauline teaching of the universal destination and mission of Christianity is as plain as that he did not regard it as a matter to be argued about in the manner of Paul. To him Christ is the light

* John xiii. 27.   † John xii. 31.

of the world, who lights every man that comes into it.
He regards Jesus as dying not for the Jews only, but that
he may also "gather together in one body the children of
God who are scattered abroad." *   Even in Samaria he
sees the fields already "white for the harvest." †   It is
true that in apparent inconsistency with this universalism
he distinctively declares Jesus to be the Messiah, and employs the Jewish designation of his person, ‡ which is not
elsewhere used in the New Testament.   But his Christ
has no national characteristics or limitations, and the
mention of him as of the seed of David occurs only as
the expression of a Jewish opinion.§   It is evident that
the writer occupied the point of view of a time when the
Pauline doctrine of the relation of man to God, and of
the office and work of Christ in salvation, held no prominent place in Christian thought.   We have already seen
that this teaching in the extreme and abstract form in
which it was presented by the apostle appeared to be
losing ground in the deutero-Pauline literature, and it is
not surprising that a writer who held such an attitude
toward the law as did the writer of the fourth Gospel
should not have regarded the deliverance of men from
obligations to it as constituting an important feature of
the saving work of Christ.   Nothing could be more incongruous with the Johannine conception of the work of
Christ than the Pauline idea that in his death he removed
the curse of the law, and representatively satisfied its
claims upon the human race.   The death and resurrection
of Christ occupy, indeed, both historically and doctrinally,
a prominent place in this Gospel, but they have not the
almost exclusive prominence which Paul accords to them.

* John xi. 52.   † John iv. 35.
‡ Μεσσίας, i. 44, iv. 25.   § John vii. 42.

Here the chief thing is the whole personality of Christ who, as the organ of revelation and the manifestation of God, communicates life and light to those who are receptive of them. He is the bread of God which those who eat will never die, the vine whose life-giving sap is communicated to those who abide in him, and apart from vital union with whom men can bear no fruit.* In the discourse of the Baptizer it is, indeed said, that Jesus is "the lamb of God who taketh away the sin of the world," † but this expression has not the sense of the Pauline representative death. Rather it is to be interpreted in accordance with the dominant idea of the Gospel as referring to the moral-spiritual influence of his whole personality and work by which sin was overcome and removed in those who received him. The Gospel has, indeed, a doctrine of faith, but no doctrine of the acceptance of men as righteous through faith in the specific Pauline sense of the words. The personal relation of men to the *living* Christ is vividly presented in the words " receive," " hear," and " come," which may be regarded as standing for " believe." ‡ Hence the Pauline opposition of faith and works finds no place in the thought of the writer of this Gospel. In adapting the gospel of Jesus to Hellenistic thinking he had no use for the great apostle's polemic against Judaism. He had advanced far beyond this point of view, which, indeed, although adapted to its time, was too one-sided and ideal in its disregard of the living personality of Jesus to answer the practical needs amid which the fourth Gospel was written. It comports with this practical point of view, indeed, that the writer

---

* John xv. 1, 4.   † John i. 19.

‡ John i. 11, 12, iii. 11, 32, v. 43, xii. 48, xiii. 20, viii. 43, 47, x. 3, 16, xviii. 37, vi. 35, 37, vii. 37.

20

disposes of the conflict between faith and works by making faith itself a work. When Jesus is asked by certain of the multitude: "What are we to do that we may work the works of God?" he is made to answer: "This is the work of God that ye believe in him whom He sent." *

It would appear, then, to be one of the characteristics of this wonderful Gospel that while it surpasses Paulinism in exalting the person of Christ, it furnishes a much-needed supplement, one may even say a correction, of the great apostle's doctrine of salvation by bringing Christian soteriology down out of the region of abstract speculation in which he had placed it, and establishing it upon a practical, rational basis. In giving prominence to the personality of Christ on the divine side of salvation it is consistent with its characteristic Logos-idea, while in putting emphasis upon works on the human side it denotes a tendency to a return to the primitive historical Christian conception of the relation of man to God which is set forth in the synoptical account of the teachings of Jesus. It introduces, however, a new principle which, since there is slight trace of it in the synoptic tradition, can hardly have received from the lips of Jesus the emphasis which is here laid upon it. This principle is that of personal attachment, love, and devotion to Jesus as an impulse to the moral and spiritual life. Accordingly, Jesus is made to say to his disciples: "If ye love me, ye will keep my commandments"; "He who hath my commandments and keepeth them, he it is who loveth me; and he who loveth me will be loved of my Father, and I will love him, and will manifest myself to him." † Likewise obedience to him confirms the abiding in his love:

* John vi. 28, 29.   † John xiv. 15, 21.

" As the Father hath loved me, so have I loved you; abide in my love. If ye keep my commandments ye will abide in my love, even as I have kept my Father's commandments and abide in his love." * Keeping the commandments or doing that which accords with the will of God and of Christ is thus made a matter of paramount importance with respect to the relation of man to God. While Paul places faith foremost, and regards love as the expression of it,† here love is first, and is the spring of the activity by which the commandments are kept. The Pauline doctrine of the impossibility of obedience finds no expression, but rather it is taught that the highest spiritual attainments are within the reach of him in whom abides the life-giving principle of love. He who loves Jesus is able to do all that Jesus requires, and among the requirements which he makes of his disciples is this, that they love one another. In accordance with the general principles of this Gospel the sphere of human activity is here connected with the divine Source of all good through the mediation of the Logos, and human love receives its supreme authentication in the love of Christ for the Father and the Father's love for him. Source and highest type of love is that love which the Father had for the Son before the foundation of the world. Because God loved the world the Son was sent forth from His bosom, and those who are drawn to him as the light of men he loves as the Father loves him. As the Son out of his love for the Father does all that the Father requires,‡ so out of their love for him should and can his followers fulfil his requirements. As he is one with God, so he prays that all believers " may be one; as Thou Father art in me and I in Thee, that they may also be in us, that

* John xv, 9, 10.   † Gal. v. 6.   ‡ John xiv. 31.

the world may believe that Thou didst send me.* " Thus
will be given them the "glory" which God has given to
him, because they are "perfect in one."† As the Son's
performance of his work is conditional upon his oneness with God, so his followers must in order to
"bear fruit" remain in oneness with him, "the
true vine." The love of believers for Christ has
its fruition in a state of supreme blessedness which
is nothing less than the enjoyment of a special expression of the divine love and a dwelling of God and
Christ with them : " If any man love me he will keep my
word, and my Father will love him, and we will come to
him, and make our abode with him."‡ This conception
is a transformation of the Old-Testament theocratic idea
of the dwelling of Jahveh with His people on condition
of their keeping His commandments;§ but here the
divine manifestation is that of the Logos in the flesh,
and the abiding of God is not in the temple and in Zion,
but a personal indwelling in the individual soul who keeps
the commandments, not by reason of an external decree,
but through a loving union with the Son. But the culmination of man's blessedness through Christ is reached
in a relation to God analogous to that which the Son himself holds. Through the mediation of Christ those who
are united with him in faith and love are given " power to
become children of God." They are born not of blood,
nor of the will of the flesh, nor of the will of man, but of
God. ‖ This new generation by which the moral and
spiritual character is transformed is probably the same

* John xvii. 21.   † John xvii, 23, 24.
‡ John xiv. 23.
§ Lev. xxvii. 3, 11 ; Ps. cxxxii. 13, 14 ; Ezek. xxxvii. 27.
‖ John i. 12, 13.

as the being born from above, without which a man cannot see the kingdom of God.*

In this highest conception of the Johannine thought, the doctrine of love, is apparent its contrast with the Pauline theory of salvation. In the former man is conceived to be brought by love into immediate union with Christ, and through him into harmony with God and divine sonship. Through love he is able to keep the commandments of Christ and do the will of God. But to Paul there stood in the way of the consummation of this simple and natural relation the obstacle of the law and the doctrine that righteousness is unattainable by works. The law has its claims which must be satisfied, its ransom which must be paid. Since this condition is conceived to be met by the death of Christ, this event becomes the factor in salvation which is of central importance. Hence the faith directed to the cross and the problem of the relation of faith and works in reference to the acceptance of men as righteous, or the doctrine of justification. In the Johannine doctrine, however, such a conception of the importance of the death of Christ could find no place. For although the author maintains, as has previously been remarked, a connection of Christianity with the Old Testament, declares Moses to have written of Christ, and believes that the preëxistent Logos was manifested to the prophets, yet his attitude toward the law as an institution was one of such lofty disregard that its claims appeared to him of slight importance. To him Christ exerts a saving activity, not especially in his death, as to Paul, but in his whole earthly mission and in the total influence of his personality. He is " the bread of God," the

* γεννηθῆναι ἄνωθεν, iii. 3.

light of the world, to those who "receive" him he gives .
power to become the children of God, and the water
which he supplies quenches forever the thirst of the soul.
As living and self-communicating, as the source of spiritual illumination and quickening, as the divine Logos who
brings God into relation with men, and men through love
for him into oneness with the Father, and not as a representative of mankind dying to abrogate an out-grown
"law," is he the Saviour of men according to this new
Hellenistic system of thought. It must be regarded as
the good fortune of Christianity that the author of this
Gospel, following and surpassing the deutero-Pauline
writers, presented a view of Christ as a Saviour by which
a direct personal relation was established between men
and the living Jesus conceived as a light and a spiritual
power. It was the weakness of Paulinism that its founder,
knowing nothing of a Christ " according to the flesh" and
apparently indifferent to such a knowledge, lost sight of
the supreme greatness and splendor of the personal life
and example of Jesus, and fixed the attention of men
upon his death and resurrection as the chief if not the
sole events in his career significant for the work of salvation.   If it must be conceded that this conception of the
mission of Christ regarded literally and abstractly has exerted a far-reaching deleterious influence upon Christian
thought and life, the importance of the Johannine teaching of the vast significance and exalted grandeur of the
personality of the living Christ as the supreme and immediate object of faith and adoring love becomes apparent.
With all its mysticism and its metaphysical Logos-speculation, it presents a view of the personality of Christ and
of his direct relation to men which meets the needs of
practical life, and corrects the Pauline interpretation in

the interest of establishing the empire of Christianity as a world-religion.

A marked peculiarity of the Johannine teaching is the doctrine of the continuation of the work of Christ after his departure by the Holy Spirit. The almost complete identification of Christ with God is indicated in the manner in which he is made to speak of the bestowal of the Spirit. Now it is the Father who will give the Paraclete that is, the Advocate, or Helper, by reason of the prayer of Christ, or who will send him in Christ's name, and again it is Christ himself who will send him.* The coming of the Paraclete is said to be conditioned on Christ's going away: " It is expedient for you that I depart ; for if I do not depart the Paraclete will not come to you." Again it is said: " For the Spirit was not yet, because Jesus was not yet glorified."† The presence in believers, and not the *existence* of the Spirit, is evidently referred to in this last passage. The existence of the Spirit is implied in the existence of God, since it is said to " proceed from the Father," and already to have been given to Christ " without measure," wherefore the latter " speaks the words of God." ‡ The Spirit appears to be regarded by the writer as shut up in God and Christ previously to the latter's departure from the earth, and to be conceived as thenceforward a personality in the character of the Paraclete. Personality is unequivocally predicated of him in several passages. He is placed beside Christ as *"another* Paraclete "—words by which it appears to be implied that by reason of the indwelling in him of the Spirit, Christ while on earth performs for his disciples in some sense the functions of the Paraclete, since he is not in the Gospel

* John xiv., 6, 26, xv. 26, xvi, 7.

† John vii. 39, xvi. 7.   ‡ John iii. 34.

distinctively called the Paraclete.   Again it is said of him that he " will bear witness" of Christ ; that he will "come" to the disciples, will be sent, and will be not merely *in* but *with* them ; he will not speak from himself, but whatever he hears, that he will speak—words which imply his dependence on and subordination to God, just as Jesus was not able to do anything of himself.   His subordination to Christ is implied in the words : " He will glorify me, for he will receive of what is mine, and will tell it to you."* He will bring to the remembrance of the disciples what Christ has already taught them.   It must be conceded, however, that there are other sayings concerning the Spirit in which his personality as distinct from the Father and the Son is not implied.   Christ is made to speak of his own personal coming and that of the Spirit in the same breath, as if the two manifestations were identical† ; and after his resurrection he is said to have imparted the Holy Spirit to the disciples by breathing upon them.‡   But it is evident that if there are three personalities in the Johannine divine triad, they are not conceived as equal and together constituting the divine Being, "three in one and one in three."   Rather there is a threefold gradation.   Under the Father is the Son, and subordinate to the Son and representing him upon the earth as the "Spirit of truth " is the Paraclete.   The Johannine thought is strictly monotheistic, and recognizes the Father as " the only true God."   If the Logos is God, it is in the sense of absolute dependence on the Father, of subordination to His will, and of inability to do anything of himself.   If the Paraclete is a personality, it is in a sense rather related to Montanism and the beginnings of the

* John xvi. 14.
† John xiv. 16-19, xvi. 13-16.   ‡ John xvi. 14.

development of Trinitarianism than to the later doctrine of the " triune God."

In its eschatology the Johannine transformation of the gospel of Jesus maintains the " spiritual " character which has been from an early time attributed to its record. In accordance with its doctrine of the exalted rank of Christ, he is made to speak of *his* kingdom,* while the kingdom of God is retired into the background. This kingdom of Christ is also said not to be " of this world," and there is no trace of the Pauline idea of a renovated earth, the groaning creation liberated from its bondage in the Messianic age to come, or of the terrestrial glorious throne of the Son of Man spoken of in the first Gospel.† In this conception of the future the Jewish-Messianic features of the early tradition and the synoptic apocalyptic find no place. " Travail-pains " announcing the approaching birth of a new age, wars, natural convulsions, and Palestinian " tribulations," have no part in the great Johannine economy of an inward spiritual development. Here there is no " abomination of desolation," no " sign of the Son of Man in heaven," no shaking of the celestial " powers," no coming of the awful Judge in the clouds " with great power and glory," and no gathering of the affrighted " nations " before his earthly throne. The future is, indeed, full of promise, but the theatre of its blessedness is not to be a " new earth " arched with " new heavens." The divine spiritual order of the Christian life is to continue with the inspiring Paraclete present forever. Christ will come, not with " the sound of a trump " or " the voice of an archangel," but in the silent power of his spirit, and even the Father too will with him make His abode in the souls of the believers. Accordingly, the sharp distinction

* John xviii. 36.   † Matt. xxv. 30.

between "the present age" and "the age to come" fades away in the conception of a continuous spiritual economy. Here, then, there is no scenic judgment at "the end of the age." Those who believe do not come into judgment, and Christ came not as a judge. The word which he has spoken carries on perpetually the inevitable separation between the children of darkness and the children of light. Satan is not bound with chains and flung into apocalyptic flames, but irresistible spiritual forces begin with the earthly mission of the all-powerful Logos to work his overthrow as prince of this world and to conquer his kingdom of darkness.

That such is the predominant idea of the Johannine doctrine of the future is manifest to the careful reader of the fourth Gospel. In accordance with it is the fact of the absence of details regarding the second coming of Christ and of a definite statement of its time. The synoptists represent Jesus to have announced it as impending, as to take place, indeed, in his own generation before the apostles should have preached in all "the cities of Israel." Paul expected that he himself and those to whom he wrote would survive it. But in the Johannine thought the time-determination appears to be lost sight of in the conception of an indefinite, endless spiritual presence of Christ and the Paraclete in the souls of believers. Yet the careful reader will find difficulty in reconciling with this vagueness about the second coming, with this evident design to spiritualize it, and with the teaching which reduces the judgment to the attitude which men may take, by a sort of gravitation according to their natures, toward the "word" of Christ, certain expressions bordering on the synoptic and Pauline apocalyptic. Such are the words concerning the raising up of believers "at the last day"

and the solemn announcement that the hour is coming in
which all who are in the tombs will hear the voice of
Christ, and will come forth, " they who have done good
to a resurrection of life, and they who have done evil to
a resurrection of condemnation." *   So deep-rooted, however, in the Christian thought of the second century was
the idea of an apocalyptic second coming of Christ to
judgment, that it is not surprising that it should find incidental expression in a writing whose author appears in
general to have left all such conceptions far behind him,
and to have subordinated all externality in his apprehension of Christianity to a predominant spirituality and
immanence.   According to the prevailing point of view of
the fourth Gospel the " condemnation " of the unbeliever
is not pronounced by an external act of judgment.   He
" is judged already " because of his unbelief.   No last-day
assize, no arraignment "on the left hand," no formal con-
signment to " everlasting punishment " finds a place in the
Hellenistic thought of this writer.   In accordance with
this " spiritual " conception he makes no mention, even
gives no intimation of a hades, a gehenna, an intermediate
state.   Rather he appears to think with Philo that " the
place of the impious is not that which is fabled to be in
hades, for the true hades is the life of the wicked man,
exposed to vengeance, with uncleansed guilt, obnoxious to
every curse."   On the unbeliever, in fact, abides the wrath
of God.   Tormented by an evil conscience, he remains in
darkness, and comes not to the reproving light.   He who
abides not in Christ "is cast forth as a branch and is
withered ; and men gather it and cast it into the fire, and
it is burned." †   If no intermediate state finds a place in

* John vi. 39, 40, 44, 54, v. 28, 29.
† John xv. 6.

this system of thought; if there is no activity in the grave; if death is the night " wherein no man can work "; what is conceived to be the fortune of those who " die in their sins "? This problem appears to be left without definite solution.   It is repeatedly said that believers will be raised up " at the last day," *i. e.*, at the second coming of Christ, as if there were no resurrection for any others, and unbelievers perished at death, in accordance with the doctrine which finds frequent expression that belief and life, unbelief and death, are inseparably connected. In the absence of a doctrine of the underworld the dead appear to be conceived of as unconscious " in the graves," and when once only there is mention of a resurrection of " those who have done evil " it is to " a resurrection of condemnation " that they come forth.   On the whole, the writer appears to see little hope for those who remain in the darkness of unbelief until they " die in their sins," and there is a remarkable absence in the Gospel of interest in the destiny of those obstinate persons who remained insensible to the light of the great Logos, and whose opposition to him culminated in the detested children of the Devil, the Jews.   Whether the overthrow of the prince of this world is conceived as the entire abolition of sin from the universe, and whether the optimistic declaration that Christ will draw all men unto him is intended in the absolute sense of a saving influence upon unbelievers in the life to come, there are no data for determining. Questions of destiny were evidently not the chief concern of the writer of this Gospel.   Only as to the destiny of the apostles does he speak with precision.   They were not to sleep the sleep of death, but Christ having prepared a place for them would come and receive them to himself in the Father's house of many mansions—a saying which reminds us of Paul's personal longing to be absent from the body and present with the Lord without passing through the gloomy realm of hades.*

* On the Johannine doctrine see : the Commentaries of Meyer, De Wette, Tholuck, Ewald, Lange, and Holtzmann's Hand-Commentar ; the Introductions of Davidson, Weiss, Holtzmann, Hilgenfeld, Westcott, and Salmon ; the works on Biblical Theology by Immer, Weiss, Baur, and Von Cölln ; Keim, Gesch. Jesu, i. pp. 103-172 ; Thoma. Die Genesis des Johannes-Evangel, pp. 177-302 ; Weizsäcker, Apostol. Zeitalter 2te Ausg. pp. 531-558 ; Hausrath, Neutest. Zeitgesch., iii. pp. 559 ff.; Pfleiderer, Das Urchristenthum, pp. 695-786 ; Tayler, The Fourth Gospel, etc.; Wendt, Die Lehre Jesu, ii. *passim* ; Lechler, Apostol. u. nachapostol. Zeitalter, 2te Ausg. pp. 455-475 ; Martineau, Seat of Authority, Bk. iii. Chap. ii. § 4, Chap. iii. § 3 ; Matthew Arnold, God and the Bible, pp. 196-244 ; Hilgenfeld, Das Evangel. u. die Briefe Johannis ; Beyschlag, Neutest. Theol., ii. pp. 462 ff ; Oscar Holtzmann, Das Johannesevangelium, pp. 48-92.

CHAPTER VI.

ANTI-GNOSTIC INTERPRETATIONS.

HELLENISTIC speculation exerted, as everybody concedes, a very considerable influence upon the early development of Christian theology. The historical critic of the New Testament, who takes account of facts without regard to their bearing upon dogma, cannot, however, accept the conclusion of Harnack's construction of the history of doctrines, that Hellenism " suddenly " invaded the Church, and attempted to take possession. of its theology. Rather he finds that its ideas gradually entered into the Christian consciousness, exerted a growing influence, and were subject to a varied development according to the different points of view from which they were regarded ; that Paul, the real founder of Christian theology, did not write without reference to them ; that they are distinctively prominent in the deutero-Pauline Epistles; that the Johannine teaching holds them in a solution of its own—in a word, that the real beginnings of the history of doctrines are not to be found altogether in the uncanonical early literature of the Church, but in its canonical writings as well. .The view of the development of primitive Christianity of which Pfleiderer has made a masterly elucidation * finds that Hellenism was not suddenly

* It is gratifying to note that this scholar is supported to a considerable degree in this view by so able and cautious a thinker as Weizsäcker. See the latter's Apostolisches Zeitalter, 2te Ausg, 1890.

bestowed by the Gnostics upon a Christianity hitherto innocent of it, but rather that gnosticism was itself a natural product of the preceding evolution of Christianity. The Pauline and deutero-Pauline Epistles and the fourth Gospel are not, indeed, Gnostic writings; but the idealization of Christ, the speculative tendencies, the spiritualization of Christianity, and the mysticism contained severally in one and the other of them, are so related to Gnosticism as to furnish an impulse toward it, to say the least. Far from seeking to belittle or overthrow Christianity, the Gnostics in endeavoring to exalt the religion of Jesus above Judaism sought the same end that the orthodox Christians were striving to achieve. Their method was peculiar, and their speculations were more comprehensive and daring than those of the Christian writers with whom they had the closest affinity. The heterogeneous and fantastic ideas which were distinctive features of their systems would no doubt, had they prevailed, have been more harmful to Christianity than the Christian mythology and apocalyptic have been. But their purpose was noble, and their mistake was the mistake of most theologians of the Church since their time, that they were too much given to speculation concerning matters which they knew and could know nothing about. Gathering their materials from the oriental cults, the Grecian philosophy, the Old Testament, and the Christian Gospels, founding upon an original opposition of matter and spirit, and imagining that the supreme God, the most spiritual essence, could not come into immediate relation with material things and with evil, they assumed a Demiurge or world-builder whom they identified with the God of the Jews and the Author of the Jewish religion, and subordinated to the God of Christianity. As the Demiurge was the mediating agent in creation, so Christ, a cosmic principle, an æon or emanation, was conceived as the mediating agent in the establishment in the world-order of the supremacy of the spiritual forces over the sensuous. The heavenly Christ was supposed by some to have descended into the earthly Jesus, while others held the Docetic view that the incarnation was only apparent, and that as a spiritual Saviour Christ could not have inhabited a real material body. It accorded with this speculative tendency that salvation was thought to consist chiefly in right knowledge, while the most contradictory practical results of the system appeared in ascetic practices on the one hand for the suppression of the sensuous nature, and on the other in libertinism and indifference to the distinction of right and wrong. The orthodox Christians were quick to see that these tendencies would, if left to take their course, result in the dissolution of the Church into numerous sects of philosophers and mystics, and they set themselves energetically to oppose them. The New-Testament writings which contain in a greater or less degree the anti-Gnostic interpretation of Christianity are the Epistles written in the name of John, the pastoral Epistles ascribed to Paul, Jude, and 2 Peter. That these were written at a time in the second century when Gnostic ideas were current is a conclusion of criticism which a careful study of them tends to confirm.

1.—THE FIRST EPISTLE OF JOHN.

The so-called first Epistle of John, which is rather a homily than an Epistle, is pervaded by a warning against certain false teachers and their doctrines, and its distinctive purpose is declared in the words: " These things I have written to you concerning those who seduce you."* These false teachers appear to have gone out of the Church into the world where they found favor with those who were "of the world," and claimed to have a knowledge of God and to dwell in Him and in the "light" as *illuminati* of a high order. In their pride of knowledge they appear to have been deficient in "brotherly love," and to have assumed a moral perfection which made them indifferent to the doctrine of redemption and atonement. "Antichrists" and "liars," they denied that Jesus was the Christ, and that Jesus Christ came in the flesh—doctrines in which have been recognized the Ebionite heresy and the Docetic Gnosis.† The heretical teaching that light and darkness were originally mingled in the divine Being appears to be combated in the declaration that "God is light, and in Him is no darkness at all"; and against the Gnostic assertion that the higher, spiritual Christ was incapable of suffering, the atoning significance of his blood is emphatically maintained.‡ In opposition to the Gnostic doctrine that Christ the Son of God descended into Jesus at the baptism, but abandoned him before the passion, it is asserted that Christ came "not in the water only, but in the water and in the blood," so that the witnesses agreeing in one are the water of baptism, the blood of the Lord's Supper, and the Spirit.§ The moral qualities which are ascribed to the false teachers make them recognizable as the Gnostics whose theories of life and conduct are described in the writings of the fathers of the Church who combated

* 1 John ii. 26.
† 1 John i. 6, ii. 4, 6, 9, 22, iv. 2 f., 15, v. 1, 5 ;   2 John 7.
‡ 1 John i. 5, 7, ii. 2, iii. 5, iv. 10.
§ 1 John v. 6-8.

them ;* and these in connection with their teachings render it extremely doubtful that Wittichen, Keim, and Haupt are correct in the opinion that the heresies in question were those of the Ebionites, or of Corinth. On the contrary, antinomistic or libertine Gnostics are evidently the objects of the writer's denunciations.

In his opposition to the Gnostic point of view the writer himself does not, however, wholly depart from it in his terminology at least. The highest knowledge of God belongs to the true Christians who have the "anointing from the Holy One, and know all things." This "anointing" is "a truth, and is not a lie," as is the teaching of the antichrists. They "know the Spirit of God," because they acknowledge that Jesus Christ came "in the flesh."† This is the true "Gnosis." An expression borrowed from the Gnostic schools is employed to designate the spirit from which proceeds this true knowledge. This is the divine "seed"‡ which dwells in him who has been born of God. He cannot sin, because His (God's) seed remaineth in him, that is the divine Spirit abides germinally in his soul in order to come to development, according to the Valentinian Gnosis as explained by Irenaeus.§ The writer, then, does not appear to reject Gnosis in itself, but only the current heretical apprehensions of it. He lays stress on the *knowledge* of God, Christ, and the truth, in accordance with the Johannine theology. But the true Gnosis is not regarded by him, as it was by the Gnostics proper, as opposed to Christian faith ; rather it is identical with it. If they claimed to be men of the

---

* Clem. Alex. Strom. iii. 4, 31 ; Iren. Adv. haer. i. 6, 2 ; Ign. Ad. Smyr. vi.; cf. Clem. Recog. ii. 22 ; Epiph. Haer. xxxviii. 1.

† 1 John ii. 20, 27, iv. 2.   ‡ σπέρμα.

§ Adv. haer. i. 6, 4 ; cf. Tertul. De anima, xi.

Spirit who were born of God, and to have left behind
them as "pneumatics" the merely "psychical" believers
of the Church, he claims that the believers in Christ are
they who are truly born of God, who have received the
anointing of the Spirit, possess the true knowledge, or
Gnosis, and have no need that any one should teach
them. The dualism of the Epistle, which has an affinity
with Gnosticism, recalls the views expressed in the fourth
Gospel. Here as there we have on the one hand the
children of God, and on the other the Devil and his
children. In opposition to the antinomistic libertinism
of the antichrists and their followers, the writer emphasizes with great force and frequent repetition the importance of right conduct and fraternal love. In him who
keeps the word of Christ is the love of God perfected,
and he who abides in him ought to walk as. he walked.*
The true fellowship with God does not, however, as the
Gnostics taught, consist in knowledge, but in a loving
disposition toward God and the brethren, together with
faith in Christ. Love is the evidence that we have
passed out of death into life, but the love which is emphasized is not that of mankind in general. The evidence
that one has passed out of death into life is that one
loves "the brethren," and for these one ought even to
lay down one's life. "Every one that loveth Him that
begot, loveth also him that hath been begotten of Him,"
that is, the Christian. "By this we know that we love
the children of God, when we love God, and do His commandments."† Faith is rather subordinated to love than
accorded the first place as a factor in the Christian life,
and is regarded as the result and manifestation of the

* 1 John ii. 5, 6, 29, iii. 9, 10, 11.
† 1 John iii. 14, 16, 17, v. 1, 2.

birth from God rather than as the cause of this spiritual state. He who has faith that Jesus is the Christ *has been born* of God. This emphasizing of the practical side of the Christian life in the exaltation of love for one another, in which evidence is given of the indwelling of God and the perfecting of His love in the heart,* together with a mysticism similar to that of the fourth Gospel, furnished a supplementing of the Pauline doctrine of justification by faith, which was required by the moral consciousness. The difficulties which the ethical judgment could not but find in the extreme statement of the Pauline doctrine are removed by this fine mysticism, which finds expression in words which have been called the greatest and most beautiful that have ever been spoken concerning religion: " God is love, and he who abideth in love abideth in God and God in him ; Love is of God, and every one who hath love is born of God and knoweth Him ; Whatever is born of God overcometh the world, and this is the victory that overcometh the world, even our faith. This is love to God, that we keep His commandments and His commandments are not burdensome ; Hereby we know that we dwell in Him and He in us, because He hath given us of His Spirit."

That the expression of the noblest religious truths and sentiments is not, however, incompatible in a New-Testament writer with susceptibility regarding doctrinal tenets to the influences of his environment, is evident in the modifications which this author made of the principles of the Johannine school to which he doubtless belonged. In opposition to the Gnostic view that the Jesus of history consisted of the man Jesus and the divine, heavenly Christ he sets up the doctrine that the divine *life* mani-

* 1 John iv. 12, 13.

fested itself in Jesus who as man was at the same time the Son of God, and avoids the original Johannine teaching of the fourth Gospel that Christ was the personal Logos distinct from God. Instead of " the Logos who was with God, and was God," he speaks of " the everlasting life which was with the Father." * Holtzmann, approved by Pfleiderer, remarks that by an elimination of the intervening Logos-conception of the fourth Gospel such a degree of unity between God and Christ is posited that in a large number of cases it is impossible to decide whether God or Christ is the subject. The point of view of the writer is evidently that of the Monarchianism of the second century rather than Trinitarianism. It would appear to be in the interest of a strict monotheism that he also avoids the Johannine doctrine of the personality of the Holy Spirit, and employs instead of formulas which recognize it the expressions: " An anointing from the Holy One " and " Spirit of God," as in the passage : " Hereby we know that we dwell in Him and He in us, because He hath given us of His Spirit." † The Paraclete as distinct from the Father and the Son is not recognized. " The reason why the writer adheres to the Monarchianistic thought of the Church of the second century was doubtless the fear that by making the Logos and the Spirit distinct personalities he might come too near the Gnostic-mythological doctrine of the divine mediate beings or æons, and slip from the solid ground of monotheism." ‡ This modification of the original Johannine thought is evidently due to the exigencies of the Gnostic controversy, but it is not prejudicial to the interests of religion. In fact, whether intentionally or no may be

* John i. 2.
† 1 John ii. 20, iv. 13.   ‡ Pfleiderer.

left undecided, the writer establishes an immediate relation of the soul to God, which Christian theologians since Paul have unhappily disregarded, apparently solicitous lest the person of Christ should not be sufficiently exalted, and his mediatorial office magnified. A distinctive feature of the Epistle, which is not found in the fourth Gospel, is the doctrine that Christ is " the propitiation for our sins." * This conception is rather akin to the idea of the office of Christ as high-priest which is represented in Hebrews than, as Pfleiderer thinks, to the doctrine in the Gospel of the moral purification which Christ effects in the " taking away " of sin. Another deviation from the Johannine teaching of the Gospel is presented in the eschatology of the Epistle. In opposition to the predominantly spiritual apprehension of the second coming . of Christ, which we have seen to be represented in the Gospel, the Epistle speaks of the time " when he shall appear " as near at hand, especially on account of "antichrist " who appears to have been expected by the readers of the author before the Parousia. The certainty that " the last time is come " appears to be intensified by the fact that already " there are even now many antichrists." † It is difficult to see reasons for regarding this with Pfleiderer as denoting only a " relative difference " in the point of view of the Epistle from that of the Gospel. Again, the doctrine that the believers had in Christ an " advocate [Paraclete] with the Father," ‡ is entirely foreign to the Gospel. There is, indeed, in the Gospel an implication that Christ is a Paraclete in the words, " I will send you another Paraclete," but the Paraclete of the Gospel is conceived as present with the believers and

* ἱλασμός, 1 John ii. 2, iv. 10, and not elsewhere in the New Testament.
† 1 John ii. 18, 28.   ‡ 1 John ii. 1.

not as "with the Father" in the character of an intercessor, "if any one have sinned." The thought of the
passage in question is evidently analogous to that conveyed in the mention of the intercession of Christ in
earlier writings of the New Testament.*

2.—THE PASTORAL EPISTLES.

The Pastoral Epistles, 1 and 2 Timothy and Titus, do
not contain an independent and original type of doctrine.
Their general point of view is Pauline, † but the writer in
applying the teachings of his master to the conditions of
the second century has modified them in many particulars,
and furnished a weakened Paulinism in which some of the
great distinctive features of the apostle's thought are wanting. That he had the heresies of the Gnostics before him
was recognized by Irenaeus and Tertullian, and is hardly
mistakable from many passages in the Epistles. The
condemnation of "the oppositions of the falsely-called
knowledge," ‡ or the antithesis of the Gnosis falsely so-
called, finds its most probable explanation in a reference
to the celebrated Gnostic Antitheses of Marcion. A
Gnostic asceticism appears to be combated in the reference,
to the "speakers of lies" who forbid to marry, and command to abstain from food. § The teaching which is here
opposed seems to have proceeded from the dualistic point
of view of Gnosticism according to which the Demiurge,
and not the good God, was the creator of matter. Gnostic
"vain babbling" and allegorizing interpretations of the
law put forth by those who desire to be teachers of the
law, but who understand neither what they say nor

* See Rom. viii. 34 ; Heb. vii. 25, ix. 24.
† 1 Tim. ii. 7 ; 2 Tim. i. 9, 11, 15, iv. 17 ; Tit. iii. 4.
‡ 1 Tim. vi. 20.   § 1 Tim. iv. 2, 3.

whereof they affirm, appear to be referred to in the declaration that " the law is good if a man use it lawfully," in
which the practical moral fulfilment of the law is placed
in opposition to Gnostic theories and speculations about
it, or perhaps to the denial by certain false teachers of all
moral value to it.   But the absence of the characteristic
Pauline doctrine regarding the law and justification is remarkable as showing the writer's attitude toward the burning questions of the time of the apostle.*   The attitude
of the Epistles toward the Old Testament favors the extreme doctrine of its inspiration, and is doubtless due to
the Gnostic depreciation of it and to the exigencies of a
time when the Church felt the need of the Scriptures as
an objective rule of faith and life in the conflict with
heresy.   Accordingly, the writer admonishes Timothy to
continue in the things which he had learned, knowing from
what teachers he had learned them, and that from a child
he had known the Holy Scriptures which are able to make
him wise unto salvation, and then adds the declaration
which, on the presumption of its divine authority, has been
made the basis of the extreme doctrine of inspiration :
" Every Scripture is inspired by God, and is profitable for
teaching, for reproof, for correction, for discipline in
righteousness, that the man of God may be perfect," etc. †
The passage presents no difficulty to the student whose
point of view enables him to see in it the beginning of a

* Schleiermacher, who may be regarded as the real founder of the criticism of the first Epistle to Timothy, misses here with clear insight the master's hand.   Werke zur Theologie, ii. p. 286.

† 2 Tim. iii. 15-17.   The translation given in the text is that of Noyes
with the exception of his probably incorrect rendering of $\pi\tilde{\alpha}\sigma\alpha\ \gamma\rho\alpha\varphi\acute{\eta}$ by
" all Scripture," and is supported by the highest authorities.   The render-
ing :   " All Scripture inspired by God is profitable," etc. is incorrect—
$\theta\epsilon\acute{o}\pi\nu\epsilon\upsilon\sigma\tau\sigma\varsigma$ as an attribute of all Scripture being tautological.   See De

definite foundation of the dogma of inspiration, or an early phase of the history of doctrines. It is noteworthy in this connection that the writer quotes a passage from the third Gospel with the formula: "The Scripture saith." * This could not have been done by Paul, for the third Gospel was not in existence in his time, much less regarded as "Scripture," and quoted in the same breath with the Old Testament as an authority.

Characteristic of these Epistles, as of the deutero-Pauline theology, is the emphasis which is laid upon the monotheistic doctrine. In apparent opposition to the Gnostic dualism the unity of God is made especially prominent, and predicates of the divine Being are multiplied to a degree not reached in the Pauline writings. † Some of these predicates border very closely on Gnostic ideas, although they are doubtless not to be taken in the Gnostic sense, ‡ and appear to be directed against the Jewish anthropomorphism at which the Gnostics took offence. Against the Gnostic teaching that the creator of the world was not the supreme God, the writer emphasizes the absoluteness of Deity and His unlimited sway over all things natural and spiritual. The one "living God" giveth life to all things, is immortal, blessed, the source of all blessedness and truth. § The application to God of the

Wette, Commentar, ii. 5, p. 49. Holtzmann, Pastoralbriefe, p. 440, and Pfleiderer, p. 805. θεόπνευστος here only in New Testament.

* "The laborer is worthy of his wages," 1 Tim. v. 18, *cf.* Luke x. 7. These words are not found in the Old Testament.

† 1 Tim. i. 1, 17, ii. 5, vi. 15, 16.

‡ See Βασιλεύς τῶν αἰώνων, 1 Tim. i. 17, king of the æons, which together give the idea of eternity, according to Wiesinger. This expression is not elsewhere found in the New Testament. See also, "inhabiting light unapproachable, vi. 16, also here only in the New Testament, as is οἰκῶν with the accusative.

§ 1 Tim. i. 11, iii. 15, iv. 10, vi. 13, 15 ; 2 Tim. ii. 13 ; Tit. i. 2, ii. 13.

designation " Saviour " which elsewhere is almost exclusively applied to Christ is a peculiarity of these Epistles. In Titus it is often applied to Him and in 1 Timothy to Him alone.* The most obvious explanation of this peculiarity is found in an intentional opposition to Gnosticism which assumed a creator-God as distinct from God as a Saviour. In the same interest is the emphasis placed upon the " mercy " of God which in two of the Epistles, is added to the " grace and peace " of the genuine Pauline greeting.

The formulas in which the doctrine of the person of Christ represented in the Epistles is expressed are essentially Pauline. Christ is emphatically called " man " in accordance with Paul's teaching, † although the distinctive terms employed by the apostle, " second Adam " and " man from heaven " are wanting. As the Pauline Christ was " born of the seed of David according to the flesh," so here we read of " Jesus Christ of the seed of David." ‡ His preëxistence is plainly implied in the expressions: " Christ Jesus came into the world," and " was manifested in the flesh." § In the words following this latter citation, " justified in the Spirit," is expressed an idea wholly foreign to Paul, who does not apply justification to Christ. The affirmation of a manifestation in the flesh reminds us of the Johannine expressions, " became flesh," " to come in the flesh," " to be manifested," ‖ and is evidently directed against the Docetic Gnosticism, which denied that

---

* 1 Tim. i. 1, ii. 3, iv. 10 ; Tit. i. 3, ii. 10, iii. 4.

† 1 Tim. ii. 5 ; *cf.* Rom. v. 15 ; 1 Cor. xv. 21.

‡ 2 Tim. ii. 8 ; *cf.* Rom. i. 3.

§ 1 Tim. i. 15, iii. 16. Tischendorf's reading of the latter passage is adopted.

‖ John i. 14 ; 1 John i. 2, iii. 5. 8, iv. 2 ; 2 John 7.

Jesus had a real human body. The justification of Christ in the Spirit can mean, according to Hoffmann, nothing else than that " he who gave himself out for something which, according to his earthly human nature he did not appear to be, was so far justified as he proved himself to be what he really was," that is by virtue of the spiritual principle which was in him he was shown by his exaltation through the resurrection to be in fact a heavenly being. The writer does not, however, reach the Johannine point of view from which Christ was regarded as the Logos who was God. The interpretation of the words : " The appearing of the glory of the great God and our Saviour Jesus Christ," * is too doubtful to afford support for a doctrine of the Deity of Christ.

The Pauline point of view is essentially represented by the writer of these Epistles in the teaching that "Christ Jesus gave himself a ransom for all." † But in the declaration that "Christ gave himself for us that he might redeem us from all iniquity, and purify to himself a people to be his own, zealous in good works," ‡ we miss the distinctive Pauline thought that Christ redeemed men from "the curse of the law," and find in the conception of redemption from iniquity the moral and educational influ-

---

* Tit. ii. 13. The correct interpretation probably requires that "of " be inserted before "our Saviour." Grammatically σωτῆρος ἡμῶν *can* be attached as a second attribute to the article τοῦ, says Meyer. Yet he decides against this interpretation for the reasons that θεός never appears as an attribute, while the conjunction of God and Christ as two subjects is common. The Parousia of Christ is evidently the subject of the writer's thought, and the coming of Christ in the "glory of the great God " is probably the idea expressed.

† 1 Tim. ii. 6, ἀντίλυτρον, "price of redemption." This is not, however, a Pauline word.

‡ Tit. ii. 14.

ence of Christ substituted for the metaphysical thought of Paul, in accordance with the post-Pauline tendency already pointed out. The difference is marked both in terminology and in conception between the abrogation of the law, and the purification of the individual from iniquity as the result of the death of Christ. Likewise the purification of "a people to be his own" * is to be understood of a moral renewal; and Schenkel remarks that the writer's "mystery of godliness" is a mystery without mysticism. In fact the Pauline mysticism is wanting in the doctrine that Christ "abolished death, and brought life and incorruption to light *through the Gospel*," † that is, by means of his teaching. The two great, fundamental facts of the Pauline theology, death and the resurrection, find in these Epistles, indeed, only incidental mention. Certain false teachers, among whose "vain babblings" was the affirmation that the resurrection had "already taken place," are censured, and charged with overthrowing the faith of some. ‡ This is evidently not the error combated by Paul of those who denied that there is a resurrection, but rather that of the Gnostics who, according to Irenæus and Tertullian, allegorized and spiritualized that doctrine. It is characteristic of the Pastoral Epistles that they do not give to faith as a factor in salvation the prominence which it receives in the Pauline theology. Rather it is put in the background or ranked along with the practical-moral virtues. Only in two passages is it mentioned as a means of salvation, § while its association with love, peace, etc., is very frequent, as: "The end of the commandment is love out of a pure heart and a good con-

---

* περιούσιος, a word peculiar to this Epistle.
† 2 Tim. i. 10.   ‡ 2 Tim. ii. 18.
§ 1 Tim. i. 16; 2 Tim. iii. 15.

science and faith unfeigned "; " With faith and love which
is in Jesus Christ "; " If they continue in faith and love
and holiness with sobriety "; " In word, in behavior, in
love, in faith, in purity "; " Follow after righteousness,
godliness, faith, love, patience, meekness." *   The especial emphasis laid upon works in many passages may be
regarded as at least relatively unpauline in the absence of
the central significance of faith. †   Faith, indeed, is sometimes regarded as the trustful appropriation of the truth,
sometimes as a body of doctrine, and again as the virtue
of fidelity, while the Pauline conception of faith is so far
lost sight of that the general notion of godliness usurps
its place. ‡   Along with all this the Pauline point of view
is distinctively maintained on occasion, as when Timothy
is admonished to be "strong in the grace that is in Christ
Jesus," and when it is declared that God " called us with
a holy calling, not according to our works, but according
to His own purpose and the grace which was given us in
Christ Jesus," and that He " saved us not by works of
righteousness which we did, but according to His mercy." §
Yet the writer appears to lay an emphasis upon works
which has been regarded as a " denial of Pauline principles," when, for example, he says that they who " have
served well as deacons gain for themselves a good standing," ‖ and when he enjoins that the rich be charged to
do good, be rich in good works, liberal in imparting, etc.,

* I Tim. I. 5, 14, ii. 15, iv. 12, vi. 11 ; *cf.* 2 Tim. i. 13, ii. 22, iii. 10 ;
Tit. ii. 2.

† I Tim. ii. 10, v. 10, 25, vi. 18 ; 2 Tim. ii. 21, iii. 17.

‡ I Tim. ii. 2, iii. 16, iv. 7, 8, vi. 3, 5, 6, 11 ; 2 Tim. iii. 5, 12, 16 ; Tit.
i. 1, ii. 12.

§ 2 Tim. ii. 1, i. 9 ; Tit. iii. 5.

‖ I Tim. iii. 13, "standing " βαθμός, probably a high degree of blessedness in heaven.

" laying up in store for themselves a good foundation against the time to come." * This ascription of merit to good works in such a manner as to make salvation depend upon them is so unpauline that it is regarded even by Weiss as " surprising." " Surprising" from the Pauline point of view certainly is the declaration that although the woman " being deceived fell into transgression," " she will be saved through child-bearing." † One can hardly think of the apostle as striking this note. For although it is doubtless a " sound thought " that woman best accomplishes her destiny morally by fulfilling her domestic duties, he could not have recognized a " saving " efficacy in their performance, since in his soteriology faith is paramount, and besides, he regarded family cares as a hinderance to the spiritual life, thinking the unmarried condition preferable " on account of the impending distress " and because " the time that remaineth is short." ‡ In this connection Pfleiderer remarks that " it must be conceded in general that the Christianity recommended in the Pastoral Epistles, that of a simple, practical piety, so far as it abandoned the empty strifes of the theorists about words and the over-strained excesses of the ascetics, deserves really to be called a sound doctrine, and is altogether practicable for the Church, more immediately practicable than the original Paulinism which, though profounder and more spiritual, abounded more for that very reason in theoretical and practical difficulties."

The manner already referred to in which faith is spoken of, not from the Pauline point of view as an attitude of the individual believer, but in the objective sense

* 1 Tim. vi. 18, 19.
† 1 Tim. ii. 15. Adam, however, was not " deceived" !
‡ 1 Cor. viii. 25, 26, 29, 34, 38.

ᴧs a body of doctrine, is an indication of the ecclesiastical interest of the Epistles. The strict, speculative doctrines of the apostle are thrust into the background in the struggle of the Church for existence, and in its place a lax Paulinism and an absorbing practical interest predominate. The conditions are those of an organized religious community, " the beginnings of the Catholic Church." It is charged against the false teachers that they have " made shipwreck concerning the faith," " have strayed away from the faith," and "have erred concerning the truth."* There is thus an opposition of orthodoxy and heterodoxy from the genuinely ecclesiastical point of view. The heterodox are they who " teach other doctrine,"† and over against this is set with commendation the "sound teaching."‡ The idea of an ecclesiastical standard of belief is so far developed as to lead to the requirement of conformity on the part of individuals. The opinion appears to be correct that in these Epistles is expressed a definite ecclesiastical consciousness, and the idea of the Church receives its dogmatic significance, as in the words, " House of God, which is the Church of the living God, the pillar and foundation of the truth."§

---

* 1 Tim. i. 19, vi. 10; 2 Tim. ii. 18 ; *cf*. iii. 8, " reprobate concerning the faith."

† ἐτεροδιδασκαλεῖν, 1 Tim. i. 3, vi. 3. The writer of 1 Timothy, while opposing the extreme Gnostic asceticism, appears not have been without some inclination toward this tendency of the time, as is evident from the requirement of the single marriage of deacons and bishops as well as of widows who should be assigned to positions of trust (v. 9). " Bodily exercise " (σωματικὴ γυμνασία) or " the exercise of conscientiousness relative to the body, such as is characteristic of ascetics, and consists in abstinence from matrimony and certain kinds of food" (Grimm-Wilke Lex.), is acknowledged to be " profitable a little," or a short time (iv. 8).

‡ 1 Tim. i. 10; Tit. i. 9, ii. 1 ; *cf.* " sound words," 2 Tim. i. 13.

§ 1 Tim. iii. 15.

For the encouragement of believers in view of the false teachings introduced by heretics who denied a future resurrection, etc., it is said of the Church or the traditional belief, that "God's firm foundation standeth, having this seal, 'God knoweth those who are His.'" As "in a great house there are not only vessels of gold and of silver, but also wooden and earthen ones, and some for honor and some for dishonor;" so in the Church are true believers and also false teachers with their "profane babblings," whose word, spreading its infection ever wider, " will eat as doth a canker." *   The conception of a well-developed ecclesiastical institution finds expression in the reference to "the office of a bishop," in the provision for the support of the heads of the Church, in the distinction of the office of teacher, in the ceremony of ordination, in special requirements as to the single marriage of bishops, whereby they are distinguished from "the rest," and in the minute directions regarding "widows." †

In opposition to the aristocratic soteriology of the Gnostics, who distinguished a class of " pneumatic " or spiritual men as by nature blessed in contradistinction from the " hylic " and "psychical" men, great stress is laid in these Epistles upon the universality of the divine grace. Hence prayer for " all men " is recommended ; it is declared to be the " will of God our Saviour that all men should be saved "; Christ is said to have given himself " a ransom for all "; and God is represented as the Saviour of all men, especially of believers," that is, not especially of those who pride themselves on their Gnosis. "The kindness and love for men of God our Saviour" are emphasized, whose " grace bringeth salvation to all

* 2 Tim. ii. 16, 17, 19, 20.
† 1 Tim. iii. 1, 2, v. 17, 18 ; 2 Tim. ii. 2 ; Tit. i. 6.

men." *   In an apparent inconsistency with this point of
view, which the author does not attempt to reconcile, is
the teaching that those who are Christians are "called
with a holy calling, not according to our works, but according to His own purpose and the grace which was
given us in Christ Jesus before the world began." †   Not
easily reconcilable, however, with this predestination are
the doctrine that in order to be "a vessel of honor" one
must "purge" oneself, and the saying which the author
puts into the mouth of the apostle that he "endures all
things for the sake of the elect, that they may also obtain
the salvation which is in Christ Jesus." ‡   A predestination which is "not according to works" is thus apparently
regarded as conditioned not only upon what "the elect"
may do for themselves, but also upon what another may
do for them.

No well-defined eschatology appears in these Epistles.
From the way, however, in which "the last days" are
mentioned the Parousia seems to be a settled article of
faith which is assumed as well understood and requiring
no definite exposition.   This point of view accords with
the late date of the Epistles.   The "impending distress"
which Paul vaguely refers to § is here regarded as at
hand, and is specifically indicated as the time when
"some [the Gnostics] will depart from the faith, giving
heed to seducing spirits and teachings of demons."   Accordingly, Timothy is admonished to "keep the commandments without spot, without reproach, until the
appearing∥ of our Lord Jesus Christ, which in His [God's]

---

* 1 Tim. ii. 1, 4, 6, iv. 10 ; Tit. ii. 11, iii. 4.
† 2 Tim. i. 9 ; *cf.* Rom. viii. 28 f ; Eph. i. 11 ; Tit. iii. 5.
‡ 2 Tim. ii. 10, 21.   § 1 Cor. vii. 26.
∥ ἐπιφάνεια, not used by Paul.   *Cf.* Tit. ii. 13 ; 2 Tim. iv. 8.

22

own times He shall show." The vagueness of the expectation of the Parousia is, indeed, indicated in the words "in His own times," but there appears to be no good reason for holding with Holtzmann that Timothy is conceived to survive the Parousia only as "the representative of future generations of officials." * Since it is uncertain that Paul taught that unbelievers would be raised at the Parousia, the declaration that Christ will "judge the living and the dead" is doubtfully Pauline.† Nearly all the distinctive features of the Pauline eschatology are wanting. There is no mention of the apocalyptic descent of Christ with the sound of a trump and the voice of an archangel, of the resurrection of the believers who had "fallen asleep" and of the "change" of the living Christians, of the deliverance of the groaning creation, of the reign of Christ until his enemies should be put under his feet, and of the saints as judges of the world. The writer does not make Paul express the hope that he may survive the Parousia, but rather the conviction that he is about to die a martyr's death, the time of his departure being at hand.‡

3.—THE EPISTLE OF JUDE.

The so-called Epistle of Jude is not addressed to any particular church or as a circular letter to a collection of churches, but vaguely "to the called, loved in God the Father and kept by Jesus Christ." It bears no marks of the apostolic age, and no traces of the Pauline-Jewish controversy appear in it. "The common salvation " is represented as in peril, and the readers are summoned "to contend earnestly for the faith which was once

---

* 1 Tim. iv. 1, vi. 14, 15 ; 2 Tim. iii. 1–6.
† 2 Tim. iv. 1.   ‡ 2 Tim. iv. 6.

delivered to the saints," on account of "certain men " who " have stealthily crept in," men "appointed beforehand for this condemnation, ungodly men, turning the grace of our God into wantonness and denying the only Sovereign and our Lord Jesus Christ." * As " an example " of the destruction which awaits these men the writer refers to the faith of unbelieving Israelites, to the apocryphal story of "the angels who kept not their principality," and have been " kept in everlasting chains under darkness unto the judgment of the great day," † and to the calamity which befell " Sodom and Gomorrah and the cities about them."   Not only was the appearance of these unbelievers and libertines foretold by " the apostles," but Enoch " the seventh from Adam " prophesied against them.‡   In view of these perils and evils the writer admonishes his readers to build themselves up on their most holy faith, looking for the manifestation of the mercy of the Lord Jesus Christ, which would be shown to them at his coming, " unto eternal life."   The theoretical errors about which the writer is filled with anxiety and against which he raises a timely warning are the denial of God as " the only Sovereign " and of the Lord Jesus Christ." Besides this denial of the fundamental Christian principles of doctrine the charge is brought against these heretics and enemies of the truth that they are morally corrupt " turning the grace of our God into wantonness."   As

---

* Jude 1-5.

† Jude 6 ; *cf.* the story in the book of Enoch of the angels who " corrupted themselves" with the daughters of men, x. 12, xv. 3.   The writer appears to regard the apocryphal book of Enoch as good Scripture.   This myth is also recorded in Gen. vi. 2, but the reference to the punishment of the angels shows the quotations in the Epistle to have been made from Enoch.

‡ The word " apostles" is not determinable.   Perhaps the writer had in mind 1 Tim. iv. 1 ; 2 Tim. iii. 1, iv. 3.   See Enoch i. 9.

libertines given over to unbridled lust, they are called
" sensual, not having the Spirit." * Not only do they
" defile the flesh," but they also " despise dominion, and
rail at dignities," *i. e.*, good and evil angels, whereby they
show a presumption greater than that of Michael who,
when contending with the Devil about the body of Moses,
dared not bring against him a railing accusation. † They
" rail at the things which they know not," and at the feasts
of love are " cliffs " on which others are wrecked, " feeding
only themselves " in the satisfaction of their fleshly lusts.

The reference to " the faith once delivered to the saints,"
as a given and accepted form of doctrine and to the
apostles as having delivered their prophecy concerning
the scoffers who would appear " at the last time," indicates
the post-apostolic age as the time of the writer. A more
precise date is furnished with great probability, and a
setting of the Epistle is given by which its distinguishing
features are explained, in the historical fact of the appearance
in Alexandria towards the middle of the second century of
Karpokrates and his son Epiphanes, whose teachings and
moral principles are so definitely referred to in it, that
Clement of Alexandria thought the author of the Epistle
prophetically announced them. ‡ In the dualism of the
Gnostics which made a sharp distinction between the
spirit and the flesh there lay the peril of moral indifference
as to the relations of men to matter, and of a tendency to

* Jude 4, 9.

† Jude 8 ; *cf.* Eph. i. 21 ; 2 Peter ii. 10. The source of this legend
of the strife about the body of Moses is unknown. Origen refers it to an
apocryphal writing, ἀνάβασις τοῦ Μωσέως. To the author of the
Epistle the story appears to be good Scripture. His conception of canonicity was evidently not more definite than that of other Christian writers of
the middle of the second century.

‡ Clem. Alex. Strom., iii. 2, 11.

regard it as a mark of true spiritual freedom to give free rein to the sensuous impulses and passions. In fact, it is reported of the Karpokratians that their doctrines threatened the overthrow of the domestic and social order. Epiphanes in a book on " Righteousness " appears to have attempted with unequalled effrontery to exalt licentiousness into a cult by advocating a community of goods and women and a disregard of the traditional rights of the marriage relation as hostile to the more sacred rights of nature. The righteousness of God, he taught, is community under the condition of equality. The natural order of absolute community and equality has been violated by the evil angels who have limited the community of goods by the institution of property and that of women by establishing marriage. The god of the Jews, the subordinate of the Supreme One, commanding that a man should not covet his neighbor's goods or wife was the cause of theft and adultery, according to Paul's doctrine that sin is known through the law. Regarding Christ he taught that he was a man like other men, the son of Joseph, and had only this advantage over others, that his remarkably strong and pure soul remembered what in his preëxistence he had seen near to God. Therefore he was loved of God, and endowed with power from on high at the baptism that he might escape the world-creator. One cannot but recognize in the Epistle the condemnation of the immorality, of the denial of the sovereignty of God, and of the current ideas of Christ, which characterized this Gnostic sect. There appear, accordingly, to be very good grounds for Mayerhoff's conjecture that the writing originated in Alexandria where the book of Enoch and the Assumption of Moses were held in high esteem.

4.—THE SECOND EPISTLE OF PETER.

The second Epistle written in the name of Peter is vaguely addressed to "those who have obtained like precious faith with us," and like that of Jude is directed against the "false teachers" who threatened to overthrow the Christian doctrine and corrupt the Church. In fact, almost the entire substance of Jude has been incorporated into it, and it may be regarded as a variation on the theme of the other without the force, directness, and clearness of the original.* The writer avoids the quotation of apocryphal books at which the author of Jude did not scruple, although ii. 11 shows an acquaintance with Jude 9 and doubtless a use of its idea in a way to avoid the recognition of an apocryphal writing. The point of view of the writer is practical and hortative rather than doctrinal. He writes in apparent ignorance of the Pauline and Johannine theologies and of the controversies of the apostolic age. "The knowledge of Jesus Christ " † is made more prominent than faith which is mentioned in connection with virtue, knowledge, etc., ‡ and nothing is said of the atonement and of the death and resurrection of Christ. A doctrine which is not apostolic, and does not find elsewhere a post-apostolic expression, is that through the promises of God believers may "become partakers of the divine nature." § Against the "cunningly devised fables" of the false teachers the writer proposes to make known to his readers "the power and coming (the Parousia) of our

---

* 2 Peter ii. 11 compared with Jude 9 is vague and flat, ii. 12 is a misinterpretation of the image in Jude 10, and ii. 17 contains a confusing of the figures in Jude 12 f. Compare further iii. 2 with Jude 17, and iii. 3–5 with Jude 18, where the original is expanded so as to change the theme entirely.

† 2 Peter i. 2, 8, ii. 20, iii. 18.

‡ 2 Peter i. 5–8. § 2 Peter i. 4, θείας φύσεως.

Lord Jesus Christ" through the personal testimony of the reputed author, Peter, in the voice from heaven at the transfiguration. Something more sure than even this is, however, "the prophetic word," or this word is made more sure by the voice heard "in the holy mount." * At any rate "the power and coming" of Christ are established by prophecy, although the place where these prophetic words may be found is not indicated, and the writer takes occasion to express the dogma of the Church in his time that the Old Testament was given by divine inspiration. "For prophecy never came by the will of man, but moved by the Holy Spirit, men spoke from God." †

The writer apparently turns aside to answer a class of "scoffers" not mentioned in Jude, those who "in the last days" ask: "Where is the promise of his [Christ's] coming? for from the time when the fathers fell asleep all things continue as then, and as they have continued from the beginning of the creation." Hereupon he takes occasion to set forth at some length his views of the second coming of Christ beginning with a peculiar cosmogony which runs to the effect that the heavens were made by the word of God, but an earth was "formed out of water and by the water," by means of which came the deluge; but the present heavens and earth are "reserved for fire against the day of judgment and the perdition of ungodly men." ‡ He then proceeds to set aside the taunt of the "scoffers" by reminding the "beloved" that "one day is with the Lord as a thousand years, and a thousand years as one day." The delay of the Parousia is on account of God's long-suffering toward them, since He is "not willing that any should perish but that all should come to

---

* The meaning of the words is doubtful.

† 2 Peter i. 16–21 ; *cf.* iii. 2. ‡ 2 Peter iii. 4–8.

repentance."   " But the day of the Lord will come as a thief, in which the heavens will pass away with a great noise, and the elements will melt with fervent heat, and the earth and the works which are therein will be burned up."*   Then follows a practical application of the teaching in an exhortation to the " beloved " to be godly, looking for and hastening (*i. e.*, by their repentance obviating the further long-suffering of God) the day, after the terrors of which are looked for according to His promise new heavens and a new earth, wherein dwelleth righteousness. †   This latter feature suggests the Pauline idea of the deliverance of the groaning and travailling creation from the bondage of corruption.   But as the crash of the heavens and the world-conflagration are wanting in Paul's conception of the end, so here we miss the apostle's humane interest in the believers who had " fallen asleep," the resurrection, the " change" of the faithful living, the ascent to meet the longed-for Christ in the air, and the blessed " forever with the Lord ! "   For the false teachers and their followers and apparently for unbelievers generally the writer of this Epistle has no words of hope.   " The judgment long ago ordained lingereth not, and their destruction slumbereth not."   " Children of a curse," their last state is worse than their first, if they have turned from the holy command-ment delivered to them. 'With " the day of judgment " is connected "the perdition of ungodly men." The un-

* 2 Peter iii. 8–10.

† This " promise" (iii. 13) is not, however, pointed out. Did the writer perhaps think that by the current method of interpretation it could be derived from the Old Testament, or had he in mind certain passages in the book of Enoch, " The former heaven will pass away, and a new heaven will ap-pear"? Enoch xc. 17 ; *cf.* liv. 4, 5, x. 27, l. 6. The idea of a conflagra-tion of the earth was probably borrowed from the ancient Greek natural philosophy.

righteous the Lord "knoweth how to reserve under punishment to the day of judgment," so that they are supposed to enter immediately at death upon their torment.
This doom is "chiefly" reserved for those who "walk
after the flesh in the lust of uncleanness, and despise
dominion." * The prominence of eschatological teaching
in the Epistle furnishes support to the opinion that its real
object was not so much to refute the false teachers of the
Epistle of Jude as those who in the time of the writer ad-
vocated the unchangeability and permanence of the world
and spiritualized the second coming of Christ or denied it
altogether.† Spiritualistic views of this sort prevailed
under gentile-Christian influence in the latter half of the
second century, and no dealing with them could have
been deemed more effective than to combat them under
the name of an apostle.‡

* 2 Peter ii. 3, 9, 15, 20, iii. 7.

† Irenaeus perhaps refers to these teachers, Adv. haer., v. 19, 2 : substan-
tiam a semetipsa floruisse et essa se natam . . . alii adventum Domine
contemnunt, etc.

‡ Besides the general works referred to at the end of the preceding chap-
ter the student may consult : Holtzmann, Die Pastoralbriefe, etc., 1880 ;
Köstlin, Lehrbegr. des Evangel. und der Briefe Johannes ; the articles on
" Johannes" and "Petrus" in Herzog's Real Encyclop., and those on
" Johannes, Briefe des," "Pastoralbriefe," and "Petrus der zweite Brief
des," in Schenkel's Bibel-Lexicon ; Hilgenfeld, Das Evangel. und die Briefe
Johannes ; Baur, Die Pastoralbriefe, etc.; Lipsius, Der Gnosticismus, sein
Wesen, Ursprung, und Entwickelungsgang, 1860, and article "Gnosis" in
Schenkel's Bibel-Lexicon ; Hilgenfeld, Die Johanneischen Briefe, Theol.
Jahrb. 1855, pp. 471 ff.; the De Wette-Brückner and Meyer-Huther Com-
mentaries on the Epistles in question.

CHAPTER VII.

JEWISH-CHRISTIAN APOCALYPTIC.

JEWISH-CHRISTIAN apocalyptic exhibits the distinctive traits of its Jewish predecessor together with certain modifications of the latter determined by a belief in Jesus as the Messiah. Common to both are fantastic ideas of God's relation to the world and a *naïve* disregard of the historical continuity of affairs. The Jewish apocalyptic literature has been described by one scholar as " an imitation of prophecy called forth by the longing of a time destitute of prophets," [*] and by another as " that species of Scripture dating from the Maccabean age, in which the prophetic spirit put forth an after-bloom which in originality and religious worth is far inferior to the writings of the old prophets." [†] A study of it with reference to the later Jewish idea of God has resulted in the definition : " A detachment of the Messianic expectations from the earthly political ideal and an enhancement of them into the supernatural." [‡] To whatever cause may be due this enhancement of the original Messianic ideal into the supernatural, it is manifestly a distinctive feature of the Jewish apocalypses from Daniel (167 B.C.) to the later productions of this literature which belong to the first century of our era. They are charac-

---

[*] Hilgenfeld, Die jüdisch. Apokalyptik, p. 10.
[†] Pfleiderer, Das Urchristenthum, p. 307.
[‡] Baldensperger, Das Selbstbewusstsein Jesu, 2te Aufl. p. 100.

terized not only by an idealization of the person of the Messiah, but also by a conception of divine judgment which proceeds catastrophically in disregard of the natural relation of cause and effect. An eschatological consummation which sets historical development at defiance, a Messianic kingdom descending from heaven, and a Messiah riding on the clouds, are fantastic traits of this strange literature.

The influence of their apocalyptic national literature upon the Jewish-Christian New Testament writers is evident from a comparison of the portions of their works which belong to this category with the former. An idealization of Jesus, the persistent tendency to which has already been frequently pointed out, corresponding to that of the expected Messiah among the Jews during the century or two preceding our era, and an ardent desire for his re-appearance in a truly glorious Messianic manifestation, were conditions favorable to the production of Christian apocalypses. The apocalyptic section in the synoptic Gospels has already been referred to, and reasons have been given for thinking that it was the product of the Messianic hopes and expectations of the Jewish-Christian followers of Jesus rather than a report of actual words of his. It is not without significance that criticism has detected a Jewish-apocalyptic kernel in this section, around which the entire apocalypse of the Parousia appears to have been constructed. Whether this critical hypothesis be tenable or no, the imitation of the apocalyptic literature of Judaism is unmistakable in the synoptic apocalypse with its Messiah on the clouds, its " throne of glory," and its general catastrophic features.

Besides the apocalyptic features contained in the genuine Epistles of Paul, which have been discussed in Chapter

III, the little apocalypse in 2 Thessalonians ii. 1–12 which forms the centre of this writing, and for the sake of which the letter was probably composed,* requires consideration here.   Apart from other reasons for its spuriousness, which cannot be discussed here, the rest of the Epistle is so manifestly an imitation of the first as to leave little room for doubt of it.   The second chapter has been characterized as " a transference of the apocalyptic eschatology into the Pauline sphere of thought." †   Here traits appear which are unpauline and irreconcilable with the point of view of the first Epistle.   In the latter " the day of the Lord " is represented as coming without any sign, like " a thief in the night," and this the Thessalonians are said to "know full well," and " as sons of the light " not to be " in darkness " that it should " overtake " them.‡ Paul himself expects to be among the " living " who shall witness the descent of Jesus from the heavens "with a loud summons, with the voice of an archangel, and with the trump of God." §   But in the little apocalypse of the second Epistle not only are the readers cautioned against thinking the great day " near at hand," but definite indications of its approach are mentioned.   It will not come, the writer declares, " until the apostasy shall have come first, and the man of sin have been revealed, the son of perdition ; he that opposeth and exalteth himself above every one that is called God, or worthy of worship, so that he sitteth in the temple of God showing himself to be God." ‖   The readers, are asked, moreover,

---

* Weizsäcker, Das apostol. Zeitalter, 2te Aufl. pp. 238 f.
† Holtzmann, Einleit., 2te Aufl. p. 240.
‡ 1 Thess. v. 2, 5.
§ 1 Thess. iv. 15, 16.
‖ 2 Thess. ii. 2–4.

if they do not remember that Paul himself had told them all these things when he was with them.   The prominent features of the section in question show more affinity with the so called Johannine Apocalypse than with the genuine Pauline eschatology which is distinguished by a soteriological interest, whose absence is characteristic of this spurious construction of " the last things."   Opposing the indolence which arose from the expectation of the Parousia near at hand and intent on introducing his peculiar eschatology, the writer deals in terms which are obscure and inexplicable.   Who is intended by " the man of sin, the son of perdition," and what is " that which re-straineth " (τὸ κατέχον) or " the one that restraineth " (ὁ κατέχων), cannot be certainly determined.   This only is certain, that the writer had in mind conditions of his own time, whether the Roman power as it was toward the end of the first century, or the heresy and heretics of the beginning of the second.   The adversary, "the satanic counterpart of the Parousia," he declares, in true apocalyptic style, " the Lord Jesus will consume with the breath of his mouth, and destroy with the mani-festation of his coming." *

The canonical Christian apocalypse *par éminence* is that traditionally ascribed to the apostle John, and known in our English Bible as the Revelation.   That it was not written by John, however, is a conclusion scarcely contest-able in view of the recent critical investigations of its character and composition, among which are deserving of especial mention the contributions of Völter, Vischer, Weizsäcker, Pfleiderer, and Weyland.   These scholars all agree that the work is the composition of different writers, whose contributions were made at different times more or

* 2 Thess. ii. 8.

less remote.* It would be foreign to the present purpose to enter into a discussion of the origin of this writing, since we are concerned with it only as an interpretation of the gospel. The question whether the groundwork of the book is Jewish or Jewish-Christian is of course important for the end in view, but as the reasons for the former hypothesis are by no means conclusive † or generally accepted, our discussion may well proceed upon the latter. The work is as to its greater part distinctively an apocalypse ($\alpha\pi o\varkappa\acute{a}\lambda v\psi\iota\varsigma$) or a revelation concerning the last things, according to the eschatological application of the term established by Paul, ‡ and is occupied with disclosures of the future fortune and consummation to which the kingdom of God on earth was supposed to be hastening. Like its Jewish prototype it presupposes a time of storm and stress, when men felt that the existing tribulation was no longer endurable, and looked with eager expectation for the intervention of the celestial powers to bring relief and effect the triumph of their cause by a violent rupture of the course of events. Since it is evident from the declarations in the first chapter that the disclosures are of " what must shortly come to pass," and that " the time is at hand," § the only hermeneutical

* Völter's division is as follows : 1. The original Apocalypse of the apostle John of the year 65 or 66 ; 2. An addition by the same hand of the year 68 or 69 ; 3. The first revision in the time of Trajan ; 4. The second revision of the year 129 or 130 ; 5. The third revision of the year 140.—Die Entstehung der Apokalypse, 1885. Vischer regards the work as an original Jewish apocalypse with additions by the hand of a Christian, Die Offenbarung Johannis, etc., 1886.

† This hypothesis is, however, supported by Harnack and Martineau. See the former's " Nachwort" to Vischer's treatise and the latter's Seat of Authority in Religion, pp. 225 f.

‡ Rom. ii. 5, viii. 19.

§ Rev. i. 1, 3.

method by which the problems of the book can be solved is the one that seeks the key to them in the circumstances of the time of the writer or writers. Its interpretation has been greatly impeded by the presumption that all its allusions to men and events must be explained with reference to the time of the apostle John, and by the allegorizing which has applied them throughout the whole extent of the history of Christendom.

With regard to Vischer's contention that the Revelation presents no unity of doctrine, Judaism and Christianity lying in it side by side without reconciliation, Holtzmann's discrimination is important, that a distinction must be made between a Jewish basis of the apocalyptic sphere of thought and a Jewish groundwork of the book as a literary product.* Evidences of the former abound in the prevailing Old-Testament modes of thought and images and the reverence and affection shown for Jerusalem, the " holy " and the " beloved " city. The earth is the theatre of the eschatological drama, and when " the first earth " has " passed away " a new heaven and a new earth are created—" an evident proof of the genuinely Jewish materiality of this contemplation of the world." But this may be also Jewish-Christian; for, as Baur remarks, the Revelation passes here only by degrees beyond the synoptic Gospels and the Pauline sphere of thought. The idea of God is Judæo-theocratic rather than Christian. He sits on his throne in heaven—that " archetypal sanctuary," for in the Jewish theology as well as in Hebrews heaven is " the idealized archetype of the earth." He is the Almighty, King, Lord ($\delta\epsilon\sigma\pi\acute{o}\tau\eta\varsigma$), and out of His throne proceed thunders and lightnings. †

* Hand-Commentar, iv. p. 266.

† Rev. i. 8, iv. 5, 8, xi. 17, xv. 3, xvi. 7, 14, xxi. 22.

He is the "only holy," the one "who is, and was, and is to come," "the Alpha and the Omega."* He reigns in magnificent state, "in appearance" on his throne "like a jasper-stone and a sardius." Twenty-four "elders," probably representing the martyrs, golden-crowned and white-robed, sit on twenty-four thrones around Him. There are seven lamps of fire, "which are the seven spirits of God," and "a sea of glass," and four "living creatures" representing perhaps the totality of created beings.† His prominent attribute is justice which expresses itself in penalty. Vengeance and retribution proceed from Him and His wrath issues in terror and blood.‡ His paternal relation to men is scarcely recognized.

The doctrine of the person of Christ in the Revelation is unique among the Christologies of the New Testament in having as its basis the Messianism of the Old Testament and the later Judaism—a fact which has influenced opinion adversely to the unity of the book. He is "King of kings" and "Lord of lords," the "lion that is of the tribe of Judah" and "the shoot from David."§ He is the ruler of the nations and governs them "with a rod of iron," a sharp sword issues from his mouth, that with it he may smite them, and "he treadeth the wine-press of the fierceness of the wrath of God Almighty."‖ The child of the theocracy, he escapes at his birth the pursuit of the Devil, "the great red dragon" and is "caught up to God and His throne." Along with these Jewish or Jewish-Christian traits appear various distinctively Chris-

---

* Rev. i. 8. *Cf*. Isa. xliv. 6. See also iv. 9, xv. 3, xviii. 8.
† Rev. iv. 3–11.   ‡ Rev. xiv. 20, xvi. 1, xix. 15, 17–21.
§ Rev. v. 5, xvii. 14, xix. 16.
‖ Rev. xii. 5, xix. 15. See Ps. ii. 9, Isa. xi. 4 ; Ps. Salom. xvii. 26.

tian designations of Christ. He is called "the first-born of the dead," the one who "overcame and sat down with my father on his throne."* The conquering of the Devil in a "war" and the casting of him out of heaven, his abode down to the time of this conflict, apparently, is celebrated as a vindication of the "authority" of Christ. This transfer of Christ's conflict with Satan from the earth, where it takes place according to the Gospel-story, to heaven, is peculiar, and accords with the indifference manifested throughout the book to the earthly life of Jesus—a trait of apocalypse, which is nothing if not unhistorical. It comports with the extravagant idealization of Christ which pervades this work that various predicates of the Deity are here applied to him. He is called "the first and the last, the beginning and the end, the Alpha and the Omega." As the exalted Lamb he receives divine worship from the angels and the entire creation, and in one place traits of "the Ancient of Days" in Daniel are ascribed to him.† An ascription to him of a divine nature does not, however, appear to be implied in these designations. He is not called Lord God, and the term Almighty is reserved for the Deity alone. In fact, he is said to have been "the beginning of the creation of God," or the first creature—an exaltation inferior to that in Hebrews i. 10, "Lord, who in the beginning didst found the earth." It is probable also that deification is not intended in the application to Jesus of the term, "the Logos of God,"‡ which is used in connection with the comparison of this agency to a sharp sword proceeding out of his mouth—a figure of his execu-

---

* Rev. i. 5, ii. 8, iii. 21, vii. 17. See xxii. 1, 3, "throne of God and the Lamb."

† Rev. i. 13, 17, xxi. 6, xxii. 13. ‡ Rev. xix. 13.

23

tion of the penal judgments of God. The designation probably signifies that it is he who discloses and fulfils the word of God. While there is an implication here of the preëxistence of Christ, the doctrinal point of view is evidently remote from that of the fourth Gospel in which Christ is conceived not as "the Logos of God," but as "the Logos" (ὁ λόγος) absolutely. We have here perhaps the beginning of the later developed Logos doctrine, the contribution of Jewish Christianity to the conception which it required the Alexandrian philosophy to complete. The ideal character of the Christology of the book comports with the apocalyptic point of view. All the exalted qualities ascribed to the Messiah are purely nominal, and have no connection with him as a concrete personality. The extravagant eschatological expectations in which the book is rooted appear to have been the motive of the Christology, and the Messiah who was to come is conceived to be endowed with qualities and powers corresponding to the imagined splendors of his advent.

With reference to the work of Christ the emphasis is laid as in Paul upon his death, and the Johannine idea of his love for the believers finds distinct expression. An ascription of praise is made to "him who loveth us, and washed us from our sins in his own blood, and made us a kingdom, priests to God his Father." * The Pauline terminology is employed in the use of ἀγοράζειν, "to buy off," to redeem: "Thou wast slain, and hast redeemed us (bought us off) to God by thy blood." † The redeemed are clothed in garments made white by "the blood of the Lamb." Through the blood of Christ is founded the kingdom of God, and believers are made

* Rev. i. 5.   † ἠγόρασας τῷ θεῷ, v. 9.

subjects and priests therein. The designation of Christ as "the Lamb" (τὸ ἀρνίον), occurring twenty-nine times in the course of the book, was probably derived from Isaiah liii. 7, where the pious remnant of the people are represented as suffering for the nation, and as brought like a "lamb to the slaughter." For Christ himself his death is represented as the means through which he gained glory and distinction. He is accounted worthy to open the seals of the book because he was "slain."* This denotes a distinct opposition to the later Johannine doctrine according to which the glory of Christ belonged to him originally, was had with the Father before the world was, and hence was not acquired by his earthly suffering. In his exaltation he shares the divine power, sits with the Father on His Throne, is Lord of lords and King of kings, Lord of the kings of the earth, and has the keys of death and the underworld.† The emphasis placed on the resurrection of Christ is Pauline, but here as in the matter of his death there is no definite appropriation of the fact for the founding of a soteriological doctrine. The book was not written by a Christian philosopher like Paul. Its prominent theme is the exaltation of Christ and the victory which he was to win. After the war in heaven which resulted in the overthrow of Satan, the conflict carried on with him by "the brethren" on the earth terminates in their victory "because of the blood of the Lamb."

With respect to man's part in salvation the Revelation represents the Old-Testament point of view. On the human side the essence of religion is the keeping of the commandments of God. Everything depends upon "works" (ἔργα): "Blessed are the dead who die in the

* Rev. v. 9. 12.　　　† Rev. i. 18, iii. 21, xvii. 14, xix. 16.

Lord, and their works follow them," *i. e.*, determine their future condition.   The dead are judged according to their works, and a judgment book is kept in which these are recorded.   The Church in Sardis is censured because its "works have not been found perfect before God." *

There is no trace in the book of the Pauline doctrine of justification by faith.   In accordance with the stress of the time the practical rather than the dogmatic aspect of faith is made prominent.   The faith in Jesus ($\dot{\eta}$ $\pi i \sigma \tau \iota s$ 'I$\eta \sigma o \tilde{v}$) which is commended and enjoined is fidelity to the confession of him so important amid the trials of the hour.   Hence faith is associated with love, ministry, and patience, and even included among the $\dot{\epsilon} \rho \gamma a$. †   The chief requirements which are made of Christians are not to deny Jesus, to keep his testimony, hold fast his word, to hold fast that which they have, not to love their lives, even to death, and not to suffer their crown to be taken from them. ‡   The Christian's life is a conflict, and especially honored are the martyrs, who shall be clothed in white, "as an evidence of the justice of their cause and of the divine approval."

The Revelation represents in general rather the Jewish-Christian than the Pauline apprehension of the mission of Christianity.   In the enumeration of the host of those who had been "redeemed" by the blood of Christ are included "men out of every tribe and tongue and people," § but gentiles are not recognized as having equal privileges and rights with Jews as denizens of the new Jerusalem.   The preëminence of Israel is expressed in

---

* Rev. iii. 2.
† Rev. ii. 19, xiv. 12.
‡ Rev. ii. 13, 25, iii. 8, vi. 9, xii. 11, 17.
§ Rev. v. 9, vii. 9.

the declaration that the one hundred and forty-four thousand who are " sealed " are from the twelve tribes, and on the twelve gates of the new Jerusalem are inscribed the names of these tribes. Censure is, indeed, not spared for those "who say they are Jews and are not, but are a synagogue of Satan," * and the crucifixion of Christ is represented as avenged upon Jerusalem, which for this crime is called spiritually Sodom and Egypt; † yet only a tenth part of the city is destroyed, and only seven thousand of the inhabitants perish, while "the rest become afraid, and give glory to the God of heaven." ‡ It is significant that the temple is spared, and that the thousand years' reign has its central point in the beloved city. "The faith of the book may be called Jewish-Christian; but it is neither the Jewish Christianity of the primitive Church nor its later Ebionitism. It distinguishes itself from the former by the wider recognition of gentile Christianity as well as by the developed doctrine of the atoning death of Jesus and the acknowledgment of the same in its total significance for salvation. It is still farther removed from that later legal and exclusive Judaism. The requirement of circumcision is throughout foreign to and irreconcilable with its spirit." §

The book contains a mythology whose fantastic features find ample room for expression in its apocalyptic purpose. Angels play a prominent part in the drama whose theatre is the celestial and terrestial regions and the underworld. An angel stands in the sun ; there is an angel of the waters ; one ascends from the East ; one stands on the sea ; there

---

* Rev. ii. 9, iii. 9.
† Rev. xi. 8.
‡ Rev. xi. 13.
§ Weizsäcker, Das apostol. Zeitalter, 2te Aufl. p. 525.

is an angel of the bottomless pit ; hosts of them stand around the throne of God ; four angels stand on the four corners of the earth ; and there are seven angels with trumpets who announce the seven plagues.*   Angels rule over the elements and execute the divine penal judgments. Michael and his angelic hosts fight against the dragon and his angels, and cast them out of heaven. The great mythologic adversary of the Church, Satan, the Devil, the dragon, the serpent, the great red dragon, plays an important *rôle* in this vivid apocalypse. A spiritual opponent of goodness, he bears a resemblance to "the prince of this world " in the fourth Gospel, and there is presented the Old-Testament idea of him as the " accuser " of the saints before God. After being cast out of heaven by the celestial generalissimo, Michael, he begins his ravages upon the earth with bitter ferocity, knowing that " he hath but a short time." The opposition and the persecutions to which the Christians are exposed are instigated by him whose function it is to "deceive the whole world." The false teachers are they who "know the depths of Satan." After being bound and sealed in "the abyss" for a thousand years, he is released to deceive the nations, but is overcome in a great cosmic conflict, and with the beast and the false prophet is cast into the lake of fire and brimstone to be "tormented day and night for ever and ever."†

As in 1 John ii. 18 the coming of Antichrist immediately precedes the near Parousia or the last days, so in the Revelation the appearance of the great antagonist Satan announces the close of the apocalyptic drama. After a series of plagues, heaven opens, and the " Logos of God "

---

* Rev. vii. 2, viii. 2, ix. 11, x. 5, xvi. 5, xix. 17.

† Rev. ii. 10, 13, 24, xii. 3, 9, 10, 12, 17, xiii. 2, 4, 11, xvi. 3, xx. 3, 10.

descends, his eyes a flame of fire, on his head many diadems, and in his mouth a sharp sword, and makes war with Antichrist and his prophet. Both are "cast alive into the lake of fire and brimstone," Satan is bound for a thousand years, and the host of allied enemies are slain, " and all the birds are glutted with their flesh." Then are raised at " the first resurrection " those beheaded on account of the testimony to Jesus," the martyrs, the marriage-supper of the Lamb and his bride begins, and they reign with Christ in Jerusalem a thousand years.* At the end of this millennial period Satan, who has been released, gathers his hosts and " encompasses the camp of the saints and the beloved city;" but " fire comes down out of heaven and devours them." The Devil, the great deceiver, is cast into the burning lake for endless torment. Now, seated on " a great white throne," God begins the final judgment. The dead great and small appear, those who had "part in the first resurrection" apparently excepted, and they are judged "according to their works" out of the things written in the books. The sea and hades give up their dead, so that the judgment is general. Death and hades are cast into the lake of fire, which receives also all whose names are "not written in the book of life." † Then are created "a new heaven and a new earth," and the new Jerusalem comes down "out of heaven from God." The new earth becomes the theatre of the kingdom of God, whose "tabernacle is with men, and He will dwell with them. Tears shall be wiped from the eyes of the blessed, and "death shall be no more." ‡

---

* Rev. xix. 7, 9, 11, 12, 19, 20, 21, xx. 4, 5, 9.
† Rev. xx. 11, 15. *Cf.* Enoch xc. 26.
‡ Rev. xxi. 1–5.

This book considered in relation to the gospel of Jesus must be regarded as such a transformation of it as would be effected in an age of hardship and violence by men who did not comprehend its precepts of loving-kindness and forgiveness. The vindictive passions of men whose patience is exhausted amid the tribulations of the time are ascribed to the Deity. The souls of martyrs in the cause of him who prayed on the cross for the forgiveness of his executioners cry out in heaven for vengeance on "those who dwell on the earth." * The terrible drama of the last things unfolds its apocalyptic horrors in relentless judgment executed in destruction, flames, and bloodshed. With respect to the consummation of the kingdom of God no stronger contrast can be conceived than that between the catastrophes herein delineated and Jesus' parables of the leaven and the grain of mustard. It is the contrast between the fretful impatience of the narrow theocratic intelligence and the calm patience of the far-seeing religious genius. It were a great mistake to suppose that the writer of these visions was not in earnest but was merely amusing himself with figures of speech. What he depicted he and his contemporaries expected to see realized—Rome annihilated, Jerusalem saved, the Messiah coming in his "wrath" so that all should see him, even "they who had pierced him." The enemies of the good cause had shed the blood of saints and prophets, and God would give them blood to drink. † One may, indeed, with Hausrath find in the book "religious ground-thoughts" of importance, such as that "worldly power, though stronger than Rome, can at the most only reach the outer fore-court, never the holy kernel of religion itself, and that the good, though crucified and buried,

* Rev. vi. 10.   † Rev. xvi. 6.

must finally alone possess the kingdom," * but one is hardly rewarded by finding these for a search through this lurid apocalypse, since one must come upon many ideas in it which are revolting to a humane sensibility and opposed to the spirit of the Christian gospel.

* Art. " Apokalypse" in Schenkel's Bible-Lexicon, i. p. 164.

CHAPTER VIII.

THE GOSPEL AND THEOLOGY.

THE foregoing study of the gospel of Jesus and of the principal interpretations which it underwent in the New Testament discloses facts of great significance to all who are interested in the Christian religion and Christian theology. The several writings which have been passed under review are seen to constitute a theological and religious literature having in the personality and teaching of Jesus a bond of unity and in the personalities and environments of their writers the conditions of marked diversities. Precisely such phenomena are presented as the student of history would expect to see emerge from the promulgation of great truths by a commanding genius and their advocacy by men of different capacities, temperaments, and interests. The conclusion which this study compels is that the different phases of doctrine in the New Testament furnish an example of development out of simple into complex and intensified forms and not merely a relation of the juxtaposition of diverse apprehensions or interpretations. The development was determined partly by varying exigencies, circumstances, and points of view, and partly by the antecedents, presuppositions, and tendencies of the men who occupied themselves with the great central theme. We have seen that the synoptic Gospels contain fragmentary reports of the teachings of Jesus as they had been preserved in antecedent writings and in the oral tradition of his followers and their successors. From these records it is doubtless possible to construct a tolerably correct portrait of the personality of the great Teacher and an account of his principal teachings which is in the main true. In them we find that the doctrines which may without doubt be attributed to him are few and simple. He accepted from the religion in which he had been reared the doctrine of one God, the paternal attributes of whose nature he so exalted and illustrated out of his own religious intuitions and experience that the divine fatherhood may be regarded as one of his original contributions to theology by means of which an impulse and inspiration of inappreciable moment have been given to the spiritual life of men. From the current Jewish doctrines he adopted that of the existence of the human soul after death, though he taught nothing definite as to the details and conditions of that existence. The chief stress of his teaching was placed upon the proclamation of the kingdom of God, or the new order of ethical-spiritual life, and the conditions of entering it, and upon righteousness, which he represented in the manner of the ancient prophets as attainable by men through obedience to God. Though "he spoke as one having authority," he claimed no divine rank, and thrust aside the dangerous crown of Jewish Messiahship. He did not appeal to mighty works for an authentication of his teachings, but left these to verify themselves in the experience of believers and in the transformation of mankind which as a "leaven" they were destined to effect. All that is highest in human ethical achievement, in love, purity, and compassion; all that is greatest in human character, in courage, fidelity, and consecration; and all that is most blessed in religious

experience, found exemplification in his life. A spotless
Rabbi, it was not without good reason that his followers
called him Master, and it has been with a just recognition
of his preëminence that the purest souls in the highest
civilizations since his time have reverenced him as spiritual
Lord.

However desirable it may be thought to be that a
faultless record of the life and teachings of the great
Master should have been made and handed down uncorrupted, it is evident that such an achievement would have
been impossible without a miraculous intervention. In
the case of such an intervention we should not have had
an historical Christianity, but a Christianity in which the
laws of historical development would be set aside. Now,
not only do all the presumptions in the case rest against
an hypothesis of this kind, but the oldest Gospels, the
synoptics, present precisely the sort of phenomena which
would be expected in an historical course of affairs in
writings composed from forty to seventy years after the
events recorded. With all the conditions present of a
transformation of the facts of the life and teachings of
Jesus it were a marvel if such a transformation should
not be made. Accordingly, the aureole of wonder
is suspended over the cradle of the infant Saviour.
A supernatural messenger announces to the trembling
virgin the mystery of a conception by the Holy Spirit,
and the sympathy of heaven with the beginnings of the
great earthly drama of redemption finds a voice in a shout
of a choir of angels, who appear to frightened shepherds
amidst the shining " glory of the Lord." Inward spiritual
facts and experiences are expressed in terms of external
phenomena and personal powers. The illumination of
the soul of Jesus by the spirit of truth is recorded as the

descent of a visible dove and an audible voice from the upper air, and the moral conflict of opposing motives in his mind becomes a personal conflict with Satan in the desert, on the pinnacle of the temple, and on a mountain-top before a magical panorama of "all the kingdoms of the world and their glory." Material wonders attest the spiritual supremacy of the great Rabbi throughout his life, and at his death the earth is shaken, the veil of the temple is rent in twain, and darkness envelops the affrighted land. The victory of his spirit over death finds a material expression in the open grave, the abandoned burial-vestments, and a bodily manifestation, while the saints who burst their cerements and come forth into the holy city herald him as the first fruits of the resurrection of "the bodies of the holy men who slept." Having incorporated into itself the ascension of Jesus into heaven, it is not surprising that the tradition of his life and teachings which took form among Jewish Christians, who believed that in declaring himself to be a spiritual Messiah he accepted the crown of the son of David, did not leave him in the celestial regions, but developed the doctrine of his early return to the earth. A Jewish-Messianic mission could find no fulfilment in the life of a homeless teacher ending in an ignominious death. Hence the tradition of the Messiah must not only give expression to the feverish hope of an advent in glory which should realize the Messianic dream, but must also contain a glowing prophecy of it in the very words of the Master. Accordingly, he is made to declare that before his generation should pass away he would come on the clouds of heaven attended by "his holy angels," and summon the nations to judgment before an earthly "throne of glory," awarding to men eternal life or eternal punishment according to the treatment which they should have accorded to his "brethren." It is not surprising that biographies of Jesus written from the Messianic point of view of the Jewish-Christian tradition should present a mingling of incongruous elements; that sayings whose profound spirituality mark them as genuine words of the great Teacher should be found not far removed from impracticable apocalyptic visions; that declarations of the spiritual character of the kingdom of God should stand in connection with an allegorical interpretation of passages from the Old Testament quoted and distorted to serve as evidences of the unspiritual and temporal mission of Christ; and that along with the lofty morality which rebuked the worldly ambition of the sons of Zebedee for places of honor in the " kingdom " for which they were hoping with the words: " Ye will indeed drink the cup that I drink and be baptized with the baptism that I am baptized with," should be found the illusive promise to the twelve apostles that, " in the renovation when the Son of Man sitteth on the throne of his glory, ye who have followed me shall also yourselves sit on twelve thrones judging the twelve tribes of Israel." It is evident that the interest and expectation which set over against each other in the evangelical tradition the teaching that the kingdom of God had already come in the mission of its spiritual Messiah, and the apocalyptic advent and the "throne of glory," might very well place side by side the pure morality which taught the doing of good without hope of return, and the promise to calculating self-interest of a hundred-fold in the time that now is, houses, lands, etc., and in the age to come everlasting life.

The religion of Jesus, which does not admit of a precise formulation, but the leading features of which were a sense of men's relation of dependence upon and responsibility to God as a righteous Father, a recognition of their capacity to hold communion with Him through their spiritual nature over which death has no power, and a practical principle of brotherhood which binds men to mutual helpfulness and love, received from his Jewish-Christian followers the Messianic-apocalyptic appendage which occupies a conspicuous place in the synoptic Gospels, determining to a considerable degree their coloring of his biography. The predominant Messianic interest of Jewish Christianity directed attention chiefly to the future as the theatre of the exaltation of Christ, and determined the apocalyptic features of its interpretation. But Paul, in whom the speculative tendency was stronger than hope and anticipation, looked backward as well as forward in his idealization of Christ, and conceived a Christology whose celestial point of departure required a metaphysical construction. To him "the man Christ Jesus," who was "born of the seed of David according to the flesh," was not simply the man of the Jewish-Christian synoptic tradition, but "the man from heaven," the "second Adam," the spiritual head and representative of the human race. The Messiahship which he conceived was a spiritualized and transfigured Messiahship, to which were wanting the original national features of the Jewish-Christian conception of Messiah. The Christ, who was not in his thought to be the restorer of the political order of Israel, but the restorer of the spiritual order of mankind, was only "according to the flesh" of the seed of David. As the "anointed" not of a people, but of the human race, he was the preëxistent heavenly man, the "image of God," and the agent of the creation. The Pauline Christology is accordingly symmetrically conceived under

the relation of means to end.   Jesus, regarding himself as
the teacher of men and their Saviour through his teachings
and example, consistently committed the fortune of his
cause to the power of his word and his life, and prophesied
with sublime confidence that the kingdom of God would
become from a little "leaven" a world-transforming
agency.   Taking his place in the current of human affairs
as an historical force, he trusted in himself as such, and
did not connect the result of his mission with a metaphysical celestial origin of his person.   But Paul, the
centre of whose "gospel" was not the life and teachings
of Jesus, but his death and resurrection, conceiving the
end of the Saviour's mission to be the abolition by his sacrifice of the "curse of the law" for all men, a great act of
atonement which should liberate the world from bondage,
also consistently took his departure in constructing his
Christology from no mere historical personality, but from
the representative spiritual Adam, the man from heaven.

This transformation of the gospel of Jesus did not,
however, stop with the construction of a new Christology,
but reached its height in a doctrine of salvation which was
as different from that of Jesus as its theory of his person
was from his teaching regarding himself.   Jesus, who knew
of no other foundation for a character than that which is
laid in hearing and doing his words, who taught nothing
of bearing "the curse of the law" in his death, of his own
satisfaction of the divine righteousness for the world, of
a representative atonement, and of a justification of men
which should be "accounted" to them through their faith
in him, did not have in view the abolition of the law, but
expressly declared that he came to fulfil it.   He would
have men attain righteousness, as he attained it, by a
trusting, worshipful obedience, by spiritual communion

with the Father, and by nurturing the sentiment of brotherly love. This easy yoke and light burden he invited men to assume, and believed in their spiritual capacity to achieve the task through the quickening of his word and his life. On the contrary, Paul's theory of salvation was grounded upon a distrust of man's ability, took no account of the teachings and life of Jesus, and was constructed with reference to a theoretical, absolute consummation, a complete satisfaction of the law, a clearing off once for all of its claims by a final settlement of its account, which partake more of magic than of rational practicability. The idea of a righteousness which is imputed to men through faith by reason of the satisfaction of the requirements of the law by one who has "redeemed them from its curse," and been "made a curse" for them, is foreign to the thought of Jesus, and altogether incompatible with his conception of the establishment of right relations between man and God. The teaching that the Father demands of the wayward son only repentance and return, that to enter the kingdom one must do the will of God and renounce the worldly possessions which encumber the spirit, that the great invitation must be accepted with joyful alacrity though the loved ones are left without adieu, and that the coming after him or the attainment of his spiritual altitude is simply to take up the cross of sacrifice and service and follow him, could not be more radically transformed than it was in the construction of this metaphysical scheme of salvation.

Paul with all his greatness was not, however, quite superior to the apocalpytic expectations of his age and race, and his conception of the consummation of the kingdom of God included a manifestation of the Messiah from heaven, and a "judgment-seat of Christ." But in

24

his doctrine of the last things the original Jewish-Christian Messianism underwent a transformation by the addition of new and strange features. In the synoptic account of the second coming of Christ there is no mention or intimation of a resurrection, and the "throne" of the Son of Man is established on the earth for the judgment of "all nations." On the contrary, the Pauline Christian apocalypse is intimately connected with the apostle's theory of salvation. To be saved was in his thought to become a sharer in the glory and life of the Messianic kingdom, and to reign with Christ at his coming. This good fortune was to be that of the believers in Christ, both those who had " fallen asleep," and those who should be "alive" and "remain" at the Parousia. The former would be " raised incorruptible," and the latter would be "changed." By reason of the Spirit dwelling in them of Him who raised up Christ from the dead, their mortal bodies would be quickened, and, clothed upon with bodies in the likeness of Christ's "body of glory," they would all enter upon the blessedness of being "forever with the Lord." This Pauline transformation of the Jewish-Christian eschatology, although including the expectation of an immediate and catastrophic consummation and such materialistic features as the deliverance of the groaning creation from " the bondage of corruption," to which it was supposed to have been subjected by the sin of Adam, and the subjection of the Messiah's " enemies," was on the whole a more spiritual apprehension of the apocalyptic end than the latter. Among its characteristic traits were a spiritualizing of the Jewish doctrine of the resurrection of the body, a relating of the inward, spiritual transformation through faith to the resurrection apprehended as a clothing upon of the soul with an incorruptible corporeity by reason of the indwelling Spirit, an ingathering of "the fulness of the gentiles," and a hope of the salvation of the beloved and much yearned-for "brethren according to the flesh." The apostle's grounds for believing in the consummation of so hopeful a soteriology within the brief time which remained before the hastening Parousia are not apparent, and there are many things besides in his eschatology which do not well accord with one another; but his doctrine of the last days agrees with his exalted conception of Christ as the divine man from heaven and the universal spiritual Messiah, and with his idea of the transforming Spirit which touches even the mortal body with its life-giving efficacy. It is distinguished by a profundity and a noble humanness and optimism which are in striking contrast with the externality and harshness of the synoptic apocalypse.

How profoundly the person of Christ impressed the early believers in him is apparent in the writings belonging to the school of Paul which have been designated as deutero-Pauline. The transformation of Paulinism by its friends took two general directions: a further exaltation of the person of Christ, and a departure from the distinctive teachings of the apostle regarding salvation. In the matter of Christology conceptions were introduced from different points of view which were not so much in opposition to those of Paul as in some degree foreign to his thought; while the succeeding soteriology was characterized by a quiet dropping out of his fundamental doctrines and a tendency to return to the original Christian idea of the establishment of right relations between man and God. The influence of Alexandrian ideas becomes unmistakably apparent, and the Christology is so far removed from that of the synoptic Gospels that the two different types of conceptions of Jesus originating at nearly the same time furnish a problem which admits of no solution from the dogmatic point of view, and can be historically explained only by the assumption of widely diverging interests, influences, and environments. The influence of the original tradition of Jesus on the one hand and a speculative tendency and interest on the other may be regarded as the most important factors in the two series of Christological conceptions and as determining the value of the one in relation to the other. Accordingly, he who conceived of himself as a teacher of righteousness, the spiritual Messiah of the ethical-religious kingdom of God, the Son of Man by reason of his preëminent and ideal humanity, and who was thought by his Jewish-Christian followers to be their national Messiah, becomes in this speculative Christology the metaphysical Son of God, "the high-priest" of redemption, "the brightness" of the divine glory, "the express image" of the being of God, and the universal providence who "upholds all things by the word of his power." The agency of Jesus in creation, somewhat vaguely expressed by Paul, is expanded into the declarations that in him were created all things in heaven and earth, visible and invisible, thrones, dominions, principalities, and powers, that he is before all things, the end of all creation, and that "in him all things subsist." As the Philonic Logos was supposed to be "filled entirely with the immaterial powers," so Christ is conceived to have contained in himself "all the fulness of the Godhead." With the disappearance of the Pauline doctrine of the representative office of Christ, prominence is given to the ethical significance of his passion, and this idea is developed in connection with mythological features, among which appear the " bringing to naught of him who hath the power of death, that is, the Devil," and the disarming of the orders of spiritual beings, "principalities and powers," which are made "a public show," and "led captive in triumph." The bond of the law which they are supposed to hold against sinful men is "nailed to the cross," so that by means of the great sacrifice the demonic powers are put to confusion and overthrown. The prince of the mythologic "powers of the air" no longer holds the souls of the faithful in his relentless grasp, for the great Champion has gained the victory in the cosmic con-test which was waged between the representatives of the two mighty cosmic forces of good and evil.

The great transformations of the gospel of Jesus which appear in the New Testament are completed in a dogmatic-mystical writing with an ostensible biographical purpose which is subordinated to a distinctive theological tendency. The fourth Gospel is a Gospel of subjective reflection upon an idealized object. It is a Christianized Alexandrianism in which the original Christology of Jesus now disappears among metaphysical abstractions, and now vaguely emerges in the shadowy outlines of a speculative biography. The author has put himself into his work to such a degree as to render its subjectivity its distinguishing characteristic among the Gospel-records. The person of Christ is the prominent theme which is accentuated in the prologue, in the discourses, and in the narratives, and his exaltation is carried to the verge of deification. The lowly Jesus of Nazareth of the synoptic tradition here becomes the heaven-descended Logos who was in the beginning with God, and was God, by whom the world was made, and through whom in the word of ancient seers a dimly-appre-hended light had shone upon the abyss of spiritual dark-ness. Assuming the functions of a mediator in the dualism whose antitheses are God and the world, light and darkness, the divine Logos becomes flesh, and takes up his abode among men to reveal the Father, to be glorified in his death and resurrection, and to return and assume the glory which he had with God " before the world was." The position assigned to Jesus in this Gospel is one of cosmic significance, and his functions transcend the limits of Jewish Messianism. As the Logos from heaven, come forth from the bosom of the Father, as a world-mediator, descended to draw to himself the children of light and of God from all nations, as the light of the world, and the beloved divine Son of God, he surpasses in rank and glory all that was dreamed or foretold of the splendor and dominion of the scion of the royal house of David. Greater than the Pauline " second Adam," he is no representative of the human race appointed to bear the curse of the law and to be made in his passion a curse for men. He offers no atoning sacrifice, and his death is not an humiliation, but a gateway through which he passes out of the darkened world into his glory. He does not suffer to satisfy the divine righteousness, and does not buy off sinful men by the payment of the precious ransom of his blood, but he draws them to himself by the attraction of his personality, and to those who receive him he gives " power to become the children of God." The Johannine interpretation of the gospel in discarding or ignoring the leading features of the Pauline doctrine of salvation preserves the spirit of the original teaching of Jesus along with manifold variations of form and content. Discharging all such externalities as the bearing of " the curse of the law " and the effecting of a representative satisfaction by Christ in his death, it emphasizes a mystical, inward relation of men to Jesus which is consummated through a faith and love by which the receptive soul is immediately connected with the life-giving personality of the Son of God. There is no roundabout justification or accounting righteous through faith by reason of the abrogation of a burdensome "law," but he who believes has everlasting life, is passed from death to life, and though dead lives again. The life-giving Christ directly communicates to the believer a spiritual principle which is in him "a well of water springing up to everlasting life." Obedience, far from being an impossible achievement, is the prompt and glad expression of the life of him who is in living union with Christ. He who loves him will keep his commandments. "Clean already by reason of the word" which Jesus has spoken, the believer has only to abide in the life-giving vine to "bear much fruit." Yet this is not all. The believer and Christ are merged in a blessed unity of everlasting life. "I in you, and ye in me" is the formula of the mystic beatitude. The spiritual blessedness of the happy children of light is finally consummated in the practical realization of their filial relation to God. They become related to the Father as the divine Son is in a higher degree related to Him. The love with which the Father loved him before the world was is now bestowed also upon those who have received him, and not only the Son, but the Father too, comes and abides with them. For the believer the future is full of promise. The blessed Paraclete will come. Receiving that which is Christ's he will communicate it to the faithful, leading them "into all truth." Death has no power over those who have been united with Christ. He will "raise them up at the last day," and they will "come forth to a resurrection of life."

The various types of teaching which are contained in the New Testament—the essential gospel of Jesus, and the

Jewish-Christian, the Pauline, the deutero-Pauline, the Johannine, and the anti-Gnostic apprehensions of Christianity—have thus far been considered only as formal differences of doctrine. It is manifest that the teaching of Jesus lies at the basis of all the others, and that it stood in a causal relation to them, furnishing partly the material and almost entirely the impulse which made them possible. It cannot but occur, however, to one who reflects upon the subject, that between the two great classes into which the New Testament may be divided—the Gospel and its interpretations and transformations—there exists a profounder distinction than that of merely formal variations. There is in fact between the two classes a distinction according to which, while the several members of the second class present coördinate differences, the two classes are distinguished by a fundamental difference of *nature*, an unlikeness which separates them " by the whole diameter of being." It is the distinction between religion as experienced and talked about by one who was spiritually in touch with divine realities and in communion with God, and the accretions which become attached to his message and his story when these are committed to the flood of oral tradition ; between the teacher in his aloneness and simple greatness, and the portraits of him drawn by his own and the immediately succeeding generations ; between a God-allied life illustrating a divine message, and human conceptions and opinions of both determined by varying interests, tendencies, and prejudices, and by tribal or provincial points of view; between a word of universal import spoken from a commanding outlook of spiritual experience, and the commentaries of the schools upon it ; between a spiritual Messiah already come with neither strife nor cry in an inward kingdom of righteousness and love, and a temporal Messiah about to come on the clouds in pomp and splendor with apocalyptic "thrones" and judgment; between the proclamation of the kingdom of God as an ethical and religious practical principle, and interpretations of it determined by the feverish Messianic hopes of an age of political ferment and fanaticism; between the intuitions of an inspired Master who in his purity of heart beholds God, and the speculations of lesser men who grope if haply they may find Him; between realities and dreams; religion and theology; revelation and apocalypse; truth and half-truths; between the clear-sighted vision which sees what is real in man and God, and the turbid reasoning which grasps at phantoms; between the self-consciousness of the Son of Man, and metaphysical Christologies; between the straight way to God through sacrifice and obedience, and abstract and mechanical schemes of redemption; between seeking the present kingdom of God and His righteousness, and "gazing up into heaven" to discern the coming kingdom—the part of one neglecting to take up the Master's yoke and burden while dreaming dreams of "the last things."

The importance and transcendent worth of the gospel of Jesus in contrast with the "undivine elements" with which it is ordinarily confused are evident as soon as it is separated from these, and regarded by itself. What is regarded as Christianity in the average thought of men is a collection of theological opinions which preponderate over the few moral and religious ideas associated with them. Accordingly, Christianity and the religion of Jesus are two things which it is necessary to clear thinking about either to keep distinct. The gospel of Jesus is a teaching which may be described as the expression of his thought and experience of man's relation to God and to his fellow-men, or of conduct in the widest sense of the word. The importance of this gospel for thought is apparent when we set it over against the accretions which, beginning in the New Testament, as we have seen, have accumulated during its history. It has the stimulus and nurture for the mind which always accrue to it from dealing with great realities. As in art, so in morals and religion, the artificial degrades and enfeebles, the real ennobles and strengthens the soul. It is a striking evidence of the unequalled greatness of Jesus that his legacy to mankind contains nothing that is factitious. He has left us not his dreams, but his experiences; not his speculations, but his intuitive judgments; not processes, but verities; not a theology, but a religion. The great verities composing the gospel of Jesus have an inappreciable worth to the mind for the ends of spiritual culture. They are fruitful of thought, quicken the higher emotions, and furnish great moral impulses. They establish man's faith in himself, in the moral and spiritual order, and in God. A purifying flame of aspiration and love burns in the soul which receives them. Trust in them produces deathless hope and indomitable courage. They enter into the structure of all true character, and constitute the vital principle of righteousness. For the ends of spiritual development one truth of Jesus exceeds in worth all the apocalypses that have been dreamed. His gospel, contrasted with the commentaries and speculations upon it which are contained in the New Testament, is as the permanent to the transient, as the divine word to varying human interpretations of it. In what striking contrast does the fruitfulness of the one stand to the dreary barrenness of the other! There is the difference between them that the one is chiefly a religion, and the other chiefly a variety of theologies. The spiritual teacher in communion with God and in fellowship with men, how near is he to us, how apprehensible to thought, how inspiring as an example! But the Messiah on the clouds, the great high-priest, the second Adam, the preëxistent Logos, what remoteness, what inacessibility, what suggestions of spiritual sterility, do these terms convey! The real Jesus who goes before us in the way of sacrifice and obedience inspires our reverence and devotion, and as we follow him we become aware of the divine presence. But the apocalyptic and metaphysical Christs stir in us no sentiment of love and consecration, no fervor of discipleship, and only excite wonder, and provoke speculation. Had only these latter been given, there would have been no disciples, no martyrs, and no Christian Church. Did the New Testament portray only these Christs, and not also the living Jesus, it were a dead book.

As a religion, then, the gospel of Jesus is distinguished from its interpretations and transformations in the New Testament by the quality of verifiability. The only verification to man of which a spiritual truth is capable lies in its appeal to his intuitions and in the tests which his experience gives to it. It can be confirmed by no outward sign which may herald it, and by no miracle which may accompany its proclamation. A teacher can only verify his mission from God by the divineness which, filling himself and his message, awakens an immediate response to the divine truth which he delivers in those to whom he ministers, and leads them into his communion with the Highest. An outward miracle, if wrought and historically confirmed, has no significance for us apart from the teacher and his message. These must be verified by the response which our nature makes to them before the other can have aught to say to us, except to tell us that a scene of wonder or of magic has been enacted, the hidden springs of which we do not know. Thus the shaken mountain and the voice from heaven become belated and superfluous witnesses to a divine fact already authenticated. Now, the life and word of Jesus have in themselves precisely this supreme verification, that they command at once the reverent assent of every human being who is sufficiently developed in his moral and religious faculties to be impressible by them. One less developed a voice from heaven might, indeed, arrest, but could not awaken to love and worship. The difference is manifest as to verification between a teaching which reveals to us the depths and heights of our being, stirs all noble impulses, shames every debasing passion, and elicits a glad response from the affections and the will, and the teaching which offers chiefly imaginary apocalypses, speculative Christologies, and dreams and dramas of "the last things." As to the former, we know that it is true because its power and truth are revealed in our experience, and by it we are led upward from strength to strength. As to the latter, it awakens no response in us except one of wonder or curiosity, and, since it leads us into no divine experience, we do not know whether he who brings it has been in touch with reality or has dreamed a dream.

The distinction here indicated, while it does not imply that the interpretations of the gospel in the New Testament are throughout worthless for religion, and does not carry a denial of the religious fervor and devotion of Paul, the religious mysticism of the fourth Gospel, and the love-breathing spirit of the first Epistle of John, does necessarily lead to the conclusion that the word of Jesus is preëminently the one revelation contained in the New

Testament. While it might be hazardous to attempt to draw a line between the teaching of Jesus and all else in the New Testament which should definitely and rigidly separate what is revealed from what is not revealed, yet if to the gospel apart from all its accretions are applied the tests of revelation, it will be found distinctively to possess the unique character of a disclosure of spiritual verities. Now, it is manifest that a revelation to man can be of such things alone as he in his nature and environment is capable of receiving. In no proper sense of the word can he receive other truths than such as are verifiable to him. Accordingly, the test of a revelation is its receptibility, or its verifiability, or simply that it can be received, that is, appropriated, and authenticated by man. Revealed truths, then, are the truths which are intuitively apprehended and made known by an intelligence more highly endowed, that is, developed, than those intelligences to which he communicates them, but truths which the latter would have been able eventually to discern of themselves. To the revelation of religious truth there is necessary a higher religiousness in the revealer than those possess to whom he communicates his revelation. He sees spiritual realities and relations which others have not yet seen. By reason of nature, genius, or inspiration—terms which may not be so fundamentally different in meaning as is commonly supposed—he stands in an exceptional relation to the divine Spirit, and is a master in the ethical-religious realm. What he declares is what he knows and has experienced, not what he imagines or dreams ; and his declaration becomes a revelation to men only so far as they are capable of knowing it as he knows it. The indispensable relation between the organ of a revelation and those who receive his communication is that of likeness of faculty, community of nature.   No revelation of visual objects can be made by a man who sees to a man born blind.   We may, then, believe that there exists such a community of nature between the divine Spirit and His human children that to a pure and spiritual soul God can make His presence felt in blessed experiences and in an illumination which fills the being of the seer; but "the fulness of the Godhead" could be revealed only to another Godhead. Between having a spiritual sense of God as Father—a manifestly relative term—and fathoming the mystery of the absolute divine being the difference is immeasurable. If it has pleased God to place within the reach of men a knowledge of the *fact* of their future existence, it is only in a very vague and general way that they have apprehended it.   Jesus appears rather to have accepted the current belief on the subject than to have made it a capital point in his teaching.   His bodily revival, appearance to the eye of flesh, and mysterious disappearance would, granting the phenomena, throw little if any light upon the problem.   The modes and conditions of a future existence are not, however, capable of revelation to us for the reason that we are incapable of apprehending them.   It is conceivable, indeed, that a human soul might occupy a plane of spiritual vision and experience from which it could make the declaration with a certainty axiomatic to its intuitions that "God is not a God of the dead, but of the living, for all live to Him"; and this declaration would be a revelation to those whose spiritual development rendered them capable of receiving it.   But if one should say that they who "obtain that world and the resurrection from the dead are like the angels," no revelation would be made to men, for angelic natures and modes of existence are entirely unknowable to them.

These examples showing what is revealable and what is not may serve to illustrate the distinction between the gospel of Jesus as a revelation by preëminence and the interpretations and transformations of it contained in the New Testament. It is a distinguishing quality of the word of Jesus that it is essentially a declaration of facts which can be apprehended··and verified by the intuitions and experience of men. So far as it makes known to men what before they did not know, so far as it leads them to new spiritual experiences, discloses hitherto hidden springs of action, and opens to them new possibilities of divine communion, it has the character of a revelation of moral and religious truth. If we may regard the whole gospel of Jesus as comprising not alone his teaching, but also his personality, the latter cannot but be seen to be a very fruitful and inspiring revelation, since it discloses an intelligible experience far above the usual order of human experience. In it are disclosed the possibilities of a life lived in communion with God, the divine intuitions of one who remains pure in heart, the repose and peace of the trusting soul, and the strength and victory to be attained through sacrifice and obedience. These phenomena have the quality of verifiability which belongs in general to the teachings of Jesus and distinguishes them as revelations and as religious verities from the speculations of the New-Testament writers. The teaching which makes love to God and man fundamental and essential in religion and morals commands at once the assent of all men whose ethical and religious development brings them within reach of his influence. It is axiomatic just as it is axiomatic that his life was good. Both propositions may be verified in the experience of men. There is one revealed religion in the New Testament, and that is the religion of Jesus. There are also many theologies in the New Testament, but they are not revealed theologies. To become aware of the distinction between the two things, between any and every truth which in its nature is a revelation and any and every declaration which in its content is essentially a speculation, one has only to contrast Jesus' sound and fruitful teaching about the righteousness which is shown in works of obedience and love, and the Pauline theory of a righteousness which is "accounted" to men by reason of faith. There is all the difference here that exists between a reality grounded in the facts of human nature and in the moral order, and a factitious scheme produced by speculation. One has also only to contrast the real character of Jesus which has left its impress upon the synoptic tradition with the Pauline "second Adam," the deutero-Pauline "high-priest forever after the order of Melchizedek," and the one in whom dwelt "all the fulness of the God-head bodily," or with the Johannine Logos who was God and with God in the beginning, to see the difference between a living and inspiring revelation which quickens, transforms, rebukes, and uplifts the soul, and barren abstractions bearing no intelligible message, no word of courage, of comfort, or of strength.

That the New Testament is not, however, merely a collection of diverse theologies, not simply a gospel and varying interpretations of it, is obvious even to the casual reader of its several writings. It is plain that one of its most striking characteristics consists in its pervasive unities. Worthy of especial consideration is it also that these unities, regarded as dominant points of view, leading presumptions, and fundamental doctrines, are found essentially in the gospel of Jesus as a centre from which they proceeded, receiving various determinations from the media through which they passed. The fundamental presumption of the religion and theology of the New Testament is the Old-Testament monotheism, the doctrine of one God, the Creator and Moral Governor of the world, to whom the historical course of affairs, particularly the saving mission of Christ, holds the relation of the fulfilment of a divine design. This theological view of the world receives in the teaching of Jesus a distinctively religious coloring through the doctrine of the Fatherhood of God, which is also, as has been pointed out,* brought into important relations with conduct. An essential unity of teaching regarding man also pervades the New Testament. He is the child or creature of God, the especial object of the divine interest, the subject of God's moral government owing allegiance, service, obedience, and honor, and finding his supreme spiritual blessedness in love and worship of his Creator. On His part God reveals Himself to man, judges, chastens, and rewards him, to the end that He may establish on the earth His kingdom of righteousness, through which man may be saved from sin. The Christological unity is apparent in the doctrine that Jesus was the Messiah—though not the national Jewish Messiah-King—the Son of God, and the Saviour of men; that his mission is a manifestation of the divine grace; that he died for the sake of mankind, and was thereafter manifested as victorious over death; and that through faith men may come into that fellowship with him which is life eternal. The practical unity is expressed in the teaching that love to God and man, the sum of the law and the prophets, and the great commandment of Jesus, is the supreme principle of the religious

* See page 81.

and moral life. The eschatological unity is indicated in a dominant note of optimism regarding destiny, with which are blended, indeed, the sombre shadings of an ominous warning of judgment upon wilful transgression. Setting aside the pervasive expectation of the second coming of Christ and its various apocalyptic expressions as of only transient importance, there are intimations of very hopeful significance in the divine interest in man manifested in the economy of salvation, in the delineation of the good shepherd and of the forgiving father of the prodigal's story, in the triumphant anticipations, expressed, indeed, in mythologic terms, of the overthrow of the powers of evil in the consummation of Christ's cosmic victory, and above all in that fundamental doctrine of Jesus, the Fatherhood of God. The reserve both of Jesus and the New-Testament writers as to dogmatic expressions regarding destiny is not perhaps remarkable when it is considered with what absorbing interest they addressed themselves to themes of more immediate concern and importance.

It must be regarded as the misfortune of Christianity that its expounders, instead of proceeding from the actual unities of the New Testament, have attempted to combine its diversities into a factitious unity. Through a radical misapprehension of the facts in the case, due to the want of the historical sense and the absence of critical discrimination, it has been sought to combine into a homogeneous dogmatic system elements which, if not antagonistic, have at least no affinity for one another. The presupposition from which this procedure sets out is the totally gratuitous one that the writers of the New Testament were inspired to formulate theologies. It was an inference from a groundless assumption that their theologies must be in accord with one another, and from this point of view have been constructed the uncritical systems of dogmatic Christian theology. The New Testament contains many theologies which, studied apart and with respect to their origin and development, are instructive to the student of the beginnings of Christian doctrine and speculation. But the attempt to unite them in the structure of a "systematic theology" can only result in a most unsystematic product. The several Christologies of the New Testament and its differing conceptions of salvation and of the means of attaining it do not admit of combination into a homogeneous system. Jesus' teaching regarding himself and the Johannine Logos-speculation as to his nature and rank are mutually exclusive, to say nothing of the relation to both of the intermediate Christologies, and the union of his doctrine about righteousness and the conditions of entering the kingdom of God with the Pauline theories of redemption and justification is unachievable by the boldest dogmatism and the most violent harmonizing. The hermeneutical principles or assumptions on which such attempts proceed are radically wrong. If the New-Testament writings are literature—that is, productions of men, they must be interpreted by the canons which are applicable to literature in general. If they are not of this character, then it is obviously necessary before proceeding to interpret them, to assign them to some other class of products, and adopt rules of interpretation which would apply to them. If they are superhuman productions, it is not only requisite to account for the human qualities which they manifest, but also to seek for a revealed hermeneutics by which they may be interpreted. The inconsequences and absurdities into which we are led the moment that we abandon the historical point of view regarding these writings make it plain that the only logical theory of dealing with them is that which recognizes them as containing theologies which are to be examined genetically and apart, and that those who have endeavored with intentions, however good, to construct out of them a " systematic theology " have rendered a great disservice to the truth and to the Church. One may quite harmlessly construct a systematic theology, if one has a talent for it, which shall represent one's philosophy of salvation and one's view of the world, but the endeavor to substantiate such a system by attempting to force into agreement the differing speculations of the New-Testament writers on the presumption that they were inspired to produce authoritative theologies is, to say the least, grossly misleading.

The character and extent of the disservice which Christian theology has done to the gospel of Jesus may be seen in its persistence in emphasizing things non-essential and unknowable to the comparative neglect of matters on which Jesus himself laid the chief stress of his ministry. The primal error of the theologian is over-confidence. He thinks that he is able to elucidate the ultimate mysteries of the universe. Believing that the most recondite things are capable of revelation to man, and holding as a cardinal principle that the whole of the New Testament is a revelation, he has seized upon the speculations of Paul and the post-Pauline writers, and elevated them as precious disclosures of heaven to the rank of essentials of faith and salvation. In the pride of certainty and the zeal of orthodoxy he has even gone so far as to deny to all men who could not accept them as divine truth the Christian name and fellowship, and to

cast doubt upon their chances of attaining eternal life.
Thus to his theoretical error, that occult theologies and
Christologies are capable of revelation to the human intelligence, he has added the practical error, that these things,
even if they could be revealed to men, have any value for
character, any fruitfulness for life, any " saving " efficacy.
Setting up as a standard of sound faith a body of speculative doctrines, he has regarded as heretics all who
could not adjust their thinking to it, and by a strange
transformation has converted the term " evangelical,"
which originally meant relating to " the good news," *
into a synonym of a popular theological metaphysics. A
popular metaphysics, indeed ! For Christian theology
has succeeded in popularizing a metaphysics. There has
always been a class of persons—a class now happily
diminishing very rapidly—for whom speculations about
the origin of things, the nature and purposes of God,
occult schemes of redemption, and human destiny, have
a strong fascination. They are attracted by any one
who claims to have disclosures to make of the divine
counsels, or who has an apocalypse to preach. They
prefer mythologies to morals, and would rather listen to
prophecies of a kingdom to come than to an exposition
of Jesus' kingdom of God, to an account of the topography
of the celestial and nether realms than to " the words of
eternal life." The discussion of a " plan of salvation "
which includes inscrutable mysteries has more interest for
them than a discourse upon the Sermon on the Mount.
It may appear upon a superficial view to be the misfortune
of Christianity that the leadership of its exposition has so
far fallen into the hands of speculative men and makers
of theological systems that its spiritual and ethical aspects

* εὐαγγέλιον.

have been obscured by the mists of metaphysics, and its
divine verities buried under a mass of crude dogma. But
a profounder apprehension of the matter discloses a divine
progressive order, and makes it apparent that these blind
guides and their followers represent but a stage in the
spiritual evolution of mankind, in the evolution of men's
understanding of the great gospel of Jesus. It was the
fortune of this gospel to be borne in its infancy upon an
apocalypse, and to be nurtured in the souls of men who,
had they not been "gazing up into heaven" to discern
the signs of the coming of their Lord, might have turned
away from him altogether in sickness of heart. Perhaps
it is a necessity of the nature of things that before the
spiritual stage of the evolution of Christianity is reached
the divine spirit of the gospel should be passed on from
age to age in apocalypses, systems of speculation, and
metaphysics, waiting for its liberation. For liberated it
is destined to be. "Spirit cannot be captured by mechan-
ism. Life outlives the theories that would tear out the
heart of its secret."

> " Grau, theuer Freund, ist alle Theorie,
> Und grün des Lebens gold'ner Baum." *

The distinction between Christianity and the religion of
Jesus, which has already been pointed out, becomes apparent in the light of the foregoing considerations.
Christianity, which properly means the religion and doctrines taught by Christ, has come to signify in the popular
apprehension and usage the generally accepted theological

---

* " All theory, dear friend, is gray,
    And green the golden tree of life."
See The Future of Liberal Religion in America, by Dr. J. G. Schurman,
in *The New World*, 1892, pp. 29 ff.

tenets of Christendom as well as certain principles of conduct. The transformation of the original gospel of Jesus,
beginning in the New Testament itself, has been so gradual
and complete, and has proceeded to such a degree for
many centuries upon the assumption of the unity and infallibility of that book, that it is scarcely recognized by
Christians generally; and to point it out is for one who
does it to run the risk of being denounced by them as a
traitor to the cause of the Master himself. Its transformation, however, almost to the point of irrecognizability
is a most obvious fact of history. The great Teacher of
the synoptic tradition could certainly not have recognized
himself in "the second Adam," "the high-priest forever
after the order of Melchizedek," the one containing "all
the fulness of the Godhead bodily," or the Logos who
"was with God in the beginning, and was God." Still
less could he recognize himself in the rank of "very God"
assigned to him in the dogma of the Trinity; or his gospel, his good news of the kingdom of God, of love, and of
righteousness, in the doctrines of vicarious atonement,
imputed righteousness, probation, the exclusion of men
from eternal life by divine decree, and the materialistic
topography of the unseen world; or his spirit in the pride
and pomp of ecclesiasticism, the splendor of worship which
has no beatitude for "the poor," the persecution of heretics, and the bitter proscription of honest and pure men
who cannot accept as the word of God the Christian mythologies and speculations. It has come about as the
result of this transformation that Christianity as generally
understood and promulgated in the Church has more
affinity with Paulinism than with the gospel of Jesus.
There is nothing more lamentable, more inexplicable, in
the whole course of Christian history than this abandon-

ment of the great Master by his professed followers. " Of the outward and inward, of the earthly and the heavenly part of his thought and teaching, the one has been taken, and the other left. On this small and mistaken base there has been heaped up an immense and widening mass of Christian mythology, from the first unstable and now at last apparently swerving to its fall. And let it fall. For it has corrupted the religion of Christ into an apocalyptic fiction ; and *that*, so monstrous in its account of man, in its theory of God, in its picture of the universe, in its distorted reflections of life and death, that, if the belief in it were as real as the profession of it is loud, society would relapse into a moral and intellectual darkness it has long left, and the lowest element of modern civilization would be its *faith*." *

Amid all these aberrations, however, there is one hopeful indication; amid all the darkened speculations, the barren creeds, the dreary dogmas, which denote the well-meant infidelity of men to the teaching and the spirit of Jesus, there is discernible a ray of light, now hidden in the gloom, now flashing out in the luminousness of some great soul or the fervid consecration of some loving heart. This constant amid the variable, this inextinguishable light in the darkness, is the sentiment of loyalty to Jesus along with whatever misconceptions of his person and his word, acknowledgment of him as Master, right appreciation of his Spirit, and devotion to his cause. It is a strange paradox that among those who have most radically misconceived Christianity have been found many who have most truly lived it. In this fact is indicated the legitimacy of drawing a distinction between its permanent and transient, its divine and undivine elements. For the distinction is

* Martineau.

practically drawn in the application of Christianity to the life of men, since it is the divine part of it, the gospel of Jesus, his religion practically realized, which constitutes its vitality and its power. In his teaching of righteousness, love, purity, and unselfishness, and in his example of obedience, self-sacrifice, and helpfulness, are contained the highest motives and inspirations of which man is susceptible. Whether this gospel be the absolute religion or no is a speculative question which it is fruitless to discuss. One day of earnest endeavor to live this religion is worth more than a cycle of discussion of its absoluteness or relativity. Let us have done with speculation and its labyrinthian aberrations. So much is certain, that no higher interpretation of life, no nobler ideal of duty than this gospel presents has ever been set before mankind as a spring of action and a goal of endeavor. No teacher has appeared among men so worthy to be reverenced by them as spiritual Master as Jesus of Nazareth. Christian union —that divine dream of the noblest spirits of Christendom— is potentially contained in his gospel. The tendencies toward it in the Church, already becoming marked in an unspoken consensus of many of the most enlightened and spiritual believers, denote the practical realization of this gospel conceived as a doctrine and a principle of life. They are manifested in the greater emphasis which is placed upon the word of Jesus, in the growing indifference to the speculations of his followers early and late, in the increasing appreciation of the reverent criticism which separates between the divine word and human traditions and specu- · lations concerning it; and in the prevalent sentiment of fraternity and toleration in which the spirit of the gospel is expressed. There will then be Christian union, and not before, when men shall have come to estimate the gospel and theology, each at its true value according to its origin and its fruitfulness ; when they shall reverence and cherish the teaching of Jesus as the word of life, and discard the speculative Christologies and metaphysical systems which have divided Christendom into opposing camps, and exalted doctrine instead of love to the rank of "the greatest thing in the world " ; when theologians shall place the emphasis of the gospel where Jesus placed it, upon conduct rather than upon dogma, practising his reserve regarding destiny and things unknowable ; and when preachers shall discourse more of righteousness and the kingdom of God and less of theologies and the kingdom to come.   Then character, and not speculative opinions, will be the test of Christian fellowship, and the only heretic will be he whose life is false because not grounded upon the word of the Master.   This consummation will denote the RETURN TO JESUS.   When the Church, having come to herself, shall gather her scattered children from their fruitless quest in the mazes of theology into a union upon the common ground of the divine gospel, she will begin to see the realization of the dream of the spiritual supremacy, which her prophets have dreamed for ages, in the quickening of her heart and in the enlistment under her banner of the totality of the most enlightened conscience and intelligence of mankind.

INDEX OF QUOTATIONS FROM THE NEW TESTAMENT.

INDEX OF SUBJECTS.

GOSPEL-CRITICISM
AND HISTORICAL CHRISTIANITY

A Study of the Gospels and of the History of the Gospel-Canon during the Second Century; together with a consideration of the Results of Modern Criticism. By Orello Cone, D.D. Second Edition, 8vo, gilt top, $1.75.

CHIEF CONTENTS.—I. THE TEXT—II. THE CANON—III. THE SYNOPTIC PROBLEM—IV. THE GOSPEL ACCORDING TO MARK—V. THE GOSPEL ACCORDING TO MATTHEW—VI. THE GOSPEL ACCORDING TO LUKE—VII. THE GOSPEL ACCORDING TO JOHN—VIII. THE ESCHATOLOGY OF THE GOSPELS—IX. DOGMATIC "TENDENCIES" IN THE GOSPELS—X. THE OLD TESTAMENT IN THE GOSPELS; OR, THE HERMENEUTICS OF THE EVANGELISTS—XI. THE GOSPELS AS HISTORIES—XII. CRITICISM AND HISTORICAL CHRISTIANITY.

"A strong book, and well worth reading by any one who knows or does not know the recent results of the higher criticism."—*Christian Union.*

"The work of a scholar who has made himself familiar with the most important recent investigations, and who appreciates the nature and bearing of the questions at issue. . . Replete with information for those who have not made the subject a specialty, and executed in a spirit of candor and rational inquiry."—GEO. B. STEVENS, *Professor of New-Testament Criticism in Yale University, in Yale Review.*

"It is not excelled in attractiveness by any work that has been written on the subject."—Prof. C. H. TOY.

"A book of rare strength and poise. . . Places its author in the front rank of American biblical scholars."—*The Unitarian.*

"Scholarly from cover to cover, and a decided addition to New-Testament literature."—*Boston Advertiser.*

"I admire its careful learning and thorough mastery of the subject, and more I admire the singular mental poise which it exhibits. . . Such a book marks a era in American scholarship."—R. HEBER NEWTON, D.D.

"A thoroughly scholarly work ; its tone is deeply reverent and spiritual, and its literary style is marked by sobriety and conspicious refinement and grace. . . . It has commanded throughout our close attention and frequent admiration."—The London *Literary World.*

"I feel very great admiration for the scholarship and wisdom shown in the treatment of the whole subject. . . The book is admirable and cannot fail to do great good among thinking men."—ANDREW D. WHITE.

G. P. PUTNAM'S SONS, NEW YORK AND LONDON.